The Story of God Bible Commentary Series Endorsements

"Getting a story is about more than merely enjoying it. It means hearing it, understanding it, and above all, being impacted by it. This commentary series hopes that its readers not only hear and understand the story but are impacted by it to live in as Christian a way as possible. The editors and contributors set that table very well and open up the biblical story in ways that move us to act with sensitivity and understanding. That makes hearing the story as these authors tell it well worth the time. Well done."

Darrell L. Bock
Dallas Theological Seminary

"The Story of God Bible Commentary series invites readers to probe how the message of the text relates to our situations today. Engagingly readable, it not only explores the biblical text but offers a range of applications and interesting illustrations."

Craig S. Keener
Asbury Theological Seminary

"I love The Story of God Bible Commentary series. It makes the text sing and helps us hear the story afresh."

John Ortberg
Senior Pastor of Menlo Park Presbyterian Church

"In this promising new series of commentaries, believing biblical scholars bring not only their expertise but their own commitment to Jesus and insights into today's culture to the Scriptures. The result is a commentary series that is anchored in the text but lives and breathes in the world of today's church with its variegated pattern of socioeconomic, ethnic, and national diversity. Pastors, Bible study leaders, and Christians of all types who are looking for a substantive and practical guide through the Scriptures will find these volumes helpful."

Frank Thielman
Beeson Divinity School

"I'm a storyteller. Through writing and speaking I talk and teach about understanding the Story of God throughout Scripture and about letting God reveal more of his story as I live it out. Thus I am thrilled to have a commentary series based on the story of God—a commentary that helps me to Listen to the Story, that Explains the Story, and then encourages me to probe how to Live the Story. A perfect tool for helping every follower of Jesus to walk in the story that God is writing for them."

Judy Douglass
Director of Women's Resources, Cru

"The Bible is the story of God and his dealings with humanity from creation to new creation. The Bible is made up more of stories than of any other literary genre. Even the psalms, proverbs, prophecies, letters, and the Apocalypse make complete sense only when set in the context of the grand narrative of the entire Bible. This commentary series breaks new ground by taking all these observations seriously. It asks commentators to listen to the text, to explain the text, and to live the text. Some of the material in these sections overlaps with introduction, detailed textual analysis and application, respectively, but only some. The most riveting and valuable part of the commentaries are the stories that can appear in any of these sections, from any part of the globe and any part of church history, illustrating the text in any of these areas. Ideal for preaching and teaching."

Craig L. Blomberg
Denver Seminary

"Pastors and lay people will welcome this new series, which seeks to make the message of the Scriptures clear and to guide readers in appropriating biblical texts for life today."

Daniel I. Block
Wheaton College and Graduate School

"An extremely valuable and long overdue series that includes comment on the cultural context of the text, careful exegesis, and guidance on reading the whole Bible as a unity that testifies to Christ as our Savior and Lord."

Graeme Goldsworthy
author of *According to Plan*

ECCLESIASTES, SONG OF SONGS

The Story of God Bible Commentary

ECCLESIASTES, SONG OF SONGS

George Athas

Tremper Longman III & Scot McKnight
General Editors

ZONDERVAN ACADEMIC

ZONDERVAN ACADEMIC

Ecclesiastes, Song of Songs

ISBN 978-0-310-49116-3 (hardcover)

ISBN 978-0-310-49117-0 (ebook)

Requests for information should be addressed to:
Zondervan, *3900 Sparks Dr. SE, Grand Rapids, Michigan 49546*

Cover design: Ron Huizinga
Cover image: iStockphoto®

Printed in the United States of America

19 20 21 22 23 24 25 26 27 28 29 /LSC/ 15 14 13 12 11 10 9 8 7 6 5 4 3 2 1

To those who often despair, and those who endure
opposition, especially from surprising directions,
while trying to pursue righteousness and truth.

Old Testament series

1 ▪ Genesis—*Tremper Longman III*
2 ▪ Exodus—*Christopher J. H. Wright*
3 ▪ Leviticus—*Jerry E. Shepherd*
4 ▪ Numbers—*Jay A. Sklar*
5 ▪ Deuteronomy—*Myrto Theocharous*
6 ▪ Joshua—*Lissa M. Wray Beal*
7 ▪ Judges—*Athena E. Gorospe*
8 ▪ Ruth/Esther—*Marion Taylor*
9 ▪ 1–2 Samuel—*Paul S. Evans*
10 ▪ 1–2 Kings—*David T. Lamb*
11 ▪ 1–2 Chronicles—*Carol M. Kaminski*
12 ▪ Ezra/Nehemiah—*Douglas J. Green*
13 ▪ Job—*Martin A. Shields*
14 ▪ Psalms—*Elizabeth R. Hayes*
15 ▪ Proverbs—*Ryan P. O'Dowd*
16 ▪ Ecclesiastes/Song of Songs—*George Athas*
17 ▪ Isaiah—*Mark J. Boda*
18 ▪ Jeremiah/Lamentations—*Andrew G. Shead*
19 ▪ Ezekiel—*D. Nathan Phinney*
20 ▪ Daniel—*Wendy L. Widder*
21 ▪ Minor Prophets I—*Beth M. Stovell*
22 ▪ Minor Prophets II—*Beth M. Stovell*

New Testament series

1 ▪ Matthew—*Rodney Reeves*
2 ▪ Mark—*Timothy G. Gombis*
3 ▪ Luke—*Kindalee Pfremmer DeLong*
4 ▪ John—*Nicholas Perrin*
5 ▪ Acts—*Dean Pinter*
6 ▪ Romans—*Michael F. Bird*
7 ▪ 1 Corinthians—*Justin K. Hardin*
8 ▪ 2 Corinthians—*Judith A. Diehl*
9 ▪ Galatians—*Nijay K. Gupta*
10 ▪ Ephesians—*Mark D. Roberts*
11 ▪ Philippians—*Lynn H. Cohick*
12 ▪ Colossians/Philemon—*Todd Wilson*
13 ▪ 1, 2 Thessalonians—*John Byron*
14 ▪ 1, 2 Timothy, Titus—*Marius Nel*
15 ▪ Hebrews—*Radu Gheorghita*
16 ▪ James—*Mariam J. Kamell*
17 ▪ 1 Peter—*Dennis R. Edwards*
18 ▪ 2 Peter, Jude—*C. Rosalee Velloso Ewell*
19 ▪ 1, 2, & 3 John—*Constantine R. Campbell*
20 ▪ Revelation—*Jonathan A. Moo*
21 ▪ Sermon on the Mount—*Scot McKnight*

Contents

Acknowledgments . . . 11
The Story of God Bible Commentary Series . . . 13
Abbreviations . . . 17
Introduction to Ecclesiastes . . . 19
Resources for Teaching and Preaching . . . 43
1. Ecclesiastes 1:1–11 . . . 45
2. Ecclesiastes 1:12–2:26 . . . 64
3. Ecclesiastes 3:1–4:16 . . . 85
4. Ecclesiastes 5:1–6:6 . . . 116
5. Ecclesiastes 6:7–8:1 . . . 140
6. Ecclesiastes 8:2–10:4 . . . 167
7. Ecclesiastes 10:5–12:8 . . . 194
8. Ecclesiastes 12:9–14 . . . 222
Introduction to Song of Songs . . . 249
Resources for Teaching and Preaching . . . 265
9. Song of Songs 1:1–2:7 . . . 267
10. Song of Songs 2:8–5:9 . . . 289
11. Song of Songs 5:9–6:10 . . . 316
12. Song of Songs 6:11–8:14 . . . 331
Scripture Index . . . 371
Extrabiblical Literature Index . . . 385
Subject Index . . . 387
Author Index . . . 399

Acknowledgments

My heartfelt thanks go to a number a people who assisted or encouraged me in writing this commentary. First, it is such a pleasure to work with my colleagues on the editorial board of the Story of God Bible Commentary series—Tremper Longman, Mark Boda, and Myrto Theocharous. Their input has been of great value to me. In addition to them, I must also thank both Katya Covrett and Nancy Erickson at Zondervan, who have poured so much energy into making this series happen, including this volume.

This commentary was written across a number of years at both Moore Theological College in Sydney, where I teach, and George Whitefield College in Cape Town, at which I am a regular visiting scholar. The facilities, libraries, and personnel of both institutions provided all the resources one could hope for in putting together a volume like this one. In particular, I wish to thank my research assistants at Moore, Susanna Baldwin and Simon Cowell, for their investigations on my behalf, as well as my PhD student, Kamina Wüst, for our discussions about the Song of Songs. I must also acknowledge the many brief but stimulating interactions I've had with the student body at Moore on the occasions when I was able to preach on Ecclesiastes in the college chapel.

Finally, my enduring thanks go to my family and friends who supported and encouraged me in various ways through the research and writing, including those moments that felt like a journey through the desert as I was framing new interpretations: my wife, Koula, and our daughters, Hosanna and Josephine; my parents, Jim and Mary, and parents-in-law, Terry and Sofia; my "Cape Town family," the Holschers; Marshall Ballantine-Jones; Ross Ciano; Sarie King; and Donald Vance.

The Story of God Bible Commentary Series

Why another commentary series?

In the first place, no single commentary can exhaust the meaning of a biblical book. The Bible is unfathomably rich and no single commentator can explore every aspect of its message.

In addition, good commentary not only explores what the text meant in the past but also its continuing significance. In other words, the Word of God may not change, but culture does. Think of what we have seen in the last twenty years: we now communicate predominantly through the internet and email; we read our news on iPads and computers. We carry smartphones in our pockets through which we can call our friends, check the weather forecast, make dinner reservations, and get an answer to virtually any question we might have.

Today we have more readable and accurate Bible versions in English than any generation in the past. Bible distribution in the present generation has been very successful; more people own more Bibles than previous generations. However, studies have shown that while people have better access to the Bible than ever before, people aren't reading the Bibles they own, and they struggle to understand what they do read.

The Story of God Bible Commentary hopes to help people, particularly clergy but also laypeople, read the Bible with understanding not only of its ancient meaning but also of its continuing significance for us today in the twenty-first century. After all, readers of the Bible change too. These cultural shifts, our own personal developments, and the progress in intellectual questions, as well as growth in biblical studies and theology and discoveries of new texts and new paradigms for understanding the contexts of the Bible—each of these elements work on an interpreter so that the person who reads the Bible today asks different questions from different angles.

Culture shifts, but the Word of God remains. That is why we as editors of The Story of God Bible Commentary, a commentary based on the New International Version 2011 (NIV 2011), are excited to participate in this new series of commentaries on the Bible. This series is designed to speak to this generation with the same Word of God. We are asking the authors to explain what the Bible says to the sorts of readers who pick up commentaries so they can understand not only what Scripture says but what it means for today. The Bible does not change, but relating it to our culture changes constantly and in differing ways in different contexts.

As editors of the Old Testament series, we recognize that Christians have a hard time knowing exactly how to relate to the Scriptures that were written before the coming of Christ. The world of the Old Testament is a strange one to those of us who live in the West in the twenty first century. We read about strange customs, warfare in the name of God, sacrifices, laws of ritual purity, and more and wonder whether it is worth our while or even spiritually healthy to spend time reading this portion of Scripture that is chronologically, culturally, and—seemingly—theologically distant from us.

But it is precisely here that The Story of God Commentary Series Old Testament makes its most important contribution. The New Testament does not replace the Old Testament; the New Testament fulfills the Old Testament. We hear God's voice today in the Old Testament. In its pages he reveals himself to us and also his will for how we should live in a way that is pleasing to him.

Jesus himself often reminds us that the Old Testament maintains its importance to the lives of his disciples. Luke 24 describes Jesus's actions and teaching in the period between his resurrection and ascension. Strikingly, the focus of his teaching is on how his followers should read the Old Testament (here called "Moses and all the Prophets," "Scriptures," and "the law of Moses, the Prophets and Psalms"). To the two disciples on the road to Emmaus, he says:

> "How foolish you are, and how slow to believe all that the prophets have spoken! Did not the Messiah have to suffer these things and then enter his glory?" And beginning with Moses and all the Prophets, he explained to them what was said in all the Scriptures concerning himself. (Luke 24:25–27)

Then to a larger group of disciples he announces:

> "This is what I told you while I was still with you: Everything must be fulfilled that is written about me in the law of Moses, the Prophets and the Psalms." Then he opened their minds so they could understand the Scriptures. (Luke 24:44–45)

The Story of God Commentary Series takes Jesus's words on this matter seriously. Indeed, it is the first series that has as one of its deliberate goals the identification of the trajectories (historical, typological, and theological) that land in Christ in the New Testament. Every commentary in the series will, in the first place, exposit the text in the context of its original reception. We will interpret it as we believe the original author intended his contemporary audience to read it. But then we will also read the text in the light of the death and resurrection of Jesus. No other commentary series does this important work consistently in every volume.

To achieve our purpose of expositing the Old Testament in its original setting and also from a New Testament perspective, each passage is examined from three angles.

Listen to the Story. We begin by listening to the text in order to hear the voice of God. We first read the passage under study. We then go on to consider the background to the passage by looking at any earlier Scripture passage that informs our understanding of the text. At this point too we will cite and discuss possible ancient Near Eastern literary connections. After all, the Bible was not written in a cultural vacuum, and an understanding of its broader ancient Near Eastern context will often enrich our reading.

Explain the Story. The authors are asked to explain each passage in light of the Bible's grand story. It is here that we will exposit the text in its original Old Testament context. This is not an academic series, so the footnotes will be limited to the kinds of books and articles to which typical Bible readers and preachers will have access. Authors are given the freedom to explain the text as they read it, though you will not be surprised to find occasional listings of other options for reading the text. The emphasis will be on providing an accessible explanation of the passage, particularly on those aspects of the text that are difficult for a modern reader to understand, with an emphasis on theological interpretation.

Live the Story. Reading the Bible is not just about discovering what it meant back then; the intent of The Story of God Bible Commentary is to probe how this text might be lived out today as that story continues to march on in the life of the church.

Here, in the spirit of Christ's words in Luke 24, we will suggest ways in which the Old Testament text anticipates the gospel. After all, as Augustine famously put it, "the New Testament is in the Old Testament concealed, the Old Testament is in the New Testament revealed." We believe that this section will be particularly important for our readers who are clergy who want to present Christ even when they are preaching from the Old Testament.

The Old Testament also provides teaching concerning how we should live today. However, the authors of this series are sensitive to the tremendous impact that Christ's coming has on how Christians appropriate the Old Testament into their lives today.

It is the hope and prayer of the editors and all the contributors that our work will encourage clergy to preach from the Old Testament and laypeople to study this wonderful, yet often strange, portion of God's Word to us today.

Tremper Longman III, general editor Old Testament
George Athas, Mark Boda, and Myrto Theocharous, editors

Abbreviations

ANET	*Ancient Near Eastern Texts Relating to the Old Testament.* Edited by James B. Pritchard. 3rd ed. Princeton: Princeton University Press, 1969
Ant.	Josephus, *Jewish Antiquities*
ASV	American Standard Version
b. Sanh.	Babylonian Talmud, Sanhedrin (tractate)
BBR	*Bulletin of Biblical Research*
BST	Bible Speaks Today
CBQ	*Catholic Biblical Quarterly*
COS	*The Context of Scripture.* Edited by William W. Hallo. 3 vols. Leiden: Brill, 1997–2002
CSB	Christian Standard Bible
EA	El Amarna Tablet
Epid.	*Epidemiae* (Epidemics)
ESV	English Standard Version
HALOT	Köhler, L., W. Baumgartner, and J. J. Stamm. *The Hebrew and Aramaic Lexicon of the Old Testament.* Translated and edited under the supervision of M. E. J. Richardson. 4 vols. Leiden, 1994–1999
HAR	*Hebrew Annual Review*
Hist.	Herodotus, *Histories*
HUCA	*Hebrew Union College Annual*
JESOT	*Journal for the Evangelical Study of the Old Testament*
JSOT	*Journal for the Study of the Old Testament*
JSOTSupp	Journal for the Study of the Old Testament Supplement
KJV	King James Version
LXX	Septuagint
m. Yad.	Mishnah, Yadayim (tractate)
MT	Masoretic Text
Nat. hom.	*De natura hominis* (Nature of Man)
NICOT	New International Commentary on the Old Testament
NIV	New International Version
NJPS	*Tanakh: The Holy Scriptures: The New JPS Translation according to the Traditional Hebrew Text*

NRSV	New Revised Standard Version
OTL	Old Testament Library
P.	Papyrus
P. Cairo Zen.	Papyrus Cairo Zenon
P. Col.	Papyrus Columbianus (Columbia Papyrus)
Qoh	Qohelet/Ecclesiastes
RBT	Reading the Bible Today
Sir	Ben Sira
t. Sanh.	Tosefta, Sanhedrin (tractate)
TOTC	Tyndale Old Testament Commentaries
VT	*Vetus Testamentum*
WBC	Word Biblical Commentary
y. Sanh.	Jerusalem Talmud, Sanhedrin (tractate)
ZAW	*Zeitschrift für die Alttestamentliche Wissenschaft*

Introduction to Ecclesiastes

Ecclesiastes is one of the most unusual and controversial books of the entire Bible. Not only are its meaning and milieu hotly contested, its theological relationship to other parts of Scripture is also. For some, Ecclesiastes fits neatly alongside the traditional theology of the Wisdom literature, representing the conservative reflections of a mature Solomon. For others, the book sets the proverbial cat among the pigeons, railing against God, the world, and the traditional theology found in other biblical books from a standpoint very late in the Old Testament period. These widely divergent explanations demonstrate how difficult this book is to interpret. This should only spur us on to closer examination.

Part of the reason for the diversity in opinion over Ecclesiastes comes from the lack of attention to its context. This can almost be forgiven, since the book itself provides remarkably few names that might help us establish a context. In fact, the only names overtly given in the book are "David" and "Jerusalem" (Eccl 1:1, 12, 16; 2:7, 9). Despite this, there are, in fact, numerous specific details throughout the book that all converge to hint very strongly at a specific context. If we are not prepared to follow these leads, and are content to read Ecclesiastes in isolation, or only with reference to other biblical literature, we will disconnect the book from the historical reality in which it arose. The Bible deals with real contexts, since it seeks to address real issues affecting real people. That is why the books of the Bible were written in the first place. The Bible is unique in its authority, but it is not disconnected from the reality around it. Even a book as seemingly abstract and philosophical as Ecclesiastes has an original context, and determining it can only improve our understanding of the book. Only then will we be able to locate Ecclesiastes properly within the larger story of God.

Therefore, throughout the course of this commentary, we will be looking at how the context of its authors impacted what they wrote, as well as how what they wrote impacted their context. As we will see, this is not a simple task, for the words or "argument" of Ecclesiastes are hazardous to negotiate. The flow of thought seems to chop and change, staggering between encouragement and despair. But diligence will yield us understanding, showing us how the book is unconventional and disturbing as well as enriching and crucially significant.

Canonicity

Within the Hebrew canon, Ecclesiastes belongs to the Writings section, which is a collection of assorted books without a specific order to the whole. Some of the other books in the Writings include the Psalms, Proverbs, Daniel, and the books of Chronicles. In Hebrew, this book is known as *Qohelet*, which is the term used within the book for the primary author. The word comes from a root meaning "to assemble" and is usually understood to imply the leader of an assembly. In Jewish liturgical tradition, Ecclesiastes is often grouped with four other books in the Writings, namely, Song of Songs, Ruth, Lamentations, and Esther. Together they are called the Five "Scrolls" (in Hebrew, *Megillot*), and each is read at a different annual festival in the liturgical calendar, with Ecclesiastes being read during *Sukkot* (the festival of Booths) in late September.

In the Greek canon, Ecclesiastes is one of the five Wisdom books. Within this division, Job, Psalms, and Proverbs appear before it, and Song of Songs comes after it. Our English Bibles follow this convention. Our name for the book also derives from the ancient Greek term, *ekklesiastes*, meaning "convener," which is how the Greek translator rendered the Hebrew word *qohelet*.

Authorship

Two authors are responsible for producing the book of Ecclesiastes. The primary author wrote the discourse that occupies most of the book (1:2–12:8). The secondary author, whom we will call the Epilogist, wrote the epilogue (12:9–14), as well as the title (1:1). We can also discern the Epilogist's hand at 1:2, 7:27, and 12:8, amongst what is otherwise the primary author's material.

Tradition identifies the primary author as King Solomon, who reigned in the tenth century BC. This comes from two pieces of data. The first is the book's title in the first verse: "The words of the Teacher, son of David, king in Jerusalem" (Eccl 1:1). Since Solomon succeeded David on the throne of Israel in Jerusalem, he is the natural candidate to be identified as "the Teacher." The second is that the author claims to have gained unparalleled wisdom and engaged in a fabulous campaign of building and wealth accumulation (1:16–2:9). This resembles the exploits of Solomon, to whom God gave unmatched wisdom and wealth (1 Kgs 3:12–13; 2 Chr 9:22).

However, this traditional identification cannot be sustained. First of all, the author is never named explicitly as Solomon. Instead, the author is called, in Hebrew, *qohelet*. The form of this word is a feminine participle. As mentioned above, the Greek translator understood it as a substantive that means "convener," which has led modern translations to use the term "Teacher" (NIV, CSB, NRSV) or "Preacher" (KJV, ASV, RSV, ESV). The NJPS renders the term as a name, "Koheleth," but with a note that this probably means "The Assembler" of either hearers or of sayings. If Solomon is the primary author of the book, we must ask why he is identified with this enigmatic term, *qohelet*, rather than more openly as "Solomon." Is Solomon trying to hide his identity? If so, why would he openly divulge other indicators of his identity, such as being a king who gained wisdom, built widely, and acquired wealth as Solomon did? This is hardly a good strategy for throwing anyone off the trail. And if he did not want to hide his identity, why is his actual name never used? Even if we treat *qohelet* as a name ("Qohelet") rather than an indicator of vocation ("convener"), we are still left wondering why Solomon's name is eschewed in favor of this otherwise unknown appellation.

These questions alone are not enough to overthrow Solomonic authorship. But other evidence mounts up against it. The author claims that, after acquiring his wisdom and wealth, he outdid all who were in Jerusalem before him (Eccl 1:16; 2:7, 9). The fact is, though, that only David preceded Solomon in Jerusalem. This is hardly an impressive boast, even if Solomon were counting the Jebusites prior to David, who do not seem to have done much building anyway (cf. 2 Sam 5:9–11). Furthermore, the crowning achievement of Solomon's reign was the construction of the temple in Jerusalem. Yet, in relating all his building enterprises, the author of Ecclesiastes never once mentions this. Also, at various points throughout the book, the author is critical of the king, both directly and indirectly. For instance, in Ecclesiastes 3:16 he decries the wickedness found in the place of justice—an indirect criticism of authorities, which also implies his inability to right this wrong. At 5:9, as we will see, he claims the land's resources are not shared equitably by all, and the one chiefly responsible for this inequity is the king. The complaint implies he is not a king, because he has no power to do anything about it. At 8:2–4 the author dispenses advice on how to deal with a king, not because he is one and is keen to hand out friendly tips but because the king is a great unknown, wielding absolute power in unpredictable ways. This sentiment is echoed in 10:20, where the author advises his readers against saying or thinking ill of the king because someone might inform on them. Thus, early in the book the author seems to pursue royal activities that bear some resemblance to Solomon's, but elsewhere he writes as though he is not a king at all but is, on the contrary, critical and even afraid of "the king." Furthermore, at the beginning of the epilogue, the Epilogist calls the primary author a sage (NIV, "wise") who taught people (12:9). He makes no mention of him being a king who ruled a kingdom.

All these observations have led many to conclude that the author is not in fact Solomon but that he adopts Solomon's persona early in his discourse to argue that wealth and pleasure cannot satisfy—a point made more forcefully when seen from the perspective of Solomon, the wealthiest of them all. But once the point is made, he discards the Solomonic persona and assumes his real identity for the remainder of the book. This view does have merit in that it explains how the author can be a king at one point in his discourse and not at another. But it does not necessarily answer why the title of the book styles the entire discourse as the words of a "son of David" (1:1).

A closer look at the more overt Solomonic allusions in the first few chapters of the book shows that the author is doing much more than adopting Solomon's persona. As we will see, the activities he refers to reflect the exploits of numerous kings of Judah, not just Solomon, and even some of the more opulent gentile kings of history. Also, since biblical tradition associates Solomon strongly with conventional wisdom (cf. Prov 1:1), the author uses him at various points through the book as a foil to expose what he perceives are the inadequacies of conventional wisdom (cf. Eccl 4:13; 5:1–7; 7:27–28; 10:14–16). Additionally, the author alludes to prophetic words and events from various stages of Judah's history, including Sennacherib's invasion of Judah in 701 BC (9:13–16) and the fall of Jerusalem to the Babylonians in 586 BC (e.g., 3:2–3; 7:10–11; 12:2–7). Thus, on a close reading of the book, and by tracing its multiple allusions to other biblical traditions, we find that the author has the advantage of considerable hindsight over Judean history and access to a vast array of prophetic material. He makes skillful use of Judah's entire biblical heritage. All this points to the primary author of Ecclesiastes writing at a late stage in the history of God's people in the Old Testament. He cannot be Solomon and have all this knowledge from the centuries after him.

So, who was the primary author of Ecclesiastes? Since he can look back to the fall of the kingdom of Judah in 586 BC as part of his people's collective memory, he must have lived after this catastrophic event. This means he could not have been an actual king. One could argue that, by adopting the persona of Solomon, the author is acting deceptively. However, this would only be the case if the author were actually trying to pass himself off as the real Solomon, in which case he does a terrible job. Yet, his concurrent allusions to several Judean kings, his echoes of the words of various prophets, his hints of major events in the history of Judah, and the way he exposes the inadequacies of traditional wisdom mean this is certainly not the case. The author is being plainly obvious in wearing the mask of a king and fully expects his readers to discern this—to realize that he is not in fact a king. He is, in other words, engaging in a kind of theater that he hopes, and indeed needs, his audience to see through to make sense of the multiple biblical echoes and criticisms throughout his discourse. If all the reader does is see Solomon, all these references will be missed. Failure to appreciate the author's theater detaches the book from the extensive biblical heritage on which it depends, making us lose touch with his message and leaving us performing some rather strained and acrobatic exegesis to make sense of what he has written.

Part of the author's purpose, then, is closely tied to the fact that he is not a real king. In the title of the book, the Epilogist identifies the primary author as "son of David" (1:1). Of course, we naturally associate this appellation with Judean kingship. Yet, it would be unusual to include the appellation in the title if it were germane only to that small part of the primary author's discourse in which he acts as a king, namely the first two chapters. It would be irrelevant to the remaining ten chapters of the discourse, and beside the point of his real identity. However, if, as the title suggests, it is not irrelevant but pertains to all "the words" (1:1) in the entire discourse, then a new understanding emerges. The author may be putting on a mask and acting the part of a king at the beginning of his contemplations, but once the mask comes off, he is still a "son of David." This title was never used as a generic designation for ordinary people in Judaism but was reserved for Davidic descendants. If neither the primary author nor the Epilogist were being purely fictional, the use of this designation for the primary author likely indicates that he was a real descendant of the Davidic dynasty. His allusions to various Davidic kings, prophetic promises of restoration, and political persons and events during the Hellenistic Era (see "Date and Context" below) show that he was living after the fall of the kingdom of Judah. He was of royal lineage, though he was himself not a reigning king. In fact, he was living as the subject of a foreign king, as all Judeans were after 586 BC. This means that, in playing the role of a king in the first two chapters of the book, the primary author is not doing something completely alien to his identity. He is acting out his own heritage by which he should be the rightful king in Jerusalem, but all the while he knows that there is someone else on the throne—a non-Davidic foreigner. Had circumstances been different, he would have needed no mask to act the king, for he would have been reigning in Jerusalem himself. But the fact that he needs the mask reveals the plight of his own noble family, as well as that of the nation more broadly, and also the seemingly failed promises of God to restore Davidic rule. And this is part of the author's purpose. By alluding to significant facets of his national heritage, he evaluates it all and demonstrates just how far the nation had fallen. It had lost everything, and God seemed uninterested in doing anything to change this. Nothing new was forthcoming.

The most obvious clue, then, of the primary author's Davidic pedigree comes from the title of the book. The adoption of a Solomonic persona in the first two chapters also plays toward this, but more subtle clues arise in other parts of the discourse. These only come to more obvious light on a second reading of the book, after one has become more attuned to the vast array of biblical allusions throughout the discourse and fully appreciated where the author ends up at the conclusion of his many thoughts. For example, in 7:11 the author says that having an "inheritance" is a good thing, with the implication that not having one is bad. This is not a reference to receiving a wealthy windfall on the death of a relative, but rather picks up the standard biblical allusions depicting Israel as the "inheritance" (in Hebrew, *nahalah*) of Yahweh and as a Davidic kingdom. The insinuation is that the author is not in possession of his rightful royal "inheritance." In 10:16–17 he feels the right to pass judgment on poor kingship and argues that a descendant of the noble Davidic family would bring blessedness to the land. Across the entire discourse he sinks into a bleak state of mind in which he feels he has lost everything. And this is not simply a personal tragedy but a national one as well. The fortunes of the Jewish nation as a whole are closely tied to his own. These and other allusions appear throughout the book, and more detailed discussion will appear at the relevant parts of this commentary. Suffice it to say that the Solomonic persona that the author adopts at the beginning of his discourse is not merely a vehicle for making a philosophical point more forcefully. It also casts his own identity for the rest of the book, setting the tone in which it must be read. He is a Davidic descendant, the son of several illustrious Judean kings. But he can only wear this heritage as a mask, not a crown. The substance of his inheritance has gone. It has become "meaningless."

Unfortunately, we do not know the primary author's name. First Chronicles 3:17–24 gives us the names of people across several generations of the Davidic royal family after the fall of Jerusalem in 586 BC, extending just beyond 332 BC when Alexander conquered the region. Yet, the name "Qohelet" does not appear among them. It is, however, doubtful that "Qohelet" is the author's real name, even though we cannot discount the possibility completely. At Ecclesiastes 12:8, the term in Hebrew appears with the definite article as *haqqohelet*—"the" *qohelet*. This would be most unusual for a name, but completely normal for a substantive ("the convener"). This is the only unambiguous time in the whole book where the term appears with the definite article.[1] One could argue on the basis of the numbers that the original text lacked the article, and that a later scribe added it, either

1. Some would add 7:27 to this count, based on a plausible redivision of the Hebrew text. This would amend the phrase from *'amrah qohelet* to *'amar haqqohelet*, correcting the gender of the predicate verb from feminine to masculine.

accidentally or on the mistaken assumption that the term was a substantive rather than a name. And, for the most part, the Epilogist seems to refer to the author as though the term *qohelet* is indeed a name.

However, there is another reason that "Qohelet" is probably not the author's real name. In 10:20 the author implies that one should not speak or even think ill of the king in case someone informs him of it. As we will see, this does not prevent the author from making some acerbic criticisms of the king and other leaders in his society. He is a potent political commentator. The explosive nature of his criticisms means he needs to cover his tracks—all the more necessary if he is a patrician member of a once ruling dynasty. Thus, "Qohelet" appears to be a pen name, probably chosen because he was associated with assemblies of people, be they groups of students or laypeople whom he taught (cf. 12:9), official gatherings of authoritative bodies of which he was a member (cf. 12:11), or both. He was a king with no kingdom, forced to divert his energies from governance to wisdom and the criticism of governance. In line with the Epilogist, we will adopt "Qohelet" as the standard way of referring to him in this commentary.

If Qohelet drops hints at his Davidic ancestry throughout his discourse, one could argue that adopting a pen name does little to mask his identity. We can make three points in response to this. First, the explicit clue to Qohelet's Davidic pedigree comes from the Epilogist, not Qohelet himself. Second, we do not know Qohelet's fate. It could be that the pen name was not enough to screen his identity and that he suffered an ignoble end for his criticisms. We simply do not know. In building a profile of him, we can say very few things about him. The Epilogist tells us that he was a sage who taught people (12:9), suggesting considerable learning and wisdom. He was evidently familiar with Jerusalem and its temple (5:1–6) and in touch with political events in his day (see "Date and Context" below). He also seems familiar with the effects of old age (12:1–7). The book does not tell us whether Qohelet died peacefully in old age or whether he suffered for his views. Third, the Epilogist reflects on Qohelet and his legacy (12:9–10) in terms that strongly suggest Qohelet had died when his words were finally "published" (cf. Ben Sira [Prologue], 33). Even if the pen name was a thin veil, Qohelet's words only seem to have been disseminated posthumously. We are, therefore, in the dark about the manner of his death and what others knew about his identity.

Date and Context

Date

The tradition that viewed Solomon as the author of Ecclesiastes assigned the book a date in the mid- to late tenth century BC. We have seen, however, that this is no longer sustainable. Since the fall of Jerusalem in 586 BC was a past event for the author, it is the earliest possible date we can assign to Qohelet's discourse. The latest possible date comes from two sources. The first is the earliest extant manuscript of Ecclesiastes, 4QQoh[a] (also known as 4Q109), which was discovered at Qumran and is dated to c. 175–150 BC.[2] The second is the deuterocanonical book Ben Sira (also known as Sirach, or Ecclesiasticus), which Jesus Ben Sira originally penned in Hebrew in c. 180 BC and was subsequently translated into Greek by his grandson in c. 117 BC. Ben Sira was himself a sage in Jerusalem, as Qohelet appears to have been. Though the tone of Ben Sira is markedly different from Qohelet's, the two authors do share a similar theological framework. Ben Sira's tone and outlook, however, bear a strong resemblance to that of Qohelet's Epilogist, making a plausible case for the influence of Ecclesiastes over Ben Sira. These two factors place the latest possible date for Ecclesiastes at the beginning of the second century BC.

Two pieces of evidence for a more precise date have guided commentators in the past, namely language and Greek influence. The language of Ecclesiastes is Late Biblical Hebrew, with an affinity for some elements of even later Mishnaic Hebrew. Many argue that since Late Biblical Hebrew is a development from the earlier form of Standard Biblical Hebrew, which prevailed in the preexilic era, the book shows clear signs of a late postexilic composition. However, recent studies have suggested that the relationship between these two forms of Hebrew is not necessarily linear, making the linguistic dating of biblical books solely on the basis of the type of Hebrew unwise.[3] Other factors need to provide a more stable framework for dating.

Two Persian loanwords that appear in Ecclesiastes seem to help in this regard. The words are *pardesim* ("parks") in 2:5, and *pitgam* ("sentence" or "decree") in 8:11. Both words are indicative of Persian dominance and influence. *Pardes* is derived from the Persian word *pairidaeza*, denoting an enclosed royal park of grand scale, while *pitgam* conveys connotations of officialdom. These can only have entered Hebrew after the Persians conquered the Babylonian Empire in 539 BC and, therefore, held royal and legislative sway over Hebrew speakers. Before this time, Persia was not significant enough to have imparted these words to Hebrew, especially since the speakers of the respective languages were so far removed from each other.[4] Those who argue that the

2. Thomas Krüger, *Qoheleth*, Hermeneia (Minneapolis, MN: Fortress, 2004), 19.

3. See the detailed analysis in Ian M. Young, Robert Rezetko, and Martin Ehrensvärd, *Linguistic Dating of Biblical Texts*, 2 vols. (London: Equinox, 2009); Robert Rezetko and Ian Young, *Historical Linguistics and Biblical Hebrew: Steps Toward an Integrated Approach* (Atlanta: SBL Press, 2014).

4. Fredericks argues that Persia's existence prior to becoming an empire is sufficient to explain the entry of loanwords into Hebrew. See Daniel C. Fredericks, *Qoheleth's Language: Re-Evaluating*

loanwords represent later updating of the language have no evidential basis for the claim. It is also precarious to argue that a scribe needed to update easily understood Hebrew terms with later Persian loanwords. At any rate, the allusions to multiple biblical traditions down to the destruction of Jerusalem in 586 BC means we cannot date the Persian loanwords before the rise of Persia in 539 BC anyway.

Others have argued for the influence of Greek philosophy upon Qohelet, be it Stoicism, Epicureanism, Cynicism, or Skepticism. It borders on prejudicial to imply that Judeans did not think deeply before the arrival of the Greeks as overlords in the late fourth century BC. Similarity of ideas is suggestive, as Krüger intimates,[5] but it is not necessarily definitive. And yet, influence can be subtle, as one need not subscribe to all the facets of a philosophy to have been influenced by it. Without quotations or unambiguous allusions to Greek philosophers, it is difficult to find objective criteria that can determine the influence of Greek thinkers upon Qohelet, let alone the extent. Determining a direction of influence is a further hurdle. While it is historically more plausible that the culture of Greek overlords would have influenced the thought of a subordinate Jewish man, we cannot legitimately rule out the possibility that Qohelet derived his thought on his own, or even that he could have influenced others.

Nonetheless, it is the manner of Qohelet's profound skepticism that is significant on this count. As we will see, his thought calls into question much of conventional Jewish wisdom and orthodoxy that suggests an ability to think "outside the box" from an alternative perspective. For instance, while he agrees with the basic covenantal dynamic in which God blesses the righteous and punishes the wicked (e.g., 3:16; 7:15), he questions its application. He looks askance at the temple and what goes on there and discourages the taking of oaths (5:1–6). He even comes remarkably close to accusing God of wrongdoing (e.g., 1:13; 3:14–16; 7:13; 8:16–9:6). While Moses urges Israel to choose life (Deut 30:19), Qohelet finds death more desirable (6:3–5; 7:1–2). His basic motto is grim: "Everything is meaningless" (1:2). Those who claim Qohelet's thought aligns perfectly well with conventional wisdom can only do so by shoehorning his profound skepticism into an orthodox shape. We must

Its Nature and Date (Lewiston, NY: Edwin Mellen, 1988), 244. However, this seems to lean more heavily on connections to Elamite culture rather than Persian. It also does not adequately account for the earliest migration of Persian tribes into what would become their homeland in the ninth century BC, their relative lack of political organization prior to the eighth century BC, or the nature of the loanwords under discussion, which suggest grand levels of authority and culture. See Reza Zarghamee, *Discovering Cyrus* (Washington, DC: Mage, 2013), chap. 1.

5. Krüger, *Qoheleth*, 73–74.

ask what gives rise to such maverick contemplation. Is it the influence of Greek philosophy tearing him away from classic biblical faith? Is it personal circumstances alone that leads him to it? Is he just a non-conformist at heart? We will see that, despite his radical musings, Qohelet is still constrained by classic biblical ideals. Yet, a context under Greek influence has considerable explanatory power for some of his thornier sentiments. It does, however, still require additional evidence to confirm it.

Qohelet's political statements provide us with the best leverage for locating him historically. He treads rather cautiously in his discourse, because his comments are theologically, philosophically, and politically explosive. Though veiled in anonymity, he makes some very specific criticisms and allusions to people and events, all of which converge on one unequivocal historical window: the reign of Ptolemy III Euergetes (246–222 BC). This places Qohelet in Ptolemaic Jerusalem and sees him as a sage very much like Jesus Ben Sira, who wrote his wisdom book a few decades later (c. 180 BC). Qohelet would have been a contemporary of Sira, the grandfather of Jesus Ben Sira. It was the business of sages not just to engage in abstract philosophy but to reflect on developments that occurred around them. Jesus Ben Sira certainly did (cf. Ben Sira 36:1–22; 50:1–24), so it should come as no surprise that this is precisely what Qohelet before him did also. To appreciate Qohelet's reflections, then, we need to understand his historical context and the developments on which he comments.

Context

Alexander the Great defeated the Persian king Darius III Codomanus, conquering the Levant and Egypt in 332 BC before going on to take the rest of the Persian Empire in the following years. After Alexander's sudden death at Babylon in 323 BC, his chief personnel and relatives were left to squabble over the pieces of his empire. Among them were two of Alexander's generals, Ptolemy and Seleucus, who would found their own dynasties.

Ptolemy quickly took charge of Egypt and, over the next few decades, extended his control across the sea to the Aegean and parts of Asia Minor. He also supported Seleucus to gain control of territories in Syria, Mesopotamia, and Asia Minor, though it was not long before they became rivals themselves. In a bid to establish his supremacy over all claimants to Alexander's legacy, Ptolemy spirited away the embalmed body of Alexander, which he entombed in Egypt (initially in Memphis) as a sign that he was Alexander's true heir. In 305 BC Ptolemy declared himself king in Egypt, thus inaugurating what has come to be known as the Ptolemaic Kingdom. To augment his rule, he developed Alexandria, on the northwestern tip of the Nile Delta, as his capital.

He eventually had Alexander's body reburied in the city. He also founded the Museum of Alexandria, including its Royal Library, thus building Alexandria into the world's leading center of Greek learning and culture, outdoing even the cities of Greece itself.

In 301 BC Ptolemy captured Jerusalem in his bid to control the Levant, slaying many of the inhabitants and deporting many survivors to Alexandria. This was the first real influx of Jews into Alexandria, which soon came to have the largest Jewish population of any city in the world. For the next century Jerusalem and Judea were part of the Ptolemaic Kingdom. Over this time, the Ptolemies would fight a series of five wars with their neighbors to the north, the Seleucids.[6] Thus, Jerusalem and Judea were caught in the middle of a perpetual struggle between two Hellenistic kingdoms, each vying for control over it. Judea, along with the coastal plain of Palestine, formed a kind of bottleneck through which numerous trade routes passed, making it a strategic and lucrative gateway. Eventually, in 200 BC, the Seleucids wrested control of Judea away from the Ptolemies after defeating them in battle at Panias.

The century of Ptolemaic control had a profound effect on the Jewish nation. The Persians had ruled their empire as practically a confederacy of autonomous satrapies, which required a stringent governmental machinery to keep the entire mechanism operating well. Though not foolproof, this system provided the people of Judea with a reasonable measure of security, as all the cogs of empire worked together to provide mutual stability to its various parts. By contrast, the Ptolemies ruled their kingdom as a singular entity, which was viewed as the personal possession of the king. There was but a single cog of government, and it could spin at the pace the king determined without any others cogs to regulate it. This meant life for those in Judea (and other parts of the kingdom) was affected far more by the decisions of the king and his lackeys than it had been under the Persians. There was little governmental machinery to provide stability through predictable structures and systems of checks and balances. The king ruled completely at his own whim.

This situation had three significant effects. First, since the kingdom was much more about the king than its citizens, power was concentrated in a single center, namely the royal capital in Alexandria. This drew people to the metropolis, which inevitably took them away from their previous locations, thus changing the constituency of those locations. This had already happened to Jerusalem when Ptolemy I deported many of its surviving inhabitants to

6. Historians talk about six "Syrian Wars," but the sixth was fought in the second century BC after the Ptolemies lost control of Jerusalem.

Alexandria in 301 BC, but it continued for centuries after, as more Jews migrated to the city that provided them such a wealth of opportunities.[7]

Second, since the kingdom was technically the personal possession of the king, the Greek culture of the king had a considerable impact on it. This was different from the Persian Empire. Though Persian culture did indeed influence its empire's citizens, the relative autonomy of the satrapies and provinces helped foster local identities and cultures rather than rival them. In the Ptolemaic kingdom, there was no such filtering of Hellenism. While it did not eradicate local cultures, Hellenism certainly changed them, and it did convert many (cf. 3 Macc 1:3). Local Egyptian culture, for instance, was affected as it began the shift from the traditional ancient Egyptian culture into what would later become Coptic culture.[8] The Jews in Alexandria quickly became Hellenistic, adopting Greek language so thoroughly that, by the 260s BC, they needed to start translating the Scriptures from Hebrew into Greek. Judea also felt this cultural colonialism acutely, coming into direct contact with the Greek culture, language, and ideals of their overlords. Though the pace of Hellenization was not as rapid as it was for their compatriots in the cultural engine room at Alexandria, the cultural winds were still strong. The emergence of Greek personal names is one telling sign of this. The Museum of Alexandria, which attracted the best thinkers in the world, advanced the arts and sciences, giving Hellenism an exciting, progressive appeal that was strengthened via the network of Greek cities (*poleis*) and military colonies (*cleruchies*) established throughout the kingdom. Since Qohelet was a man of considerable learning who appears to have been well informed of events on both the local and international stage, it becomes implausible to argue that he was untouched in any way by Greek influence. All of Judaism was. The very fact that he engages in a kind of theater, acting the part of a king in the first two chapters of Ecclesiastes, is actually a rather Greek endeavor. It is not inconceivable that he had even traveled to Alexandria (cf. Sir 34:9; 39:4; 51:13).

Third, radical centralization affected the economics of the kingdom, as Alexandria exerted a pull on the flow of goods. One of the most important

7. The prologue to Ben Sira demonstrates that the allure of Alexandria continued even after the Ptolemies lost Judea to the Seleucids in 200 BC. Matthew 2:13–15 supports the idea that it continued into the Roman Era, as Jesus's family itself migrated to Egypt for a time, presumably to the Jewish community in Alexandria.

8. The adoption of Christianity in later centuries was a more consequential factor in this, as "Coptic" Orthodoxy shows, but the process of cultural change began in the Hellenistic Era. An uprising in Upper Egypt shortly after 217 BC, which established a traditional Egyptian state for two decades, is evidence that native Egyptians recoiled under the cultural pressure they experienced under the Ptolemies.

developments in this regard occurred during the reign of Ptolemy II Philadelphus (283–246 BC), when coinage replaced bartering as the basic means of economic exchange (see Listen to the Story for Eccl 8:2–10:4). This allowed for the one-way flow of goods, with Alexandria and the opulent royal court being the chief beneficiaries of it. The Ptolemies also imposed a considerable tax burden on their subjects. Those responsible for collecting taxes were invariably individuals with a personal relationship to the king. Ambition and whim often motivated such individuals, and the lack of real governmental machinery meant they could easily take advantage of ordinary citizens for their own personal gain. State-sanctioned extortion became commonplace. All this saw a massive redistribution of wealth toward those associated with the royal court. Since the entire kingdom was the personal possession of the king, his cronies did not view this as untoward. Everyone and everything existed for the king's pleasure. The closer you were to the king, the closer you were to wealth and comfort. It resulted in the wholesale dispossession of thousands of citizens, who were driven to the economic wall. Many fell into poverty, were forced into slavery, or even faced execution. Death and taxes were indeed certainties in Ptolemaic Judea. These economic conditions created a fabulously wealthy elite around the king, who controlled land and the means of production, and a landless peasantry in economic servility. Under such conditions, migration to Alexandria and the adoption of Hellenism became an attractive option for many.

All these factors are significant for understanding the specific people and events that Qohelet alludes to throughout his discourse. In 4:13–16 Qohelet relates an anecdote about a poor but wise youth who succeeds an old but foolish king. Commentators debate the details of the anecdote, especially whether there is a "second youth" who appears in the story or not. The ambiguities, however, fall away when we realize how precisely the anecdote maps onto the details of the politics of the time. At the end of the Second Syrian War in 253 BC, Ptolemy II Philadelphus concluded a peace deal with his Seleucid opponent in Syria, Antiochus II Theos (261–246 BC). The terms included the marriage of Ptolemy's daughter, Berenice, to Antiochus, which required Antiochus to exile his previous wife, Laodice, and her two sons, Seleucus and Antiochus Hierax. The purpose of this move was to produce a new heir to the Seleucid throne who was closely bound to the Ptolemies, thus leading to the eventual subordination of the Seleucid kingdom. After marrying Berenice, however, Antiochus foolishly returned to his first wife, only to be fatally poisoned by her in 246 BC. On his death, his estranged teenage son, Seleucus, rose up and took power back for himself. Antiochus II is the old but foolish king in the anecdote, while his son, Seleucus II, is the poor but wise youth who rises from exile to power. Before long, though, Seleucus was contending for power with his younger brother, Antiochus Hierax, who garnered widespread support among the disparate peoples of Asia Minor, becoming a king there in his own right for some time. Eventually, though, he lost his support base and died a fugitive's death in 227 BC. Antiochus Hierax is, therefore, the "second youth" (Eccl 4:15).[9] Qohelet's anecdote is obscure in both its detail and meaning until we see the precision with which he relates this Seleucid succession.

The reason Qohelet tells the anecdote in the first place is because of the effect it had on the political situation in Jerusalem in the 220s BC, to which he was a party. By then, Judea had felt the effects of Ptolemaic rule for over seventy years. Traditional Jewish culture was in a tug-of-war with Hellenism for the hearts and minds of its people, with many being drawn to life in Alexandria while those who remained struggled under the economic burdens the Ptolemies imposed. The Jewish High Priest in Jerusalem at the time was Onias II (*Ant.* 12.156–85). As high priest, he held charge (in Greek, *prostasia*) over the Jews in Judea, but he was required by oath to pay the Ptolemaic crown twenty silver talents for the privilege—an exorbitant amount. Ptolemy III was then on the throne in Alexandria. Onias seems generally to have had an anti-Ptolemaic tendency, which may have led Ptolemy III to demanding an oath for his allegiance. As mentioned above, Seleucus II had by this time pried the Seleucid kingdom away from the claws of the Ptolemies. And now, he was consolidating his power in Syria in the wake of his brother's losses. His bolstered position tempted Onias to switch his pledged allegiance from Ptolemy III to the Seleucid monarch, thereby extricating himself from his debt of twenty silver talents and aligning Judea with the Seleucids against Ptolemy III. Sometime in the 230s BC, Onias broke his oath and refused to pay Ptolemy III the fee for his position. Onias's actions upset the balance of power in the region, but for some years he went unchallenged by Ptolemy III. Then, in c. 228 BC, Ptolemy demanded Onias pay up and prove his loyalty.

Jerusalem now descended into chaos. Ptolemy threatened military action if Onias refused to pay, sending the people of Jerusalem into panic. The king sent an envoy to pressure Onias into paying the fee, but the high priest still refused (cf. Eccl 5:6). Onias put his position on the line, as he risked the wrath of both his imperial overlord, Ptolemy III (cf. 10:1–4), and his God,

---

9. The NIV translates this phrase as "the youth, the king's successor," giving the impression that the anecdote contains just two characters (the old king and the youth). However, the Hebrew text literally reads "the second youth," making it clear that the anecdote contains three characters. For a fuller discussion see George Athas, "Qohelet in His Context: Ecclesiastes 4,13–16 and the Dating of the Book," *Biblica* 100.3 (2019), 353–72.

in whose name he had sworn an oath to pay the monarch. In the eyes of the population, this could only spell disaster for the Jewish nation, and Qohelet agreed (cf. 5:1–7). The Ptolemaic burden on Judea was agonizing, so in one sense Onias's sentiments were understandable. But his delay in paying the fee came at a time when Ptolemy III was still in firm control of Judea. Thus, the high priest's recalcitrance threatened catastrophe, as the full might of Ptolemy's army would fall not on the Seleucids, but on Jerusalem itself. According to Qohelet, discretion was the better part of valor (cf. 7:11), for Onias could never have known whether his gamble would pay off (cf. 1:6; 11:3). Indeed, it did not. He was, therefore, foolish to favor the Seleucids in the north so flagrantly over the Ptolemies in the south (cf. 10:2). Despite being implored to change his mind and head to Alexandria to avert disaster, Onias remained resolute in defiance (cf. 10:15).

Just when all seemed lost, Onias's nephew, Joseph Tobias, stepped forward. Joseph was the son of Onias's sister and Tobias, a local Jewish aristocrat in Transjordan with decidedly Hellenistic leanings, who had been in good standing with the Ptolemies. Full of charisma and political acumen, Joseph canvassed enough support to act as the city's spokesman in Onias's stead. He even won over the confidence of the masses after holding an assembly in the temple and promising to resolve the crisis (cf. Eccl 8:10; *Ant.* 12.164–65). With popular support behind him, Joseph used his personal charm and aplomb to gain favor with Ptolemy's envoy. He then gained further backing from local magnates to head to the royal court in Alexandria, where he fawned over the king and his queen and managed to satisfy Ptolemy that Onias did not pose any substantive threat and that Judea was not in rebellion against Ptolemaic rule. Disaster had been averted, and Jerusalem was spared. Joseph Tobias had saved the day.

However, while Joseph was in Alexandria, he was present for the negotiation of rights to farm taxes throughout Syria, which included Judea. The burden over the region was already breaking the backs of lowly citizens. Yet, with brazen audacity and the opportunism that comes from unbridled ambition and greed, Joseph pledged to gather twice the amount of taxes for Ptolemy (*Ant.* 12.169–85). Joseph most likely sensed that Ptolemy did not wish to appear weak in the face of Onias's defiance, thus presenting him with the perfect means of appeasing his wrath, saving face, displaying strength, and filling his coffers even more. Joseph had backed his uncle, Onias, into a corner, thus giving himself considerable power over the Jewish nation, in addition to the prospect of lining his own pockets by taking a substantial cut of the tax revenues he raised. So Ptolemy awarded Joseph the right to farm taxes in a deal that was mutually beneficial for both of them but horrendous for the population of Judea and its neighbors. If life had been difficult for citizens before this moment, it now became abject misery (cf. Eccl 3:16; 5:17; 7:15).

Onias had been outmaneuvered by his nephew, Joseph. Ironically, he now owed his survival in priestly office to Joseph. This became even more apparent when, just two years later in 225 BC, Seleucus II fell from his horse and died, leaving Onias without any support among the Seleucids. He now had to grovel back to Ptolemy, with Joseph as his only "ally." It is hard to know whether Qohelet wrote before or after Seleucus's demise; either way, he deplored Onias's supreme irresponsibility, which had handed so much power to the avaricious and thoroughly Hellenistic Joseph, at such cost to the Jewish nation. All these actions took place amid the tectonic pressure that Hellenism was already exerting on Judaism. They were not, therefore, of minor significance. They threatened the very future of the Jewish nation itself, turning it into the tinderbox that would erupt into blazing revolution under the Maccabees in 167 BC.

Qohelet makes frequent allusions to these developments that imperiled Jerusalem between 230–225 BC. I have given a very quick overview of the events here, but they will be discussed in greater detail, particularly the way they intersect with Qohelet's discourse, as they arise throughout the commentary. Suffice it to say that these allusions are not sparse and ambiguous, but numerous and conspicuous. At certain points, it is only knowledge of the historical events that helps us make sense of what are otherwise strangely specific sayings with peculiar meanings (e.g., 4:13–16; 8:10; 10:15). Knowing the context, in other words, saves us from needing to perform acrobatic exegesis. Qohelet employs what seem to be many generic altruisms, but not because he is engaging solely in general philosophy and wisdom.[10] It is, rather, his rhetorical strategy as a sage. He clothes the specific circumstances of his day in proverbial generalities in order to highlight the general wisdom principles that guided his evaluations. He invites the reader to consider his critique of the people and events of his day from the perspective of classic biblical wisdom. But, in doing this, he not only critiques the people and events in his sights but also enables the reader to see the shortcomings of cherished conventional wisdom for making sense of them or solving them. It is one of the ways he demonstrates that "everything is meaningless" (1:2). It is similar to the kind of parable-strategy that Jesus used, which encouraged the one who has ears to hear, to hear (cf. Matt 11:15).

10. Contra Tremper Longman, "Determining the Historical Context of Ecclesiastes," in *The Words of the Wise are Like Goads: Engaging Qohelet in the 21st Century* (ed. Mark J. Boda, Tremper Longman, and Cristian G. Rata; Winona Lake, IN: Eisenbrauns), 89–102.

Message

As mentioned previously, commentators have derived a range of interpretations of the book of Ecclesiastes. For some, it is a book wholly in keeping with traditional biblical wisdom, while for others it is a radically unorthodox manifesto. One of the interpretive cruxes for determining the interpretation is the ideological relationship between Qohelet and the Epilogist. I will reserve most of the analysis of this question for the treatment of the epilogue itself (12:9–14), but I see the Epilogist as endorsing Qohelet's thought and giving further caution beyond it.

One of the temptations with Ecclesiastes is to align the book's message with that of other books of the Bible. This is enticing, particularly when Qohelet's thought seems opaque or when he uses words or ideas that have parallels in other biblical books. This interpretive strategy is often described as "Scripture interpreting Scripture." However, it fails to let each biblical writer say what they want to say in their own context before understanding them within the larger configuration of Scripture. Sometimes this occurs inadvertently, because we can't help but import the ideas associated with similar words in other parts of the Bible into the text we are reading. Nevertheless, it is an interpretive error whereby we make all of Scripture sing the same note rather than listen more carefully for its chorus of harmonies. In Qohelet's case, we can claim to be listening to him when, in fact, we are listening to someone else's voice and thinking it is coming from Qohelet's lips. Alternatively, we might only listen to Qohelet when he strikes a note we have heard elsewhere in Scripture. Qohelet is evaluating the biblical heritage of his own Davidic ancestry and of his Jewish nation more generally. He is also conversing with what seems to be popular opinion or conventional wisdom. He will, therefore, draw on many ideas that can be found in other parts of Scripture. However, such reference does not necessitate his wholesale agreement with them. We must remember that Qohelet was not writing into the ether but was impacted by his specific historical context even as he sought to speak into it. Once we discern the contours of the historical events and persons in Qohelet's discourse, we are in a better position to determine how he deals with ideas found elsewhere in Scripture and so appreciate his distinctive message and its contribution to the wider scriptural chorus.

Most commentators view Ecclesiastes as a philosophical reflection of some kind. That is, they see Qohelet (and the Epilogist) asking ultimate questions about the meaning of life. In this endeavor, Qohelet weighs up evidence and counter-evidence to derive a perspective on human life under the sovereignty of God, with some viewing his musings as positive and others as negative.

There is considerable truth to this view, since Qohelet is indeed a sage examining philosophical issues. But he is doing so much more than this. To leave Qohelet's thought solely in the realm of philosophical reflection is to lift him out of his historical context and miss just how embedded he is in Israel's history, not just its thought and traditions. He is not just contemplating life in general, but life in a specific circumstance. This circumstance was, broadly, the era "Before Christ" and, more narrowly, the era of Ptolemaic sway over Judea in the late third century BC. We need to understand this circumstance in order to listen properly to what he (and the Epilogist) have to say. Failure to see how Qohelet interacts with his immediate context leads to an absolutizing tendency, in which we elevate his statement to the level of polished doctrinal formulation that transcends a particular context. But this is like letting go of the balloon and letting it float untethered into the ether, where the winds of our own concerns take Qohelet's words in whatever direction our subconscious blows. To do justice to Qohelet, we must not relinquish the historically embedded nature of his reflections or impose our expectations on what he has produced.

We encounter Qohelet's basic message in his motto, which appears at 1:2 and 12:8, with echoes of it a further twenty-eight times throughout the book: "Meaningless! Meaningless! Everything is meaningless!" This deeply pessimistic note resounds ubiquitously throughout his discourse. Again, more detailed discussion will follow in the commentary, but, by way of introduction we should note two things. First, the keyword of his motto is the Hebrew word *hebel*, which the NIV translates as "meaningless." It has a range of meanings, which include such connotations as "vapor," "transient," "worthless," "absurd," and "pointless," to name but a few. This often leaves commentators reaching for one particular connotation that dominates Qohelet's discourse, but his pessimism is so pervasive that, through the course of his contemplations, he cycles through them all. Second, Qohelet does not qualify the statement at all. For example, it is not as though he is saying that life *without God* is meaningless. It is an absolute statement that takes in all of life "under the sun," including his biblical heritage. He sees absolutely everything as "meaningless" (*hebel*). It is a rather hopeless message.

The reason for Qohelet's profound pessimism is twofold. First, death is the great leveler of humanity that renders all human endeavor worthless. Life is a zero-sum game (cf. 5:16). And since humanity inevitably gains no "profit" from it, life loses its value. Part of Qohelet's thinking on this is that death is the effective end of all human existence (9:1–6), and he is agnostic about any notion of post-mortem judgment (3:21). For him, death is the final line in the ledger of life. Second, Qohelet's Ptolemaic context has a deep impact on his psyche. Since Jerusalem fell in 586 BC, there had been no independent kingdom of Judah. The nation had been subject to a series of foreign empires, with conflicts being concentrated in the century or so prior to the writing of the book. Qohelet perceives the cultural threat of Hellenism even as he seems partially influenced by it. He also rails against the economic burdens that the Ptolemies and Joseph Tobias imposed on people, filling their lives with misery and frustration (5:17). These had led him to observing the incongruous situation of the righteous suffering and the wicked prospering, with no sensible way of dealing with this perverse reality (7:15–18). And having experienced the consequences of Onias's political gambling and Joseph Tobias's rank opportunism, Qohelet feels that he is witnessing the final death of his nation and their hopes of restoration. His despair is reminiscent of the poet in Lamentations, who had experienced the catastrophe of 586 BC.

Qohelet's despair, therefore, does come from classic biblical hopes, particularly as expressed in the prophets for the restoration of an independent Davidic kingdom in the land of Israel. He longs for a return to the glories of the past, even acting them out to some extent in the first two chapters. Alas, he feels they are now beyond reach. The folly and evil of human beings have imperiled the nation's future.

One of Qohelet's primary purposes in writing is to expose the limitations of conventional wisdom, which he feels cannot right the injustices he observes throughout society. The national covenant included the principle of retribution, whereby God blessed the righteous and punished the wicked. But this had been upended in Ptolemaic society. Instead, the inversion of justice had been institutionalized. Thus, Qohelet feels that the nation was so far gone that nothing could save it from oblivion. He did not believe conventional wisdom was somehow wrong, but rather that it was hopelessly inadequate for dealing with the current crisis, for just "a little folly outweighs wisdom and honor" (10:1). Qohelet converses at length with traditional wisdom, often quoting popular proverbs and coining new anti-proverbs in response, to demonstrate how wisdom simply did not have the necessary clout to rescue the nation from an ignoble end. It left him not knowing where to turn. Everything was meaningless.

It seems odd, then, that Qohelet punctuates his discourse with advice to enjoy life (2:24; 3:12–13; 5:18; 8:15; 9:7–10; 11:8). Some commentators latch onto these encouragements to eat, drink and find satisfaction in work as proof of Qohelet's optimism, characterizing his theology as a positive biblical form of *carpe diem* ("Seize the day!").[11] However, this usually comes

11. For example, see Michael A. Eaton, *Ecclesiastes*, Tyndale Old Testament Commentaries (Leicester: Inter-Varsity Press, 1983), 73–77; David A. Hubbard, *Ecclesiastes, Song of Songs* (Dallas, TX.: Word

from a lack of awareness of Qohelet's historical context and must overlook the prevalence of his motto and the titanic pessimism that weighs him down at every point. One has, for example, a very hard time reconciling a positive outlook with his arresting claim that the most blessed person in all human existence is the stillborn baby who has never experienced life "under the sun" (6:3–5). Qohelet's thoughts stem from a sense that life should not be a misery—that it should be enjoyed (3:22). In concert with this, he feels that God should make good on his historic promises of restoration. However, he does not think these to be realistic possibilities in the dire straits of Ptolemaic Jerusalem, with the nation's death brewing (1:4–11). Since he sees no real hope for the nation, he encourages his readers, as far as it is possible for them, to salvage crumbs of joy in their wretched existence before it comes to a dismal end.

Yet Qohelet even sees the attainment of such meager scraps of enjoyment as the result of chance, which is ultimately up to God's decision, not human effort (1:13, 15; 3:10, 14; 7:13–14; 9:11). This comes from Qohelet's orthodox conviction that Yahweh, the God of Israel, is supremely sovereign over all human life. God directs the course of history and assigns to each person their "lot" in life (3:1–11; 5:18–19; 7:13–14). This does not mean humans have no responsibility for their decisions. On the contrary, Qohelet's criticisms of Ptolemy III, Onias II, and Joseph Tobias attest to his understanding that humans do have genuine choices in life that can be evaluated as wise or foolish, good or evil. However, he sees this working in concert with the pervasive sovereignty of God.

This and the lamentable situation of Ptolemaic Judea in the 220s BC leaves Qohelet with a profound theological problem: If God is sovereign over human affairs, and God says that he works according to the principle of retribution as stipulated in the national covenant, and God has promised to restore the nation as a Davidic kingdom, why has God allowed the nation to sink irredeemably into such a dark abyss? The sovereignty of God and the reality of his context leave Qohelet thoroughly flummoxed and despondent. On the one hand, it leads him very close to the theological precipice of charging God with evil intent. Yet, he never does so. Qohelet is still a pious Jew constrained by orthodoxy. In fact, he is genuinely afraid of God, seeing him as wielding absolute power in a baffling and unpredictable way, so Qohelet dares not attribute wickedness to him. He believes God has imparted to humans

Books, 1991), 92–93; David George Moore and Daniel L. Akin, *Ecclesiastes, Songs of Songs*, Holman Old Testament Commentary (Nashville: Broadman & Holman, 2003), 32–34; Sidney Greidanus, *Preaching Christ from Ecclesiastes: Foundations for Expository Sermons* (Grand Rapids: Eerdmans, 2010), 50, 53–54.

a sense that there is a purpose to history, but knowledge of this purpose is beyond human reach (3:11). Not even wisdom, or fear of the Lord that is the beginning of knowledge (cf. Prov 1:7; Eccl 12:13), can give humans insight into the depths of God's mind. God's ways are inscrutable, and so wisdom has only limited value, which had been curtailed even further after recent events upended justice and threatened to snuff the nation out completely—events that God himself must have ordained. It leads Qohelet to the conclusion that God directs history so that human beings become scared of him (3:14), as Qohelet himself was. But this leaves Qohelet with no way of making sense of God's dealings with his covenant nation throughout history. Everything was meaningless.

The Epilogist agrees with Qohelet's grim assessment of life in Ptolemaic Jerusalem. But rather than despair, the Epilogist gives expression to a more traditional mindset that has a measure of hope attached to it. This initially seems at odds with Qohelet's pessimism, but the Epilogist is not contradicting him. He is, rather, injecting a shot of marshal austerity and steely resolve into the readers precisely because Qohelet's assessment was right. The nation was in grave danger of oblivion. So, he advises the readers to "fear God and keep the commandments" (12:13). The Epilogist does not believe this will somehow rescue the nation, for, as Qohelet has shown, traditional wisdom does not have the power to achieve this. Instead, as we will see when discussing the Epilogist's words (12:9–14), the Epilogist's outlook is shaped by apocalyptic eschatology, which looked to God for direct intervention in human affairs to rescue the Jewish nation from the cultural and historical abyss. Indeed, the development of apocalyptic thinking in Judaism arose at this very time, when Jewish identity and hopes were under grave threat.

When we see Qohelet's place in history and his bleak evaluation of life and hopes for the Jewish nation, we are in a far better position to appreciate the coming of Jesus. We can discern the historical, cultural, and theological tides that were beating against the Jewish nation in the centuries leading up to Jesus's bursting onto the scene. It lets us see that he was not a religious genius who appeared out of the blue with a new philosophy. Rather, we see his life and ministry in the bigger story of God's dealings with his covenant people, Israel. Time for the nation was running out, and Jesus was its last hope. He was sent to the "lost sheep of Israel" (Matt 15:24), whom he came to seek and to save (Luke 19:10). His prophetic ministry, his miracles, his teaching, and ultimately his death and resurrection are seen from within the story of God's people. And, as we will see, this gives us a far better appreciation of how Jesus's death and resurrection opens the gates of salvation to people from all nations.

Genre and Structure

The Epilogist is responsible for the "publication" of Qohelet's discourse, which he framed with a title (Eccl 1:1) and an epilogue (12:9–14).[12] His hand is also evident briefly at 7:27, where he interrupts Qohelet's words and refers to him in the third person. We do not know exactly when the Epilogist published Qohelet's work, but his familiarity with Qohelet suggests he knew Qohelet personally and issued the book soon after his death. It might have coincided with the death of Ptolemy III in 222 BC, the accession of Simon II to the high priesthood in place of his father, Onias II, in c. 219 BC,[13] or developments in the aftermath of Ptolemy IV's surprising victory over Antiochus III at the Battle of Raphia in 217 BC (see 3 Maccabees).

Qohelet's material (Eccl 1:2–12:8) is written in the first person as a single discourse. It contains several passages where Qohelet overtly expresses his own thoughts or observations (e.g., 7:15–22), but these are mixed with poems (e.g., 3:1–8), proverbs (e.g., 9:17–10:3), and other such wisdom material (9:11–12). The first "monologue," in which Qohelet plays the part of a king (1:12–2:26), initially has the feeling of a royal autobiography, until it becomes apparent afterwards that Qohelet is not actually a king. There are also Qohelet's many political comments, which are dressed as observations or wise counsel. There is, therefore, an eclectic mix of genres within Qohelet's work, making it difficult to classify the whole. We must also account for the way Qohelet's historical context, personal situation, and theological heritage impact his thought. Perhaps the most elastic category that the book fits into is "theological and philosophical soliloquy."

Qohelet's train of thought begins in orderly fashion, with a poetic introduction (1:3–11), his royal theater (1:12–2:26), and a poem on the seasons of life (3:1–8). Thereafter, the train of thought seems to meander haphazardly, making it notoriously difficult to discern a deliberate structure beyond that point. Three potential structural markers present themselves by their frequency: (1) the introduction of a new observation (e.g., 4:1); (2) the reiteration of a form of the motto (e.g., 2:11); or (3) the advice to enjoy life (e.g., 2:24). The coincidence of some of these does provide a sense of transition

---

12. The book of Ben Sira follows a similar strategy.

13. The timing of Simon II's accession to the high priesthood is not known precisely, as the sources give us a conflicting picture. Josephus states that Onias died and left the high priesthood to his son, Simon II, at about the same time that Joseph Tobias died (*Ant.* 12.224), which was c. 205 BC. However, 2 Macc 3 sees Simon II in office by the time the Battle of Raphia occurred in 217 BC. Both sources have significant issues, but Simon II's accomplishments and generally stellar reputation suggest he came to office well before 205 BC. Thus, most historians place his accession to the high priesthood in c. 219 BC, shortly before the Battle of Raphia.

(e.g., 3:19–22), but they often do not align perfectly. There is, therefore, a sense that most of Qohelet's thought after the poem in 3:1–8 lacks a specific structure until the very end, when he relates a haunting poem on old age and death, which itself reflects what he sees as the death of his nation (12:2–7). In fact, it seems that most of Qohelet's discourse deliberately lacks structure as a rhetorical device to demonstrate his motto that all is meaningless. It begins with what at first appears orderly, then descends into the disorderly, before expiring with one last discernible sigh at the end. There is no clear literary seam between these stages. The whole movement gives a sense of uncontrolled, heavy descent into darkness and oblivion, capturing perfectly Qohelet's sense of the fate of humanity and, more particularly, the Jewish nation.

Qohelet is, therefore, quite a sophisticated thinker and author. The form of his discourse—or rather, its lack of form—helps create his message. Additionally, throughout his reflections, he employs several rhetorical techniques that further his purpose. For example, he uses the strategy of *reductio ad absurdum*, by which he takes a claim to its logical extreme to expose its faults (e.g., 7:15–18). He uses juxtaposition to show how two seemingly contradictory statements each have an element of truth, thereby demonstrating the logical knots that can arise within conventional wisdom (e.g., 7:13–14; 8:12–13). He measures theory against reality to show the shortcomings in orthodoxy and wisdom (e.g., 7:19–20). He also coins anti-proverbs that enshrine what he sees as the impotence of wisdom in the crisis of his own time (e.g., 7:1). He uses these techniques not because he is a rogue thinker wanting to tear down bastions of orthodoxy and wisdom, but because his penetrating thought leaves him in an utter quandary about God, humanity, life, and history. The form, tenor, rhetorical techniques, and content of Qohelet's thought, therefore, lead me to deny that there is any immediate positive in his message. Contrary to some commentators, I do not see his encouragement to "eat, drink, and find satisfaction in their own toil" (2:24) as redeeming the negative aspects of his thought. Rather, all his techniques reinforce his pervasive pessimism.

For the purposes of this commentary, I have divided the text into units that, for the most part, dwell on a couple of themes, thus providing the best opportunity to expose the message of the book. I do not pretend that this is the only way to divide the book, for, as just mentioned, Qohelet's structure is deliberately vague. But I have tried to work with the more obvious transitions and give a sense of Qohelet's purpose when they are not so obvious. Thus, my division is motivated by a combination of Qohelet's own content and pragmatics arising from the aims of this commentary series. Accordingly, the commentary will proceed on the following structure:

1:1–11	**Introduction**
1:1	Title
1:2	The Motto
1:3–11	The Preface
1:12–2:26	**Royal Theater**
1:12–18	Testing Wisdom
2:1–16	The Pursuit of Happiness
2:17–23	A Legacy of Frustration
2:24–26	Clutching at Straws
3:1–4:16	**The Sovereignty of God over Human Life**
3:1–8	A Time for Everything
3:9–15	Hapless Humans Before an Awful God
3:16–22	Dehumanizing Humans
4:1–3	The Tears of the Oppressed
4:4–6	The Greed of the Upwardly Mobile
4:7–12	Working Hard for Nothing
4:13–16	Changing Fortunes
5:1–6:6	**Folly and Evil**
5:1–7	Folly in Sacrifice and Breaking Oaths
5:8–12	The Vicious Circle of Corruption
5:13–6:6	Grievous Evils
6:7–8:1	**The Limits of Wisdom**
6:7–12	Deconstructing Conventional Wisdom
7:1–14	Devaluing Conventional Wisdom
7:15–24	The Limits of Orthodoxy and Wisdom
7:25–8:1	The Superficiality of Conventional Wisdom
8:2–10:4	**The Good, the Bad, the Meaningless**
8:2–15	Defying the King
8:16–9:6	The Same Destiny Overtakes All
9:7–12	Enjoying a Meaningless Life
9:13–10:4	Folly Outweighs Wisdom
10:5–12:8	**The Approaching End**
10:5–15	The Consequences of Folly
10:16–20	Criticizing the King
11:1–6	Playing it Safe
11:7–8	Attempting to Enjoy Life
11:9–12:8	Living in the Shadow of Death
12:9–14	**Epilogue**
12:9–10	The Work of Qohelet
12:11–12	The Words of the Sages
12:13–14	The Conclusion

Resources for Teaching and Preaching

The monographs and commentaries detailed in the footnotes of this volume represent a wide range of interpretations of Ecclesiastes, which is testament to the difficulty of interpreting the book. The works I found most stimulating and valuable in my endeavors were those by Barbour, Fox, Krüger, Longman, Shields, and Sneed. The following works will buttress further study into the message and background of Ecclesiastes.

Alter, Robert. *The Wisdom Books: Job, Proverbs, and Ecclesiastes*. New York: Norton, 2010.

Athas, George. *Bridging the Testaments*. Grand Rapids: Zondervan (forthcoming).

Dell, Katharine J. *Interpreting Ecclesiastes: Readers Old and New*. Critical Studies in the Hebrew Bible 3. Winona Lake, IN: Eisenbrauns, 2013.

Grant, Michael. *From Alexander to Cleopatra: The Hellenistic World*. London: Weidenfeld & Nicolson, 1982.

Perdue, Leo G. *The Sword and the Stylus: An Introduction to Wisdom in the Age of Empires*. Grand Rapids: Eerdmans, 2008.

Schäfer, Peter. *The History of the Jews in the Greco-Roman World*. Rev. ed. London: Routledge, 2003.

VanderKam, James C. *From Joshua to Caiaphas: High Priests after the Exile*. Philadelphia: Fortress, 2004.

CHAPTER 1

Ecclesiastes 1:1–11

LISTEN to the Story

1The words of the Teacher, son of David, king in Jerusalem:

2"Meaningless! Meaningless!"
says the Teacher.
"Utterly meaningless!
Everything is meaningless."
3What do people gain from all their labors
at which they toil under the sun?
4Generations come and generations go,
but the earth remains forever.
5The sun rises and the sun sets,
and hurries back to where it rises.
6The wind blows to the south
and turns to the north;
round and round it goes,
ever returning on its course.
7All streams flow into the sea,
yet the sea is never full.
To the place the streams come from,
there they return again.
8All things are wearisome,
more than one can say.
The eye never has enough of seeing,
nor the ear its fill of hearing.
9What has been will be again,
what has been done will be done again;
there is nothing new under the sun.
10Is there anything of which one can say,
"Look! This is something new"?

It was here already, long ago;
it was here before our time.
[11]No one remembers the former generations,
and even those yet to come
will not be remembered
by those who follow them.

Listening to the Text in the Story: 2 Samuel 7; 1 Chronicles 3:19–24; Psalm 89; Isaiah 65:17; Epic of Gilgamesh, Tablet III (Old Babylonian version); *Harper's Song* from the Tomb of Intef; Satrap Stele of Ptolemy I; Pithom Stele of Ptolemy II; Canopus Decree of Ptolemy III.

Ecclesiastes begins with a title and a preface introducing us to the main speaker and his ideas. The main speaker is in some way connected to King David (Eccl 1:1). Davidic rule began when God chose a young David to replace a wayward Saul as king over God's covenant people, Israel (1 Sam 16), toward the end of the eleventh century BC. Of particular importance is 2 Samuel 7, which relates the covenant that Yahweh made with David. The basic premise of this milestone revelation was that Yahweh would adopt David's heir as God's own son to rule Israel on his behalf. This was a permanent arrangement that placed David's dynasty at the fore of human authority within the people of God. Through the prophet Nathan, Yahweh announced to David, "Your house and your kingdom will endure forever before me; your throne will be established forever" (2 Sam 7:16).

Israel split into two kingdoms after the reign of David's son, Solomon. While there was an unhealthy turnover of dynasties in the northern kingdom of Israel, the house of David ruled fairly steadily in the southern kingdom of Judah. It all came to an end, though, in 586 BC when the Babylonians destroyed Jerusalem, its temple, and the entire kingdom of Judah, deporting many Judean survivors, including members of the royal family, to the environs of Babylon. This would have seemed inconceivable when Yahweh initiated the covenant with David. Psalm 89 captures the theological confusion that the dynasty's demise produced. "You have renounced the covenant with your servant and have defiled his crown in the dust," the psalmist vents at God (Ps 89:39[89:40][1]). He goes on to beg God to change this dismal situation before he dies.

1. In instances where the verse numbering differs between English versions and the original Hebrew text, the Hebrew verse(s) will be noted in square brackets, as is the case here.

How long, LORD? Will you hide yourself forever?
    How long will your wrath burn like fire?
Remember how fleeting is my life.
    For what futility you have created all humanity!
Who can live and not see death,
    or who can escape the power of the grave?
        (Ps 89:46–48[89:47–49])

The psalmist's despondency takes on an air of accusation, for not only does God's apparent rejection of the Davidic dynasty seem whimsical in light of the covenantal promises, but human death also seems to depict God as toying monstrously with creation. The psalmist's anger is mixed with despair, as is often the case when someone goes through adverse circumstances beyond their control. We see the psalmist pining for God to change the present and do something new—something the author of Ecclesiastes also desires (cf. Eccl 1:10).

Judeans were eventually permitted to return to their homeland after Cyrus the Persian conquered Babylon in 539 BC. The last Davidic descendent to have wielded official power of any sort was Zerubbabel, who spearheaded the reconstruction of God's temple in Jerusalem (c. 520 BC). His efforts at the time were seen as the first step in restoring the Davidic kingdom they had lost some seventy years earlier. Zerubbabel may have been crowned locally as king in Jerusalem, but, even if so, it was short lived. Darius I took over the Persian Empire and, with an iron fist, crushed perceived rebellion throughout his domain during his first few years of rule.[2] From that time onward, the Davidic royal family receded into the background of life in Jerusalem. By the time of Ezra (458 BC) and Nehemiah (444 BC), they held no official power at all. The genealogy of 1 Chronicles 3:19–24 tells us the names of eleven generations of Zerubbabel's descendants, taking us past Alexander's conquest of the region in 332 BC and down to the time Ptolemy I captured Jerusalem in 301 BC. The Davidic royal family could certainly be identified at the beginning of this Hellenistic Era, but they were at most minor celebrities by then. By the first century AD, they were nothing more than plebs who could live quiet lives as tradesmen in the backwaters of Galilee. Up to that point, the fortunes of the house of David looked grim, as God seems not to have addressed the psalmist's cries in Psalm 89.

---

2. While no specific biblical text relates the crowning of Zerubbabel, there are texts that provide strong circumstantial evidence that it did occur. Zerubbabel was probably crowned in late 520 BC during a spate of "rebellions" across the Persian Empire, only to be removed from power barely weeks later by the forces of Darius I (reigned 522–486 BC). See Hag 2:20–23; Zech 4:1–14; 6:9–15.

From the very outset of Ecclesiastes, we encounter a tone of pessimism stemming from the universal human experience of death. Reflections on death are not, of course, unique to biblical writers but are found in writings from all cultures. One of the earliest epics in human literature is the Epic of Gilgamesh. In the Old Babylonian version (c. 1800 BC), the protagonist, King Gilgamesh, declares his intention to journey to the Cedar Forest where he will take on its dangerous guardian, Huwawa.[3] His alter ego, the originally wild, but now increasingly civilized, Enkidu, tries to dissuade him, since it will put Gilgamesh in mortal peril. Gilgamesh, however, retorts, "Who, my friend, can scale heaven? Only the gods live forever under the sun. As for mankind, numbered are their days; Whatever they achieve is but the wind!"[4] In other words, Gilgamesh points to the universal human experience of mortality to say that he will have to die some day. It is a pessimistic outlook but, for Gilgamesh, one that instills him with current bravery for a death-defying task he hopes might yield him some gain. "Should I fail," he says, "I shall have made me a name: 'Gilgamesh'—they will say—'against fierce Huwawa has fallen!'"[5] Renown is, for Gilgamesh, some measure of consolation, and therefore he begins his journey feeling he has little to lose. While he vanquishes Huwawa, his journey ironically leads to the death of Enkidu. This sets Gilgamesh on another quest for the secret of immortality—a quest that ultimately fails. Instead, his own earlier words are confirmed: only the gods live forever, and humans are destined to die. But while Gilgamesh dies, his name and exploits survive. A key lesson of the epic, therefore, is that the best human beings may hope for in life is to be someone who will be remembered by later generations.

Yet even this outcome is questionable. From Egypt come a variety of funerary reflections on death known as *Harper's Songs*. Most of these praise the traditional Egyptian notion of an afterlife, but some take a more skeptical view that is resigned to death as the ultimate end of human existence. One version that was originally inscribed on the Middle Kingdom tomb of Pharaoh Intef I (c. 2100 BC), but copied subsequently, dejectedly declares:

> A generation passes,
> Another stays,
> Since the time of the ancestors.
> The gods who were before rest in their tombs,
> Blessed nobles too are buried in their tombs.

3. Huwawa is also known by the Assyrian name, Humbaba.
4. Tablet III, lines 5–8. See *ANET*, 79.
5. Tablet III, line 13–15. See *ANET*, 79.

(Yet) those who built tombs,
Their places are gone,
What has become of them?
I have heard the words of Imhotep and Hardedef,
Whose sayings are recited whole.
What of their places?
Their walls have crumbled,
Their places are gone,
As though they had never been![6]

The song describes the transience of all human beings, even the most renowned, in terms very similar to those the author of Ecclesiastes uses in 1:1–11.

Ancient Near Eastern monarchs frequently depicted royal scenes beneath a winged sun disk representing the divine realm. This can be observed, for example, in Assyrian, Babylonian, and Persian reliefs. More relevant to our endeavors are the depictions from Egypt, where the winged sun disk was also flanked by rearing cobras (the double "uraeus"). This was a symbol of divine protection and authority that also adorned the brow of many a Pharaoh. After Alexander the Great died in 323 BC, his general Ptolemy established his own dynasty in Egypt, quickly adopting the traditional trappings of the Pharaohs. The Ptolemies depicted the winged sun disk differently than their Egyptian predecessors. Rather than adopting a compact design,[7] the Ptolemies elongated the sun disk's wings and curved them to form a dome over the scene beneath. We see this, for example, on Ptolemy I's Satrap Stele, the Pithom Stele of Ptolemy II (reigned 285–246 BC), and the Canopus Decree of Ptolemy III (reigned 246–222 BC).[8] This stylization gave the impression that every activity occurred "under the sun" (that is, the divine realm). It also implied the Ptolemaic Dynasty was divinely sanctioned—an idea reinforced by gold coins depicting a deified Ptolemy III wearing a crown of solar rays. This would have been a difficult ideology to accept in Jerusalem at the time, particularly amongst those who still hoped for the revival of an independent Davidic kingdom. Indeed, it is precisely in this period of history that apocalyptic eschatology, which longed for radical historical transformation, really gained momentum (see discussion of 12:13–14). Ptolemy I captured Jerusalem in

6. Miriam Lichtheim, *Ancient Egyptian Literature: A Book of Readings. Volume I: The Old and Middle Kingdoms* (Berkeley: University of California Press, 1973), 196.

7. A good example of the compact design is on the famous "Israel Stele" of Merneptah (c. 1210 BC).

8. Günther Hölbl, *A History of the Ptolemaic Empire* (translated by Tina Saavedra; London: Routledge, 2001), 82–83, 107 (figures 3.2, 3.1, and 3.6 respectively).

301 BC, deporting many residents to Alexandria.[9] His dynasty held sway over Judea for the next century, but throughout this time the Seleucids in Syria sought to pry Judea and the cities along Palestine's coast away from Ptolemaic control. Thus, the Ptolemies and the Seleucids were in perpetual conflict, fighting five wars through the course of the third century BC. The attempts of the high priest, Onias II, to align Judea with the Seleucids against Ptolemaic sovereignty affected the balance of power in the region (see "Date and Context" in the "Introduction to Ecclesiastes"). The Jewish nation was, therefore, blown by the constantly shifting political winds of this larger geopolitical struggle.

EXPLAIN the Story

Introduction (1:1–11)

Ecclesiastes is essentially the monologue of one man's search for the meaning of life in a particular historical circumstance. Rather than let us discover his conclusions through the course of the book, his conclusions are announced at the very start: "Everything is meaningless (1:2)." The preface that follows (1:3–11) clarifies that human death is the trigger for the author's investigation. He seeks to discover whether humans have any positive outcome from life. However, his negative conclusion resounds loudly throughout his search.

The Title (1:1)

The book opens with a title attributing authorship (1:1). This title was not written by the main author of the book but by a later editor—the "Epilogist." This editor also quotes the main author's motto in 1:2 before giving way to the main author's monologue (1:3–12:7). The editor then closes the monologue in 12:8 by quoting the author's motto again, and then appends a short interpretive epilogue (12:9–14).

The NIV states that the main author is "the Teacher" (Heb: *qohelet*), but this is not the usual Hebrew word for "teacher."[10] The NIV acknowledges this with a footnote offering "the leader of the assembly" as an alternative. In ancient Israel, the assembly was any gathering of able-bodied male citizens who

9. The exact date of Ptolemy I's capture of Jerusalem is a matter of conjecture. He may have taken the city in 312 BC after his capture of Gaza. If so, he probably held it for very little time, as he was soon forced to pull out of the region. More likely, Ptolemy took Jerusalem in 301 BC on his fourth attempt to seize control of the region. Zechariah 13:78–14:2 probably alludes to this.

10. The usual Hebrew word for teacher is *moreh* (e.g., Isa 30:20).

could function as guarantors of Israelite society (see Deut 23:1–8).[11] While the assembly would gather *en masse* for worship during the great pilgrimage festivals, such as Passover, smaller assemblies could gather at local city gates to conduct business and hear legal cases. The term *qohelet*, therefore, could apply to someone with authority to summon or preside over the dealings of such an assembly—an "assembler." In that case, the author's station in life was not that of a teacher but rather a recognized community leader. However, as discussed in the Introduction, we can also understand the Hebrew term here as a name of some kind. It may be the author's actual name, though the term appears once (Eccl 12:8) with a definite article attached to it (*haqqohelet*). If this is intentional, it may indicate the term is a pen name derived from the title of a recognized leader in the Jewish community. Throughout this commentary, I will refer to the main author as Qohelet on the understanding that this probably was a pen name.

The title also identifies the author as "son of David, king in Jerusalem" (1:1). At first this suggests he was not just any community leader—he was royalty! Indeed, this opening verse is part of the reason why tradition associated Ecclesiastes with Solomon, the son of David who ruled in Jerusalem. Nevertheless, as discussed in the Introduction, and as we will see from hints throughout the book, it is unlikely that the author was a reigning king. Indications are that the author was a Jewish man living in Hellenistic era Jerusalem during the third century BC—well after the time of the Davidic kings. More than this, however, the author seems to have been a descendant of the Davidic kings. Qohelet thus had a unique vantage point for his project of evaluating Jewish life. The legacy of his royal forebears belonged to him personally. He was a member of a family that could boast not just of having ruled a kingdom for over 400 successive years, with such illustrious names as David, Solomon, Hezekiah, and Josiah regaling the dynasty, but of also having been granted God's unconditional commitment that they would always have someone to rule on their ancestor David's throne (2 Sam 7:11b–16). Now, centuries later, they had experienced the downfall of their house, the failure to restore it, and had watched as authority over Jerusalem and God's people passed from one foreign empire to the next. Even as the house of David may have hoped to regain power one day, each passing season must have made it feel less and less likely. Its members must surely have questioned the purposes and faithfulness of God. Qohelet was part of a disenfranchised dynasty in a steep and steady decline into nameless obscurity. Even his name, "Qohelet,"

11. This was similar to the concept of citizenship in ancient Rome, before its more liberal application after the Edict of Caracalla in AD 212.

was obscure. Did it perhaps point to a bitter irony that he was not a king who could assemble the entire nation of Israel at his command (unlike Solomon in 1 Kings 8:1), but was just a minor local "assembler" (a *qohelet*)? Certainly, the fact that he can only play the role of a king in Jerusalem (Eccl 1:12–2:26) is testament to just how much the house of David had crumbled. Thus, Qohelet was heir to both the highs and the lows of the house of David, uniquely positioned to appreciate the heady heights of royal heritage as well as the struggles of a commoner. And if he was a recognized community leader, he would also have been familiar with the various classes of people in between, attempting to get ahead in life. He could legitimately evaluate life from the perspective of the prince, the pauper, and all people in between. This is precisely what he endeavors to do in the book of Ecclesiastes.

The Motto (1:2)

Qohelet's first quoted words reveal his disenchantment with life: "Meaningless! Meaningless! Utterly meaningless! Everything is meaningless" (Eccl 1:2). It's hardly an inspiring start! Yet, this will be Qohelet's motto throughout the book, including the note on which his monologue finishes (12:8).[12] Three questions arise from this motto: (1) What does Qohelet mean by "everything"? (2) What exactly does "meaningless" mean? And (3) why does Qohelet see "everything" as "meaningless"?

First, when Qohelet refers to "everything," he is talking about life in its entirety. The Hebrew word for "everything" here (*hakkol*) includes the definite article, which underlines Qohelet's universal purview. He is commenting about "the whole lot"! We see this also from the next verse, in which Qohelet poses one of the most basic questions of his investigation: "What do people gain from all their labors at which they toil under the sun?" (1:3) It is a very philosophical and timeless question that is all-encompassing. Essentially, Qohelet wants to know the meaning of life. Yet even before we get to that question, Qohelet's motto trumpets a resoundingly pessimistic answer: life is meaningless! It is also important to notice that Qohelet's motto does not add any qualifications. For example, it does not announce that life is meaningless "without God."[13] Qohelet is pursuing his thought within the context of Second Temple Judaism, which presumed God at every point. Even the influence of Hellenism, with its emphasis on reason and philosophical thought, never took God out of the picture in Judaism. Qohelet sees God firmly lodged in the picture—indeed,

12. The last word in Ecclesiastes goes to the book's editor (the "Epilogist"), who adds an epilogue (Eccl 12:9–14) after the end of Qohelet's discourse.

13. Contra Jim West, *Ecclesiastes and the Song of Solomon: For the Person in the Pew* (Quartz Hill, CA: Quartz Hill, 2007), 12–15.

at the helm of the entire universe (e.g., 1:13; 2:24–26; 3:10, 18; 5:2; 6:2; 7:13–14; 8:17; 9:9). That is what makes Qohelet's motto not merely wistful, but caustic. It throws down a virulent challenge to basic orthodoxy within Second Temple Judaism. When all things are considered, even with God in the picture, Qohelet sees the whole lot of it as utterly meaningless.[14]

This leads to our second question: What exactly does "meaningless" mean here? The Hebrew word is actually a noun, *hebel.* Of the seventy-three occasions that Old Testament authors use *hebel,* Qohelet leads the way with thirty-eight. It is evidently a primary concept in his thought. When we scan the way other authors use the word, we see how versatile a noun it is. For instance, it can denote a puff of breath, thus pointing to ideas of transience (e.g., Job 7:16; Ps 39:5–6, 11[39:6–7, 12]; 144:4; Prov 31:30; Isa 57:13). It can denote worthlessness, making it fit to describe things that lack power, like idols (e.g., 2 Kgs 17:15; Jer 10:3, 15), useless help (e.g., Isa 30:7; Lam 4:17), or empty words (Job 35:16). It can indicate something trivial (e.g., Ps 62:10[62:9]; 94:11) or troubling (e.g., Ps 78:33; Prov 13:11). It can also describe something that has no goal, outcome, or point, thus leading to notions of futility and absurdity (see Job 9:29; 27:12; Isa 49:4). Additionally, *hebel* is paired with ideas of falsehood and illusion (e.g., Zech 10:2), ignorance and stupidity (e.g., Ps 94:11; Jer 10:8), mockery (e.g., Jer 10:15), and even death (e.g., Prov 21:6). While all these nuances have different words in English, they are all possible meanings and associations of the one Hebrew word, *hebel.* A pivotal notion among these concepts is lack of substance. This might be seen in physical, temporal, logical, ethical, vital, or practical terms. The notion is applicable to a wealth of contexts, ironically giving it substantial meaning for Qohelet's purposes in Ecclesiastes.[15] As he meanders through his philosophical investigation of life, he looks for meaning in a number of contexts, only to come up short each time. This variety of contexts raises for Qohelet all the nuances of *hebel* at one point or another.[16] Thus, his motto will, at different moments, proclaim that life is meaningless, transient, worthless, absurd, pointless, vain, vexing, and illogical.

14. Tremper Longman argues that "Qohelet's worldview does not allow him to take a transcendent yet immanent God into consideration in his quest for meaning." See Tremper Longman, *The Book of Ecclesiastes,* NICOT (Grand Rapids: Eerdmans, 1998), 66. However, it is precisely because God is part of Qohelet's consideration that his discourse is so confronting.

15. Cf. Ibid., 64.

16. Contra Michael V. Fox, who sees "absurd" as the essential meaning of *hebel* in Ecclesiastes, based on his theory that Qohelet's purpose is to observe apparent contradictions. See *A Time to Tear Down and a Time to Build Up: A Rereading of Ecclesiastes* (Eugene, OR: Wipf & Stock, 1999), 30–34; *Qohelet and His Contradictions,* JSOTSupp 71 (Sheffield: Almond Press, 1989), 31. Although "absurd" is indeed a valid inference in many instances, Qohelet is interested in weighing life against the inevitability of death. This is a slightly wider purpose than Fox allows.

Such torrential pessimism saturates Qohelet's discourse and makes his book difficult to wade through. Indeed, the difficulty of weathering both his topic and his tenor has led many commentators to try to find something positive to hold onto.[17] This desire is born of wishful thinking and misunderstanding, for there is no sandbagging against the tide of Qohelet's despair. His motto floods every crevice of his discussion. As we will eventually see, Qohelet does make the odd positive statement in his own quest to find some solid ground against the swell of his observations. Yet each such statement feels more like driftwood than *terra firma*. His motto cries out that there exists nothing in life that has enough substance to provide anyone with stability, surety, or purpose. It is a deeply despairing message.

The obvious question that now arises is *why* Qohelet sees "everything" as "meaningless" (*hebel*). The answer lies in the rest of Ecclesiastes. Qohelet is on a quest to find some kind of positive substance to life, but to no avail. When we understand his own predicament as the scion of a displaced royal family, we begin to sense something of his dissatisfaction with life. But his is more than longing or bitterness at what might have been. For while Qohelet will examine life from the perspective of a would-be king, he will not stop there. He will seek solace from other vantage points also: the perspective of a wise man, a commoner, and a pious man. Yet as he surveys the spectrum of experience, he finds no solace. On the contrary, there is no part of life that provides him with any substance. His survey does aim for a measure of objectivity, so his conclusions are not purely subjective. Nevertheless, pessimism soaks him to the bone. And so, we launch out with Qohelet on his quest to find substance, knowing that ultimately it will be a fruitless endeavor.

The Preface (1:3–11)

Qohelet begins his quest with a preface (1:3–11). While it lacks first-person pronouns and is introductory in feel, this preface does not sit so apart that we should separate it as distinct from Qohelet's monologue. It sets the tenor and direction of his thought, and so should be understood as a deliberately generalized beginning of the monologue itself. In it, he raises what is perhaps his most basic question: "What do people gain from all their labors at which they toil under the sun?" (1:3) At first glance this seems to be a question about work. Indeed, Qohelet deliberately employs economic language here. The word for "gain" (Heb: *yitron*) can equally be translated "profit"—that is, that

---

17. Kaiser, for example, insists that "the mood of Ecclesiastes is one of delight"—something that seems totally incongruent with Qohelet's motto in Eccl 1:2. See Walter C. Kaiser, *Ecclesiastes: Total Life*, Everyman's Bible Commentary (Chicago: Moody, 1979), 42.

which is left over after accounting for expenditure.[18] Qohelet is interested, therefore, in seeing whether humans come away from their "labors" with any kind of positive return for themselves.

However, his word for "labors" (Heb: *'amal*) is not simply about economic production. Rather, he has all human endeavor in mind. In Hebrew, the noun is singular, demonstrating that he is viewing life as a singular whole. In the course of his investigation, he will examine multiple facets of life, like work, leisure, relationships, authority, worship, and death. But he is seeking meaning in all of these combined.

His word choice here is also interesting for its connotation. The noun *'amal* indicates hardship—a frustrating exertion of effort that is more trouble than it is worth (cf. Deut 26:7). It focuses not on the joy of achieving something, nor even the ability to produce something, but on the pains to which one must go in trying to achieve anything. It is a distinctly negative characterization that views life as a burden and a struggle. To ensure his audience hears this, he pairs the noun with a verb from the same root in almost redundant fashion. Thus, he talks about the "labors" (*'amal*) at which a person "toils" (Heb: *ya'amol*), or, to put it another way, "the struggles in which a person struggles." This makes his question in 1:3 quite loaded, for it already implies that humans invest an extraordinary amount in life—so much, in fact, that he can only reach a negative assessment about it. Qohelet wonders whether such an investment is worth it, for he asks not how much a person gets in return for their investment in life, which might imply there is some gain, even if meager. On the contrary, he asks whether there is any gain at all. Qohelet will employ this terminology throughout his discourse, and each time he does we get a taste of his ultimate conclusion, already signaled in his motto (1:2), that life is a bitter pill to swallow.

Qohelet also frames his depiction of life with the phrase "under the sun" (1:3). This phrase is not original to him, though. Its earliest attestation is in the Old Babylonian version of the Epic of Gilgamesh (c. 1800 BC), in which it stands for the totality of the universe. Even the gods exist "under the sun" in Gilgamesh. This is perhaps a nod toward the classic polytheistic idea that idols contained the essence of the gods they represented, and these idols could be placed within human-made temples on the earth. However, this is not the case in Ecclesiastes, for Qohelet has a classic Jewish view of the divine. There is only one God and he is transcendent—practically beyond knowing (a notion

18. The Aramaic cognate of this word has this economic connotation. See Stuart Weeks, *Ecclesiastes and Scepticism*, Library of Hebrew Bible/Old Testament Studies 541 (New York: T&T Clark, 2012), 35.

he will explore at later points in his discourse). God exists not "under the sun," but above it "in heaven" (Eccl 5:2), from where he orchestrates all that happens in creation below.[19] There exists for Qohelet, then, a clear divide between the divine and created realms. God holds sway over both, but human beings only ever experience created life "under the sun." For human beings, the divine realm is impossibly out of reach, which Qohelet takes to mean that human beings ultimately cannot understand God. As earthbound beings, humans are unable to see beyond their own horizon. They are certainly unable to catch a view of life from the vantage point of heaven, from where God views all. This means humans are limited to figuring out the meaning of life purely by what they can glean "under the sun."

Qohelet will, therefore, use empirical observation and reason in the attempt to discern the meaning of life. To that end, he will often talk about what he sees (e.g., 3:10) and what he says in his heart (e.g., 2:15).[20] This does not mean Qohelet is a materialist or only a humanist. Since he works within a classic Jewish framework, he understands the possibility of divine revelation. He is, after all, a member of the Davidic royal family, whom God chose to rule Israel from Jerusalem centuries earlier. The significance of his family is itself a divine revelation. Yet such revelation comes to humans in their struggles "under the sun" and therefore, along with experience more generally, forms just one means of total knowledge. Divine revelation, as it comes from the history and Scriptures of Israel, provides the furniture of Qohelet's thought world, but he uses experience and reason to arrange it all in different ways to see if he can find a favorable (that is, comprehensible) configuration. In other words, Qohelet feels free to use experience and reason to critique divine revelation, but his purpose is not to debunk it. Rather, since he finds life a struggle, he wants to use all possible sources of knowledge "under the sun" in his quest for meaning and substance. In so doing, he will call into question much of the received orthodoxy and conventional wisdom in Second Temple Judaism, and for this he offers no apologies. As we have already seen by his motto (1:2), Qohelet does not intend to sugarcoat his conclusions, and he is not after easy answers. But his purpose is experimental, evaluative, and skeptical, rather than cynical or polemical. This will become more apparent throughout his discourse, but also when the editor will have the final word (12:9–14). The editor will confirm the veracity and weight of Qohelet's unconventional conclusions while also advocating an orthodox response to them.

19. Also noteworthy here is that Qohelet works with a classic ancient understanding of the universe as a system of levels ranging (in descending order) from (1) God's abode in heaven; (2) the sky and the celestial bodies; (3) the earth surrounded by oceans; and (4) the underworld beneath the earth.

20. The NIV usually translates this with the phrase, "I said to myself."

More speculatively, the phrase "under the sun" may have some veiled political reference to the Ptolemaic dynasty that held sway over Judea during the third century BC. Qohelet would certainly have been familiar with the ideology of Ptolemaic sovereignty. He may also have been familiar with their iconography, in which the all-encompassing winged sun disk became the symbol of their authority. Not only was this a symbol of foreign mastery over the Jewish nation, but it also represented a direct counterclaim to any Davidic aspirations Qohelet may have harbored. It is not inconceivable, then, that by using the phrase "under the sun" Qohelet is offering a sharp but subtle critique of the Ptolemies. The implication of such subtle rhetoric would be that the Ptolemies, though novel in the sweep of history, actually represented nothing new (cf. 1:10). God, not the Ptolemies, was the one in charge of the world, and the Jewish nation still struggled on without substantial gain. In this way, Qohelet criticizes not just Ptolemaic authority but also holds God's ways up to scrutiny. In later sections of his monologue, Qohelet will imply some stinging things about God's character.

Mortality is the main trigger for Qohelet's evaluation of human life (1:4). As the universal human experience, death is ever at the fore of his thought. It is, for Qohelet, not a threshold to a blessed afterlife, for, like the *Harper's Song* from Intef's tomb, he is actually skeptical about the existence of such an afterlife (see Eccl 3:21).[21] It is, rather, the ultimate destination of all human beings as far as he knows. The classic view of the Old Testament, which Qohelet shares, is that when people died, regardless of whether they had been righteous or wicked, they ended up in "Sheol." The NIV often translates this Hebrew word as "the grave" (e.g., Ps 89:48[89:49]; Hos 13:14) or the "realm of the dead" (e.g., Isa 14:9). It was understood as a shadowy place beneath the earth (e.g., Num 16:30–33) where the dead slept or were in a state of suspended animation, unable to do anything (Eccl 9:10), not even praise or relate to God (Ps 6:5[6:6]). The only time the dead were roused within Sheol was to welcome prominent new arrivals to share their impotent, obscure existence (e.g., Isa 14:9–11; cf. 1 Sam 28:11–19). Sheol was thus the great leveler that brought every person low, from the Davids, the Solomons, and the Ptolemies to the countless nameless peasants. Qohelet confirms that Sheol is the final fate of every human being (Eccl 9:10).

21. Ecclesiastes 3:21 must be balanced with 12:7, in which Qohelet states that the human "spirit" returns to God at death, while the "dust" (i.e. flesh) returns to the earth. However, he does not seem to be talking in terms of a human soul at that point, for 3:21 affirms that even an animal has a "spirit." These two references would seem to have more of a material focus that speaks of the compositional elements of physical existence. As such, "spirit" (Heb: *ruah*) is probably best rendered "breath" in these two verses. Thus, he affirms that human death is the moment when God takes back the breath as one of the basic elements necessary for earthly life. See discussion of 3:16–21 below.

This is what makes Qohelet's comparison between human existence and the physical environment in which human life occurs so poignant and tragic. As Qohelet states, "Generations come and generations go, but the earth remains forever" (1:4). The grand sweep of human history chronicles not just the rise and fall of dynasties like David's, but the rise and inevitable fall of all people in death.[22] The Egyptians reflected on this in their *Harper's Songs*, dolefully mourning the passing of even their wisest and most powerful. In Mesopotamia, even the giants like Gilgamesh succumbed to this ultimate fate. Here in Ecclesiastes, Qohelet states that people come and go in their generations, and this demonstrates humanity's ultimate transience. But the sun, wind, and rivers come and go (1:5–7), demonstrating creation's permanence.[23] The contrast is stark, sober, and depressing. The beauty and finely tuned nature of the earth's cycles, with all their delicate poise and regularity, become, for Qohelet, not a thing of wonder and amazement but of oppression and despair. When viewed against the inevitability and finality of human death, the earth, which survives and continues on, utterly mocks human existence. Everyone must die, and the earth will simply leave everyone behind as it blissfully continues on without them, as though they had never even existed.

Qohelet also captures Judea's geopolitical situation in 1:6 as he describes the wind shifting from the south to the north and its aimless swirling round and round. The Ptolemies, who were in control of Judea in the 220s BC, when Qohelet wrote, were situated in the "south," while the Seleucids, whom the high priest, Onias II, sought to align with, were in the "north." Indeed, these designations of "south" and "north" are how the book of Daniel refers to the respective kingdoms of the Ptolemies and the Seleucids (Dan 11). Thus, Qohelet is not merely describing the cycle of human life on the enduring earth. He is also locating his contemplations within the political struggles that Judea was caught in during his day. The Ptolemies and Seleucids were perpetually struggling with each other, with the balance of power constantly shifting from the south to the north and back again. Judea was in unstable circumstances, but far from indicating perennial change, the constant political shifts kept Judea in constant subservience to foreign powers. The reality was

22. Graham Ogden suggests that "generations" here refers to the cycles of nature rather than generations of humans. However, not only does this stretch the word's semantics, it misses the contrast the preface here makes between the transience of humans and the permanence of the earth. See Graham S. Ogden, "The Interpretation of *dôr* in Ecclesiastes 1.4," *JSOT* 34 (1986): 91–92.

23. Fox, responding to Ogden (Ibid.), argues that "the earth" in 1:4 "does not mean the physical earth, but humanity as a whole." He sees the verse saying that "the movement of generations does not change the face of humanity." See Michael V. Fox, "Qohelet 1.4," *JSOT* 40 (1988): 109. Fox rightly sees a contrast here between humanity and the earth but reverses its intent. Qohelet's appeal to death, however, focuses very much on humanity's transience.

that Judea was not in control of its destiny, and God's promises seemed very far from fulfilment.

And so, Qohelet concludes, "All things are wearisome" (1:8a). The NIV pairs this statement with the next, "more than one can say," as a way of intensifying the conclusion. However, the structure of the Hebrew expression also allows us to join that second statement with the two similarly structured clauses that follow: "No person can speak. The eye never has enough of seeing, nor the ear its fill of hearing" (1:8, author's translation).[24] In this way, Qohelet again neatly contrasts the never-ending nature of human endeavor and observation with the never-ending cycles of nature, showing that human activity is ultimately to no avail. No matter what humans do, nor how much they do it, they still can do nothing to stymie death. More than this, Qohelet feels, as we will see in subsequent chapters, that no one can do anything to stave off the death of the Jewish nation and its hopes. Thus, all of life, and all of Israel's history, has been a dreary struggle for naught.

When Qohelet asks whether there is anything truly new in the world (1:10a, b), he asks not to question human creativity and ingenuity: he is going beyond questioning whether God can do something to restore the house of David to power. On this front alone, Qohelet expresses extreme doubt. He recycles the phrasing of prophecies that had called excitedly for a "new thing"—a restoration of the Davidic kingdom out of exile (Isa 42:9; 43:19)—and declares them essentially to have failed.[25] Indeed, his own situation as a Davidic descendant without a Davidic kingdom centuries later accentuates his despondency and skepticism. More than this, though, Qohelet wants something to deal with the more fundamental problem that the psalmist in Psalm 89 touches upon. The psalmist expresses bewilderment at the fall of the Davidic kingdom (Ps 89:19–51[89:18–50]) but also frustration at the harsh reality of death (Ps 89:48[89:49]). Qohelet seeks something that might put a stick in the spokes of humanity's inexorable fate, or at the very least produce something of substance that death does not steamroll into a useless pulp. Alas, he concludes, no such thing exists (Eccl 1:10c, d).

History unequivocally proves Qohelet's conclusion. As he turns to discuss the memory of previous generations (1:11), he states that no one remembers them. He is not here arguing that current generations do not know or care about the past, though as a distant descendant of David he might have felt such

24. The three clauses have a similar structure that is a convincing argument for keeping them together as a tripartite unit. Each of the three clauses begins with the Hebrew negative particle "not" (*lo'*), which negates a *yiqtol* verb connected to a human function, and ends with an infinitive.

25. Jennifer Barbour, *The Story of Israel in the Book of Qohelet: Ecclesiastes as Cultural Memory* (Oxford: Oxford University Press, 2012), 51.

ignorance and apathy keenly. On the contrary, the very nature of his statement proves that Qohelet knows something of the past. Indeed, in his own royal experiment in the very next section (1:12–2:26), he clearly knows the exploits of his august predecessors in Jerusalem (1:16; 2:7, 9). As the Epic of Gilgamesh shows, people can make a name for themselves that might endure beyond their death. God had even made the name of David "like the names of the greatest men on earth" (2 Sam 7:9). But this is scarce comfort for Qohelet, who now lives only with the tatters of such greatness. In any case, even the heights of fame are ultimately of no substance, for they can never prevent the person's death in the first place. Life is a zero-sum game, and there is no gain to be taken from it.

Thus, in 1:11 Qohelet argues not that people are ignorant of history (though they often are!) but that current generations fail to remember that previous generations came, saw, and failed to conquer death. So, like their forebears, they too will try but fail to outmaneuver the grave. They do not see that their efforts to achieve something of substance are in vain. If they did, they would desist from trying and realize instead that life is a terrible investment that ultimately pays nothing. Yet, they strive in vain for gain. For Qohelet, this failure to learn is an amnesia that clouds every generation. So generations are fated to repeat the efforts of those who have gone before in a never-ending cycle of vanity. Human striving is, for Qohelet, proof that humanity does not learn from the past.

There is a further "sting in the tail" of Qohelet's preface, as we note the close correspondence between his words here and Isaiah 65:17. In Isaiah 65:17 God announces that he will create something new—new heavens and a new earth—and that former things will be remembered no longer. Qohelet picks up on these phrases and recycles them here in Ecclesiastes 1:11 to express his own skepticism: yes, former things will indeed be remembered no longer, but that is because humanity should not expect anything new. Through the ages nothing has changed, and everybody continues to die. It is an expression of disappointment in God's failure to intervene in history and prevent the tragedy of human death or even restore a Davidic kingdom. His tone even takes on a sinister sarcasm as a vote of no confidence—a "disavowal of the past prophetic hopes."[26] Instead, Qohelet resigns himself to a world of no change and no future. Qohelet is not a romantic pining nostalgically for a bygone era, though as a Davidic descendant we might forgive him for that. He is also far from an idealist with hope for a brighter tomorrow, though he seems to want one desperately. Rather, he is a skeptic jaded by the universality of human fate that turns life and all history into a relentless pursuit of nothing.

Everything, he concludes, is utterly meaningless!

---

26. Ibid., 53.

LIVE the Story

In September 2015 the lifeless body of toddler Aylan Kurdi was found washed up on a Turkish beach. He had perished in his family's attempt to find refuge after escaping the war and terror plaguing their native Syria. Their road from Damascus was one of terrible suffering. Reaction to this little boy's tragic death ranged from deep grief through to rage. There was something terribly obscene about the death of one so young and vulnerable. He had been robbed of life when it had barely started for him. His life had been utterly wasted, and it was not fair!

Death is rightly a catalyst for serious reflection on life and all that is wrong with the world. When someone dies in the prime of life, we find it particularly difficult to swallow. We say the person was taken "before their time." Parents who have had to bury their children know all too well just how bitter and devastating death is. Those who have walked among the countless headstones in the war cemeteries of Western Europe know that the current tranquility belies the horrors of hostility, suffering, and death in previous generations. Qohelet's contemplations highlight not just the tragedy of untimely death but the tragedy of all human death. Whether it is the death of a toddler, a solider, or a centenarian, death is obscene. It steals away life, breaks relationships, cements regrets, and smothers all potential and possibility. Qohelet does not point to the opening chapters of Genesis to explain death as the rightful wages of sin because he is not after the theological cause of human death.[27] Rather, he focuses on the fact of death and its effects. He concludes that death robs human life of all substance, and there is nothing anyone can do to stop it.[28]

At least that used to be the case.

For one Sunday morning in the first century, just outside the walls of Jerusalem, something new happened: Jesus of Nazareth, whom the authorities had executed as a criminal the Friday before, walked out of his tomb alive. The resurrection of Jesus was the game changer, and the world will never be the same again.

---

27. William P. Brown claims Qohelet (like others in Israel's wisdom tradition) is scarcely interested in Israel's history. See William P. Brown, *Ecclesiastes*, Interpretation (Louisville, KY: John Knox, 2000), 11–12. This is perhaps an overstatement, though, for Qohelet is connected to one of the most prominent figures in Israel's history: David (Eccl 1:1).

28. Russell L. Meek argues that Qohelet has the Eden narratives of Genesis in mind throughout his discourse, demonstrated chiefly by his use of *hebel*, which is also the Hebrew form of the name "Abel." See Russell L. Meek, "The Meaning of הבל in Qohelet: An Intertextual Suggestion," in *The Words of the Wise Are Like Goads: Engaging Qohelet in the 21st Century*, ed. Mark J. Boda, Tremper Longman, and Cristian G. Rata (Winona Lake, IN: Eisenbrauns, 2013), 241–56. While Qohelet does use echoes of the Genesis narratives in his phrasing at various places, his purpose is nonetheless oriented toward a very different goal, namely the exploration of the effect of death upon the ultimate outcome of human life. He is not interested in the origins of sin, evil, or death.

As we read Ecclesiastes today, we must remember that its author, Qohelet, lived in a "BC" world—an era before the final revelation of God in Christ. He knew that God was sovereign and somehow working out his plans for the world. He knew that humans are finite and all are destined to die. But he did not know the Christ would suffer and rise again on the third day (cf. Luke 24:5–7, 25–27). Qohelet's generation came and went, but there was more of God's story to come. So although Qohelet's perspective is weighty and true, his is not the final word. He speaks from a standpoint of incomplete revelation.

For this reason I want to tell Qohelet about Jesus. I want him to know that a loyal son of David—a pleb from Galilee—was none other than God the Son who came down from heaven and shared our lot "under the sun." I want him to know that in Christ, God himself has experienced human death. But I also want him to know that, in Christ, death has been swallowed up in victory and lost its sting (1 Cor 15:54–55). The resurrection shows us that life is not a zero-sum game after all. There is substance and meaning in life: it is found in knowing the Father and Jesus Christ, whom he has sent (John 17:3). Life is now not merely under the *sun*, but under the *Son*. God has now revealed the purpose of his will, which is "to bring unity to all things in heaven and on earth under Christ" (Eph 1:9–10). For this reason, God has highly exalted Jesus through his resurrection and ascension, and given him "the name that is above every name" (Phil 2:9).

When the apostle Paul reflected on the course of his life in his letter to the Philippian Christians, he presented them with quite a résumé. He had the privilege of his Jewish heritage, his education, fervor, and upright standing in the Jewish community (Phil 3:4–6). Many today might point to similar accomplishments of their own. But Paul wrote, "I consider everything a loss" (Phil 3:8a). This was not because he knew that one day his death would bring it all to naught. "I consider everything a loss," he wrote, "because of the surpassing worth of knowing Christ Jesus my Lord" (Phil 3:8). Paul had encountered the risen Jesus on the road to Damascus (Acts 9:1–20), and this changed everything for him. "I want to know Christ," he wrote, "yes, to know the power of his resurrection and participation in his sufferings, becoming like him in his death, and so, somehow, attaining to the resurrection from the dead" (Phil 3:10–11). For Paul, being united to Christ by God's Spirit secured for him eternal life. The grave, therefore, was not his final destination. And so he proclaimed with complete confidence, "For to me, to live is Christ, and to die is gain" (Phil 1:21). The resurrection of Jesus and the hope of eternal life in him turns back the tide of Qohelet's pessimism. It does not mean we will be spared the swells of suffering and death. Paul knew this fact all too well.

Yet for the person who, like Paul, puts their faith in Christ, in suffering and death there is actually great gain.

Furthermore, in Christ there is indeed hope for something truly new. The Christian looks forward to the resurrection of her own body—a future in which death is no longer a reality. God has promised new heavens and a new earth (Isa 65:17), and with the resurrection of Jesus we can affirm that God is indeed going to deliver on this promise. "If the Spirit of him who raised Jesus from the dead is living in you, he who raised Christ from the dead will also give life to your mortal bodies because of his Spirit who lives in you" (Rom 8:11). We may feel the challenges, disappointments, and tragedies of our current existence keenly, as Qohelet also did. These may even lead us to express doubt in God's goodness or power to deliver, as they did for Qohelet. Yet in those moments, we must turn to Christ and be reassured by his resurrection that God has not reneged on his promises to transform and renew.

The universality of human death highlights the need that every human has for Christ. He is the only one who has broken the power of death. Salvation can be found in no name but his (Acts 4:12). Although we all now live on this side of the cross and empty tomb, not all of us know this sure hope that may be found in Christ. This is why Qohelet's contemplations are still so valuable for us today. He expresses for us a "BC" view of life—life before the knowledge of Christ comes. He soaks us with the heaviness of death, forcing us to evaluate our own lives and the prospect of our own mortality. And he concludes that there is no meaning or substance to be found in it. But this must drive us to Christ, who is the rock that gives us ultimate security against the rising tides of hardship and death (cf. Matt 7:24–25).

CHAPTER 2

Ecclesiastes 1:12–2:26

LISTEN to the Story

[12]I, the Teacher, was king over Israel in Jerusalem. [13]I applied my mind
to study and to explore by wisdom all that is done under the heavens.
What a heavy burden God has laid on mankind! [14]I have seen all the
things that are done under the sun; all of them are meaningless, a chasing
after the wind.

[15]What is crooked cannot be straightened;
what is lacking cannot be counted.

[16]I said to myself, "Look, I have increased in wisdom more than anyone
who has ruled over Jerusalem before me; I have experienced much of
wisdom and knowledge." [17]Then I applied myself to the understanding
of wisdom, and also of madness and folly, but I learned that this, too, is a
chasing after the wind.

[18]For with much wisdom comes much sorrow;
the more knowledge, the more grief.

[2:1]I said to myself, "Come now, I will test you with pleasure to find out
what is good." But that also proved to be meaningless. [2] "Laughter," I said,
"is madness. And what does pleasure accomplish?" [3]I tried cheering myself
with wine, and embracing folly—my mind still guiding me with wisdom.
I wanted to see what was good for people to do under the heavens during
the few days of their lives.

[4]I undertook great projects: I built houses for myself and planted
vineyards. [5] I made gardens and parks and planted all kinds of fruit trees
in them. [6]I made reservoirs to water groves of flourishing trees. [7] I bought
male and female slaves and had other slaves who were born in my house.
I also owned more herds and flocks than anyone in Jerusalem before me.

8I amassed silver and gold for myself, and the treasure of kings and
provinces. I acquired male and female singers, and a harem as well—the
delights of a man's heart. 9I became greater by far than anyone in Jerusalem
before me. In all this my wisdom stayed with me.

10I denied myself nothing my eyes desired;
  I refused my heart no pleasure.
My heart took delight in all my labor,
  and this was the reward for all my toil.
11Yet when I surveyed all that my hands had done
  and what I had toiled to achieve,
everything was meaningless, a chasing after the wind;
  nothing was gained under the sun.
12Then I turned my thoughts to consider wisdom,
  and also madness and folly.
What more can the king's successor do
  than what has already been done?
13I saw that wisdom is better than folly,
  just as light is better than darkness.
14The wise have eyes in their heads,
  while the fool walks in the darkness;
but I came to realize
  that the same fate overtakes them both.

15Then I said to myself,

"The fate of the fool will overtake me also.
  What then do I gain by being wise?"
I said to myself,
  "This too is meaningless."
16For the wise, like the fool, will not be long remembered;
  the days have already come when both have been forgotten.
Like the fool, the wise too must die!

17So I hated life, because the work that is done under the sun was grievous
to me. All of it is meaningless, a chasing after the wind. 18I hated all the
things I had toiled for under the sun, because I must leave them to the one
who comes after me. 19And who knows whether that person will be wise or

foolish? Yet they will have control over all the fruit of my toil into which I have poured my effort and skill under the sun. This too is meaningless. [20]So my heart began to despair over all my toilsome labor under the sun. [21]For a person may labor with wisdom, knowledge and skill, and then they must leave all they own to another who has not toiled for it. This too is meaningless and a great misfortune. [22]What do people get for all the toil and anxious striving with which they labor under the sun? [23]All their days their work is grief and pain; even at night their minds do not rest. This too is meaningless.

[24]A person can do nothing better than to eat and drink and find satisfaction in their own toil. This too, I see, is from the hand of God, [25]for without him, who can eat or find enjoyment? [26]To the person who pleases him, God gives wisdom, knowledge and happiness, but to the sinner he gives the task of gathering and storing up wealth to hand it over to the one who pleases God. This too is meaningless, a chasing after the wind.

Listening to the Text in the Story: 1 Kings 21:1–16; 2 Kings 20:20; 21:18, 26; 1 Chronicles 22:14; 27:25–31; 2 Chronicles 1:1–10:19 (paralleled in 1 Kings 3:1–12:19); 17:5; 26:9–10; 32:27–30; 35:7; Esther 1–2; Proverbs 1:7a; 8:1–36; 25:1; Daniel 4:29–30; The Mesha Stele (*COS* 2.23); The Siloam Tunnel Inscription; The Annals of Thutmose III in the temple of Amun at Karnak (lines 94–102; *COS* 2.2A); Herodotus, *Histories*, 1.27–32, 50–52, 75–88; 4.166; Xenophon, *Agesilaus* 8.6; Arrian, *Expedition of Alexander*, 6.29; Atheneus, *Learned Banqueters* 5.196a–203d; 12.536e; the Tomb of Cyrus, Pasargadae; Darius' Apadana Hall in Persepolis.

Our world today is made up predominantly of nation states, which we tend to think of as entities in and of themselves. The ancient Near East was very different from this. There were no such self-evident states. Rather, through the power of military force, economics, ideology, and tradition, particular men built up personal estates for themselves, which enabled them to extend their will directly over the lives of others within the estate. They tried to ensure that control of their estate remained within their family by passing it on to a son. In other words, they formed what we call "kingdoms." This was the basic governing model throughout the ancient Near East.[1]

1. There was the occasional departure from this model, but these lay mostly in the West. For example, because of the excesses of its kings, Rome overthrew its monarchy and formed a republic

This helps us understand why ancient Near Eastern kings were so keen to have their virtues and achievements extolled in inscriptions, annals, and other documents. It was not so much an exercise of personal vanity as of statesmanship. They boasted of their military exploits and the spoils they captured to demonstrate that they were a force to be reckoned with. They also listed other accomplishments, such as civic works and construction of official buildings. These created the infrastructure of their rule by which they cemented their will over the lives of others. Wealth could ensure power, privilege, the approval of the gods, and perhaps even happiness.

In Israel and Judah, the most famous example is Solomon. When God urged Solomon to ask anything of him, and Solomon chose wisdom, God ensured he would also receive wealth (2 Chr 1:7–12). And so, in the chapters pertaining to his reign (2 Chr 1–9),[2] we read of Solomon's vast achievements, which included the construction of his palace and the temple of Yahweh in Jerusalem. He is said to have made silver and cedar wood abound (2 Chr 1:15; 9:27)[3] and earned an income of 666 talents of gold in one year (2 Chr 9:13).[4] He also produced ceremonial and decorative items made of gold, traded in horses and military hardware, and imported luxury goods, exotic animals, and spices (2 Chr 1:14–17; 9:15–28). "King Solomon was greater in riches and wisdom than all the other kings of the earth" (2 Chr 9:22) and boasted some 700 wives and 300 concubines (1 Kgs 11:3). The Queen of Sheba expresses her marvel when, after visiting Solomon and seeing his wisdom and wealth, she declares to him, "How happy your people must be! How happy your officials, who continually stand before you and hear your wisdom! Praise be to the Lord your God, who has delighted in you and placed you on the throne of Israel. Because of the Lord's eternal love for Israel, he has made you king to maintain justice and righteousness" (1 Kgs 10:8–9)

---

in c. 509 BC. It viewed the state as bigger than any person involved in running it. At the same time, Athens established a democracy, in which the state was identified with a particular class of people ("citizens") within it.

2. Solomon's reign is the subject of 1 Kings 3–11, which is paralleled (with some modification) in 2 Chronicles 1–9. Qohelet's consideration of Solomon's legacy seems predominantly drawn from the Chronicler's account.

3. While cedar is widely used today, it was not so in the ancient world. Cedar only grew at high altitudes in the mountains of Lebanon, which stand almost 10,000 feet above sea level. To use it required sending logging teams up into these mountains, manually sawing through the thick trunks, cutting these into smaller logs, transporting them all the way down the mountains to urban centers, then transporting them to the relevant construction site, which might be weeks or months away. It was a difficult and costly endeavor.

4. This is the equivalent of approximately 25 tons of gold, which would be worth over $1 billion today. The NIV implies that this was Solomon's annual income ("The weight of the gold that Solomon received yearly was 666 talents"). However, the Hebrew verb used in this clause (a *qatal* verb) more likely implies "One year, the weight of the gold that Solomon received was 666 talents."

Solomon is not the only one in the Bible known for the accoutrements of power. The Chronicler portrays his father, David, as wealthy enough to provide 100,000 talents of gold[5] and one million talents of silver for the construction of the temple, not to mention the countless amounts of bronze and iron (1 Chr 22:14). This is in addition to the storehouses, farming lands, vineyards, olive groves, fig trees, livestock, camels, and donkeys David owns (1 Chr 27:25–31). King Jehoshaphat "had great wealth and honor" (2 Chr 17:5). Uzziah built defensive towers, carved many cisterns, and owned livestock, fields, and vineyards (2 Chr 26:9–10).[6] Hezekiah is credited with vast stores of silver, gold, gems, spices, grain, wine, oil, and livestock (2 Chr 32:27–28). He also built towns and tunneled through the bedrock under Jerusalem to bring water from the Gihon Spring to the Pool of Siloam within the confines of the walled city (2 Chr 32:29–30; 2 Kgs 20:20). The Siloam Tunnel Inscription also commemorates this feat. It describes how, after digging from opposite ends, the two excavation teams met in the middle of the winding tunnel, "ax upon ax," and water flowed from the spring to the pool.[7] Hezekiah's son and grandson, Manasseh and Amon, were both buried in a private garden (2 Kgs 21:18, 26). King Josiah owned enough livestock to provide 30,000 lambs and goats and 3,000 cattle for pilgrims at Passover (2 Chr 35:7). King Ahab of Israel so desired the vineyard of his neighbor, Naboth, that he conspired to murder him and joined the vineyard to his own property (1 Kgs 21:1–16). The book of Daniel also portrays King Nebuchadnezzar "walking on the roof of the royal palace" and boasting of having built Babylon by his own power and for his own majesty (Dan 4:29–30).

There are numerous examples of similar rhetoric outside Israel and Judah, too. From the fifteenth century BC, the walls of Amun's temple at Karnak relate how Pharaoh Thutmose III increased his personal estate after victory at Megiddo. Among "his majesty's" takings were the enemy's horses and military paraphernalia, thousands of livestock, gems, luxury items, thousands of slaves, and his enemies' wives (lines 96–102). In his stele,[8] Mesha, the king of Moab (c. 850–820 BC), boasts of recapturing towns that the Israelite dynasty of Omri had once ruled. He then outlines the building program he pursued throughout his kingdom, including the construction of water reservoirs, town walls, gates, towers, a palace, a moat built by Israelite slaves, roads, and temples (lines 8–9, 21–31).

---

5. This is approximately 1383 tons of gold, equating to almost $62 billion today.

6. Uzziah is known as "Azariah" in 2 Kings 14:21 and 15:1–7.

7. People can still walk through Hezekiah's Tunnel in Jerusalem today. However, the inscription has long been removed and housed at the Istanbul Archaeological Museum.

8. A stele is an upright stone slab with a commemorative inscription or pictorial relief carved onto it.

During the fourteen years of his reign, Croesus, king of Lydia (c. 560–546 BC), developed the reputation of being one of antiquity's richest men. He is famed for being the first ruler to standardize gold coinage. The Greek historian, Herodotus, describes how Croesus conquered vast territories in Asia Minor, bringing the flow of tribute into his capital city, Sardis (*Hist.* 1.27–28). He was also renowned for making vast offerings to Apollo through the oracle at Delphi, including thousands of animal sacrifices, 117 ingots of gold,[9] and numerous other items of opulence that later became famous relics on display throughout the ancient Greek world (*Hist.* 1.50–52). The wisest men in the Greek world visited Croesus, including Solon, the well-traveled lawmaker of Athens (*Hist.* 1.27–32).[10] After showing Solon his extensive treasuries, Croesus asked him whom he deemed the happiest and most prosperous of men. To Croesus's chagrin, Solon named others ahead of him. Upset by this, Croesus pressed Solon to explain why he was not Solon's first choice. Solon replied,

> Human life is pure chance. You seem to be very wealthy, and you rule over many people, but I cannot yet tell you the answer you asked for until I learn how you have ended your life. . . . The man who has great wealth but is unhappy outdoes the fortunate man in only two ways, while the fortunate man outdoes him in many ways. The former is more capable of gratifying his passions and of sustaining himself in adversity, but the fortunate man, although he does not have the same ability to sustain himself in adversity or passion, avoids these anyway by virtue of his good fortune. Moreover, he has no injury, no sickness, no painful experiences; what he does have is good children and good looks. Now if, in addition to all these things, he ends his life well, too, then this is the man you are looking for; he alone deserves to be called happy and prosperous. But before he dies, refrain from calling him this—one should rather call him lucky. (*Hist.* 1.32)

For Solon, possessions and privilege signified luck more than happiness. Only the totality of a person's life could afford a proper estimation of true happiness and prosperity. In this regard, death provided the only accurate measure, and before it, no person could be considered truly happy.

9. This is approximately 236 talents, or nine tons of gold, which would be worth almost $400 million today.

10. Herodotus also mentions a visit by either Bias of Priene or Pittakos of Mytilene, both of whom, along with Solon of Athens, were among the seven proverbial wise men of ancient Greece. See Robert B. Strassler, ed., *The Landmark Herodotus: The Histories*, trans. Andrea L. Purvis, Reprint edition. (New York: Anchor Books, 2009), 17.

As fortune had it, Croesus's luck ran out when he rushed foolhardily into conflict with Cyrus of Persia. Cyrus had recently conquered the growing kingdom of Media (550 BC), and Croesus now drew him into war. But in 546 BC Cyrus captured Croesus's capital, Sardis, and so acquired all of Croesus's wealth. Herodotus records Cyrus sentencing Croesus to be burnt alive on a blazing pyre. While resigning himself to this fate, Croesus recalled Solon's assessment that no living person could be called truly happy and prosperous. Cyrus then had a change of heart and spared Croesus, making him an advisor in his court (*Hist.* 1.86–88).[11]

With his newly acquired wealth, Cyrus developed his Persian capital at Pasargadae. This included the creation of a walled royal park containing various kinds of trees, irrigation channels, lawns, meadows, pavilions, and a palace.[12] The Persians gave the term *pairidaeza* ("walled around") to such parks. This made its way into Greek as *paradeisos*, from which we derive the English word "paradise." A precursor to such parks had been built by Sennacherib in Nineveh (705–681 BC), so the idea of a royal park was not new,[13] but the use of "paradise" as a technical term for such a park—and Qohelet uses this term in Ecclesiastes 2:5—comes from the Persians.

Cyrus's successors continued his legacy with even more extravagant displays of opulence, leaving a lasting impression in the minds of both biblical and Greek writers of the obscenely rich Eastern despot.[14] Darius I (522–486 BC) established the city of Persepolis with its ornate palace and Apadana Hall. According to Herodotus, "Darius had set his heart on leaving behind a memorial to himself unlike any of those left by other kings" (*Hist.*, 4.166). In the book of Esther, Xerxes I (486–465 BC) enjoys a fanciful six-month banquet in his lavishly decorated garden in Susa (Esth 1:1–8), surrounded

11. Croesus became the stuff of legend among the Greeks, so despite Herodotus's account, Croesus's actual fate is not definitively known. The Nabonidus Chronicle from Babylon refers to Cyrus invading Urartu and executing its king (2.15–17). The timing of this comports with the conquest of Croesus's kingdom, but the label of "Urartu" is problematic. Thus, we cannot determine whether this refers to the fate of Croesus, or of someone else.

12. The second century AD historian, Arrian (*Anabasis of Alexander* 6.29.4–5), preserves a brief description of Cyrus' royal park, written originally by Aristobulus of Cassandreia, who had seen it on campaign with Alexander the Great (330 BC) and had been commissioned to decorate it (see Strabo, *Geography*, 15.3.7). The accuracy of this description has been verified by archaeological surveys conducted in the twentieth century. See D. Stronach, "The Royal Garden at Pasargadae: Evolution and Legacy," in *Archaeologia Iranica et Orientalis: Miscellanea in Honorem Louis Vanden Berghe*, ed. L. de Meyer and E. Haerinck, vol. 1 (Ghent: Peeters, 1989), 475–502.

13. The Hanging Gardens of Babylon—one of the seven wonders of the ancient world—have never been found. The legend most likely derived from Sennacherib's elaborate garden at Nineveh, which was watered by an aqueduct of ancient engineering marvel descending from the mountains to the north.

14. Barbour, *The Story of Israel in the Book of Qohelet*, 30–36.

by fawning courtiers, an extensive harem, luxuries aplenty, and the ability to express his every whim (Esth 1–2).[15] Xenophon, a contemporary of Artaxerxes II (404–358 BC), writes, "It was the belief of the Persian king that by possessing himself of colossal wealth, he would put all things in subjection to himself. In this belief he tried to engross all the gold, all the silver and all the most costly things in the world" (*Agesilaus*, 8.6). The fall of Persia to the Greeks did not bring this pattern to an end. Ptolemy II Philadelphus (283–246 BC), whose empire included both Egypt and Judea, is said to have celebrated a victory parade in Alexandria with the most ostentatious display of wealth ever seen. Atheneus describes the parade at great length (*Learned Banqueters*, 5.196a–203b), leading him to remark, "What kingdom . . . has ever been so rich in gold?"[16] He goes on to say that Ptolemy II "was richer than many kings and made a vigorous effort to win glory in everything he did" (*Learned Banqueters* 5.203c–d).

All these examples demonstrate that kings were the most privileged of people in the ancient world. In forming and maintaining their royal estates, they could accomplish so much, but this meant they also had much to lose. Whether they were the happiest or most fulfilled people of their time is, therefore, a poignant question. Testament to this poignancy are two anecdotes. The first comes from Atheneus regarding Ptolemy II Philadelphus:

> The second Ptolemy to become king of Egypt was the most august of rulers and as devoted to learning as anyone ever has been, he was so deluded and corrupted by his inopportune addiction to luxury that he imagined that he was going to live forever and claimed that he alone had discovered the secret to immortality. So when he was tortured by gout for many days, and then eventually recovered and looked out a window and saw average Egyptians having lunch on the riverbanks, eating simple food and lounging on the sand, he said: "Poor me—I wish I was one of them!" (*Learned Banqueters*, 12.536e)[17]

The second anecdote comes from the fact that Cyrus erected his own tomb within his "paradise" at Pasargadae. Apparently, it once carried an inscription

15. The Masoretic Text gives the name of the Persian king as "Ahasuerus," which is usually understood to be Xerxes. However, the Greek version of Esther translates his name as "Artaxerxes," presumably the son of Xerxes.

16. Atheneus was a Greek writer from Egypt in the second century AD. His description of Ptolemy II's parade is based largely on quotes from Callixeinus of Rhodes, who was Ptolemy II's contemporary.

17. Atheneus's recollection of this anecdote is taken from Book 22 of Phylarchus's *History*—a work from the third century BC, which is now lost to us.

that read, "O man, I am Cyrus, who acquired the empire for the Persians, and was King of Asia. Grudge me not, therefore, this monument" (Strabo, *Geography*, 15.3.7).[18] The tomb still stands today, though Cyrus's body, sarcophagus, and inscription have long since been pilfered. Today's visitors may scarcely imagine how lush and verdant Cyrus's "paradise" had once been, for the entire site is now dry and dusty.

EXPLAIN the Story

Royal Theater (1:12–2:26)

In this section of Ecclesiastes, Qohelet takes on the persona of a king for the purposes of an experiment. He uses this persona as a platform to test whether power and privilege provide any real profit to those at the very top of human society. He concludes that even the elite have no ultimate gain in life, so he reiterates the substance of his motto (1:2) that life has no substance.

In 1:12, Qohelet claims the title "king over Israel in Jerusalem." Along with 1:1, this verse has been traditionally used to identify Qohelet as Solomon, for no one else could possibly be a son of David ruling over "Israel" (as opposed to just Judah) from Jerusalem. However, as we have seen in the Introduction, there are numerous difficulties with this traditional identification. Qohelet does not name himself as Solomon here, for he is not actually Solomon, nor even a reigning king. Rather, he is here adopting the "mask" of a king, in the same way someone in an ancient theater would have put on the mask of the character they were playing. Yet, despite not being a reigning king, we have also seen that Qohelet is probably an heir of the Davidic kings. This means he is rightfully king of Israel, even if in reality he is not. This provides him with a wistful perspective for evaluating the achievements of his ancestors. This is more than just playacting for him. It is a solemn contemplation of his own heritage.[19]

His contemplation takes in more than Solomon alone. The litany of accomplishments he presents between 1:12 and 2:26 reflects the achievements of many Davidic kings who ruled in Jerusalem, especially as they are presented in 1 and 2 Chronicles. We see reflected the deeds of David, Solomon, Jehoshaphat,

---

18. Other sources give slightly different wording to the inscription, but all convey the same tenor.

19. In this way, Qohelet's reflection is like a literary rendition of the Roman practice of eulogizing the dead through the production of *imagines*—ancestral masks. These masks were portraits of deceased nobles and could be worn by an actor at the funeral of the deceased. The masks were then usually placed on a wall in the home, often accompanied by a brief description of the deceased's accomplishments.

Uzziah, Hezekiah, Manasseh, Amon, and Josiah. As Barbour puts it, "we are seeing the sum of what the king sitting on the throne in Jerusalem saw, and what this pastiche king sees is therefore a palimpsest of all Israel's history."[20] But Qohelet's contemplation goes even further than this, as it also resonates with the deeds of famed foreign kings, such as Croesus of Lydia, the great kings of Persia, and Ptolemy II Philadelphus of Egypt. Qohelet's "king" is a composite character whose achievements are a mosaic of the most illustrious and legendary monarchs of the ancient world. Indeed, the manner of his exploits, which are all for his personal pleasure, embody the basic ideology of the Ptolemaic king, who in Qohelet's day was Ptolemy III Euergetes. Qohelet's accomplishments, therefore, deliberately caricature the royal ideology of the Ptolemies.

Yet, nowhere does Qohelet name any of these royal figures. He exemplifies them all while only hinting at their identities. This reinforces the idea expressed in the verse immediately preceding this section: "No one remembers the former generations, and even those yet to come will not be remembered by those who follow them" (Eccl 1:11). After all, "What has been will be again," for "there is nothing new under the sun" (1:9). The exploits of past grandees and the dark obscurity that engulfs them takes in both the highs and lows of Israel's experience within the wider ancient world, leading inexorably to the conclusion that it has achieved nothing. No one has learned the lessons of the past. By also embodying the experience of self-aggrandizing foreign kings, Qohelet extends his observations to the time after the decline and fall of Israel—a time like his very own, when there was no Davidic king ruling in Jerusalem and the Jews were subject to the Ptolemaic dynasty of Egypt. In Qohelet's estimation, God has done nothing new to change the floundering fortunes of Israel and its rightful Davidic dynasty. Qohelet finds in the experience of both Israel and foreign empires a tragic similarity: there is nothing new under the sun, and there is nothing of substance to be found. God has not done anything to alter this stark reality. Even if Israel's history led to naught, the course of foreign history is no different. Qohelet's contemplation, then, becomes a skeptical critique of Israel's entire history—a means for questioning all the orthodoxy and received wisdom of Israel's past, including, by inference, questioning God's role in not policing orthodoxy or coming to Israel's rescue. It also becomes a snub toward those empires conceited enough to think they possessed any superiority over Israel, especially the kingdom of the Ptolemies who prided themselves on great learning and wealth. Even more than demonstrating historical amnesia, "King Qohelet" has subtly engaged in *damnatio memoriae*—the erasure from the record of the great names of the past.

20. Barbour, *The Story of Israel in the Book of Qohelet*, 29.

Testing Wisdom (1:12–18)

Qohelet begins his contemplation by evaluating life and wisdom (1:12–18). The paragon of wisdom among his ancestors was undoubtedly Solomon, whose wisdom was divinely granted (2 Chr 1:7–12). He is credited with speaking three thousand proverbs (1 Kgs 4:32), presumably including those preserved in the book of Proverbs (Prov 1:1; 25:1). Wisdom here incorporates both intellect and savvy—empirical knowledge of the world and what to do with that knowledge.

Inhabiting the persona of wise King Solomon, Qohelet conducts an extensive theatrical study of what occurs "under the heavens" (Eccl 1:13)—a phrase evoking God's sovereignty over every endeavor on earth. It is not just one or two activities that Qohelet considers, but the totality of what humanity does on earth. Nothing is beyond his purview. It is as though Qohelet is subtly putting God on trial.

His verdict is shocking. The NIV expresses it as a cry: "What a heavy burden God has laid on mankind!" (1:13). The underlying Hebrew expression, however, is even more stark: "It is a bad task that God has given to the children of humanity to occupy it" (author's translation). The word "task" here (*'inyan*) denotes an activity requiring exertion, and the word "bad," which describes this task, could also be translated "evil." The phrase "to occupy it" (*la'anot bo*) can also mean "to oppress it." There may be a pale allusion to Genesis 2–3 here, in which God employs the man he has formed to tend the garden he has planted in Eden and then condemns the man to hard labor for his disobedience (Gen 2:8, 15; 3:17–19). However, Qohelet nowhere alludes to humanity's sinfulness, so he does not see this task as a just punishment for sin.[21] Furthermore, the hard labor in Genesis 3:17–19 is a result of God cursing the ground—a curse that is lifted in Genesis 8:21.[22] Qohelet's study takes in every human pursuit in every time and place and views it all as essentially harmful to humanity. The scope of Qohelet's study makes his conclusion universal. It is unnerving, as it casts God in the role of humanity's cosmic oppressor.

This evidently brings into question the character of God. What kind of God does this? Is humanity trapped by this harsh task? Does God trifle with humans? Is there a way to deal with the enormity of the situation? At this point, Qohelet's pessimism rings loudly as he reiterates his motto that "everything is

21. A key task in biblical interpretation is to let each book of the Bible speak on its own terms before bringing it into conversation with other books in the Bible. This avoids "cross pollination" and imposing the thoughts of one author on another. Thus, Qohelet is not here denying the veracity of Genesis, but he simply has other concerns.

22. Noah's fabulous success in planting a vineyard (Gen 9:20–21) is evidence of the lifting of this curse.

meaningless" (1:14, author's translation). He even exclaims that all of life is "a chasing after the wind."[23] This ingenious little phrase, which Qohelet uses elsewhere, slips easily from the lips in Hebrew: *re'ut ruah*. It can be taken a few ways, making this phrase versatile in various contexts. It can indicate the attempt to "shepherd the wind"—something over which one has absolutely no control, making it an impossible task. It can also indicate the attempt to grasp something that turns out to be nothing but air—a disappointing task. It can indicate a "desire" for something devoid of substance or gain, which reveals only the self-delusion of the desirer. Or it can indicate the "pursuit of the wind"—a task both aimless and fruitless. There is significant overlap between these possible meanings, so it is difficult to know if Qohelet has only one in mind here. In any case, each possibility would confirm his conclusion that all human endeavor is a terrible waste, which seems like a cruel and arbitrary sentence for God to impose.[24]

The proverb Qohelet quotes in 1:15 amplifies the pessimism. The NIV translates the first part as "What is crooked cannot be straightened." However, this is not necessarily true. The final word in this clause does not contain any causative sense in the Hebrew.[25] It is better rendered, "What is crooked cannot be straight," indicating that something cannot exist in one state and its opposite state simultaneously. This is self-evidently true. Qohelet implies that if all human endeavor is meaningless pursuit, it cannot somehow be meaningful at the same time, and no one can make it meaningful, because there is no meaning to be found anywhere. After all, "what is lacking cannot be counted" (1:15)—you can't quantify what is not there. Humanity is, therefore, trapped in a hopeless situation. Qohelet will reiterate this in 7:13, when he will imply that God has "made crooked" the human predicament, and no human has the power to alter what God has done.

This defeatism does not stop Qohelet from pursuing alternative routes to meaning, though he knows these too will end in failure. He has already concluded that every human endeavor is meaningless, so why should he think he will find anything different down other avenues? Yet, he wants his study to be exhaustive, so he takes up the challenge and continues his royal experiment.

Having used wisdom to come to his depressing conclusion, he now questions his method. Does the fault lie with wisdom itself? He undertakes an

---

23. A similar expression is found in Hos 12:1[12:2].

24. For further discussion of the phrase *re'ut ruah*, see Fox, *A Time to Tear Down*, 42–49. Although Fox assigns the specific meaning of "senseless mental activity" (46), his analysis still shows how adaptable the phrase is.

25. The word is an infinitive in the *qal* stem, which indicates a plain, basic action or state ("to be straight"). The causative sense ("to straighten") would be conveyed by the *piel* stem.

examination of wisdom and weighs it against "madness and folly" (1:17a). The Hebrew word for "madness" here (*holelot*) is best translated "ignorance." In other words, Qohelet evaluates wisdom by comparing it to both its passive and active opposites: ignorance (a lack of intelligence) and folly (deliberate stupidity). As expected, his conclusion is no different from what he has already demonstrated: it is "a chasing after the wind" (1:17b). Qohelet here uses a slightly different form for this phrase to the one he uses in 1:14, though it preserves the same possible meanings and in Hebrew still rolls easily off the tongue: *ra'yon ruah*. As pleasing as the phrase sounds, its implications are somber: the more you know, the more sorrow you experience (1:18), because the vanity of human existence simply gets writ larger. Qohelet's ancestor, wise and wonderful Solomon, celebrated in biblical literature for shining glorious light on the lives of others (2 Chr 9:5–8; Prov 1:1–7), now cuts a tragic, forlorn figure in Qohelet's dim theater.[26]

The Pursuit of Happiness (2:1–16)

On this dispiriting note, Qohelet turns to the pursuit of happiness (2:1). The NIV renders the Hebrew word *simhah* as "pleasure," which certainly accounts for many of Qohelet's exploits in this chapter. However, the word has a wider range of meaning than the excitement of the senses. It can describe the gladness that comes from relief (Jer 41:13), a sense of satisfaction (Jon 4:6), a cheerful cry or sound (1 Chr 15:16), or a solemn celebration (Lev 23:40). In turning to "pleasure," Qohelet is not merely looking for thrills, but for general happiness. He wants to determine whether there is anything that humans might do under God's sovereignty ("under the heavens") that can bring them any satisfaction or gain (2:3). He will test this by moving from pure observation and intellectual engagement (1:12–18) toward experience (2:1–11). This does not mean he will abandon the use of rational thought, for he needs this to evaluate his experience (2:3). Rather, he now adds "field work" to his experiment.

As his experiment grows, so does Qolehet's *dramatis persona*. He now becomes bigger than Solomon and incorporates into his role all his royal forebears who had occupied the Davidic throne in Jerusalem, and their deeds: David himself, Jehoshaphat, Uzziah, Hezekiah, Manasseh, Amon, and Josiah. His persona even takes on the airs and trappings of famed foreign rulers: rich Croesus, who prided himself on being the happiest of men for

26. First Kings 11 relates the tragedy of Solomon's apostasy. However, this flaw is not part of the Chronicler's depiction of Solomon, from which Qohelet seems to draw much impetus for his playacting here. Nonetheless, Solomon's apostasy would not alter any of Qohelet's conclusions.

his wealth; Cyrus, Darius, Xerxes, and Artaxerxes II of Persia; and Ptolemy II Philadelphus of Egypt, in whose kingdom Qohelet had probably lived.[27] These were kings from well beyond Jerusalem's horizon, whose empires extended across vast lands. They ruled the lives of millions, including Jews, and their wealth afforded them every pursuit and pleasure. By adopting them all into the single stereotype of the "oriental despot," well known in Second Temple Judaism and the wider ancient world,[28] Qohelet can amass "the treasure of kings and provinces" (2:8) in his theater and boast, "I became greater by far than anyone in Jerusalem before me" (2:9). Thus, his experiment becomes a truly universal test of all human pursuits "under the heavens" (2:3). For "King Qohelet," nothing is beyond imagination.

His exploits are grand in the extreme, ranging from the construction of palaces to Persian style "paradises" (NIV: "parks"). In addition to property, his possessions include people, animals, and luxury goods. He denies himself nothing (2:10). But while other kings would list their achievements and wealth to promote their own glory and extend their sway over others, Qohelet lists his in order to gain some kind of sway over his own life. Perhaps in these things he might find happiness or the meaning he so desperately desires.

Yet, despite the seemingly limitless possibilities his wealth can afford him, he finds only a transient modicum of joy. The NIV depicts this as "delight" and a "reward" for his toil (2:10), which sounds positive. Yet, the underlying Hebrew expression is not so glowing: "Indeed my heart was cheered by all my effort, but this was my lot out of all my effort" (author's translation). The word "lot" (*heleq*) can indicate a share in spoils of war (1 Sam 30:24) or a piece of land (2 Kgs 9:10)—an apt word given Qohelet's accumulation of wealth. But in the larger context of Qohelet's experiment, it conveys the notion of one's "lot in life," with the distinct sense of something paltry dished out callously by God.[29] When coupled with the term for "effort" (*'amal*), it sounds decidedly negative. Qohelet's joy is real but meager. The implication is that he received little profit from his exorbitant investment—certainly not enough to justify the expenditure. Far from being an enduring inscription to fame and fortune that lauds gods and kings, Qohelet's anti-boast is a monument to failure and gloom that indicts God.

The ultimate reason for Qohelet's grim assessment is the universal reality of death. After considering ignorance and stupidity (2:12), he surmises that

27. Qohelet probably did not live in Egypt, but rather in Judea. However, from 301 to 199 BC Judea was part of the empire that the Ptolemies ruled from Alexandria in Egypt. The Ptolemies were very active throughout the eastern Mediterranean, and quickly developed a reputation for opulence.

28. Barbour, *The Story of Israel in the Book of Qohelet*, 33.

29. Fox, *A Time to Tear Down*, 109–11.

wisdom does provide a certain advantage during life, just as light provides advantage over darkness (2:13–14a). Yet the bleak reality is that the same fate awaits both the sage and the fool (2:14b, 16). For the Greek sage, Solon, a person's death gave the opportunity for someone else to evaluate the entire life of the deceased, with the possibility of concluding that the person had lived a good life and died well. For Qohelet, however, death is the ultimate leveler that robs everyone of any meaning in life (2:15–16). The cheer that pleasure brings and the light that wisdom sheds, then, ultimately come to nothing. They have no lasting value and merely reinforce the transience and meaninglessness of all things.

A Legacy of Frustration (2:17–23)

Qohelet's short lived joy (2:10) now turns to hate (2:17–18) and despair (2:20). The lack of meaning in life causes him to revile all efforts to find it. The momentary cheer he had experienced through pleasure seeking was, therefore, illusory. This taunts him to the point of utter frustration and resignation. Life becomes an object of his hate.

As if this were not enough, "King Qohelet" then considers an added point of frustration. As king, he must contemplate the issue of succession. When he dies, another will take not just his throne but the entire estate he has worked so hard to acquire (2:18–21). The magnitude of Qohelet's royal persona, incorporating so many royal figures with so many achievements and riches into one, underscores the enormity of death's criminal nature: it robs Qohelet of all his vast possessions, forcing him to leave them to someone else (2:18). There are certainly shades of Rehoboam, the son of Solomon, in 2:19, when Qohelet asks concerning his successor, "And who knows whether that person will be wise or foolish?" After Solomon's death, his son, Rehoboam, foolishly failed to heed the advice of elders and took instead the advice of his peers. The result was the permanent loss of half his kingdom, as the nation of Israel split into two distinct entities (2 Chr 10). This moment of fracture and loss is significant, for although some illustrious Davidic kings followed Rehoboam, centuries later, their descendant Qohelet finds himself without a kingdom, and God's people find themselves under foreign rule. The glories of the past are gone, and the prophetic hopes for restoration remain unfulfilled. Qohelet is king in his theater only, not in actuality. When he removes his royal mask, we see a forlorn figure with little to his name. And what little he has he will one day surrender to death's fiendish hand anyway. His fate is ultimately the same as the grandest of his grandfathers: he will come to naught. All this leads Qohelet to conclude that existence is *hebel*—meaningless and a chasing after the wind (Eccl 2:17, 23).

Clutching at Straws (2:24–26)

Qohelet's reasoning to this point has demonstrated that human existence is but the temporary delay of oblivion. It may be surprising, then, that in 2:24–26a Qohelet comes up with apparently positive advice: "A person can do nothing better than to eat and drink and find satisfaction in their own toil."[30] Some commentators read this as reference to "fleeting yet profoundly redemptive moments of joy amid the toil"[31]—the heart of Qohelet's philosophy, which proves it not to be despairing, but optimistic.[32] However, this evaluation is perhaps wishful thinking and misses Qohelet's point. This advice does not mute Qohelet's motto from being the first and last word of his discourse: "Meaningless! Meaningless! Everything is meaningless!" (see 1:2; 12:8). Indeed, it does not dislodge the same basic motto from bracketing this seemingly positive advice here (2:23, 26b). We must see this advice in 2:24–26, therefore, within Qohelet's larger message. He is not endorsing "a wholesome enjoyment of the 'good life'" as a way through life's challenges.[33] Rather, he is clutching at straws—attempting to salvage even a mangled bit from the wreckage of human existence. That he does this shows he is trying to be objective. He is not simply storming off in despair before he has accounted for all the facts. The magnitude of his royal experiment alone demonstrates this. He is honestly trying to gain a grip on reality and find something hopeful. Yet, what he pulls from the wreckage of human existence is so mangled that it provides little substantive hope.

In 1:13 Qohelet exclaimed of life, "It is a bad task that God has given to the children of humanity to occupy it" (author's translation). His subsequent royal experiment bore this conclusion out, demonstrating how meaningless and futile human life seems to be. In the midst of life's terrible task, humans cannot expect anything better than trying to find some satisfaction in the basics: eating, drinking, and working.[34] Although Qohelet's royal experiment

30. The Hebrew Masoretic Text of this sentence reads, "There is nothing good in the person who eats and drinks and shows himself good in his toil." However, this makes littles sense in the context. It seems that a single Hebrew letter (*mem*), which changes the meaning to that given in the NIV, has fallen off the front of the word *sheyyo'kal* ("who eats"). This can be explained as the result of haplography, in which two instances of the same letter appear one after the other but only one is copied. The previous word in Hebrew, *ba'adam* ("in the person"), ends with the letter *mem*. Thus, the word *sheyyo'kal* ("who eats") should read *misheyyo'kal* ("than that he should eat").

31. Brown, *Ecclesiastes*, 38–39.

32. For example, see Eaton, *Ecclesiastes*, 73–77; Hubbard, *Ecclesiastes, Song of Songs*, 92–93; Moore and Akin, *Ecclesiastes, Songs of Songs*, 32–34; Greidanus, *Preaching Christ from Ecclesiastes*, 50, 53–54.

33. Contra Daniel C. Fredericks and Daniel J. Estes, *Ecclesiastes & the Song of Songs* (Nottingham, England: Inter-Varsity Press, 2010), 101.

34. As Seow notes, Qohelet is not limiting the possibility of satisfaction only to eating, drinking, and working, but rather using these to indicate "a general attitude toward life." See Choon-Leong Seow, *Ecclesiastes: A New Translation with Introduction* (New York: Doubleday Religion, 1997), 157.

has made him a connoisseur of life, he is not saying this with any relish, but with resignation: "Since life is utterly meaningless, this is as good as it will ever get. Enjoy it while it lasts!" There is some joy to be found in eating, drinking, and working (cf. 2:10), but this is not really an antidote for Qohelet's despondency, because death makes it ultimately meaningless (2:26).[35] The implication is that enjoying the basics of life is akin to a prisoner on death row enjoying his last meal. Any satisfaction derived from it will be squashed by death. It is just *hebel*: "transient" at best and "useless" at worst.

Furthermore, Qohelet maintains that there is no guarantee of finding transient satisfaction in eating, drinking, and working. Rather, satisfaction is God's to give, and without his sanction, no one can find it, try as they might (2:24–25). The implication is that satisfaction may be real, but attaining it is something of a lottery. Qohelet is not claiming that meaning is found in receiving joy from God or in eschewing a secular perspective of the world in favor of a theistic one.[36] On the contrary, he is subtly indicting God as the cosmic oppressor of humanity (cf. 2:10), giving to some and not to others. Yet, as a faithful Jew, he never comes out with a plain charge against God. He only implies it through circumlocution. Thus, in 2:26, Qohelet expresses the basic dynamic of Israel's national covenant: God blesses those who please him but curses the sinner who disobeys him. It is essentially a reiteration of Proverbs 13:22. This initially seems to provide reliable guidelines for seeking happiness and perhaps attaining it. However, he perceives a circularity in the covenantal dynamic here: if God blesses those who please him with wealth procured from sinners (2:26), then sinners are necessary to the economy of blessing. This implies that God almost needs sinners in order to bless the righteous. Yet, Qohelet's observations later in his discourse will undermine this possibility, too, as he sees many wicked who prosper and many righteous who suffer (7:15–17; 8:14). Death means that even the righteous must surrender their wealth to others anyway, so that there is no real advantage to being righteous or wealthy (cf. 2:16, 19).[37] No human can win at life! Regardless of their wisdom, ignorance, or folly, humans appear to be mere pawns in God's cosmic game of chess, and ultimately in control of nothing. Everything is meaningless!

The overall effect of these considerations is scandalous: God may be all sovereign, but there are serious questions about his goodness. He has not fulfilled

35. Contra Seow. See Ibid.

36. Contra Eaton, *Ecclesiastes*, 76–77; and Greidanus, *Preaching Christ from Ecclesiastes*, 54. For Qohelet, the reality of God is a given assumption. He never entertains a "secular" worldview in which God is not present or active.

37. Seow, *Ecclesiastes*, 158.

Israel's prophetic hopes. He does not grant happiness to all people. Everyone, regardless of their station in life, comes to nothing in death. Qohelet's philosophical musings question some of the most basic tenets of Israel's cherished orthodoxy. Yet, he is reticent to blame God directly. The best he can do is point to what God gives humanity and label it as "bad" (2:10). So, Qohelet must grapple with the possibility that individual humans are fated to whatever it is God has decreed for them, be that good or bad. It is to this issue he turns in chapter 3.

LIVE the Story

It seems difficult to redeem anything from Qohelet's devastating conclusions about God, humanity, and life. However, we must remember that Qohelet's understanding of God, humanity, and life is a "BC" understanding. He does not have the benefit of God's full revelation in Christ, so we cannot take Qohelet's view as the final word. Our temptation is to think that because Qohelet is a biblical author, he must be making absolute statements that are generically true. To some extent, he is indeed grasping for ultimate truth. As he seeks it, he raises issues pertaining to the very meaning of life and reaches conclusions that are not just sobering, but depressing and even frightening. It is not that Qohelet's observations and conclusions are wrong. The final editor endorses their veracity (12:9–10), so we can affirm that Qohelet was indeed inspired by the Spirit of God in his deliberations. However, in seeking absolute truth, Qohelet was limited by his historical vantage point. He lived before the final revelation of God and his purposes in the person of Jesus Christ. Thus, Qohelet's conclusions are provisional at best—located in the Old Testament and in much need of fuller light from the New Testament.

The Fulfiller of God's Promises

Qohelet's discussion implies the failure of God's promises. Although God had made a covenantal commitment to David (2 Sam 7), both the kingdoms of Israel and Judah ultimately failed. Despite hopes for restoration expressed by the prophets, and hopes for a new work of God in history, these had not materialized by Qohelet's day in the third century BC. Qohelet himself was a tragic testament to this.

Yet, this was not the end of the matter. Jesus was himself descended from David (Rom 1:3) and came proclaiming the kingdom of God—a time of great fulfilment. John's Gospel tells us that "He came to that which was his own"—his own people, his own estate—and yet "his own did not receive him"

(John 1:11). He came eating and drinking with them, and they called him a glutton and a drunkard (Matt 11:19). He was rejected by his own people, abandoned by his followers, executed by foreign overlords as a failed "King of the Jews," and forsaken by the God he trusted (Matt 27:46). Qohelet had questioned the goodness of God on the basis of his seeming inaction to make good on his promises, but the terrible irony is that when Jesus showed up to make good on those promises, humanity rejected and killed him. The death of Jesus, the righteous one, demonstrates the utter sinfulness of humanity. So, if anyone in human history had reason to hate life and despair of it all, it was Jesus in the moment of his crucifixion. At that moment, he seemed even less of a true king than Qohelet in his theatrical experiment. As his wrecked body was unfastened from the timber of his cross and laid lifeless in a tomb, it appeared that death had once again had the final say. It all appeared so utterly meaningless.

The genius of God, however, is displayed by the fact that in this chief expression of humanity's rejection of him, God was fulfilling his ancient promises and reconciling humanity to himself through the forgiveness of sins. By his resurrection, Jesus demonstrated that the grave was not the ultimate end that Qohelet had thought it was. Humans may have killed Jesus, but Jesus killed death. His opened tomb opens up the hope of eternal life to all. As John's Gospel puts it, "Yet to all who did receive him, to those who believed in his name, he gave the right to become children of God" (John 1:12).

Furthermore, at his ascension, Jesus was granted all authority in heaven and on earth (Matt 28:18). The one who was executed as "King of the Jews" was made King of the world. This grant of authority was no mere playacting, as Qohelet's royal experiment was, but a real endowment with power over all creation. Subsequently, through the ministry of his apostles, King Jesus fulfilled God's promises and restored Israel. As the gospel of his death and resurrection was proclaimed to Jews and Samaritans, many came to place their faith in him as their messiah and took hold of the hope of eternal life (Acts 1–8). This hope was then proclaimed to all people in all nations. As Paul said to the Corinthians, "For no matter how many promises God has made, they are 'Yes' in Christ. And so through him the 'Amen' is spoken by us to the glory of God" (2 Cor 1:20).

This Life Matters

In the person of Jesus Christ, God entered the world and revealed the true meaning of life: to know the only true God, and Jesus Christ, whom he has sent (John 17:3). In knowing Jesus—the fulfiller of God's promises, the conqueror of death, and the reigning king of all creation—we find that life is not utterly meaningless or a chasing after the wind. Instead, we find purpose, meaning, and hope. The resurrection means death is not the final word for humans. Death has lost its sting (1 Cor 15:55), so what we do in this life matters. Every life matters. Everyone's life is of value and has eternal significance. Knowing Jesus is the most significant thing any person can do in life.

It is sometimes said that the Christian hope for eternal life means that Christians care more about the life to come than this life they currently live. This is unfortunately often true, but it should not be. It is because death has been conquered that this current life matters so much. Our words, actions, and thoughts have eternal consequences. This means that our sin weighs heavily upon us, but this underscores the significance of Jesus' sin-bearing death that brings us forgiveness. It also means that the other aspects of our lives are significant, too. It's not as though every minute aspect of our lives carries the same weight and consequence, that we should agonize over even the simplest decisions. Rather, we need to get on with living life in a thoughtful and deliberate manner, living the good works for which God intended us (Eph 2:10). It is not these works that guarantee our eternal hope—that comes only from faith in the one who conquered death—but neither must we underestimate their value.

As Qohelet despondently clutched at straws, he looked to eating, drinking, and working to find a modicum of joy. When our eternal future is secured in Christ, these mundane activities of life can indeed be a source of real joy. They are no longer meaningless activities—the mere façade of a life condemned to demolition. They are some of the pillars on which we support the edifice of our lives. They can indeed bring genuine joy, to be received with thanksgiving (1 Tim 4:3–4). Faith in Christ is no guarantee that these activities will be joyful. For many, eating, drinking, or working is a source of much pain and frustration, especially for those of us in developing societies or under oppressive regimes. This fact should motivate us to work for the bettering of human society—for constructive activity that makes eating, drinking, and working a substantive source of satisfaction. After all, every society and regime exists under the current reign of the risen and ascendant Lord Jesus. Since every life matters, we must work for the good of all.

However, for a person whose eternal future is not secured, Qohelet's "BC" perspective is a stark reminder that this life is as good as it gets. A Christless life is a life whose pillars are crumbling. Those of us with the stable foundation of Christ and sturdy pillars resting on him are obliged to those who despair in life or who are attempting to build it on a false foundation. This is what makes both evangelism and social action such constructive activities for followers of the risen and ascendant Lord Jesus.

Wealth

In his theatrical pursuit for meaning and happiness, "King Qohelet" accumulated "the treasure of kings and provinces" (Eccl 2:8). Qohelet never evaluates this as wrong or sinful—only that it was misguided, as it did not provide him with the answers to life. As Qohelet discovered, the pursuit of happiness through wealth can be deceptive. No one takes their possessions with them into death. Despite the common practice of the ancient world to bury the famous dead with the trappings of their lives, as the Egyptians did with their Pharaohs and Cyrus did with his paradise tomb, death always prizes our hand away from our possessions, no matter how tightly we may grip them. Qohelet lamented that he would have to relinquish his accumulated wealth to another. The saying, "He who dies with the most toys wins," is simply not true.

Wealth is not of itself wicked. Wealth can do many good things, such as afford opportunities and provide latitude of choice, but it can never plumb the deepest questions of life. In fact, the human heart can be so shallow that it is often fooled into thinking life is simply a pursuit of wealth. We have institutionalized this to such an extent that economics is usually the driving factor in government policies and household decisions. That Jesus can call even the poor "blessed" (Matt 5:3) shows that the meaning of life is not found in possessions.

The reality of death means we must hold our possessions lightly. The reality of resurrection means we must use our possessions wisely. As Jesus himself said, "What good is it for someone to gain the whole world, yet forfeit their soul?" (Mark 8:36). "Every good and perfect gift is from above, coming down from the Father of the heavenly lights" (Jas 1:17), so wealth is not to be shunned when it is given. It is there for enjoyment and generosity (Acts 20:35), yet it cannot be the ultimate end of human life either. True life consists in knowing God and Jesus Christ, whom he has sent (John 17:3). We must subordinate our wealth to this ultimate pursuit. To that end, we must ask for God's wisdom (Jas 1:5), seek his kingdom above all things (Matt 6:33), and learn contentment in all circumstances (Phil 4:12). Jesus's words are apt advice for the shallow human heart: "Do not store up for yourselves treasures on earth, where moths and vermin destroy, and where thieves break in and steal. But store up for yourselves treasures in heaven, where moths and vermin do not destroy, and where thieves do not break in and steal. For where your treasure is, there your heart will be also" (Matt 6:19–21).

CHAPTER 3

Ecclesiastes 3:1–4:16

LISTEN to the Story

[1]There is a time for everything,
and a season for every activity under the heavens:
[2]a time to be born and a time to die,
a time to plant and a time to uproot,
[3]a time to kill and a time to heal,
a time to tear down and a time to build,
[4]a time to weep and a time to laugh,
a time to mourn and a time to dance,
[5]a time to scatter stones and a time to gather them,
a time to embrace and a time to refrain from embracing,
[6]a time to search and a time to give up,
a time to keep and a time to throw away,
[7]a time to tear and a time to mend,
a time to be silent and a time to speak,
[8]a time to love and a time to hate,
a time for war and a time for peace.

[9]What do workers gain from their toil? [10]I have seen the burden God has
laid on the human race. [11]He has made everything beautiful in its time. He
has also set eternity in the human heart; yet no one can fathom what God has
done from beginning to end. [12]I know that there is nothing better for people
than to be happy and to do good while they live. [13]That each of them may
eat and drink, and find satisfaction in all their toil—this is the gift of God.
[14]I know that everything God does will endure forever; nothing can be added
to it and nothing taken from it. God does it so that people will fear him.

[15]Whatever is has already been,
and what will be has been before;
and God will call the past to account.

[16]And I saw something else under the sun:

In the place of judgment—wickedness was there,
in the place of justice—wickedness was there.

[17]I said to myself,

"God will bring into judgment
both the righteous and the wicked,
for there will be a time for every activity,
a time to judge every deed."

[18]I also said to myself, "As for humans, God tests them so that they
may see that they are like the animals. [19]Surely the fate of human beings
is like that of the animals; the same fate awaits them both: As one dies,
so dies the other. All have the same breath; humans have no advantage
over animals. Everything is meaningless. [20]All go to the same place; all
come from dust, and to dust all return. [21]Who knows if the human
spirit rises upward and if the spirit of the animal goes down into
the earth?"

[22]So I saw that there is nothing better for a person than to enjoy their
work, because that is their lot. For who can bring them to see what will
happen after them?

[4:1]Again I looked and saw all the oppression that was taking place
under the sun:

I saw the tears of the oppressed—
and they have no comforter;
power was on the side of their oppressors—
and they have no comforter.
[2]And I declared that the dead,
who had already died,
are happier than the living,
who are still alive.
[3]But better than both
is the one who has never been born,
who has not seen the evil
that is done under the sun.

[4]And I saw that all toil and all achievement spring from one person's envy of another. This too is meaningless, a chasing after the wind.

[5]Fools fold their hands
    and ruin themselves.
[6]Better one handful with tranquillity
    than two handfuls with toil
    and chasing after the wind.

[7]Again I saw something meaningless under the sun:

[8]There was a man all alone;
    he had neither son nor brother.
There was no end to his toil,
    yet his eyes were not content with his wealth.
"For whom am I toiling," he asked,
    "and why am I depriving myself of enjoyment?"
This too is meaningless—
    a miserable business!
[9]Two are better than one,
    because they have a good return for their labor:
[10]If either of them falls down,
    one can help the other up.
But pity anyone who falls
    and has no one to help them up.
[11]Also, if two lie down together, they will keep warm.
    But how can one keep warm alone?
[12]Though one may be overpowered,
    two can defend themselves.
A cord of three strands is not quickly broken.

[13]Better a poor but wise youth than an old but foolish king who no
longer knows how to heed a warning. [14]The youth may have come from
prison to the kingship, or he may have been born in poverty within his
kingdom. [15]I saw that all who lived and walked under the sun followed
the youth, the king's successor. [16]There was no end to all the people who
were before them. But those who came later were not pleased with the
successor. This too is meaningless, a chasing after the wind.

Listening to the Text in the Story: Epic of Gilgamesh, Tablet V (Standard Akkadian version); Gezer Calendar; Zenon Papyri; Josephus, *Antiquities* 12.154–185; Deuteronomy 28:30; 2 Samuel 7:1–16; 1 Kings 11:9–13; 11:26–12:19; 2 Kings 3:9–25; 25:1–10; Psalm 126; Isaiah 57:14–21; Jeremiah 1:1–10; 12:14–17; 23:1–5; 31:10–14; Ezekiel 34:1–31; 36:33–38; Hosea 6:1–3; Amos 9:11–15; Zechariah 7:1–7; 8:18–19.

Ancient life was governed by the rhythms of the earth in ways that those of us in modern cities today perhaps do not fully appreciate. The four seasons and the cycles of the moon dictated the nature of life throughout the whole Mediterranean world. The Gezer Calendar provides us with an excellent example of this. It is a small limestone inscription that was probably a practice tablet for a scribe in training some time during the tenth century BC. Written in a Canaanite dialect,[1] it outlines the course of an agricultural year:

Two months, gathering.
Two months, sowing.
Two months, late sowing.
A month, cutting flax.
A month, harvesting barley.
A month, harvesting and finishing.
Two months, pruning.
A month, summer fruit.[2]

There is a beautiful simplicity in this "calendar." Its repetition produces a rhythm attuned to the agricultural activity of consecutive months, conveying a sense of appropriate activity for each respective month. This makes the calendar both descriptive and prescriptive, telling us what *is* done at various times of the year but also signifying what *should* be done. Thus, it produces a sense of orderliness and productivity. The calendar's repetition and annual "grid" also make it cyclical. This is an unchanging and unceasing rotation of time aligning the earth with human activity upon it.

Qohelet picks up similar ideas in this next section of his monologue. His poem in 3:1–8 bears some similarity to the Gezer Calendar. However, Qohelet

1. The language of the inscription is still debated today. I have estimated it to be a late Canaanite dialect. Others, however, view it as an archaic form of Hebrew, or perhaps Phoenician. All these options are closely related, and the distinction between them can sometimes be difficult to discern.

2. My translation.

is doing more than just talking generally about what is done on earth and when. He is evaluating the activity of an all-sovereign God in the world and how humanity fits into this. In his evaluation, Qohelet alludes to the story of God's dealings with Israel. His word choices resonate with particular ideas and events within this national story. As Barbour puts it, "there seems to be a shadow of Israel's historical experience behind the language here, which supports the idea that this is the outworking not only of theory but also of experience."[3] There isn't the space here to recount this entire experience, so we will confine ourselves to the broadest of outlines and save more specific discussion, including of some of the biblical passages listed above, for our exegesis of Qohelet's words.

Israel's national story begins with their exodus from Egypt and the granting of the law at Sinai. After a generation of wandering through the desert, Israel entered and settled in the land of Canaan, which Yahweh, their national deity, had promised them. Initially a loose association of tribes governed locally by judges and priests, Israel eventually adopted monarchy. The first king, Saul, foolishly incurred Yahweh's anger and so failed to establish a dynasty. He was instead replaced by David, who garnered Yahweh's favor. Yahweh forged a covenant with David that promised to plant Israel securely within the land and give David a permanent dynasty over the nation in Jerusalem (2 Sam 7:1–16). His heir, Solomon, built Yahweh's temple in Jerusalem as the essential symbol of this covenant and the focal point of Israel's national life. Solomon was lauded as the wisest of men, but he permitted worship of foreign gods in Israel. As a result, the prophet Ahijah told him that Yahweh would tear most of the kingdom away from the Davidic dynasty (1 Kgs 11:26–39). This occurred in the reign of Solomon's son, Rehoboam. He acted foolishly toward his subjects and occasioned the kingdom's fracture in two. The northern half tore away from the Davidic dynasty, setting itself up as the kingdom of Israel. It experienced apostasy from Yahweh and tumultuous dynastic changes. Two centuries later the Assyrians obliterated this kingdom. Many of its inhabitants were scattered to other areas in the region, while other peoples were brought in to mix with those who remained.

The southern half of the nation, however, continued under the Davidic dynasty as the kingdom of Judah. Yet it, too, faced difficulties in obeying Yahweh. Prophets like Jeremiah continually sounded warning calls for the nation and its leaders to amend their ways (Jer 1:1–10; 12:14–17; 23:1–5; 31:10–14). Yet, Judah also failed. Consequently, the Babylonians warred against Judah and won. They demolished Yahweh's temple, sacked Jerusalem,

3. Barbour, *The Story of Israel in the Book of Qohelet*, 57.

and exiled many of the inhabitants. The exiles in Babylon and the few left behind in Judah mourned their loss of nationhood.

This exile presented a considerable theological challenge to Yahweh's covenant with David. Despite his promise of the dynasty's permanence, Israel had been uprooted from its land and there was no more Davidic kingdom. This raised uncomfortable questions about Yahweh's ability and faithfulness. Yet, Yahweh's prophets insisted that he was not done with the Davidic dynasty or the nation (Ezek 34:1–31; Amos 9:11–15).

Against the political odds, the Persians permitted Judeans to return to their homeland and rebuild Yahweh's temple in Jerusalem. This reversal of fortunes turned people's mourning into laughter (Ps 126). Those who returned to Jerusalem rebuilt the temple, but they never managed to reestablish the Davidic kingdom. Instead, they were passed as the possession of one foreign empire to the next. God's promises remained unfulfilled, right down to the time of Qohelet in the third century BC. In his day, Jerusalem and the whole region of Judea was the object of a continued tug-of-war between the Ptolemies of Egypt and the Seleucids of Syria. In fact, these two kingdoms fought six protracted wars with each other over the course of a century,[4] ensuring Judaism was caught in a Hellenistic vice that challenged traditional modes of thinking.[5] Qohelet himself was a product of this to some degree.

To compound this situation, the tax burden on Jews increased significantly under Ptolemaic rule. This is demonstrated by the Zenon Papyri, an archive of over 1800 documents kept by Zenon, an agent of Apollonius, the treasurer (*dioiketes*) of Ptolemy II. Forty of Zenon's documents relate to his tour of Judea, Transjordan, Phoenicia, and southern Syria in 259 BC to audit their administration and the collection of taxes. In addition to evidence of trade focused on getting goods to Egypt, they attest to tax farming throughout the region, the use of intimidation, resistance by locals, the payment of gifts and bribes, and the trading of slaves.[6] Jewish historian Josephus (*Ant.* 12.158) also relates how the Jewish high priest, Onias II, refused to pay taxes to Ptolemy III Euergetes (246–222 BC). In doing this, he was probably seeking to ally

4. These are usually termed the "Syrian Wars" and are numbered accordingly. The First Syrian War began in 274 BC, though conflict between Ptolemaic Egypt and Seleucid Syria began a generation earlier. The Sixth Syrian War ended after Rome threatened to intervene in 167 BC, and also played into the Jewish Maccabean Revolt (167–164 BC). Qohelet, who seems to have been writing in c. 225 BC, would have lived through at least three of these.

5. Hellenism is the influence of Greek culture on other cultures, which began during the fourth century BC.

6. For further discussion, see Campbell Cowan Edgar, *Zenon Papyri in the University of Michigan Collection* (Ann Arbor: University of Michigan Press, 1931), 15–19; Martin Hengel, *Jews, Greeks and Barbarians: Aspects of the Hellenization of Judaism in the Pre-Christian Period*, trans. John Bowden (Philadelphia: Fortress, 1980), 23–28.

himself with Ptolemy's enemies, the Seleucids, who had their own internal squabbles at the time. Onias's nephew, Joseph Tobias, then took advantage of this situation. Joseph's father, Tobias, is mentioned in the Zenon Papyri. Joseph managed to placate Ptolemy, thus saving Jerusalem from reprisal, but then used the opportunity to offer twice the amount of taxes to Ptolemy. This earned him the position of chief tax farmer throughout the entire region in 227 BC. To enforce collection of these taxes, Joseph Tobias employed violence and military force (see "Context and Date" in the Introduction for further discussion).[7] Jews, therefore, found themselves under foreign oppression and being fleeced by their own compatriots.[8] Qohelet's Judea, therefore, was a place of frequent conflict, changing fortunes, cultural pressure, economic brutality, and perpetual disappointment in the purposes of God.

EXPLAIN the Story

The Sovereignty of God over Human Life (3:1–4:16)

In the previous section, Qohelet subtly indicts God as the cosmic bully of humanity. He now chases this idea further in almost lyrical fashion. He portrays God as the only one who truly understands the course of history, yet he sees God as trifling with human beings. For their part, humans seem trapped in the matrix of times that God has imposed on them. Qohelet sees little prospect of coming out of life with any gain, let alone for seeing justice during it. Once again, this leads him to the conclusion that everything is meaningless.

A Time for Everything (3:1–8)

Chapter 3 begins with a poem (3:1–8) that bears some resemblance to the Gezer Calendar but has a far more philosophical purpose. Its cadence and poignancy make it undoubtedly one of the most famous passages of Ecclesiastes. It is often understood to imply that there is a right time for things to happen. Wiersbe, for example, asserts, "The inference is plain: if we cooperate with God's timing, life will not be meaningless. Everything will be 'beautiful in His time' (v. 11), even the most difficult experience of life."[9] Yet the very first pair of activities mentioned in the poem are almost completely beyond human

7. For yet further discussion, see Mark R. Sneed, *The Politics of Pessimism in Ecclesiastes: A Social-Science Perspective*, Ancient Israel and its Literature 12 (Atlanta: Society of Biblical Literature, 2012), 95–98.

8. Cf. Sirach 13:3–7, 19, which reflects this kind of situation in 180 BC.

9. Warren W. Wiersbe, "Time and Toil: Ecclesiastes 3," in *Reflecting with Solomon: Selected Studies on the Book of Ecclesiastes*, ed. Roy B. Zuck (Grand Rapids: Baker Books, 1994), 264.

control: the time of birth and the time of death (3:2). It is nonsensical to talk about cooperating with God in these actions to give them meaning. Furthermore, a positive view of the poem would require Qohelet to repudiate his oft stated motto, "Everything is meaningless!" While we must allow for varying contours in Qohelet's discussion, such a view of the poem here requires a wholesale change of landscape. All the indications both in and around the poem are that Qohelet is continuing his melancholy exploration of life under God's sovereignty and arriving at pessimistic conclusions.

First, let's look at the moorings that anchor Qohelet's poem to his larger discussion. Qohelet finishes the previous section by declaring the way God deals with both those who please and displease him as "meaningless, a chasing after the wind" (2:26). In the very next verse, he commences his poem about time. He declares the scope of the poem's subject to be "everything" and "every activity under the heavens" (3:1). This can hardly be different to the "everything" in his motto, "Everything is meaningless!" (1:2). At the conclusion of the poem, he asks what "gain" workers have for their "toil" (3:9). This is the same question he asks in 1:3. Thus the poem is in a frame expressing the most essential ideas and tensions of Qohelet's pessimism. It prompts the same response from him. To further underline this, his next statement evaluates human life as a task that God has given humanity to occupy (or oppress) it (3:10). This echoes 1:13, where Qohelet makes the same bleak claim. From there he moves on to declare numerous aspects of life as "meaningless" (3:19; 4:4, 7–8, 16). There can be no doubting, therefore, that, despite the poem's lovely aesthetics, its underlying tenor is of resignation, which does not swerve from Qohelet's motto that all is meaningless.

Qohelet headlines his poem with the claim, "There is a time for everything, and a season for every activity under the heavens" (3:1). We must note that he is considering all human endeavor here. Yet, this is human endeavor conducted "under the heavens." After the exile, Jews began relating to God not only as their national deity but as the sole deity who is sovereign over the whole world. As such, they gradually jettisoned use of the divine name, Yahweh, in favor of more generic monotheistic conventions, such as "God" (e.g., Neh 8:18), "Lord" (e.g., Dan 1:2), and "God of heaven" (e.g., Neh 1:4–5).[10] The phrase "under the heavens" is Qohelet's way of indicating human life as it is under the sovereignty of God. There is nothing humans do that is not under God's jurisdiction. Thus, the poem is not merely exploring the kinds of activities humans engage in so much as how God is in control of them.

10. These conventions continued into New Testament times. This is, for example, why Matthew refers to the "kingdom of heaven" (e.g., Matt 3:2), Mark and Luke refer to the "kingdom of God" (e.g., Mark 1:15; Luke 4:43), and the divine name is otherwise consistently replaced with the word "lord" (in Greek, *kyrios*).

The terminology in this headline is crucial for understanding the poem. Qohelet uses two nouns for time in 3:1. The first, *zeman*, indicates a set time. The second, *'et*, is a generic word for time or season (cf. Ps 62:8[62:9]), and is often characterized by an activity, such as a "time of harvest" (Jer 51:33). In this case, the NIV characterizes it as "a season for every activity under the heavens" (3:1). The word for "activity" (*hepets*) conveys an action that someone wants to do. In other contexts, it indicates a desire or wish whose fulfilment results in satisfaction (cf. 1 Sam 15:22; 1 Kgs 5:10[5:24]). It conveys the notion of purpose—an "activity" that enacts someone's will.

This prompts the question of whose will these activities are enacting. Since the poem lists human endeavors, our initial response may be to think that Qohelet is interested in human will. Fredericks takes this view, claiming "this 'poem of the times' emphasizes the decisions of life" and that "humanity is encouraged to accomplish wisely many timely acts."[11] But though the actions Qohelet lists may have human agents, some of them can hardly be willed or wanted by those proponents (e.g., birth, death, loss). Critically, Qohelet is considering every activity "under the heavens" (3:1), and he goes on to state that God "has made everything beautiful in its time" (3:11). This suggests it is God's will that Qohelet is evaluating. The poem examines human affairs as part of the divine enterprise (cf. 7:14). It is not so much about when humans ought to do things, or even humans collaborating with God. Rather, it is about God deciding when humans will do things as per his sovereign will.

For Qohelet, then, human life is simply the enactment of God's will. This is not a denial of human free will, as Qohelet imparts advice to his readers with the expectation that they can choose to follow it or not (e.g., 5:1–9). However, he does see God as actively involved in human life, shaping its quantity, quality, and course. For Qohelet, humans can make genuine decisions, but they are hemmed in by constraints that God imposes on them. Rudman describes it this way:

> This viewpoint may be illustrated with the hypothetical case of a slave working on the estate of a large landowner. The slave is not an autonomous being in his own right, but a tool, an extension of the master's will. The actions of the slave are entirely determined by the will of this master and he works not for himself but for another. Well might this slave ask himself "what benefit do I get from all my work?"[12]

11. Fredericks and Estes, *Ecclesiastes & the Song of Songs*, 117, 119.

12. Dominic Rudman, *Determinism in the Book of Ecclesiastes* (Sheffield: Sheffield Academic, 2001), 90. Interestingly, Rudman's analogy here finds close parallel with Jesus's parable of the tenants (Matt 21:33–46).

Thus Qohelet concludes that life is a struggle and that God is its taskmaster (3:9–10).

The poem itself consists of fourteen "time" pairs, each of which represents a set of opposite activities. This "catalogue of seasons"[13] does not advocate a right time for humans to decide to perform these activities. Rather, it states merely that they happen at times as God determines them. It is about God's set timing.

As a whole, these fourteen time pairs demonstrate some key facts for Qohelet. First, God is in sovereign control over human life. Second, life includes a huge diversity of experiences. Third, these experiences can be anything from sheer pleasure to utter vexation. Life is full of multifarious hues. Fourth, this means life can be unpredictable, as humans are not ultimately in control of their own existence "under the heavens"; God is. Fifth, humans are, therefore, ultimately at the whim of God. And finally, it is difficult for humans to figure out if there is a rhyme or reason to God's will. The swinging cadence of the poem gives a sense of to-ing and fro-ing between different experiences, which ultimately produces a sense of aimlessness. Humans move between life's highs and lows, but there is no way of knowing what it accomplishes or what it means. God is an inscrutable monarch who cannot be approached, let alone understood.

Yet the poem is doing more than just talking about life's generic experiences. The words Qohelet uses echo experiences from Israel's history. Barbour captures it well:

> A book as literary and as late in the Hebrew Bible as Qohelet can plausibly be said to be haunted by the texts that have gone before it and against which it chafes . . . . [W]e can hear the ghosts of those texts in this poem. In the "everything" that happens in front of the gaze of the observer, some—though not all—of those events and accidents will trigger wider reverberations, and the undertow of communal currents will be felt beneath the stream of individual experience.[14]

As we consider each of the time pairs in Qohelet's poem, we will not only examine how they relate generically to life, but also, where appropriate, how they echo the history of Israel through inner biblical allusion. In this, we will observe how Qohelet here critiques God's sovereignty over both the individual and his chosen nation.

---

13. Ibid., 91.
14. Barbour, *The Story of Israel in the Book of Qohelet*, 58.

A time to be born and a time to die (3:2a): The first phrase here is better translated as "a time to give birth."[15] In any case, this first pair presents the two extremities of life and is therefore a fitting way to exemplify the poem's scope and purpose. Schoors describes it as follows:

> The lesson of this poem is not, as is often suggested, that everything has its opportune time which should govern our action, but that everything happens at its fixed time. This appears from the first pair, life and death, which lie beyond human control. We do not hold our life in our hands; it is one big adventure in which we experience a great number of experiences, but we cannot control our life, nobody can change anything about these fixed times.[16]

A time to plant and a time to uproot (3:2b): As the Gezer Calendar shows, there were appropriate times in the annual agricultural cycle to sow or plant seed and to uproot or harvest what the seed produced. Yet the idea of planting is also integral to the Davidic covenant. God promised David, "I will provide a place for my people Israel and will plant them so that they can have a home of their own and no longer be disturbed. Wicked people will not oppress them anymore" (2 Sam 7:10). For a time, this was Israel's experience. However, the fracture of the nation under Rehoboam led eventually to the Assyrians annihilating the northern kingdom of Israel (723 BC). At a later time (586 BC), the Babylonians wiped out the southern kingdom of Judah. The result was the uprooting of God's chosen nation from their native soil and their scattering to other lands (Jer 12:15). In commissioning Jeremiah as a prophet during the kingdom of Judah's downfall, God told him, "See, today I appoint you over nations and kingdoms, to uproot and tear down, to destroy and overthrow, to build and to plant" (Jer 1:10). The permanence associated with the imagery of God "planting" his people within the land had been replaced by the reality of their "uprooting." Even though some returned under the Persians, in Qohelet's day, the Jewish diaspora was spread across Ptolemaic Egypt and the various lands of the Seleucid Kingdom. God had promise to "completely uproot and destroy" those nations who continued to oppress his people (Jer 12:14–17), but his people continued to suffer under foreign oppression. What did all this say about God's commitment to the permanent Davidic covenant? The God who once had promised to plant his own people securely had now uprooted

15. The infinitive used (*ledet*) is in the *qal* stem, which suggests giving birth, rather than in the *niphal* (*hiwaled*) which would indicate being born.

16. Antoon Schoors, *Ecclesiastes*, Historical Commentary on the Old Testament (Leuven: Peeters, 2013), 229.

them, and wicked people oppressed them. Had he simply changed his mind? For Qohelet, an heir to the Davidic promises, it was difficult to perceive what God might be doing. Indeed, it appeared meaningless.

A time to kill and a time to heal (Eccl 3:3a): The first activity in this pair is not referring to execution but more generically to slaying—depriving another of life. Such violence is an unfortunately familiar part of human experience. Sometimes, though, people are brought back from the brink of death and healed. Furthermore, the order of this imagery echoes Israel's experience of exile. God had shown Ezekiel a plain of dry bones, representative of the "slain" nation in Babylonian exile, and commanded him to prophesy to the wind, saying, "Come, breath, from the four winds and breathe into these slain, that they may live" (Ezek 37:9). "A time to slay," therefore, reflects the reality of Israel's exile from their land, and "a time to heal" suggests the opportunity to return to it. Indeed, some did. In the Book of the Twelve,[17] Hosea 6:1 urges, "Come, let us return to the LORD. He has torn us to pieces but he will heal us; he has injured us but he will bind up our wounds." Yet the persistent realities of foreign empires and a Jewish diaspora would cause Jews to ask why, if God was in control of all things, he had not chosen to occasion such a healing in Qohelet's day. If it was not the time, then when would be the time? Or perhaps God had simply decided against it altogether? This time pair, then, also alludes to the ambivalence of God's will in history.

A time to tear down and a time to build (Eccl 3:3b): The word for "tear down" here (*perots*) is not the ordinary word for demolition. It tends to describe breaking through defenses in a siege (cf. Mic 2:13). On the one hand, then, Qohelet is depicting a hazard of ancient life: siege warfare and the destruction it wrought on infrastructure and lives, as well as the necessary rebuilding that must occur after it. On the other hand, he is also considering Israel's historical experience. In his covenant with David, God promised that David's son would build Yahweh's temple in Jerusalem and the throne would be secure evermore (2 Sam 7:12–13). But after the Babylonians breached the walls of Jerusalem in 586 BC, they destroyed the temple, the king's palace, important buildings, people's houses, and tore the city walls down, too (2 Kgs 25:1–10). Zerubbabel rebuilt the temple in 516 BC, and Nehemiah repaired the walls in 445 BC.[18]

17. The "Book of the Twelve" refers to the fact that the twelve Minor Prophets (Hosea–Malachi) were compiled into a single work on a single scroll, in either the late Persian or, more probably, early Hellenistic era (early third century BC). Our modern convention of splitting this work into twelve discrete books is a somewhat artificial division.

18. It is likely that Jerusalem's walls had been rebuilt earlier than this. Zechariah 2:1–5[2:5–9] preserves memory of an aborted attempt to rebuild Jerusalem's wall in Zerubbabel's day, which left Jerusalem unprotected for quite some time. Yet, when Nehemiah received word that Jerusalem's walls were in ruins and its gates destroyed by fire, it seemed to be news to him that caused sudden mourning

Even so, the Davidic kingdom was no longer a reality. In 301 BC, Ptolemy I besieged Jerusalem and claimed the city for himself. Ptolemaic rule was the reality Qohelet knew. This line, therefore, reflects some painful episodes in Jewish history and the waning memory of a Davidic kingdom.

A time to weep and a time to laugh, a time to mourn and a time to dance (3:4): These two pairs of opposites take in the joys and pains of everyday life. But once again, they resound with Israel's national experience. The destruction of Jerusalem and subsequent exile were times of weeping and mourning (Ps 137:1; Lam 1:2–4; Zech 7:1–3). By contrast, Psalm 126 celebrates the opportunity to return by reminiscing, "When the Lord restored the fortunes of Zion, we were like those who dreamed. Our mouths were filled with laughter, our tongues with songs of joy" (Ps 126:1–2). Jeremiah pictures the regathering of God's people in Jerusalem as a time when "young women will dance and be glad, young men and old as well" (Jer 31:13; cf. Zech 8:18–19). Yet the failure to reestablish a Davidic kingdom after the exile meant the pallor of mourning persisted within the people of God and cast continuing shadows over God's will.

A time to scatter stones and a time to gather them, a time to embrace and a time to refrain from embracing (Eccl 3:5): The first pair here (3:5a) has sparked much debate as to its meaning. The most fanciful interpretation comes from medieval Jewish midrash that takes the pair as euphemisms for sexual activity and abstinence.[19] This would be more obvious for the second pairing (3:5b), but if both pairings are playing off each other's meaning, a sexual connotation for the first pair cannot be completely discounted. Nonetheless, it's possible that 3:5a refers to knocking down the stones of prominent buildings and regathering them for reconstruction. This would certainly be evocative of the destruction and rebuilding of Jerusalem. However, the term for "scatter" here (*hashlik*) suggests "throwing" stones, and this has further possibilities. It may refer to using stones with a sling in battle or to the practice of littering an enemy's field with stones to prevent agricultural use and the subsequent need

(Neh 1:1–4). If the walls had not been rebuilt since the Babylonians pulled them down 130 years earlier, Nehemiah, as cupbearer to Artaxerxes I (a significant political office), would surely have known it. This suggests that Jerusalem had experienced a conflict shortly before Nehemiah's appointment as governor in 445 BC, which caused damage to the city's fortifications. This conflict is best identified as the rebellion of Megabyzus (c. 449 BC), Satrap of Trans-Euphrates. Ezra 4:12–16 describes the building of Jerusalem's wall as part of a satrapy-wide rebellion (cf. Ezra 4:16), and Artaxerxes used force to disrupt the building (Ezra 4:18–23). In the conflict, the half-built walls of Jerusalem suffered damage, and the city was almost completely abandoned. When Megabyzus' rebellion ended with his reconciliation to Artaxerxes, Nehemiah used his personal standing with the king to petition for Jerusalem's rehabilitation, which included the rebuilding of its walls (Neh 2:3–6).

19. *Qohelet Rabbah* 3:5. See also Fox, *A Time to Tear Down and a Time to Build Up*, 207–8; Longman, *Ecclesiastes*, 116.

to clear the field to work it (cf. Isa 5:2).[20] In any case, we again hear echoes of incidents from Israel's famous but now fading past: a brave David facing Goliath (1 Sam 17:40, 49) and past military successes (2 Kgs 3:19, 25).

A time to search and a time to give up, a time to keep and a time to throw away (3:6): The NIV has translated the second action here as "giving up" a search—an action that, though regrettable, may still be wise. However, this phrase is better translated as "a time to lose" or "a time to destroy." There is rarely if ever a good time to "lose," which demonstrates that Qohelet's poem is not about knowing good times for specific actions but about God determining human history. As Levine and Barbour also point out, the first pair of actions evokes shepherding imagery.[21] Passages like Jeremiah 23:1–5 and Ezekiel 34 portray Israel's leaders before the fall of Jerusalem as shepherds who had lost their sheep (that is, the people of the nation) and caused their destruction (exile). God promises to search for his lost sheep and even tend them himself via a Davidic descendant (Ezek 34:15–16, 23–24). By Qohelet's day, this had simply not happened. Once again, Qohelet questions God's will in relation to Israel's history. Has God failed to keep his promises? In light of this apparent failure, should his people persist in keeping his commands, or should they throw them out (3:6b) and adopt other values and prospects, such as those afforded by Hellenism?

A time to tear and a time to mend, a time to be silent and a time to speak (3:7): On the surface of it, the first pair refers to the wear and tear that clothing suffers. However, clothing also has symbolic significance in Scripture. When a desperate Saul tore the edge of Samuel's garment, Samuel told him, "The Lord has torn the kingdom of Israel from you today" (1 Sam 15:28). When Ahijah prophesied the fracture of Israel at the end of Solomon's reign, he symbolically tore his new cloak into twelve pieces, giving ten to Jeroboam, who would eventually break away from the Davidic dynasty with ten of Israel's tribes, leaving just two tribes for the Davidic dynasty to rule (1 Kgs 11:29–33). Again, therefore, Qohelet subtly recalls what God has done in Israel's history, drawing special attention to the losses suffered by the Davidic dynasty, to which Qohelet was an heir. This raised the question of whether God ever intended to "mend" the kingdom as he had promised. He had spoken this intention via the prophets in days gone by but was yet to fulfill it. For Qohelet, God's speaking may as well have been silence, for his will continued to baffle.

20. Roger N. Whybray, *Ecclesiastes*, New Century Bible Commentary (Grand Rapids: Eerdmans, 1989), 71.

21. Baruch Levine, "The Semantics of Loss: Two Exercises in Biblical Lexicography," in *Solving Riddles and Untying Knots: Biblica, Epigraphic, and Semitic Studies in Honor of Jonas C. Greenfield*, ed. Ziony Zevit, Seymour Gitin, and Michael Sokoloff (Winona Lake, Ind.: Eisenbrauns, 1995), 137–58; Barbour, *The Story of Israel in the Book of Qohelet*, 61–62.

A time to love and a time to hate (3:8a): In addition to representing extreme human emotions, this pairing recalls God's relationship with Israel. In Malachi 1:2–3 God states, "I have loved Jacob, but Esau I have hated." This statement of Israel's election is set against God's rejection of others. And yet, the hardship that Israel continued to experience under foreign regimes like the Ptolemies cast aspersions on the substance of God's love. If God's love seemed strangely absent, had he now decided to hate Israel and love another nation? Should Israel continue to love Yahweh their God (cf. Deut 6:5), or not? This highly emotional pairing expresses Qohelet's ambivalence toward God's character.

A time for war and a time for peace (3:8b): This final pair sums up the pendulum swing of society's fortunes and expresses the changing circumstances of Israel. After the peaceful days of Solomon centuries earlier, Israel succumbed to conflict and conquest. Qohelet's reality was one of continual strife (cf. the Syrian Wars), to which there did not seem to be an end. War could never be described as "good," so again Qohelet is drawn to these states of affairs as determinations of God, wondering what God is doing. If God was the one who established peace for his people (cf. Isa 26:12), and his zeal would establish the rule of a prince of peace (cf. Isa 9:6–7[9:5–6]), had God's zeal simply run out?

Hapless Humans before an Awful God (3:9–15)

As Qohelet explores God's control of history and human experience, he leaves us questioning God's purposes. Qohelet comes to some conclusions in this next section. The first is phrased as a rhetorical question: "What do workers gain from their toil?" (Eccl 3:9). As in 1:3, Qohelet is not interested solely in work here, but in all human activity. He uses the word "toil" as a generic summary of all the activities he has explored in his poem (3:1–8). The essence of his question is that, if God ultimately controls the course of human history according to his own purposes, does human effort change or achieve anything? Is there anything in it for humans? The answer is at best unknown, and at worst "no." As he says in the following verse (3:10), God assigns the tasks according to his own purposes, and this seems oppressive to human beings. This is scarce comfort for anyone, even amid seemingly pleasant experiences. Qohelet's musings drain the color from life, leaving only pallid hues. Rudman's analogy of the slave on the estate of a large landowner (see above) captures well the sense of entrapment that Qohelet feels.[22]

This makes Qohelet's conclusion in 3:11 seem incongruent: "He has made everything beautiful in its time." This claim is sometimes used to justify the

22. Rudman, *Determinism in the Book of Ecclesiastes*, 90.

poem in 3:1–8 as positive, seeing each of the activities and their timing as a divine gift to humans.[23] So out of place does this statement seem that it has even led some to argue that it is a later pious gloss.[24] However, in light of our analysis above and Qohelet's insipid pessimism, this is hard to justify. When we understand that Qohelet's poem is about God's determination of history, we can see Qohelet here characterizing things from God's point of view. To God, whose will and power over the times are untrammeled, everything is "beautiful" (*yapeh*) and nothing out of place. His every desire and purpose is fulfilled, and thus everything has its "appropriate" or "fitting" (also viable translations for *yapeh*) place in God's estimation. This may be "the greatest statement of divine providence in the whole of Scripture," as Fredericks asserts, but for Qohelet it is definitely not "the theorem from which the believer's hope is derived that all things work together for the good for those who love God (Rom 8:28)."[25] It is as though he wants this to be true, but he can find nothing to confirm it.

His next statement (3:11b) bears this out. Qohelet affirms that God is probably up to something in history and has given humans a sense of this by setting "eternity in the human heart." The word "eternity" (*'olam*) can denote all the distant past, all the distant future, or even the current age, understanding each of these possibilities as long periods of history consisting of multiple successive generations. Qohelet uses it in the current context as a parallel to "what God has done from beginning to end" (3:11b). Thus, Qohelet uses it here to denote all history—past, present, and future. The rhythms of life and the course of Israel's history demonstrate that there may be a method to the madness of the world. God has certainly signaled his mighty intentions through the prophets, and it includes bringing all Israelites together under a Davidic king. And yet, because God has not fulfilled these intentions in Qohelet's current age, it is mighty difficult to determine what exactly God is up to. Although Qohelet, a would-be Davidic king, might want to fulfill these intentions, he has no power to do so. Perhaps God has not revealed things to humans that would dispel such cognitive dissonance, but such things would be hidden, so who is to know? God may have his own purposes and timing and hinted at this to humans, "yet no one can fathom what God has done from beginning to end" (3:11b). This merism ("beginning to end") summarizes all the actions Qohelet surveys in 3:1–8 and shows they are but a small selection of God's purposes. The aimlessness of the poem finds expression here in the

23. See Roland E. Murphy, "Worship, Officials, Wealth and Its Uncertainties: Ecclesiastes 5:1–6:9," in Zuck, *Reflecting with Solomon*, 286.

24. See discussion in Schoors, *Ecclesiastes*, 255.

25. Fredericks and Estes, *Ecclesiastes & the Song of Songs*, 117.

assertion that no one knows what God is doing (3:11b) and no one can add or subtract from it (3:14). Humans go about "under the sun" and can see only to their own horizon. They cannot, therefore, discern a greater picture "under the heavens," let alone change it.

On the one hand, this could inspire blind trust in God. If his will always prevails at the right time, then could not one rest in God's sovereignty? But Qohelet does not advocate such blind trust, because he cannot determine what God is really doing in the world. This is not because he sees Yahweh as the God of Deism, who sets the world in motion and then steps away, leaving it to its own devices. On the contrary, Qohelet sees God's fingerprints all over human life and history. Rather, it is because the reality of Jewish life in the third century BC—before the revelation of the Christ—was barely cause for such trust. It was, rather, reason for alarm, anxiety, and disappointment. As time wore on, it became harder to see how God could possibly fulfill his stated purposes given the current circumstances that he himself was apparently responsible for. With his people scattered across multiple fronts and moving in different directions, the sun of Hellenism rising, and the Ptolemies and Seleucids jostling for control of Judea while David's descendants waned into powerless obscurity, what hope could there possibly be?[26] Qohelet leaves room for God to act, since God is all-sovereign, but all the indications tell him that he won't.

This might lead Qohelet to wonder whether God had lost control over history—that things had gotten out of hand. As a pious Jew, he cannot come to this conclusion. Qohelet is constrained by both the revelations of his Jewish heritage and the realities of his experience. He affirms that nothing can undermine God's sovereignty over all things (3:14a). Therefore, Qohelet concludes, God must do what he does so that humans might fear him (3:14b). Since the "fear of the Lord" is usually a good thing in Scripture (cf. Prov 1:7), many view this phrase positively—that God enacts his will to earn respect and honor ("fear") from his creatures. Yet, this view does not account adequately for the searing pain in human experience, which Qohelet surveys in his poem, as well as the challenge that he sees history poses to making sense of God's purposes. To think that suffering and confusion lead to applauding the one who inflicts them is perverse and trivializes human suffering. Qohelet is under no illusion about the depth of the human plight (cf. Eccl 4:1–3). The reality of human

26. This historical circumstance helps us understand both the split between Jews and Samaritans within Palestine, as well as the rise of liberal thinking in Judaism at the time. It sought to embrace Hellenism and move Judaism away from conservative orthodoxy. This trend set the battle lines for the eventual outbreak of conflict between liberal and conservative Judaism during the persecution of Antiochus IV Epiphanes (167 BC).

suffering means Qohelet can either affirm God as good but not omnipotent, or as omnipotent but not good. Qohelet's pessimism testifies to how sharp the horns of this dilemma are.

Once again, however, his piety will not allow him to accuse God of evil. Instead, Qohelet adapts the soundly orthodox notion of fearing God and subverts it from denoting reverence for God to terror of God.[27] If God is omnipotent in life and history, and both are puzzling and painful, God is indeed a frightening being and incomprehensible to humans. Fredericks takes exception with this view, arguing that this is "quite contrary to the giving God" we encounter in this passage,[28] but this misses the contours of Qohelet's depiction. Qohelet does not accuse God of wrongdoing, nor does he trivialize human suffering. By subverting the concept of fearing the Lord, Qohelet is not departing from orthodoxy but emphasizing one aspect of it. The idea of God frightening humans is integral to his revelation. Israel's encounter with God at Horeb, where he formed them as a nation, was an utterly terrifying experience (Deut 5:5, 23–37). Just as Israel had come close to God in that experience, so also Qohelet here tries getting close to God in order to apprehend him. Like Israel, though, as he approaches closer, what he finds scares him. God can inspire both positive and negative fear. He can be awesome and awful. Either way, before his supreme power, humans are hapless, and this scares Qohelet.

In light of this, Qohelet insists once more that all humans can do is try to enjoy the basics of life (3:12–13). Since God is sovereign over human experience, any ability to do so must inevitably come from his decision. When Qohelet describes such enjoyment as a "gift of God" (3:13b), he is not portraying God as generous. Rather, he is depicting enjoyment of life as a rare and surprising decision of God to give something good to humans. The underlying idea is that no one should expect it, as he will explore further in 5:18–20[5:17–19]. Indeed, the variability of human experience and the disappointment in Israel's history, which Qohelet knew all too well, mean no person has any assurance that they will see happiness in life or that God will fulfill what he has promised to Israel. God may just choose to withhold such happiness and inflict pain and disappointment instead. This makes God scary and humans powerless before him.

Dehumanizing Humans (3:16–22)

The next section reinforces the idea that God's frightening sovereignty means the best that humans can do is enjoy the basics of life, if such enjoyment

27. Tremper Longman, "The 'Fear of God' in the Book of Ecclesiastes," *BBR* 25.1: 13–21.
28. Fredericks and Estes, *Ecclesiastes & the Song of Songs*, 119.

happens to come their way. Qohelet observes wickedness in the place of justice (3:16) and is powerless to do anything about it. As Longman notes, this powerlessness demonstrates that Qohelet cannot be a genuine king, for he cannot change this situation.[29] Again, this recalls God's failure to reestablish the Davidic kingdom. The brevity of Qohelet's observation easily masks how profoundly distressing injustice is. And yet, this was Qohelet's reality.

Since he is helpless to effect change, he appeals to God's judgment by affirming the orthodox tenet of divine retribution: "God will bring into judgment both the righteous and the wicked" (3:17). It is easy to bring to this statement the later concept of eschatological or post-mortem judgment. There probably were Jews in Qohelet's time who held to such a notion. However, Qohelet is skeptical about it, as we will see. Instead, he is more likely thinking about God's judgment during life and within history.

Qohelet's skepticism turns on the meaning of the question in 3:21. First, Qohelet uses the word *ruah* here, which can denote wind, breath, or spirit. Second, this *ruah* belongs to both humans and animals (3:19). This suggests that Qohelet is not talking about the human "spirit" as the imperishable personal soul, but the impersonal animating principle that makes something alive. "Breath" or "life force" is perhaps the best way of capturing this idea. Once taken from a living entity, that entity ceases to be. In 12:7 Qohelet affirms that this life force returns to God at a person's death, but the idea there is not that someone's personal soul survives death and enters God's presence, but that death is God's decision to revoke the state of life. All creatures are contingent beings who derive their own being from God, the source of all life. God can, therefore, recall a life force at any time. Some equate the *return* of a person's life force to God in 12:7 with its potential *ascent* in 3:21.[30] However, the terminology differs critically between these verses. Since Qohelet states that there is no difference between humans and animals regarding their *ruah* (3:19), we must conclude that the death of animals should also be described as the return of their *ruah* to God. It is simply an acknowledgement that they, too, like humans, are contingent beings (cf. Jon 3:7; 4:11). This can only mean that Qohelet equates the return of the *ruah* to God with the *descent* of the *ruah* described in Ecclesiastes 3:21. In that sense, Qohelet affirms the classic Old Testament notion that all people, whether righteous or wicked, *go down* to "Sheol" (the Underworld). The ascent of the *ruah* in 3:21, therefore, must be referring to something else.

29. Longman, *Ecclesiastes*, 127.

30. For example, Eaton, *Ecclesiastes*, 87–88; Wiersbe, "Time and Toil," 268; Fredericks and Estes, *Ecclesiastes & the Song of Songs*, 123.

It seems, therefore, that Qohelet understands the ascent of the human *ruah* as the possibility of the human soul's survival after death. This was evidently an idea that had started to gain some traction in Judaism, perhaps under the influence of Greek thinking,[31] but it had not become the dominant paradigm.[32] The notion would distinguish humans from animals and make it possible to talk about God enacting post-mortem judgment. Perhaps in that case, God might achieve justice by rewarding the righteous and punishing the wicked, thus overcoming any imbalances of justice experienced during the course of physical life. But Qohelet is deeply skeptical about the whole notion. He simply does not know if such a thing occurs (Eccl 3:21). In fact, all the indications for him are that it does not, and this throws the hope that injustice might be addressed into jeopardy. As Fox puts it, "we cannot rationalize a known injustice by appeal to an unknown remedy."[33]

The judgment Qohelet has in mind in 3:17, therefore, can only really be judgment during one's lifetime, as was the standard expectation in Israel (cf. 1 Sam 24:15; 1 Kgs 8:32; Ps 2). This possibility is disappointing for Qohelet, though, because not only can no one divine the future to ensure such justice will prevail (Eccl 3:22), but injustice pervades human life. According to Qohelet's poem, this must be because God ordained it to be so. After all, "there is a time for every activity," as God has willed. This is indeed the "sting in the tail" of 3:17. God may have set a time for judgment, but he must also have set a time for injustice to occur. Humans, therefore, are trapped like animals in God's zoo. This sorry state of affairs leads Qohelet to conclude that the world is one big case of entrapment. God is testing humans (3:18), but there is nothing humans can do to get out of their circumstances, be they

31. The author of the apocryphal book, Wisdom of Solomon, is a case in point. He seems to have been a Jew living in Alexandria, the center of Hellenistic Judaism, during the first century BC. In chapter 2 he describes the kind of belief that the ungodly teach, which includes a denial that the soul survives death (Wis 2:1–5), and other attitudes closely reminiscent of Qohelet's statements.

32. Daniel 12:1–3 is certainly a step closer to the notion, but even it presumes that people are woken *up* from death for judgment. It presents eschatological judgment, as opposed to personal post-mortem judgment. Thus, while the passage is more confident than Qohelet that justice will prevail after death, this is eschatological in nature, not immediate, and this still configures pre-eschatological death as a descent, as does Qohelet. Daniel 12:1–3 does, however, represent a theological development beyond Qohelet's position, though the notion of personal post-mortem judgment is beyond Daniel 12 also. Furthermore, the influence of Greek thought upon Judaism is not in question, but the extent of that influence upon this issue during Qohelet's time (third century BC) is not definitively known.

33. Fox, *A Time to Tear Down*, 215. Contra Davis, who states that Qohelet's "goal was not to have readers understand the details of life after death, but rather to have them recognize the fact of the existence of an afterlife so that they might live eternally purposeful lives here and now." This cuts completely against the grain of Qohelet's argument. See Barry C. Davis, "Death, An Impetus for Life: Ecclesiastes 12:1–8," in Zuck, *Reflecting with Solomon* 364.

righteous or wicked. This shows humans that they have no advantage over animals, with which they share the same fate. To put it another way, Qohelet sees God's sovereignty as dehumanizing, and he finds this deeply disturbing.

The only solace Qohelet can find is to salvage even the smallest sense of humanity—to enjoy the basics of life, if God happens to allow this (3:22). It is the same conclusion he came to in 3:12–13, and that he has stated earlier in his monologue. This is not a "joyful confidence in the pursuit of earthly responsibilities and the pleasures they bring,"[34] but a crestfallen attempt to snatch of scrap of dignity and relief in a caged existence. "Everything is meaningless" (3:19b).

The Tears of the Oppressed (4:1–3)

If that were not somber enough, Qohelet continues to sink in the sands of despair in chapter 4 by noting further examples of the vanity of human life "under the sun" (4:1). He evaluates four situations, coming to a morbid conclusion about the first (4:1–3) and labeling the other three (4:4–6, 7–12, 13–16) "meaningless."

In his first observation (4:1–3), Qohelet sees "the tears of the oppressed" (4:1), continuing the theme of injustice from the previous chapter. These are the working classes and the poor—those in economic servitude to those who could bend justice and exploit others. He acknowledges their weakness before their powerful oppressors. The pain seeps out of his words as he states twice that "they have no comforter." Qohelet is considering things from a human perspective "under the sun," so this is clearly a denouncement of all who wield power to the detriment of others, past, present, and future. This was undoubtedly the Ptolemies and their lackeys, like Apollonius and Zenon in a previous generation and Joseph Tobias in Qohelet's day. The perfidy of Joseph is especially in view here, since he had acted initially to save the people from Ptolemy III's wrath, only to bring down an even harsher burden on people in an act of supreme opportunism motivated by greed.

But there is also a subtle indictment of God here, for in the previous chapter Qohelet has shown that God is the one who holds utmost power. Isaiah 57:14–21 depicts God as the one who punished Israel in the past for their wickedness but who would heal them of their stubbornness and their plight. "I will guide them and restore comfort to Israel's mourners," he promises (Isa 57:18). "There is no peace for the wicked," he affirms (Isa 57:21). Yet Qohelet sees the complete opposite as the reality. It leads him to view death as a more blissful state than life (Eccl 4:2), remembering that for Qohelet this

34. Eaton, *Ecclesiastes*, 89.

means essentially non-existence (see discussion above). The NIV's translation of 4:2 is somewhat tame, as Qohelet goes so far as to say, "I lauded the dead who had already died" (author's translation). Even more despondently, he sees the one who has never existed and therefore never experienced life in all its cruelty as the most fortunate of all (4:3). It is difficult to conceive of a more melancholic mindset than this.

The Greed of the Upwardly Mobile (4:4–6)

If that is an indictment of God and society's most powerful, Qohelet's second observation (4:4–6) indicts the upwardly mobile in society. He sees the hard toil that people engage in and the skill they exert, driven by jealousy of others, and labels it "meaningless, a chasing after the wind" (4:4). The motive of jealousy is crucial to understanding Qohelet's point. He is not indicting the working class and the poor who must work to survive because they are exploited by others. Rather, he is looking at those who could afford to work less, yet work more, because jealousy drives them to have more than their neighbors. These are the middle class and elite who strive to acquire more power and all the wealth that comes from it. Qohelet acknowledges that laziness is not an option, as he quotes part of Proverbs 6:10 affirmatively in Ecclesiastes 4:5. However, he critiques the upwardly mobile who greedily crave wealth. This is undoubtedly a critique of the avarice displayed by the likes of the high priest Onias II and, even more so, Joseph Tobias. Indeed, 4:6 seems to be a deliberate allusion to Joseph: "Better one handful with tranquility than two handfuls with toil and chasing after the wind." This doubling theme coupled with the motive of jealousy resonates with Joseph Tobias' bid to exact twice the amount of taxes for Ptolemy III than other would-be tax farmers bid in 227 BC. The "toil" or trouble associated with this probably alludes to the fact that Joseph Tobias made many enemies by this move and had to resort to violence and intimidation to make good on his pledge. This is not to mention the strife it caused for those who suffered under the arduous tax burden. This does not cause Qohelet to envy the likes of Joseph but rather to see their actions as a self-defeating pursuit of the wind.

Working Hard for Nothing (4:7–12)

Qohelet's third observation (4:7–12) is an anecdote in which a man without close relations exerts himself to make wealth without enjoying any of it. He sees this as "meaningless" (*hebel*) and "a terrible task" (4:7–8).[35] There are two implications here. First, hard work should yield the ability to enjoy the

35. The NIV translates this phrase as "a miserable business."

basics of life, and second, enjoyment is heightened when shared with others. Considering the despondency with which Qohelet views life, this is a critical admission. If there is any consolation to salvage from the meaninglessness of life, it should not be squandered. We see here Qohelet's belief that humans have some measure of control over their lives, even if this is constrained by God's sovereign will. It is a crying shame, then, to have the opportunity for some joy amidst the melancholia of life and not take it.

Qohelet's further thoughts on this in 4:9–12 are sometimes taken to refer to the benefits of marriage, especially because 4:11 implies the intimacy of sharing a bed.[36] However, Qohelet prefaces these thoughts with an observation about a wealthy man without son or brother. He evidently is not restricting his thoughts to marriage but looking more broadly at beneficial relationships, be they familial or otherwise. His appeal to "a cord of three strands" further underlines this. His logic runs like this: If one alone is bad, but two is good, then three must be even better. This "cord of three strands" does not refer to marriage[37] but to mutual defense. Indeed, 4:12 is almost certainly recalling an ancient proverb that goes all the way back to the ancient Epic of Gilgamesh. As Gilgamesh prepares to fight the monster, Huwawa, his companion, Enkidu, turns to flee, but Gilgamesh seeks to prevent him. The text is fragmentary (Tablet V), but Gilgamesh cites a proverb that considers the difficulty one person has on their own, followed by the claims, "A slippery path is not feared by two people who help each other . . . a three-ply rope cannot be cut."[38] It implies that two or three people stand a better chance of success against an assailant than just one. Nonetheless, the meaninglessness that Qohelet draws from all this suggests that he sees the "three strand" unity required for successful defense as ultimately unattainable. In other words, considering God's sovereignty over human affairs, as well as human folly, it is a very rare thing to find harmony enough to bring people together in a mutually beneficial endeavor. The solitary man who works hard for nothing (4:8) is proof of this.

Changing Fortunes (4:13–16)

Qohelet's final "meaningless" observation is another anecdote (4:13–16). The ambiguities in Qohelet's phrasing make this anecdote notoriously difficult

36. Robert Gordis, *Koheleth: The Man and His World* (Northvale, NJ: J. Aronson, 1995), 242.

37. This is despite the nice symbolism sometimes imposed on it, in which the three strands symbolize husband, wife, and God.

38. See Aaron Shaffer, "New Information on the Origin of the 'Threefold Cord,'" *Eretz Israel* 9 (1969): 159–60; Aaron Shaffer, "The Mesopotamian Background of Qoh 4:9–12," *Eretz Israel* 8 (1967): 246–50, cited in Longman, *Ecclesiastes*, 143.

to decipher. It is ostensibly a story about an old, foolish king and a poor but wise youth who succeeds him. Qohelet observes that the youth is better than the old king (4:13), but beyond that the details are difficult to untangle for two reasons. First, the anecdote is related with anonymous characters. Second, Qohelet keeps using pronouns ("he" and "him") that resist precise identification. Thus, although the NIV states that it is "the youth" who came from prison in 4:14, the Hebrew text merely says, "he" came, without specifying whether "he" is the older king or the wiser youth. The NIV also states that all who lived under the sun followed "the youth, the king's successor," whereas it literally says that they followed "the second youth" (*hayyeled hasheni*) without specifying whether this is the wise youth mentioned previously, or an entirely different youth who has not been mentioned before. It sounds like Qohelet has specific people in mind, but commentators have been unable to identify them definitively.

There is, however, a way of solving this riddle, which allows us to identify the players in Qohelet's anecdote accurately with figures contemporary to him.[39] It revolves around the interpretation of 4:14. First, most English versions follow the ancient Greek translation in rendering the Hebrew phrase *bet hasurim* as "prison" (literally, "house of binding"). However, this requires an emendation of the Hebrew text to *bet 'asurim*. If the Hebrew text is not emended, it reads, "the house of removal." The root of the second word in this phrase (*sur*) is often used to indicate the removal of someone from a position of power (e.g., Judg 9:29; 1 Kgs 15:13; 20:24). A "house of removal," then, should be understood as residence in exile after such a demotion. Second, the final word in the verse, *rash*, is interpreted as "poor," and a link is thereby drawn to the "poor" youth in 4:13. The Greek translation of Ecclesiastes uses the same Greek word (*penes*) for both these instances, but the Hebrew word for "poor" in 4:13 (*misken*) is completely different to that used in 4:14. This raises the question of why Qohelet would opt for such a different term in 4:14 if he were still talking about the same thing as in 4:13. There is another possibility, though. The word *rash* may be an Aramaism of the Hebrew word *rosh*, meaning "head" or "first." Alternatively, without changing the consonantal Hebrew text, we can instead read a different vowel for the final word in 4:14, so that we read the word as *rosh* ("first").[40] Both options amount to the

39. The argument here is a condensed form of the more detailed argument I present in my article, "Qohelet in His Context: Ecclesiastes 4,13–16 and the Dating of the Book," *Biblica* 100.3 (2019): 353–72.

40. This word is normally spelled with a quiescent *aleph* (*ro'sh*), so both suggestions here require the *aleph* to drop out of the word. This is not implausible, though, for by Qohelet's day this *aleph* was frequently dropped, as it contributed nothing to pronunciation. We see comparable pronunciation to the suggestion *rash* in 2 Sam 12:4, and plene forms of *rosh* without the *aleph* throughout the Dead Sea Scrolls.

same reading. So, without any emendation to the consonantal Hebrew text, we may translate 4:13–16 as follows:

> Better a poor but wise youth than an old but foolish king, who no longer knows how to take advice. For he came from the house of exile to reign, even though within his kingdom he was born first. I saw all the living who walk about under the sun following the second youth who would take his place. There was no end to all the people—to all who were before them. But even those who come later will not celebrate him. For this too is meaningless, and chasing the wind.

With this rendering, a clear identification of the respective figures emerges. It requires us to understand the second youth of 4:15 as a separate youth to the poor but wise youth of 4:13. The old, foolish king is the Seleucid king, Antiochus II Theos (261–246 BC), and the poor but wise youth is his eldest son, Seleucus. After the stalemate of the Second Syrian War (260–253 BC), Antiochus agreed to marry Berenice, the daughter of his erstwhile foe, Ptolemy II, in order to make peace. To do this, Antiochus needed to divorce his first wife, Laodice. He confined her to exile in the province of Asia with her two sons, Seleucus and Antiochus Hierax, much to the chagrin of Laodice and her supporters at court. This effectively removed Seleucus from the position of crown prince, with that honor going instead to the son Antiochus had by Berenice. In political folly, though, Antiochus returned to his first wife, Laodice, who was still seething from being spurned for Berenice. Consequently, she poisoned Antiochus in 246 BC and simultaneously arranged the murder of Berenice and her infant son. She then had her eldest son, eighteen-year old Seleucus, declared the new king of the Seleucid Kingdom. Seleucus II (246–225 BC) thus came out of demotion and exile to rule his kingdom, though he had once occupied the position of crown prince within it as his father's firstborn.

Soon after, however, a rivalry arose between Seleucus II and his younger brother, Antiochus Hierax. Qohelet alludes to this in 4:15–16. Antiochus Hierax is the "second youth," being so called because he was the second son of Antiochus II and an adolescent when his brother took the throne. Seleucus II sought to reassert sovereignty over Asia Minor since his father's grip over the region had weakened. Over the coming years, however, his younger brother, Hierax, garnered the support of their uncle, Alexander, who governed Lydia, as well as Mithridates of Pontus, and Galatian mercenaries who came from Celtic tribes that had migrated to the region from Gaul a generation earlier. Hierax, therefore, had wide-ranging support, including amongst peoples whose origins lay at the edge of Qohelet's known world. Antiochus Hierax defeated Seleucus at Ancyra in 237 BC and seems to have supplanted Seleucus in portions of Asia Minor, while Seleucus retreated to rule in Syria. But Hierax's success was short lived, as he was soon defeated by other rivals. He was eventually killed as a fugitive in Thrace in c. 227 BC.[41]

The ambiguity of 4:16 makes it difficult to know whether Qohelet knew of Antiochus Hierax's death, anticipated it, or simply assumed it had occurred. He seems at least to have known of his political demise, for without it, his point is not made. In any case, Qohelet relates this anecdote because it had an influence on Judean politics. Sometime in the late 230s BC, the Jewish high priest, Onias II, defied his overlord, Ptolemy III, by refusing to pay the fee for his charge (*prostasia*) over the Jewish nation. Instead, he seems to have entertained an alliance with one of the Seleucid brothers, presumably Seleucus II, whose star was rising over that of his brother, Hierax. Onias's actions brought the threat of reprisal from Ptolemy, which threw Jerusalem into panic when Ptolemy demanded Onias's payment in c. 227 BC. This allowed Onias's nephew, the magnate Joseph Tobias, to save the day by placating Ptolemy. However, Joseph then used his newfound favor with Ptolemy to win the tax-farming rights over the region with the promise of doubling revenues.

As he will elaborate in 8:2–15 (see discussion there), Qohelet viewed Onias's actions as foolish, since they opened the door for Joseph to make a bad situation in Judea even worse. He uses the anecdote of the Seleucids themselves to show the benefit of wisdom over folly (cf. 2:12), particularly since fortunes can change so suddenly and radically. Qohelet criticizes Onias while philosophically inviting his readers to make the most of opportunities given them within reason, since God is ultimately in control of human affairs. The story also demonstrates the lack of foresight humans have—another jab at Onias—such that they cannot anticipate the times or prevent sudden changes of fortune (cf. 3:1–8). This underlines Qohelet's point in 3:22 that no one can see the future, so it is best to enjoy the lot that one is given by God, if that is possible. This is rammed home even harder if Qohelet was writing after 225 BC, for in that year Seleucus II fell from his horse and died unexpectedly. Onias was, therefore, left without a substantive ally against Ptolemy III,

41. K. D. Schunck had proposed a similar identification for the figures of Qohelet's anecdote in 4:13–16. He identified the old king as Antiochus II and the first youth as Seleucus II (as here) but identified the second youth as Antiochus III. This latter determination is not convincing, but the rest of Schunck's argument is cogent. Having written in German, his perspective has received scarce attention in English-speaking scholarship. See K. D. Schunck, "Drei Seleukiden im Buche Kohelet?" *Vetus Testamentum* 9 (1959): 192–201. For further details about Antiochus II, Seleucus II, and Antiochus Hierax, see John D. Grainger, *The Rise of the Seleukid Empire (323–223 BC): Seleukos I to Seleukos III* (Barnsley: Pen & Sword Books, 2014), chaps. 13–15.

whom he had offended. It left him needing to grovel back to the king. Unlike Antiochus II, his younger son Antiochus Hierax, and Onias, wisdom helps someone come to terms with their lot in life, so that they do not take foolish risks that backfire on them.

We should again note that Qohelet tells this anecdote with anonymous characters. This achieves two goals. First, it allows Qohelet to veil his criticism of Onias behind a screen of generalization and so avoid the charge of direct slander (cf. 10:20). In other words, he clothes his obervations in the terms of generic wisdom. Second, it permits us to discern a pattern within the story in addition to the immediate historical referents in Qohelet's day. As Barbour puts it, "Qohelet recognizes in current events a recurring pattern from his own literary tradition, and as he tells his present-day tale he sets out the events on that ancient template."[42] Thus, this rags-to-riches sketch with its interplay between wisdom and folly, which maps precisely onto contemporary Seleucid politics, also echoes incidents from Israel's biblical story in a looser way. Barbour justifiably sees numerous such incidents.[43] For example, the old but foolish king resembles Solomon, and the poor but wise youth who rises from exile to the throne resembles Jeroboam I, who became the first king of the northern kingdom after Israel's fracture under Rehoboam (cf. 1 Kgs 11:40; 12:20).[44] The difficulty with this suggestion is trying to fit Solomon's son, Rehoboam, into it, since he does not fit the bill for the second youth. Yet this does not actually matter, because Qohelet's anecdote is meant to spark a vague memory of Solomon and Jeroboam rather than recount their story with precision. In that way, the anecdote also imprecisely echoes the rise of a young David (despite not being a firstborn) during the madness of Saul, who scorns the advice of his firstborn, Jonathan (1 Sam 19–20). Similarly, it evokes memory of an older David, whose folly (2 Sam 12:9–10) causes him to struggle with heeding advice (2 Sam 14:1–24) and leads to a coup by his son, Absalom (2 Sam 14:25–19:8). Finally, it recalls a foolish (2 Sam 24:10) and eventually senile David, who is initially succeeded by his presumptuous son, Adonijah, who is then outwitted by the younger but wilier Solomon (1 Kgs 1:1–2:25).

As Barbour notes, these stories would have been familiar enough to Qohelet's audience that the "standard outline" would have been enough to evoke the "social memory" of their pattern.[45] In this way, Qohelet skillfully

42. Barbour, *The Story of Israel in the Book of Qohelet*, 86.

43. Ibid., 86–92.

44. Barbour follows the translation of "prison" rather than "house of exile" in 4:14, but she still notes that Jeroboam came from exile in Egypt to rule (88). The proposed reading here helps align her suggestion even more closely with the text.

45. Barbour, *The Story of Israel in the Book of Qohelet*, 92. She builds on the work of James Fentress and Chris Wickham in *Social Memory* (Oxford: Blackwell, 1992), 68.

achieves two outcomes. First, in evoking Israel's social memory through contemporary politics, Qohelet demonstrates that there is indeed nothing new under the sun (cf. Eccl 1:9; 3:15). Second, by making the characters anonymous and the biblical allusions imprecise, he simultaneously recalls the biblical characters and effectively expunges them from memory. Once again, he has engaged in *damnatio memoriae* (cf. 1:11), practically relegating God's grand designs to eras of the distant past and reinforcing the notion that no one can fathom what God is doing from the beginning of history to its end (cf. 3:11).

LIVE the Story

The Mystery of God's Will

In his "BC" world, Qohelet felt lost and trapped. He found God's sovereignty over history overwhelming. When coupled with his inability to deduce what God was doing in history, it produced a disturbing sense of disorientation. This was not simply epistemic angst at being unable to figure out a mental puzzle, but a deep-seated fear of being feebly small beneath a colossal God of unknowable purpose and inexhaustible potency. The deeper Qohelet investigated the meaning of life and God's involvement with Israel through the ages, the weaker he found humanity and the scarier and more puzzling he found God.

It is easy to see how the historical machinations of the Second Temple era might have scuttled the hope of many Jews that God would act in their favor. Qohelet certainly appeared to be sinking under the weight of disappointment in the third century BC. The tenor of his argument shows that he desperately wanted things to be different, but he was powerless to do anything about it.

Two and a half centuries later, though, everything changed. God made himself fully known. In Ephesians Paul states that God, in his wisdom and understanding, made known the mystery of his will, which was to bring unity to all things in heaven and on earth under Christ. This was his purpose all along, and it happened at the fulfilment of the times (Eph 1:8–10). The unpredictability of life and the twists and turns of history enabled Jesus, a descendant of David, to come from the obscurity of Nazareth and minister to the poor and oppressed of Israel. During his ministry, Jesus claimed that God the Father had committed all things to him, granting him the kind of ascendancy associated with the longed-for Davidic king (cf. Ps 2:7–8; Isa 9:6–7). He had made God the Father known to those whom he had chosen and invited the weary and burdened to receive rest from him (Matt 11:27–28).

As Paul says to the Roman Christians, it was at precisely the right time, while Israel was weak, that the Christ died for the ungodly (Rom 5:16).

To know God, then, one must know Jesus Christ. Jesus does not reveal the answer to every minute question of life, but he does reveal the purpose of history and the nature of the God who shapes its course. In Colossians 1:15–19 Paul states that Jesus is the image of the invisible God, with all the fullness of God dwelling within him. All things were created through him and for him. In his death, Jesus dealt with human weakness and sin, reconciling humans to God. In his resurrection, he justified humans before God and extended the hope of eternal life. And in his ascension, Jesus received all power and authority under the heavens, and will one day return to judge. God's intention for Israel, and indeed the world, was for Jesus to rule the world in peace and justice—"That in everything he might have the supremacy" (Col 1:18). Jesus's rule of the world commenced at his ascension, but it will be fully realized on the day he returns. While the time of his return is unknown, it is sure to happen.

The advent of Christ, then, anchors the world into God's purposes. History is not a matrix of random events tumbling out one after the other in aimless fashion but an intricate and grand design to crown Jesus as lord of all creation. Although we continue to experience the unpredictability of life, with its highs and lows, thrills and disappointments, joys and pains, we now know the course that God has set for the history of the world. Sometimes life and the events of history seem untethered from any purpose, and we feel like hapless riders on a rudderless raft at the mercy of raging rapids. It can leave us battered, bruised, and baffled. But Jesus has shown that, despite the rapids and bends, the river of history is heading to the tranquil ocean of his lordship. Though we do not know when we will get there, God has ensured that it is our destination. When we get there, justice will indeed prevail. Though Qohelet was unsure whether God would put right the world's wrongs, in Christ we know definitively that he will bring all to account on the last day (Acts 17:31). Qohelet's disorientation need not be ours. What he longed to know has been revealed in Christ.

If We Were God

In his own circumstances, Qohelet found God frightening in power. But in Christ, God is revealed to be loving and good. It is not that God changed, or even that the God Qohelet knew was different to the God we find in Christ. The second-century teacher, Marcion, believed that the God of the Old Testament was different from the God of the New Testament and so rejected the former in favor of the latter. This was a mistake. We are not dealing with two deities or a sudden about-face by the one God. Rather, in the Old Testament,

God had not yet fully revealed himself because his purposes had not yet been fulfilled. It is only in Christ that God becomes fully known. Qohelet's knowledge of God toward the end of the Old Testament era was true knowledge, but it was incomplete.

Jesus's ministry reveals a God who desires to bless. Jesus proclaimed good news for the poor and freedom for the oppressed (Luke 4:18). He came to bless those whose lot was poverty, mourning, and exploitation (Matt 5:3–4, 10) and to offer repentance to exploiters like the tax collectors. Yet, the leaders of the Jewish nation rejected Jesus and had him executed by the Romans. His own experience, therefore, was one of oppression and violence. Astoundingly, this was part of God's plan, because it was through this means that Jesus was crowned not just King of the Jews, but Lord of creation.

God does stick to his plans, though at times it may seem to us that he does not. He does this in his own timing, and in his own manner, and it is ultimately good. If we were God, we would undoubtedly do things differently on the assumption that we would probably do a better job. British comedian and actor Stephen Fry was once asked what he would say to God if he ever met him. He responded, "How dare you create a world in which there is such misery that is not our fault? It's not right. It's utterly, utterly evil. Why should I respect a capricious, mean-minded, stupid God who creates a world which is so full of injustice and pain?"[46] Like Qohelet, Fry clearly grapples with the reality of pain and suffering against the notion of an omnipotent deity. Qohelet's survey of God's pervasive sovereignty reveals that nothing is beyond God's control. God does not face history passively as we humans who experience it do. History happens to us, but God actively shapes it. Fry's charge has some sting to it.

The marvel of the incarnation, however, means that in Christ the sovereign God who determines the course of history became human and experienced it "from the inside." God has both an objective and subjective knowledge of human existence, as both its author and its content. As humans, however, we only have knowledge "under the sun." We only see in part.

If we were to do God's job, then, we would lack both his objective and subjective knowledge, not to mention his wisdom and understanding. We would certainly do things differently. It would be disastrous. We would be like a child at the controls of the space shuttle. Indeed, it is precisely the desire to be God and do what he does that creates our own troubles. We are

46. Henry McDonald, "Stephen Fry Calls God an 'Evil, Capricious, Monstrous Maniac,'" *The Guardian*, February 1, 2015, https://www.theguardian.com/culture/2015/feb/01/stephen-fry-god-evil-maniac-irish-tv.

our own worst enemies. As inherently self-centered beings, we would impose our own will on the world to our own and others' harm. Indeed, when God submitted himself to human will in Jesus, we killed him. There is no better demonstration of what we would do if we were God (Acts 2:23). Thankfully, this was part of God's plan. As the apostles later recognized, the authorities of their day willingly conspired against Jesus and executed him, but they did what God's power and will had predetermined (Acts 4:27–28).

This leaves the question of why there are times of suffering in our world. While Jesus does not provide us with the answer in every instance, we can appeal to both Qohelet's argument and the love of God as a way forward. Qohelet understood that humans have a will, though it is God's will that ultimately prevails. God does not force his will on people. Rather, he confines our wills within the limits of our created nature. We each have a created human will, with all the limitations that entails. Rudman's analogy of the slave on the estate of a large landowner is helpful,[47] as it reflects something of the limitations we face. Jesus's parables of the tenants (Matt 21:33–46), the Wedding Guests (Matt 22:1–14), and the Prodigal Son (Luke 15:11–32) also illustrate the point well. God gives us genuine freedom within the limits of creation, but we use that freedom in ways that harm ourselves and others. If God imposed his will forcefully on us, no one would love him. Forced love is not love at all, for love requires freedom to truly love. God desires relationship with his human creatures because he is love, and therefore he gives us freedom. We, however, use that freedom by trying to dethrone God. Since none of us would use our God-given human freedom to love God of our own accord, he himself became human so that we might be given access to the deepest love that exists between the Father and the Son. As the Spirit regenerates believers, he does not override our wills but redeems them, enabling us to respond rightly with faith and repentance.

The Trinitarian God whom Christians love and worship, therefore, is both immensely powerful and profoundly loving. Human power is seen when one person denies the will of another to impose their own will on others. Qohelet knew this all too well, and we see examples of it throughout human history. Yet God's power is seen in the fact that he permits us our own will while still achieving his own will at all times. That is all-pervasive power. But it is power motivated by love, not selfishness or force. The loving God who is revealed to us in Christ and made present to us in the Spirit is even bigger than Qohelet perceived.

47. Rudman, *Determinism in the Book of Ecclesiastes*, 90.

CHAPTER 4

Ecclesiastes 5:1–6:6

LISTEN to the Story

1Guard your steps when you go to the house of God. Go near to listen rather than to offer the sacrifice of fools, who do not know that they do wrong.

2Do not be quick with your mouth,
do not be hasty in your heart
to utter anything before God.
God is in heaven
and you are on earth,
so let your words be few.
3A dream comes when there are many cares,
and many words mark the speech of a fool.

4When you make a vow to God, do not delay to fulfill it. He has no
pleasure in fools; fulfill your vow. 5It is better not to make a vow than to
make one and not fulfill it. 6Do not let your mouth lead you into sin. And
do not protest to the temple messenger, "My vow was a mistake." Why
should God be angry at what you say and destroy the work of your hands?
7Much dreaming and many words are meaningless. Therefore fear God.
8If you see the poor oppressed in a district, and justice and rights
denied, do not be surprised at such things; for one official is eyed by a
higher one, and over them both are others higher still. 9The increase from
the land is taken by all; the king himself profits from the fields.

10Whoever loves money never has enough;
whoever loves wealth is never satisfied with their income.
This too is meaningless.
11As goods increase,
so do those who consume them.

And what benefit are they to the owners
  except to feast their eyes on them?
12The sleep of a laborer is sweet,
  whether they eat little or much,
but as for the rich, their abundance
  permits them no sleep.

13I have seen a grievous evil under the sun:

wealth hoarded to the harm of its owners,
  14or wealth lost through some misfortune,
so that when they have children
  there is nothing left for them to inherit.
15Everyone comes naked from their mother's womb,
  and as everyone comes, so they depart.
They take nothing from their toil
that they can carry in their hands.

16This too is a grievous evil:

As everyone comes, so they depart,
  and what do they gain,
  since they toil for the wind?
17All their days they eat in darkness,
  with great frustration, affliction and anger.

18This is what I have observed to be good: that it is appropriate for a
person to eat, to drink and to find satisfaction in their toilsome labor under
the sun during the few days of life God has given them—for this is their
lot. 19Moreover, when God gives someone wealth and possessions, and the
ability to enjoy them, to accept their lot and be happy in their toil—this is
a gift of God. 20They seldom reflect on the days of their life, because God
keeps them occupied with gladness of heart.

6:1I have seen another evil under the sun, and it weighs heavily on man-
kind: 2God gives some people wealth, possessions and honor, so that they
lack nothing their hearts desire, but God does not grant them the ability
to enjoy them, and strangers enjoy them instead. This is meaningless,
a grievous evil.

[3]A man may have a hundred children and live many years; yet no matter how long he lives, if he cannot enjoy his prosperity and does not receive proper burial, I say that a stillborn child is better off than he. [4]It comes without meaning, it departs in darkness, and in darkness its name is shrouded. [5]Though it never saw the sun or knew anything, it has more rest than does that man—[6]even if he lives a thousand years twice over but fails to enjoy his prosperity. Do not all go to the same place?

Listening to the Text in the Story: 1 Kings 3:4–28; 8:1–9:9; Zenon Papyri (esp. Papyri 1, 4, 6; P. Col. 66; P. Cairo Zen. 59.012); Tax Edicts of Ptolemy II (Vienna Papyrus); Josephus, *Antiquities* 12.156–185.

Solomon's reign forms an important backdrop for Qohelet. Not only has Qohelet borrowed Solomon's persona in earlier portions of his discourse, he also alludes to the illustrious king in this next section. Of interest to Qohelet here are Solomon's dreams, the temple he built, and his legendary wisdom. Early in his reign, Solomon went to the shrine at Gibeon to offer a thousand burnt offerings to Yahweh (1 Kgs 3:4). In return, that very night, Yahweh appeared to Solomon in a dream and offered to grant him anything he wished. Solomon famously requested "a discerning heart to govern your people and to distinguish between right and wrong" (1 Kgs 3:9). Yahweh granted his request, and Solomon demonstrated his gift of wisdom to all and sundry. Solomon subsequently built the temple to Yahweh in Jerusalem, fulfilling the prophecy that the son who succeeded David would do so (2 Sam 7:12–13). At its dedication, Solomon and the assembled people sacrificed "so many sheep and cattle that they could not be recorded or counted" (1 Kgs 8:5). After his dedication prayer, Solomon is said to have sacrificed 22,000 cattle and 120,000 sheep and goats on the altar as fellowship offerings (1 Kgs 8:63). After this, Yahweh appeared to him in a dream once again and ratified both the Davidic and national covenant (1 Kgs 9:1–9).

This narrative is important for picking up the allusions in this part of Qohelet's discourse. However, there is also a more subversive purpose in this. Qohelet uses wise King Solomon here as a foil to expose inadequacies in conventional wisdom. While wisdom is meant to apprehend the structures of the world and suggest ways of adapting favorably to it, Qohelet surveys his world in the third century BC and finds that mainstream wisdom does no such thing. He finds it incongruous with reality, providing little hope in a world rife with injustice, corruption, and dissatisfaction.

To appreciate the injustices within Qohelet's world, we need to know about the Ptolemaic administration of their kingdom and how it fostered forms of oppression and systemic corruption. The kingdom was divided into numerous administrative units. This included over forty "nomes" throughout Egypt and a disparate network of districts (in Hebrew, *medinot*) in Palestine, Transjordan, Phoenicia, Syria, Cyprus, and portions of Asia Minor. While the exact configuration of these districts outside Egypt is not known, most seem to have centered on prominent cities, such as Ashkelon and Jerusalem. Some of these cities took on the status of a Greek city (*polis*) or housed military units, which effectively made them Greek colonies (*cleruchies*). We know, for example, that during the reign of Ptolemy II (283–246 BC), Tobias, the father of the infamous tax farmer Joseph Tobias, was the *cleruch* of Philadelphia in Ammanitis (today's Amman, Jordan, in the ancient territory of the Ammonites). Though the prominent Tobiad family was Jewish, as their Hebrew names and connections with the priestly Oniad family in Jerusalem demonstrate, they were often disparaged as foreigners.[1] In the third century BC they were certainly pro-Ptolemaic and overtly Hellenistic, as the Zenon Papyri and the *Antiquities* of Josephus (12.160–185) ably prove. Jerusalem, on the other hand, resisted becoming a Greek *polis*, but this, of course, did not stem the tide of Hellenistic influence or Ptolemaic control.

The elite of society jockeyed for rank in the Ptolemaic administration or, like Tobias and his son Joseph, sought ways to engage with those in the higher echelons of power. This yielded not only political power but meteoric economic prospects. Those appointed to administrative positions, or who managed to ingratiate themselves with the Ptolemaic bureaucratic network, were able to amass fortunes at the expense of the general populace. Some were able to control the supply and demand of markets in their districts, enforce high rates of taxation, and forcibly take goods and assets from the people who produced or owned them previously. In short, Ptolemaic administration enabled the elite to extort the citizenry and confine most people to cycles of poverty and dependency. While such practices were evident even before the Ptolemies took control of Jerusalem in 301 BC (cf. Ezra 9:9), it appears the Ptolemies fostered it in increasing measure.

Primary historical evidence that this was standard practice in the Ptolemaic bureaucracy comes from the Zenon Papyri. Zenon's employer was Apollonius, the treasurer (*dioiketes*) of Ptolemy II. Apollonius mingled the affairs of state

1. The name Tobias or Tobiah was popular throughout the Tobiad family's generations, probably reaching back to the return from exile in Babylon in the late sixth century BC (cf. Ezra 2:60; Neh 7:62; Zech 6:10). Tobias's ancestor, Tobiah, who was an opponent of Nehemiah in the mid fifth century BC, is specifically characterized as "Tobiah the Ammonite," (Neh 2:19), showing that the family had by that time settled in the traditional territory of the Ammonites.

with his own, using his official capacities for personal benefit. This was by no means extraordinary in the Ptolemaic bureaucracy—in fact, it was standard practice. Thus, from Zenon's archive, we can determine that Apollonius owned at least two royally bequeathed estates in Egypt and at least one personal estate in Galilee.[2] On them he had hundreds of workers beholden to him. He commercially traded the products of his vast holdings and exploited numerous other mercantile channels to import and export goods for personal gain, thus dominating both supply and demand in a number of centers.[3] For this purpose, he maintained an extensive network of agents throughout Ptolemaic territories, Zenon being one of them. Zenon was specifically responsible for oversight of Apollonius's estate at Philadelphia in the Fayyum Oasis in Egypt. But, as mentioned in the previous chapter, Apollonius sent Zenon to Palestine and Syria in 259 BC to audit revenue streams and consolidate tax collection. The trip benefited Apollonius as well as King Ptolemy II. We have, for instance, documents detailing the sale and gifting of slaves to Zenon by Tobias (P. 1, 4). More telling, however, is a letter from a certain Alexandros, which outlines that Zenon had sent a representative named Straton, possibly a hitman, to collect money from a Jewish man named Jeddous (P. 6).[4] The attempt, however, met with resistance:

> [Alexan]dros to Oryas, greeting. I have received your letter, to which you added a copy of the letter written by Zenon to Jeddous saying that unless he gave the money to Straton, Zenon's man, we were to hand over his pledge to him (Straton). I happened to be unwell as a result of taking some medicine, so I sent a lad, a servant of mine, with Straton, and wrote a letter to Jeddous. When they returned they said that he had taken no notice of my letter, but had attacked them and thrown them out of the village. So I am writing to you (for your information).[5]

---

2. This estate was located at the biblical site of Beth Anath (Josh 19:38; Judg 1:33) in what is today southern Lebanon. For more details integrating evidence from the papyri about Apollonius and Zenon, see Edgar, *Zenon Papyri in the University of Michigan Collection*, 5–50.

3. The extent of Apollonius's estate at Beth Anath is demonstrated by his importation of 80,000 vines from the Aegean island of Cos for planting within it. See Hengel, *Jews, Greeks and Barbarians: Aspects of the Hellenization of Judaism in the Pre-Christian Period*, 24. A summary impression of the tax rates comes from P. Cairo Zen. 59.012. This papyrus stipulates taxes of up to 50 percent on the value of goods imported for the benefit of Apollonius in 259 BC. See Michel M. Austin, *The Hellenistic World from Alexander to the Roman Conquest: A Selection of Ancient Sources in Translation*, 2nd Augmented Edition (Cambridge: Cambridge University Press, 2006), §298.

4. The name Jeddous is a Hellenized form of the Hebrew name Jaddai (cf. Ezra 10:43) or Iddo (cf. Zech 1:1).

5. Translation taken from Victor Tcherikover, Avigdor Tcherikover, and Alexander Fuks, eds., *Corpus Papyrorum Judaicarum*, vol. 1 (Jerusalem: Magnes Press, Hebrew University, 1957), 130.

Though this attempt to exact money from Jeddous failed, it highlights the antipathy Jews held toward the Ptolemaic bureaucracy and its demands. While we do not know how Zenon responded to Jeddous, other documents in Zenon's archive, as well as two tax edicts of Ptolemy II from 261 BC (Vienna Papyrus), demonstrate the punitive measures that were sometimes taken against defaulters. Ptolemy's edicts, which related the registration of cattle and slaves for taxation purposes in Syria and Phoenicia, stipulate:

> The heads of villages are to register at the same time the cattle in the villages, and their fathers' names and their home district and by whom it is pastured, and likewise also as much (cattle) as they know is unregistered . . . And they will make registrations annually at the same times, and they will pay dues . . . . Those who do not comply with some aspect of the public notices, such as those who register their own cattle by another name, will be liable to the penalties thereof. Whoever is willing to inform will receive of the penalties being exacted . . . one-third of the property which is confiscated to the royal treasury . . . . If someone does not register or does not pay taxes for a slave, the slave will be confiscated and payment of 6,000 drachmae per slave will be exacted for the royal treasury, and the king will judge him.[6]

Another papyrus (P. Col. 66) is a letter written in 256 BC by a man who knew no Greek but whom Zenon had left in Syria (or more accurately Palestine) to work. The man complains of not having been paid by Zenon's local agents for months and therefore being "compelled to run away to Syria to avoid dying of hunger" and being "in distress summer and winter."[7] All this demonstrates a strict tax regime and opportunities for exploitation. A citizen could expect to pay tax on virtually every aspect of life, to make extortionate payments, be forced into taking ruinous loans that made him dependent on his creditor, need to bribe, tip, or provide favors, have assets confiscated, forego pay, do forced labor, spend time in prison or the stocks, experience intimidation and violence, be informed upon by a neighbor, be enslaved, sell children into slavery, or even face death.

Joseph, son of Tobias, is another prime exemplar of these tactics. When he pledged to double the amount of taxes for Ptolemy III, the king granted him the right to farm taxes throughout Palestine and Syria in 227 BC (*Ant.*

6. Lawrence H. Schiffman, *Texts and Traditions: A Source Reader for the Study of Second Temple and Rabbinic Judaism* (Brooklyn, NY: KTAV, 1998), § 4.2.6 (141–42).

7. Austin, *The Hellenistic World from Alexander to the Roman Conquest*, §307.

12.180–85). Overnight, then, the already heavy tax burden in Qohelet's world doubled. Joseph employed soldiers to intimidate people into paying these exorbitant rates of tax. When prominent citizens refused to pay up, Joseph would round them up, execute them, and confiscate their assets, thereby amassing his own sizeable fortune. This in turn usually convinced the citizens of other cities to comply, though discontent never died down. Thus, the Jewish historian Josephus states, "By this means he [Joseph] gathered great wealth together, and made vast gains by this farming of the taxes; and he made use of what estate he had thus gotten, in order to support his authority" (*Ant.* 12.184). So injurious was the taxation burden and the redistribution of assets throughout the region from this time that its beggaring effects were still being felt in Jesus's day during the first century.[8] The average citizen in the Ptolemaic Kingdom bore a crippling burden of taxation that fed the ever-deepening coffers of the authorities. While the court of the Ptolemies was legendary for its opulence, the life of most people in Qohelet's world was of hardship and economic servitude.

This situation arose in Judea because of the actions of Onias II, the uncle of Joseph Tobias. Onias broke his oath by refusing to pay Ptolemy III the fee for his custodianship of the Jewish people, seeking instead to align himself with the Ptolemies' enemies, the Seleucids in Syria. Not only was Onias defying his political overlord, Ptolemy III, but he was breaking an oath he had sworn to God. Ptolemy sent an envoy to Judea to coerce Onias into paying his fee, with the threat of punitive military action if he did not. When Onias persisted in his refusal, Joseph Tobias became the people's champion by negotiating with Ptolemy's envoy and then placating Ptolemy himself in Alexandria. It was while he was there on his diplomatic mission that Joseph then seized the further opportunity to be appointed as tax farmer for the region, doubling the tax burden on the population. The people's champion had sold them out, and the people found themselves in even worse economic conditions than before (see "Context and Date" in the Introduction for further discussion).

---

8. The attitude toward taxation and tax collectors in the Gospels, Jesus's statements about wealth and abuse of the poor, as the reality of begging all testify to this (cf. Matt 5:3; 6:24; 18:23–35; 21:33–46; 22:15–22; Mark 12:40–44; Luke 12:57–59; 16:1–13, 19–31; 19:1–10). Josephus's later claim that Joseph Tobias "brought the Jews out of a state of poverty and meanness, to one that was more splendid" (*Ant.* 12.224) refers to events at the very end of Joseph's life, when he and his sons helped lever Judea away from the Ptolemies, enabling the Seleucid king, Antiochus III, to gain control over the region. Under Antiochus III, Jerusalem experienced an economic renaissance. See George Athas, *Bridging the Testaments* (Grand Rapids: Zondervan, forthcoming).

EXPLAIN the Story

Folly and Evil (5:1–6:6)

In this next section of Ecclesiastes, Qohelet continues to explore how the immense power of God affects human endeavor. The dominant subject of his musings is the abuse of power—how injustice impacts people and what people should and should not do in response. His best advice is to accept that injustice is a fundamental aspect of a meaningless world and try to cope by enjoying small pleasures when they are possible. Once again, Qohelet adroitly brings God's purposes into question and reveals his own dejection and disenfranchisement.

Folly in Sacrifice and Breaking Oaths (5:1–7)

Having discussed how hapless humans are before a mighty God, Qohelet here dispenses advice about conduct in formal matters relating to this God. His advice pertains to two related spheres: sacrifice at the temple altar (5:1–3)[9] and the making of vows (5:4–7). As we will see, his advice is not generic but contains cutting political comment.

Verse 1 shows that Qohelet was familiar with the Jerusalem temple ("the house of God"). He warns his readers to watch carefully what they do there, encouraging listening above sacrifice. This implies that auditory rites occurred at the temple, which presumably included the reading of authoritative works, such as the Law (cf. Neh 8) and psalms, including perhaps homilies as well as public declarations.

The Hebrew wording of 5:1b is odd, making the second half of the verse difficult to interpret. Though some commentators understand the verse to demonstrate that Qohelet fully advocates the orthodox theology of other parts of the Old Testament,[10] the broader sweep of Qohelet's discourse must make us think twice about this. Indeed, the various ways this verse may be understood show that the issue is not so clear-cut.

There are several ways to understand the verse. First, most translators, including the ancient Greek translator, understand Qohelet to advise coming to the temple to listen, "rather than to offer the sacrifice of fools, who do not

9. The versification of the Hebrew text makes 5:1 the last verse of the previous chapter (4:17). Both the Hebrew and English versification are late impositions on the text, which originally was not broken up into verses. But as Longman notes, the English versification makes more sense, since 5:1 clearly belongs to the subject matter that follows it. See Longman, *Ecclesiastes*, 148.

10. Barry G. Webb, *Five Festal Garments: Christian Reflections on the Song of Songs, Ruth, Lamentations, Ecclesiastes and Esther*, New Studies in Biblical Theology 10 (Leicester: Apollos, 2000), 97; Fredericks and Estes, *Ecclesiastes & the Song of Songs*, 282.

know that they do wrong" (so NIV). This could mean that Qohelet sees the entire notion of sacrifice as a foolish and "wrong" activity. Why he would think this is not immediately apparent, but if this is Qohelet's intended meaning, he is offering a strong critique of the temple cult. It may be that he sees the entire enterprise as useless because sacrifice changes nothing—it is "meaningless" (*hebel*)—or that the proceeds from it are pilfered by the elite, be they Onias and the Jewish temple personnel or the Ptolemaic hierarchies. Essentially, he would be labeling anyone who offers sacrifices to such an ineffective or corrupted system a fool. Alternatively, it might mean that Qohelet approves of sacrifices but discourages fools from offering them. This could imply that fools wrongly rely on ritual to be right with God while being blind to their own unethical behavior as they fail to heed the kind of warnings taught in the temple (cf. 4:13). In this case, Qohelet would be promoting "a cautious but reverent attitude to the cult that is not essentially different from the usual [prophetic] critique of cultic abuses."[11] A third way to interpret the verse is to see Qohelet calling the temple elite "fools." It encourages listening "rather than giving fools a sacrifice, because none of them know that they do wrong." This option is a more strident critique of temple personnel who benefited economically from sacrifices.[12]

There is, however, a better alternative, which works with the flow of thought from Qohelet's anecdote about the Seleucids in the previous verses (4:13–16). It is likely that Qohelet has the high priest, Onias II, in his sights here. By refusing to pay the fee for his charge over the Jewish nation, Onias had broken an oath of loyalty to Ptolemy and aligned Judea with Seleucus II in the north.[13] Onias's oath had presumably been made in the temple in the name of the God whom he served as high priest, and this would have been sealed with a sacrifice. Onias's attachment to the Seleucids (cf. 8:2–15), demonstrated by his refusal to pay the fee to Ptolemy, brings the sincerity of his oath and sacrifice into serious question. In the eyes of Qohelet and the people of Jerusalem, Onias had acted foolishly, for not only had he been disloyal to Ptolemy, bringing the

11. Murphy, "Worship, Officials, Wealth and Its Uncertainties: Ecclesiastes 5:1–6:9," 283.

12. Priests and Levites were entitled to some sacrificial meat, as well as the fleeces of victims, which could then be sold on. They also had access to the funds that people deposited for safekeeping in the temple, which came to function much like a bank, as well as donations and the payment of fulfilled vows. In Jesus's day, they also ran money-changing businesses and sold animals for sacrifice, meaning they benefited twice (Matt 21:12).

13. A story of some relevance to this situation is found in Josephus's discussion of the establishment of Alexander's hegemony over the region (*Ant.* 12.8). Josephus mentions that "the people of Jerusalem were most faithful in the observation of oaths and covenants" and that Jews who migrated to Alexandria were required to swear oaths of allegiance to Alexander's successors. It is not implausible to discern from this that Onias, who had been given *prostasia* of the Jewish nation in Jerusalem, was also required to take an oath of allegiance to the Ptolemies.

threat of war upon the city, he had also incurred divine wrath. He had broken an oath sworn in the name of God, sealed with a sacrifice offered on the altar in Jerusalem. In that case, Qohelet's advice here is, "Do not be foolish like Onias, who offers sacrifices to God with complete insincerity."

This gives 5:2 a grim feel, as it reveals the ultimate source of danger for the community. It is not Ptolemy III; it is God. In the previous chapter Qohelet gave a picture of a menacingly powerful God that makes the contrast with humans here stark: "God is in heaven and you are on the earth." "Heaven" for Qohelet is indicative of God's unrestricted view and authority over human affairs. This is contrasted with the feeble limitations that humans have "on the earth." Onias might have thought he could dupe Ptolemy, but he was a patent fool for thinking God would not know about the duplicity of his sacrifice. He is, rather, completely exposed and vulnerable before a God of unfathomable power and knowledge. Sacrifice does not domesticate him or throw him off the scent. Since God determines the highs and lows of human experience, it is unwise to tempt him by folly into using his raw power against you. Yet, this is precisely what Onias had done, and now the whole nation was suffering for it. He, the high priest, had lied to God and hidden behind ritual, bringing the nation he led under the judgment of God. Onias had "poked the bear." Qohelet draws a lesson from this, that it is far wiser to "lay low" in the temple by not saying or offering too much to God. God is, after all, frightening (cf. 3:14).[14]

This leads naturally onto the issue of making vows (5:4–6). Again, Qohelet is criticizing Onias's folly in reneging on his avowed commitment to Ptolemy and to God, but he also draws lessons from this for his readers. "When someone made a vow, they usually asked for God's help in some matter, and in return pledged to give something back to God, usually in the form of a donation to the house of Yahweh."[15] Since such vows were taken in the temple before witnesses, temple staff could be expected to foreclose on repayment (5:6). Indeed, the idea that God might "destroy the work of your hands" for failing to pay for a vow could also be translated as "impound the work of your hands" (5:6[5:5]),[16] referring to the confiscation of property. The implication is that temple staff work on God's behalf and that one endangers their own possessions earned through hard work by taking a vow. In 5:4 Qohelet cites the beginning of Deuteronomy 23:21 to affirm that those who make such vows to God should not delay in fulfilling them. Unlike Deuteronomy, though, Qohelet does not associate the certainty of punishment with failure to repay a

14. Cf. Longman, "The 'Fear of God' in the Book of Ecclesiastes," 16.

15. George Athas, *Deuteronomy: One Nation under God*, RBT (Sydney: Aquila, 2016), 277.

16. In an unpointed text, the Hebrew root *hbl* could be either in the *piel* stem ("destroy") or the *qal* stem ("foreclose"). See James L. Kugel, "Qohelet and Money," *CBQ* 51.1 (1989): 33.

vow, though he implies it may well happen. Qohelet's God is transcendent, but not aloof. As Shields states, Qohelet "consistently maintains that there is no way to know or predict God's behavior in a specific matter."[17] The implication is not that someone might get away with using God or paying him off but that someone should not test God's ability to punish. Trying to exploit God is a dangerous business.

This makes Onias's broken oath all the more foolish. It was no small thing for the high priest to go back on an oath sworn to the God he served. Qohelet is, therefore, characterizing Onias as supremely irresponsible, because his defiance put the entire Jewish nation, whom he represented, at risk of reprisal from Ptolemy and God. If Onias could use his own personnel to demand payment of vows from others who had similarly sworn oaths to God in the temple, then why would Onias think that God might not foreclose on his failure to pay on his oath? Onias certainly could not complain when Ptolemy sent his envoy to demand payment from him. This is, indeed, what Ptolemy did, and Qohelet alludes to it in 5:6[5:5] when he refers to "the messenger." The NIV translates this as "the temple messenger," but the word "temple" is not present in the Hebrew text. Onias's refusal to pay put Jerusalem into panic, opening the door for Joseph Tobias to take advantage of the situation (*Ant.* 12.154–66). God, it seems, was "foreclosing" on the nation for Onias's broken vow.

Throughout Qohelet's discussion are also allusions to Solomon, which he uses to critique both human wisdom and raise questions about God (once again). Qohelet's references to the temple (5:1) and dreams (5:3, 7) evoke Solomon's construction of the temple, which is bookended by two revelatory dreams. The wording of 5:3[5:2] literally reads, "For the dream comes with much toil." In a generic way, this signifies that much activity leads to much dreaming, both literally, by engendering the sleep of fatigue (cf. 5:12), and figuratively, by fostering hopes for betterment. In a suggestive way, though, it also alludes to *the* dream Solomon had at Gibeon and the grand scope of his building works that flowed from it. For the ordinary person, much dreaming comes with much work, but for Solomon, much work came with much dreaming. Though Solomon gave a grandiloquent speech at the dedication of the temple, loudly proclaiming God's faithfulness to his promises to David, Qohelet advises against such theatrics. This is where Qohelet turns conventional wisdom on its head. God granted Solomon divine wisdom, with which he built the temple and dedicated it with great fanfare and prolific sacrifice, but it never stopped him permitting the worship of other gods and

17. Martin A. Shields, *The End of Wisdom: A Reappraisal of the Historical and Canonical Function of Ecclesiastes* (Winona Lake, IN: Eisenbrauns, 2006), 160.

bringing disaster upon Israel. As Samuel told a wayward Saul, "To obey is better than sacrifice, and to heed is better than the fat of rams" (1 Sam 15:22). For all Solomon's wonderful, wise words, folly still befell him. He "poked the bear," and God in heaven took action against the folly on earth. Solomon, therefore, represents the antithesis of Qohelet's advice. Qohelet sees through such "wisdom" that builds grand temples but destroys kingdoms and human lives. Centuries later, Qohelet still lived with the effects of Solomon's folly and God's frightening action, as the Jewish nation lay broken, strewn across foreign empires, and under the foolish leadership of Onias. And still God had not followed through with his later promises to restore the nation. Instead, the nation was now under serious threat because of Onias's duplicitous sacrifice and disobedience. He may have had dreams of breaking Judea away from Ptolemaic control, but he would have been wiser fearing the God he served. Qohelet thus concludes that life would be easier for all if people dreamed less, spoke less, and were afraid of God (5:7).

The Vicious Circle of Corruption (5:8–12)

Alas, Qohelet's world is run by ambitious dreamers who are not afraid of God. The harsh realities of life in Judea in the third century BC now come through, as Qohelet examines the injustice and exploitation around him. Again, this recalls Onias's folly and the schemes of his nephew, Joseph Tobias, who made the Ptolemaic yoke even heavier on the necks of the populace. Qohelet even sees the excesses of Ptolemaic power as providing little benefit to the powerful themselves. In his estimation, the configuration of society under the Ptolemies is rampantly ruinous for all.

Verse 8 sets the bleak tone for the remainder of the chapter, as it oozes with sinister irony. Qohelet advises his readers to expect the oppression of the poor in a district, and the denial of justice (5:8a). The term *medinah* (NIV, "district") is, on one level, a mundane term for a unit of jurisdiction, such as the nomes and *cleruchies* that the Ptolemies maintained throughout their territories. But the word itself comes from the Hebrew root *din*, which means to establish or defend justice. Thus, on another level, Qohelet exposes the lack of justice in the very place it should be.[18] Instead, Qohelet sees systemic corruption maintained by the hierarchy of officials who prop up the avaricious Ptolemaic administration (5:8b). These were people like Apollonius (treasurer of Ptolemy II), his agent, Zenon, and, of course, the unscrupulous Joseph Tobias—all representative of the various levels of Ptolemaic bureaucracy who literally took their toll on the lower working classes of Judea. The ordinary

18. Seow, *Ecclesiastes*, 202.

Hebrew word for tax farmer is *gobeh*, but here Qohelet uses the term *gaboah* (literally, "high one") to describe these officials.[19] The play on words is almost a portmanteau.[20] It disparagingly contrasts these "high" and haughty bureaucrats with the low and humble poor. A hierarchy should have provided a measure of protection against injustices to protect these poor and vulnerable. However, as Brown puts it, what Qohelet observes is "not so much a structure of checks-and-balances as a network of corruption in which royal personnel, driven by pride and ambition, ensure their mutual advantage over the dispossessed, a sanctioned conspiracy of corruption."[21] Power in Qohelet's society is infested with villainy, and the oppressed are powerless to eradicate it. Since Qohelet is not a real king, he can do nothing about it either. So, he advises his readers to resign themselves to debilitating disenfranchisement. This is hardly a satisfactory situation, but Qohelet's rhetoric is not about a stoic approach to hardship, but a stark exposé of exploitation and a sigh of vexation.

The Hebrew syntax of 5:9[5:8] is highly problematic, making it notoriously difficult to translate. It literally reads, "And a profit of land is in all, a king to a field is worked." There are questions here not just about how the words relate to each other but how the sentence fits into Qohelet's train of thought. So problematic is the verse that Seow proposes redividing the words to derive an entirely different sentence: "the advantage of the land is in its yield, that is, if the field is cultivated for [its] yield."[22] The ancient Greek translator, though, saw the words as they are in the Masoretic Text, making the suggestion unlikely. This means Fox's suggestion to emend the text, though attractive, is also problematic.[23] Eaton translates the verse, "But an advantage to a land for everyone is: a king over cultivated land," and interprets this to mean that "bureaucratic officialdom does not totally override the value of kingly authority."[24] However, this is not only a difficult imposition on the words, it also reverses Qohelet's stark rhetoric in the previous verse, as well as his general attitude to human authority. Brown commendably tries to pick up Qohelet's line of reasoning by suggesting an echo to Proverbs 29:4 ("By justice

---

19. Kugel suggests emending the Hebrew text from *gaboah* ("high one") to *gobeh*, which he translates as "payment taker." However, the use of wordplay suggests this meaning without the necessity of emending the text. Kugel entertains such a wordplay, but sees the current Masoretic Text as reflecting a pious emendation, which he wants to reverse. See Kugel, "Qohelet and Money," 35–38; Seow, *Ecclesiastes*, 203–4.

20. A portmanteau blends two different words into one new word. Some English portmanteaus have become common words, such as "brunch" (breakfast + lunch) and "motel" (motor + hotel). However, some are simply novel, like "evilangelist" and "totalitolerance."

21. Brown, *Ecclesiastes*, 58.

22. Seow, *Ecclesiastes*, 204.

23. Fox, *A Time to Tear Down*, 234.

24. Eaton, *Ecclesiastes*, 101. Cf. Fredericks and Estes, *Ecclesiastes & the Song of Songs*, 141.

a king gives a country stability, but those who are greedy for bribes tear it down").[25] Yet, other than the words "king" and "country" (i.e. "land"), it is hard to see any substantive connection. Another common proposal is to translate the second half of the verse, "for even the king is subject to the land."[26] The implication is that everyone needs the land to survive, from the poorest right up to the king. Yet, while a plausible fit for the words, it is tangential to Qohelet's argument.

Longman (along with the NIV) opts to see the verse continuing the description of "all" the corrupt bureaucrats from the previous verse: "*even the king* himself takes advantage of his politically powerful position to get the *profit of the land*."[27] This seems contextually closer to the mark, though we may refine the idea even further. The previous verse establishes a contrast between the powerful and the powerless, and this may be extended to 5:9 as a contrast between king and commoners ("all"). Thus, we can read the verse, "Though the profit of the land should be for all, yet it is a king who is served by the field." The implication is that the earth's resources are not enjoyed by all, least of all by those who actually work it. On the contrary, only the upper echelons of society enjoy the earth's bounty, like Apollonius enjoying the fruits of his vast estates. This has even more sting in it when we realize the consequences of Onias's refusal to give the king his pledged share—the "profit of the land." Though Onias may have been right to feel the injustice of the situation, since the land's resources should be shared by all, yet by withholding the payment to the king, he allowed Joseph Tobias to fleece the land even more. Onias's folly, Joseph's scheming, and Ptolemy's avarice had, to borrow an image from Deuteronomy, thoroughly "muzzled the ox that treads the grain" (Deut 25:4).

In 5:10–12 Qohelet reflects on the motivations of the powerfully corrupt by commenting on what seems to be a chain of proverbs. He starts with a proverb about how wealth never satisfies (5:10). The implication is that those who love money never cease to accumulate it in search of satisfaction, and this propels the vicious circle of exploitation of the poor—a sentiment matching that of 5:8. The suggestion that the wealthy are never satisfied with their level of wealth makes the entire money-gaining enterprise meaningless. It yields little satisfaction to those who accumulate it (cf. 6:7), and it embattles the poorer masses who are robbed of it. Nobody wins! This never-ending cycle of dissatisfaction means that the more goods are produced, the more the wealthy consume without satisfaction (5:11). Qohelet has the tax farmers and

25. William P. Brown, *Ecclesiastes*, 59.
26. Gordis, *Koheleth: The Man and His World*, 250.
27. Longman, *Ecclesiastes*, 158.

bureaucrats, like Apollonius, Zenon, and Joseph Tobias, in mind in 5:11, not to mention the Ptolemaic kings themselves. It is also another sideways jab at Onias, whose folly enabled the increased oppression of the masses. Qohelet's criticism is that the wealthy always seek to take more from the poor, and yet it is impossible for them to enjoy personally so much acquired wealth. One could not possibly have the time, opportunity, or energy to consume it all. One could only gaze at such wealth—a literally useless situation. Thus, Qohelet critiques the Ptolemaic taxation system as irresponsibly wasteful and dissatisfying even for the elite. It leaves the poor unjustly dispossessed of the benefits of their own labor. Qohelet even extends this wide discrepancy between the rich and the poor to sleep (5:12). The poor person will sleep well despite their circumstances because their hard labor fatigues them and their conscience is clear. The rich of Ptolemaic society, however, never stop mulling over gaining more wealth. It keeps them awake at night, and their conscience never permits them rest.

Grievous Evils (5:13–6:6)

The cruelty and meaninglessness of society that Qohelet observes leads him now to consider three "grievous evils" relating to wealth (5:13–15; 5:16–17; 6:1–2). He punctuates these with two comments about what he thinks is "good" (5:18–20; 6:3–6), but even these are disenchanting.

The first "grievous evil" is "wealth hoarded to the harm of its owners" (5:13b). The NIV term "hoarded" suggests intemperate collection of wealth, but the Hebrew word simply means "kept" (*shamur*) and so has a neutral connotation. Since Qohelet has observed the powerful exploiting the poor, it is appealing to see this as a case of accumulated wealth backfiring upon powerful owners. This may be wishful thinking and does not adequately consider the Ptolemaic context Qohelet was critiquing. The NIV begins 5:14 with the word "or," suggesting the verse describes a similar evil to the one mentioned in 5:13b. However, the Hebrew wording is more generic and suggests an expansion of the scenario from 5:13b, rather than an alternative one.[28] It describes a man (the verbs are singular, despite the plurals used by the NIV) who loses some unspecified wealth, leaving him with nothing to pass on to his son. Qohelet does not elaborate on the nature of the loss, but given his discussion in the previous verses, his words resonate strongly with the situation in Ptolemaic Judea. Onias had attempted to keep wealth by withholding payment from Ptolemy. This backfired on him, since the Seleucids he was courting soon died, forcing

28. The relevant word is *we'abad*, which uses the generic conjunction *waw* ("and"). The resultant *weqatal* verb form frequently continues an earlier thought.

him to pay Ptolemy anyway. Yet, Onias's actions had ruinous repercussions for the whole population, who now had even more of their assets taken under the villainous tax burden of Joseph Tobias. Qohelet's scenario captures this well. It sees a man earn his wealth through hard work, only to attract the sybaritic attention of the elite, who forcibly take it from him. It sounds very much like the situation of Jeddous from the Zenon Papyri, though unlike Jeddous, Qohelet's hapless man was unsuccessful in his attempt to keep his assets. The situation also resembles the intimidation and violence perpetrated by Joseph Tobias in collecting taxes (*Ant.* 12.180–85). Thus, Qohelet's observation was a tragically common experience. The "grievous evil" Qohelet sees, then, is not that the man had kept wealth per se, or stored up treasures on earth rather than in heaven,[29] but that the folly of leaders and the predatory greed of the powerful robbed him of his rightful possessions. The man was thus unjustly left with nothing for his toil. As Qohelet describes the indisputable fact that no one takes wealth with them when they die (5:15), he also implies that the poor man's situation was like a living death. He had been forced to surrender his hard-earned wealth even before death took it from him.

That this scenario is one of exploitation is confirmed by Qohelet's second "grievous evil" (5:16–17). This essentially expands the thought of 5:15. Since nobody takes anything with them when they die, there is no lasting profit for anyone seeking to accumulate and hold on to wealth. If the elite do not take it first, death eventually will (cf. 2:18). And no one is exempt from that final comprehensive payment, not even the elite. We see here another subtle indictment of Onias's folly. Qohelet implies that, since Onias could not take his wealth to the grave, he should simply have paid up when Ptolemy demanded. But because he tried to defy Ptolemy, life for most people in Judea was now utterly miserable. "All their days they eat in darkness with great frustration, affliction and anger" (5:17; cf. 2:23).

Though Qohelet's heart bleeds for the masses, he can offer only dim hope. This he does in 5:18–20 with an observation of what is "good" in such wretched circumstances. It echoes what he has already said previously: one should try to salvage some positivity in life by enjoying the basics of eating, drinking, and working (2:24–25; 3:13). It is a call to make the most of a bad situation. He extends this to the attempt to enjoy wealth if one has it. Finding this joy provides a rare distraction from the harsher realities of life. However, the two "grievous evils" he has just observed—the man whose wealth was confiscated (5:13–15) and the relentless reality that condemns most to a life of poverty, discontent, and eating in darkness (5:16–17)—makes the possibility

29. Fredericks and Estes, *Ecclesiastes & the Song of Songs*, 151.

of experiencing such "good" remote. This is why Qohelet appeals here to what God gives. The power to enjoy the basics of life or hard-earned wealth is beyond the capacity of most, for their "lot" in life is simply too grievous. It is, therefore, a rare gift of God if one can achieve it, especially in the political and economic climate of Ptolemaic Judea. Once again, there is a subtle yet penetrating critique of God here for being complicit in the oppression of the poor and failing to give them even scant joy in life. For the majority in Qohelet's Judea, a life of comfort was but a fantasy.

The critique continues in 6:1–2, as Qohelet returns to the notion of having one's wealth confiscated. It is unclear whether Qohelet is here describing the same man in 5:13–14, who has his assets confiscated but survives (again, the Hebrew uses singular terms, despite the NIV's plurals), or a different man who is killed in order to have his assets seized, like some of Joseph Tobias's more prominent victims. Though the NIV describes this as "another evil under the sun" (6:1), the word "another" is not there in Hebrew. The NIV also has Qohelet state that the situation "weighs heavily on mankind." In addition to this possible translation, Qohelet may be saying, "it is prevalent across humanity."[30] Whichever the case, Qohelet frames the situation with reference to what God does and does not give. God gives assets to some people, but not the power to enjoy them. Instead, God gives that power to "a foreign man" (NIV: "strangers")—a reference to both Ptolemy III, who legally demanded Onias's fee after Onias's oath, and to the Ptolemies' lackeys more generally—folks like Apollonius and Zenon. This might even be a disparaging label specifically for Joseph Tobias, whose family was of disputed nationality. Qohelet's language also picks up the curse of Deuteronomy 28:33, which foreshadows Israel's exile: "A people that you do not know will eat what your land and labor produce, and you will have nothing but cruel oppression all your days."[31] Thus, Qohelet effectively indicts God for collusion with the Ptolemaic elite, under whom Israel continues to languish, as it has since its exile. He concludes that it is all "meaningless, a grievous evil" (6:2).

At this juncture Qohelet responds with an observation of what is "good," but once again it is miserable comfort (6:3–6). In 6:3 he paints an exaggerated picture of a man who has it all—a hundred sons and very long life, and then magnifies this exponentially in 6:6. This man does not find satisfaction in his wealth. The NIV translates this phrase as "he cannot enjoy his prosperity" (6:3), which seems to allude back to the dispossessed man in 5:13b–14 and 6:2.

---

30. This translation understands *rabbah* as referring not to "great" weight, but rather to "much" occurrence.

31. Barbour, *The Story of Israel in the Book of Qohelet*, 117–18.

The phrase certainly does this, as the reference to not receiving proper burial (6:3) suggests the kind of victim Joseph Tobias often left in his wake. But the Hebrew reads "his soul [or appetite] is not satisfied with goods," which also encompasses the elite in 5:11, who, though they seize the possessions of others, are still not satisfied by them. Thus, Qohelet's "man" here takes on the experience of both the exploited majority, as well as the privileged elite living off that exploitation.

Better than such a man, he says, is the stillborn baby (6:4). This is a horridly morbid claim that gives us a glimpse into the desperate plight of people in Ptolemaic Judea. Qohelet uses the keyword of his discourse, *hebel* ("meaninglessness"), to describe the coming of a stillborn. The nuances of transience and futility are evident here in the notion of bringing forth a new life that is not actually alive. The NIV translates 6:5a as "Though it never saw the sun or knew anything." However, the object of knowing is probably also the sun, which yields the reading, "Though it neither saw nor knew the sun." Qohelet uses this phrase to point out that the stillborn baby is blissfully ignorant of the grievous evils, dissatisfaction, and epidemic injustice of life "under the sun." For Qohelet, life is puzzling, painful, and depraved—so much so that, in his estimation, the champion of human existence is not the long-lived man surrounded by family, nor even the Ptolemaic king, but the stillborn baby. "It has more rest than does that man" (6:5b).

LIVE the Story

The Coming of the Kingdom of God

The social and economic injustices of Qohelet's day had lasting repercussions for the Jewish nation. There was some temporary relief when the Seleucids wrested Judea from Ptolemaic control in 199 BC during the Fifth Syrian War. The Seleucid conqueror, Antiochus III (222–187 BC), extended tax breaks to numerous members of the Jewish community, including a three-year tax exemption for those who returned to Jerusalem after it suffered heavy damages during the war and a one-third reduction of the nation's overall tribute payment to the king (*Ant.* 12.143–44).[32] Yet, it was not to last. Within a few years, Antiochus III's losses to Rome imposed a massive debt on the Seleucid kingdom, which now included Judea, and paralyzing economic liabilities returned.[33] In the decades following, the economic and

32. See also Hengel, *Jews, Greeks and Barbarians: Aspects of the Hellenization of Judaism in the Pre-Christian Period*, 42–43; Athas, *Bridging the Testaments*, forthcoming.

33. Rome defeated Antiochus III in 190 BC, and imposed reparations of almost 12,000 talents on him at the Peace of Apamea in 188 BC (Polybius, *Histories* 21.42).

cultural pressure within Judea erupted into conflict (the Maccabean Revolt). Though this established Jewish self-rule in Palestine for a century, it did not completely alleviate the economic suffering of the masses. Rather than directing funds into the coffers of foreign monarchs and their lackeys, funds were now diverted into the temple coffers in Jerusalem. Jewish nationalists used Jewish identity and law observance, with which most Jews were willing to identify, as a means of political and financial gain. Sacrifice and tithing were no longer just tokens of worship and piety but now imposed as a means of control and oppression.

When the Romans arrived in 63 BC, the economic constraints tightened again. The Romans permitted the temple elite to continue exacting dues from their compatriots but also imposed their own taxes on the population. The census that Luke reports under Caesar Augustus (Luke 2:1–3) was a measure that only occurred to update registers of taxpayers and their assets. Thus, Jesus's birth occurred in the kind of world that Qohelet bemoaned. Temple personnel took advantage of people's piety, and the Roman overlords imposed their own financial demands, which not only overtaxed the population but put a chokehold on Davidic hopes. And yet, the fact that Jesus's parents, Joseph and Mary, went to register themselves in Bethlehem, the city of David, was most poignant (Luke 2:4–5). On the one hand, it demonstrated their political and economic subjugation to Rome. On the other hand, it was a statement of hopeful defiance, aligning themselves with the classic hope that God would raise a descendant of David—a member of their own clan—to put things right, just as he had promised.[34] It was in Bethlehem, the city of David, that Jesus was born.

When Jesus began his ministry, Jewish society consisted of a fabulously wealthy ruling elite based predominantly at the temple (Sadducees, other priests, Levites, and elders), religious movements promoting strict piety that upheld the status quo (e.g., Pharisees), tax farmers[35] who extorted people for a living, and a browbeaten populace attempting to meet the demands of them all. We must not underestimate the economic disparities and frictions in Jewish society when Jesus began calling people to repent (Mark 1:15). We get

34. The NIV translates Luke 2:3 as "And everyone went to their own town to register." However, the word order in Greek is slightly different, and should be read, "And everyone went to register, each in his own town." The Greek word order leaves open the possibility that most people did not travel to register themselves, but rather did so in the town of their residence—a more logical and logistically plausible process. But Luke has Joseph and Mary travel from Nazareth to Bethlehem—a considerable journey. This seems to be a deliberate choice rather than an inconvenient necessity.

35. Most English versions call them "tax collectors," but this term does not necessarily convey the self-interest of its practitioners or the ingenuity with which they sought to grow their tax base and maximize their takings. They farmed taxes—not just collected them.

a sense of this when the Pharisees and Herodians attempted to trap Jesus by asking, "Is it right to pay the imperial tax to Caesar or not?" (Matt 22:17). They figured that if Jesus admitted it was right, he would put the impoverished masses offside and potentially lose his following. If he claimed it was not right, however, the authorities could legitimately pursue him as a dangerous insurrectionist. The dilemma demonstrated the polarity in Jewish society, but Jesus's response was ingenious: "So give back to Caesar what is Caesar's, and to God what is God's" (Matt 22:21). It was clever not only because Jesus extricated himself from a tight trap, but because it issued a cutting challenge in return. Jesus was not dividing authority into separate worldly and spiritual spheres, as though he were separating "church" and "state." Rather, he was urging his audience to ponder where true authority lay: with Caesar or with God? If they claimed God held true authority, as the Pharisees did, then they would readily give to God what was his, including recognizing Jesus as God's chosen messiah, and repenting in accordance with his message. If they did not do so—if they denied Jesus's status as messiah, and sought to maintain their own power and standing, they would be acknowledging Caesar as the ultimate authority, thus exposing their own treachery and the bankruptcy of their own piety and ethics.

Qohelet, in his day, could barely perceive a difference between the authority of God and the authority of oppressive powers. He observed a world of heart-rending injustice perpetrated by monarchs and magnates, yet acknowledged God's sovereignty over them all. Jesus, however, came to demonstrate that the kingdom of God consists not in the social, political, and economic subjugation of others, but in a transformed world in which grace and love establish justice and peace. In identifying himself as Israel's messiah, Jesus took on the hopes of the oppressed for the nation's salvation—hope that a Davidic descendant would overthrow the heavy yoke upon them and establish a kingdom of justice and peace. This is precisely what the crowds expressed when Jesus entered Jerusalem on a donkey: "Hosanna to the Son of David! Blessed is he who comes in the name of the Lord. Hosanna in the highest!" (Matt 21:9, author's translation). The term "Hosanna" means "To the rescue!" Though the NIV translates the last cry as "Hosanna in the highest heaven," the word "heaven" is not there in the Greek text. The crowds were not expressing a heavenly delight at proceedings or simply praising God but rather willing Jesus on to "the highest" levels of power to rescue them from their languishing plight—to establish God's kingdom above that of Caesar and any other human authority. It was a potent political statement.

Today, we often think that Jewish hopes for the overthrow of the Romans and the oppressive authorities were misguided—that people wanted a political messiah when they should have hoped for a spiritual messiah. Such thinking is actually wrong, for in Jesus's ministry, both the political and spiritual dimensions of Israel's hope came together. Jesus's message about the forgiveness of debts was spiritual in that it entailed forgiveness of sins and turning back to God, but it was also political in that it entailed the cancelling of debts and oppressive demands. Jesus criticized the leadership of his day for their oppressive practices that confined people to lives of hardship and perpetuated meaninglessness. He accused the teachers of the law, for example, of using their demands for piety as a weapon to "devour widows' houses" and witnessed one such widow putting the last two copper coins she had to live on into the temple coffers (Mark 12:40–44). In noting her costly piety, Jesus exposed the villainy of the leadership that desired her sacrifice rather than extended her mercy. He lambasted them for valuing the tokens of oppression—the gold kept in temple coffers and the animals sacrificed on the altar—over the temple itself or the God who dwelt in it, especially when it came to taking oaths (Matt 23:16–22). It is why he urged a member of the Jewish elite not just to follow the commandments of the law but to sell his fortune, give it to the poor, and follow him to Jerusalem. This was not a command to asceticism but an encouragement to join Jesus, overcome selfishness, and undo the ills that harmed so many. Alas, the man was unwilling to part with his wealth, leading Jesus to opine, "How hard it is for the rich to enter the kingdom of God! Indeed, it is easier for a camel to go through the eye of a needle than for someone who is rich to enter the kingdom of God" (Luke 18:18–25). Jesus's message was of profound social, political, and economic significance. Though his kingship was not derived from earthly spheres of power (John 18:36), yet he conquered the world (John 16:33). The means of his conquest was not foreseen, as the authorities dispossessed Jesus of everything and killed him. They embodied the worst excesses Qohelet had observed and lamented centuries earlier. But as Paul notes, "having disarmed the powers and authorities, he [Jesus] made a public spectacle of them, triumphing over them by the cross" (Col 2:15). Jesus conquered all the authorities of this world through his selfless death, receiving the name that is above every name, to which every knee in heaven, on earth, and under the earth will bow and whom all will confess as messiah and lord (Phil 2:6–11).

Jesus's gospel, then, had a sharp social, political, economic, and spiritual edge. It is, indeed, a radical development that one of Jesus's twelve apostles was a repentant tax farmer, Matthew (Matt 9:9–13), who joined the ranks of Peter, Andrew, James, and John, who ran a fishing business that Matthew had almost certainly oppressed. In following Jesus, justice was achieved and these men were reconciled. It is a marvel that Zacchaeus, a tax farmer in the affluent city of Jericho, not only welcomed Jesus into his home but subsequently pledged half his wealth to the poor and promised to pay people back four times the amount he had swindled from them (Luke 19:1–10). It is remarkable that wealthy women like Mary Magdalene, Joanna, and Susanna supported the ministry of Jesus with their own means (Luke 8:2–3).[36] What we see in the lives of these people Jesus impacted is a reordering of society away from forms of oppression that damaged people's lives toward forms of justice and mercy that promoted community and wellbeing. We see the ethic of love at work, which seeks to love God to the fullest capacities, and to love neighbor as self; to move from meaninglessness to meaningfulness. What Qohelet longed to see, but which was patently missing from his world—grace—came through Jesus Christ.

Secular Power Today

This discussion may lead us to ask why, if Jesus now reigns supreme over the kingdom of God, do we continue seeing oppressive regimes and harsh economic conditions in our world? Why did Jesus not dismantle the power of Caesar and displace all who rule corruptly or engage in exploitation? The question picks up the same concerns Qohelet had as he surveyed his world in the third century BC and came away disillusioned, even to the point of indicting God for being seemingly complicit in injustice.

Qohelet did not have the clarity that comes from knowing God's work in Christ. For God's ultimate power is not seen in the use of force that quashes and subjugates but in the work of his Spirit that regenerates, transforms, and unites people to Christ. God, as three persons in perfect loving singular union (Father, Son, and Spirit), is by nature other-person centered. The truest expression of God's nature is not the use of suppressing force, but the active expression of love that promotes the good of others. The kingdom of God, which Jesus inaugurated, is therefore not an external imposition of authority but an internal transformation that expresses itself in love. While Jesus could have annihilated all authority, just as he could have commanded twelve legions of angels to prevent his arrest (Matt 26:53) or had his followers fight for him (John 18:36), he did not. Instead, he revealed to us the inner nature of God, which is perfect love—an inner working of God's Spirit. When the Pharisees asked Jesus when the kingdom of God would come, he replied, "The coming of the kingdom of God is not something that can be observed, nor will people

36. Contrary to popular perception, Mary Magdalene was not a prostitute, but a woman from whom Jesus had driven out seven demons. Luke's mention of her alongside Joanna and Susanna (Luke 8:2–3) shows that she was a woman of considerable wealth, though the nature of this wealth is not explained.

say, 'Here it is,' or 'There it is,' because the kingdom of God is in your midst" (Luke 17:20–21). Thus, Christ has not suppressed all authorities in our world, but he has disarmed them.

Our challenge, therefore, is to proclaim the gospel of Christ by which the Spirit works to transform people. No one is beyond the pale. The gospel leads people into repentance and lives that are in step with the Spirit, promoting the genuine good of all under God. Christians are not to find their identity in power, wealth, or rampant materialism. Rather, they are to find their identity in union with Christ, recognizing that the Christian life is not merely spiritual but also social, political, and economic. Like Jesus, we are to seek to love others genuinely from the heart, overcoming injustice, oppression, and degradation through the proclamation of the gospel and loving works of service. This does not mean Christians cannot hold positions of secular power, produce wealth, or own assets. Rather, Christians are to recognize that these things do not transform people into lovers of God and humanity. It is the Spirit of God working through the proclamation of Christ alone that does this. The love that comes from this is both disarming and transformative. It disarms us, transforming us from enemies of God into reconciled children of God, and compels us to love others by proclaiming and living out the gospel of love.

Taxation and Financial Systems

The adage says that there are only two certainties in life: death and taxes. For Qohelet, the two barely seemed separate. His context involved ruinous taxation that made life for many utterly miserable. Under similar conditions, Jesus called tax farmers to repentance, with the likes of Matthew and Zacchaeus complying. This raises the issue of how Christians should approach taxation today. Taxation in the ancient world worked differently than the way it works today. In the modern world, taxation is a means by which money is collected from the population to fund government and public works, like social welfare, infrastructure, education, defense, and the like, which generally benefit most people. This is different from the ancient world, in which taxation was a way that rulers took money from populations as a form of recognizing their authority. Funds came to rulers directly, who then used them as they saw fit. Sometimes this included public works, but more often than not, taxes simply enriched the powerful. Moreover, tax farmers extracted more taxes than the authorities required, pocketing the surplus for themselves and leaving taxpayers with little for making ends meet. In fact, it often left people destitute.

While nobody enjoys paying taxes, we should appreciate the way taxation systems today seek to benefit the public rather than beggar people. It is not the level of taxation that matters so much as the benefit that accrues from it.

The Christian ethic of love, in which we give for the genuine benefit of others, should motivate us to honesty and obligation toward our neighbors so that we willingly pay our dues.

It should also enable us to evaluate the financial systems of our respective contexts. Many of us live in democracies, where we have the ability to criticize, protest, vote, and seek change. We should not evaluate these systems purely from motives of self-interest. The transformative work of the Spirit should motivate us to evaluate our financial systems, whether they be governmental, corporate, or household, with the best interests of others in mind. This is often difficult, especially when it hurts our own hip pocket. But our love of God and neighbor must compel us in this regard. It should also embolden us to call out instances of injustice and oppression in financial systems, such as wasteful spending, abuse of labor, irresponsible lending, mismanagement of resources, and even gambling. It should also compel us to seek change in oppressive regimes that do not have the interests of citizens at heart. The gospel teaches us that people matter more than economics. It calls us to live responsibly and intelligently, but above all, lovingly.

CHAPTER 5

Ecclesiastes 6:7–8:1

LISTEN to the Story

7Everyone's toil is for their mouth,
yet their appetite is never satisfied.
8What advantage have the wise over fools?
What do the poor gain
by knowing how to conduct themselves before others?
9Better what the eye sees
than the roving of the appetite.
This too is meaningless,
a chasing after the wind.
10Whatever exists has already been named,
and what humanity is has been known;
no one can contend
with someone who is stronger.
11The more the words,
the less the meaning,
and how does that profit anyone?

12For who knows what is good for a person in life, during the few and
meaningless days they pass through like a shadow? Who can tell them what
will happen under the sun after they are gone?

7:1A good name is better than fine perfume,
and the day of death better than the day of birth.
2It is better to go to a house of mourning
than to go to a house of feasting,
for death is the destiny of everyone;
the living should take this to heart.
3Frustration is better than laughter,
because a sad face is good for the heart.

4The heart of the wise is in the house of mourning,
but the heart of fools is in the house of pleasure.
5It is better to heed the rebuke of a wise person
than to listen to the song of fools.
6Like the crackling of thorns under the pot,
so is the laughter of fools.
This too is meaningless.
7Extortion turns a wise person into a fool,
and a bribe corrupts the heart.
8The end of a matter is better than its beginning,
and patience is better than pride.
9Do not be quickly provoked in your spirit,
for anger resides in the lap of fools.
10Do not say, "Why were the old days better than these?"
For it is not wise to ask such questions.
11Wisdom, like an inheritance, is a good thing
and benefits those who see the sun.
12Wisdom is a shelter
as money is a shelter,
but the advantage of knowledge is this:
Wisdom preserves those who have it.

13Consider what God has done:

Who can straighten
what he has made crooked?
14When times are good, be happy;
but when times are bad, consider this:
God has made the one
as well as the other.
Therefore, no one can discover
anything about their future.

15In this meaningless life of mine I have seen both of these:

the righteous perishing in their righteousness,
and the wicked living long in their wickedness.
16Do not be overrighteous,

neither be overwise—
why destroy yourself?
17Do not be overwicked,
and do not be a fool—
why die before your time?
18It is good to grasp the one
and not let go of the other.
Whoever fears God will avoid all extremes.
19Wisdom makes one wise person more powerful
than ten rulers in a city.
20Indeed, there is no one on earth who is righteous,
no one who does what is right and never sins.
21Do not pay attention to every word people say,
or you may hear your servant cursing you—
22for you know in your heart
that many times you yourself have cursed others.

23All this I tested by wisdom and I said,

"I am determined to be wise"—
but this was beyond me.
24Whatever exists is far off and most profound—
who can discover it?
25So I turned my mind to understand,
to investigate and to search out wisdom and the scheme of things
and to understand the stupidity of wickedness
and the madness of folly.
26I find more bitter than death
the woman who is a snare,
whose heart is a trap
and whose hands are chains.
The man who pleases God will escape her,
but the sinner she will ensnare.

27"Look," says the Teacher, "this is what I have discovered:

"Adding one thing to another to discover the scheme of things—
28while I was still searching

but not finding—
I found one upright man among a thousand,
but not one upright woman among them all.
29 This only have I found:
God created mankind upright,
but they have gone in search of many schemes."
8:1 Who is like the wise?
Who knows the explanation of things?
A person's wisdom brightens their face
and changes its hard appearance.

Listening to the Story in the Text: Deuteronomy 27–28; 1 Kings 11; Lamentations 5; Job 28; Proverbs 7; Josephus, *Antiquities* 12.160–85

In this next portion of his discourse, Qohelet weighs up conventional wisdom and orthodoxy. To understand the texture of his rhetoric, we need to keep the covenantal dynamic of the law in mind. Simply put, it sees God blessing the righteous and punishing the wicked. To be righteous was not merely about being generically moral but, more specifically, about following the customs and meeting the standards stipulated in God's law. This made someone righteous—that is, it gave one the right to continue as a member of the covenantal community of Israel. To be wicked was to disobey or disregard these customs and standards and so imperil one's standing within covenantal Israel or put oneself outside it completely. Deuteronomy 27–28 lays out the respective blessings and curses for obedience and disobedience. The essential difference was that God granted success and prosperity to the righteous but meted out punishment to the wicked. Thus, the righteous could expect to have healthy children surviving to adulthood, healthy livestock, successful harvests, full barns, and security from enemies. These blessings combined the natural outworking of an orderly society following good laws, as well as the divine reward for concerted obedience. The wicked, on the other hand, could expect short life expectancy, disease, drought, foreign invasion, and ultimately ejection from the land God had given Israel.

There were some shining moments in Israel's history, the age of Solomon being perhaps the pinnacle. But the Old Testament tells the story of the people's wickedness, and not even Solomon was immune from this. First Kings 11 describes how his harem of a thousand women led him astray into idolatry. Ultimately, the nation endured hardship and judgment and was exiled from the land—first the northern kingdom in 723 BC, and then Judah in 597 BC and 586 BC.

The book of Lamentations is a collection of five poems expressing the trauma of Jerusalem's fall to the Babylonians in 586 BC. The final poem (Lam 5) is especially poignant for this next section of Qohelet's discourse. It describes the hardship of living under foreign oppression:

> Our inheritance has been turned over to strangers,
> our homes to foreigners. . . .
> We must buy the water we drink;
> our wood can be had only at a price. . . .
> We submitted to Egypt and Assyria
> to get enough bread.
> Our ancestors sinned and are no more,
> and we bear their punishment.
> Slaves rule over us,
> and there is no one to free us from their hands. . . .
> The crown has fallen from our head.
> Woe to us, for we have sinned!
> Because of this our hearts are faint,
> because of these things our eyes grow dim
> for Mount Zion, which lies desolate,
> with jackals prowling over it.
> You, LORD, reign forever;
> your throne endures from generation to generation.
> Why do you always forget us?
> Why do you forsake us so long?
> Restore us to yourself, LORD, that we may return;
> renew our days as of old
> unless you have utterly rejected us
> and are angry with us beyond measure. (Lam 5:2, 4, 6–8, 16–22)

The pain of the poet is palpable. The "inheritance" (Heb: *nahalah*) he refers to (Lam 5:2) is rich with the significance of Israel's life under God. It is the term used to describe Israel as the "property" of Yahweh (cf. Deut 4:20; 9:29; 1 Kgs 8:51, 53). It describes the land of Israel, which God gave his people as their "property" (Deut 4:21; 12:9). It also describes the "share" or vested interest that people had in the Davidic dynasty, which the northern tribes renounced when the nation fractured (1 Kgs 12:16; cf. 2 Sam 20:1). The poet claims that all this was lost when Jerusalem fell in 586 BC. In describing the crown that "has fallen from our head," he alludes to the downfall of the Davidic dynasty. This contrasts with the reality of now living under foreign rule and leads the poet to urge God, whose throne is eternal, to act to restore them. The poet also contemplates the frightening possibility that God has permanently rejected the nation. Indeed, this is the logical outcome of the covenantal dynamic. Wickedness leads to God's rejection of the nation and its eviction from his land. Now, some three centuries after the kingdom's downfall, Qohelet still lived in the ambivalence of this rejection. Though parts of the nation had returned to the land, and Qohelet himself appears to be a resident in Jerusalem, they were still under foreign rule. Qohelet, a son of David, was not a king on a throne, but a plebeian who could only pretend to be a king—powerless to effect any change.

Qohelet also appraises conventional wisdom in this upcoming section. Job 28 provides a good foil for Qohelet's discourse. It is a poem that interrupts the flow of exchange between a suffering Job and his three "friends." It compares the pursuit of wisdom to the mining of gems and precious metals. Humans must go to extreme lengths to extract the minerals from the ground, and yet it can be done. "But," the poem asks, "where can wisdom be found? Where does understanding dwell?" (Job 28:12). It finds wisdom elusive because it is of such great value. "It cannot be bought with the finest gold, nor can its price be weighed out in silver" (Job 28:15). Nevertheless, the poem claims wisdom dwells with God alone, who declares to humanity, "The fear of the Lord—that is wisdom, and to shun evil is understanding" (Job 28:28). Thus, the poem aligns wisdom with the classic expressions of it elsewhere (cf. Prov 1:7; 3:5–18). Qohelet also mentions the wily woman who ensnares men (Eccl 7:26)—an allusion to the classic wisdom motif of the adulterous woman. Proverbs 7 is perhaps the best extended treatment of this motif. It depicts a married woman cunningly seducing a young man while her husband is away. "Her house is a highway to the grave, leading down to the chambers of death," the proverbial father figure warns his son (Prov 7:27). Qohelet will have opportunity to ponder this motif in light of his observations about the pervasiveness of human sinfulness, leading to some confronting claims about conventional wisdom and orthodoxy.

EXPLAIN the Story

The Limits of Wisdom (6:7–8:1)

After observing the cruel injustices of his world in the previous section, Qohelet now turns to reevaluate the utility of wisdom (cf. 7:23). Wisdom is meant to provide guidance by discerning what is "good" and what is "bad." On the one hand, Qohelet acknowledges that wisdom does sometimes prove useful. However, he finds wisdom often limited or in need of correction. Life in Qohelet's world is so tumultuous and makes so little sense, wisdom does not provide the ultimate answers to life that he desires. The cognitive turmoil this produces in Qohelet now begins to tie him in philosophical knots. Indeed, many of his statements in this next section are confusing, sometimes contradictory, and even nonsensical. This has caused much angst for commentators seeking to discern a singular line of reasoning here from Qohelet, especially if they judge that reasoning to be at one with conventional wisdom.[1] It has led some to hammer Qohelet's statements into an orthodox shape that denies the more critical and skeptical aspects of his discourse. But Qohelet is deliberately giving mixed signals—a jumble of positive and negative statements that all ring true, but which leave him lamenting the possibility of making sense of life. Indeed, the confusion of it all demonstrates the essential motto of his monologue: "Everything is meaningless!"

Deconstructing Conventional Wisdom (6:7–12)

Qohelet's staggering statement that the stillborn child is better off than the long-lived man surrounded by family (6:3–6) is cause for further reflection on life. For, unlike the stillborn, Qohelet's readers are very much alive "under the sun" and in need of guidance to cope with life's grievous evils. Proverbs are often useful means of capturing the hums of life in punchy quips. They represent wise ways of understanding and responding to the world. So, in 6:7–12, Qohelet takes some of them and intermingles them with rhetorical questions. Qohelet's purpose is not to confirm the conventional wisdom of proverbs but to correct it subtly in light of his observations. This was the kind of activity Qohelet was known for in life (12:9). Consequently, the proverbs take on new shades of meaning that reflect his dim view of life and echo the sentiments in his introduction (1:2–11).

The first proverb in 6:7 captures the essence of the never-ending nature of work. Everyone needs to eat, so they work. But people always need to eat, for the appetite is never finally satisfied, so work must always continue. In isolation, the proverb neutrally portrays the cyclical connection between work and eating. It could even be taken as motivation for work, but in Qohelet's discourse the proverb signals a life of drudgery and degradation. The prospects for most people in Qohelet's world are to "eat in darkness, with great frustration, affliction, and anger" (5:17) because of oppression. The ongoing

1. See, for example, Greidanus, *Preaching Christ from Ecclesiastes*, 160–61.

need to work, therefore, exposes the average person to the avarice of the elite. The elite also need to eat, so their oppression of the dispossessed masses will continue. And yet, the elite will, in turn, fail to find satisfaction in their amassed wealth, leading to still more oppression of the poor. Qohelet uses the proverb to characterize the life of both the poor and the rich. Like the never-ending cycles of the sun, winds, and rivers (1:5–7), which accentuate the meaninglessness of human existence, Qohelet sees all people trapped in a constant rhythm of futility.

So, there is no advantage for the wise person over the fool, and the perceptive poor will achieve nothing through their perception (6:8). Qohelet's rhetorical questions in 6:8 show that all people, regardless of their station in life or personal savvy, are ensnared at one point or another in life's cycle of drudgery and degradation. There is a further kick in this verse. Since Qohelet has taken what seems to be a popular proverb (6:7) and realigned it to his pessimistic outlook, he is once again critiquing conventional wisdom. The wise person has no advantage over the fool, because conventional wisdom needs correction.

Qohelet proves his point again in 6:9. He quotes another proverb: "Better what the eye sees than the roving of the appetite." The saying implies that a person should be content with what is before them rather than greedily craving what they do not have, for the latter might lead them into strife. But in 5:11 Qohelet demonstrates the sinister wastefulness of the Ptolemaic elite who obtained wealth by seizing the assets of others and accumulated so much wealth that they could not possibly use it all. Instead, all they could do was "feast their eyes" on it (5:11). Despite this, their hunger for more wealth was never satisfied. Even if the privileged of Ptolemaic society were content with what they could see, this would still amount to considerable robbery of the underprivileged and scandalous wastefulness. The proverb, therefore, fails to impart advice that adequately responds to the ills in Qohelet's world. His observations to this point deconstruct this proverb, which leads him to conclude, "This too is meaningless, a chasing after the wind" (6:9b).

The beginning of 6:10 is essentially a rewording of 1:9, in which Qohelet stated that "there is nothing new under the sun," because "what has been will be again." When put with the second half of the verse, which observes that the weak cannot contend with the strong, Qohelet's emerging point is that no one should expect the world to change. The injustice, oppression, and hardship within Ptolemaic society are nothing new. They simply reveal the darker structures of the human heart. They are, therefore, here to stay as a permanent fixture of human life. The Hebrew word Qohelet uses to describe the weak "contending" (*din*) with the strong has a legal connotation, which means Qohelet is alluding to the futile attempts of people to prevent officially sanctioned exploitation, like that which Zenon and Joseph Tobias engaged in. But there is, again, a subtle indictment of God, who is *the* strongest of all, who oversees the times and controls the course of human history. As much as Qohelet wants to change the pitiful plight of people, he knows he does not pull the strings. God ultimately does, and Qohelet does not see God changing things any time soon.

In Qohelet's estimation, therefore, conventional wisdom, which seeks to apprehend the world and provide guidance, does not really do much. If everything is meaningless (*hebel*), all that wisdom does, as it proliferates words, is to proliferate meaninglessness (6:11). Qohelet finds conventional wisdom of no substantive benefit. It cannot recommend anything truly good for humanity, whose existence is ultimately meaningless, nor can it provide hope for the future, since nothing ultimately changes (6:12).

Devaluing Conventional Wisdom (7:1–14)

After starting to deconstruct conventional wisdom, Qohelet continues the endeavor in 7:1–14. Seow demonstrates how the keywords and sentiments of 6:10–12 are the same as those in 7:10–14. This connection comes out more obviously in the Hebrew vocabulary:[2]

6:10 "Whatever exists . . ." (*mah-shehaya*)	7:10 "Why were . . . ?" (*meh hayah*)
6:10 "no one can . . ." (*lo' yukal*)	7:13 "Who can . . . ?" (*mi yukal*)
6:11 "profit . . ." (*yoter*)	7:11 "benefits . . ." (*yoter*)
6:12 "a shadow . . ." (*tsel*)	7:12 "a shelter . . ." (*tsel*)
6:12 "after they are . . ." (*aharayw*)	7:14 "their future . . ." (*aharayw*)

The similarities show Qohelet questioning whether anyone can make such sense of the world that their future might consist of hope rather than a dismal expectation of shadowy darkness. He is, however, skeptical to the point of despondency. Thus, like in 6:7–12, Qohelet here (7:1–14) deconstructs wisdom. Throughout the section he states what is "good" or "better" in life (7:1, 2, 3, 5, 8, 10, 11, 14; cf. 6:9, 12), which is the classic aim of wisdom. However, he now starts coining his own anti-proverbs. There are some deeply

2. The table is adapted from Seow, *Ecclesiastes*, 241. Seow sees the verses as the beginning and end of one unit (6:10–7:14), whereas I have understood them as the respective ends of two sections of similar purpose (6:7–12 and 7:1–14).

discouraging moments here when his wisdom becomes something of a dark and farcical art. It is, however, all part of his attempt to realign wisdom to his pessimistic outlook.

He begins by quoting a short and beautifully crafted proverb: "A good name is better than fine perfume" (7:1a). In Hebrew, the sounds slip pleasantly from the lips: *tob shem mishemen tob*. The similarity between the words for "name" (*shem*) and "perfume" (*shemen* [literally, "oil"), along with the mirror structure they produce, make for a lovely sounding statement whose aesthetics demonstrate the comparison being made. The proverb echoes conventional wisdom motifs pertaining to the value of a good reputation (cf. Prov 22:1; Song 1:3). Given the economic hardships he has observed in his world, this proverb might encourage Qohelet's readers to take a stoic approach and invest their hopes in the more intangible assets of morality and reputation. However, Qohelet then thumps this proverb on the head with an anti-proverb: "the day of death is better than the day of birth" (7:1b). As Seow notes, this statement "is without parallel anywhere in the wisdom literature of the ancient Near East."[3] It is a proverb of Qohelet's own making. He is not claiming that pondering one's death is wiser than pondering one's birth.[4] Rather, it is a stark assertion that death is better than life, extending Qohelet's arresting claim that the champion of human existence is the stillborn child (6:3–6). It is as though Qohelet takes to the initial proverb in 7:1a with a blunt instrument, beating the beauty out of it. The realities of his world make a good name of little value. In fact, "a bribe corrupts the heart" (7:8), which effectively makes a good name a mere commodity that can be traded, just like fine perfume. It can be used, and then it is gone.

Qohelet continues to wallow in morose thoughts by advising that the house of mourning is better than the house of feasting or pleasure (7:2, 4). Again, this is not about imparting wise sobriety but about desiring death, which, after all, is everyone's destiny. In stating that "the living should take this to heart" (7:2), Qohelet is not advising his readers to reflect on death deeply so that they might live more wisely. The expression Qohelet uses here is literally "to give one's heart to something." It can have the sense of desiring—of doing what the heart wants. Qohelet used the same expression in 1:13, where he expressed his desire to examine and explore wisdom. He was not saying that he was *pondering* the examination and exploration of wisdom but that he *wanted* to examine and explore wisdom, so he applied himself to it. Thus, Qohelet is here actively encouraging his readers to want death. This also helps

3. Ibid., 244.
4. So Greidanus, *Preaching Christ from Ecclesiastes*, 161.

explain why he finds frustration better than laughter (7:3). He says that it is because "a sad face is good for the heart." This initially seems absurd, and the temptation is to read this also as an encouragement to sober thought that enables one to appreciate life and live it more wisely. However, this is out of step with Qohelet's macabre reasoning, which lifts the experience of the stillborn child above all others (6:3–6). For Qohelet, a sad face is good for the heart, for it leads to the heart desiring death (7:2). It is the heart of fools that desires feasting and pleasure (7:2, 4), which commits them to participating in a world that is brutally depraved. This is not about salvaging the meager enjoyment of the basics of life that Qohelet has advised previously (2:24; 3:13; 5:18), but a heady and futile pursuit of the wind. Qohelet likens the laughter of such fools to the crackling of thorns (*sirim*) beneath a pot (*sir*) on the boil (7:6); the noise is indicative of its own destruction.

When we perceive the "rhetoric of subversion"[5] that Qohelet employs here, we can discern the skillful use of ambiguity throughout 7:5–12. On the surface of it, 7:5 seems to be a conventional proverb: "It is better to heed the rebuke of a wise person than to listen to the song of fools" (7:5). It echoes the kind of wisdom found in Proverbs 13:18 and 15:31–32, which places value on constructive criticism. But the wording in Hebrew allows for an ambiguity: "the rebuke of a wise person" may be understood subjectively as "a wise person who rebukes another" or objectively as "someone who rebukes a wise person." Since Qohelet is himself upending conventional wisdom with critiques and anti-proverbs, it seems more in line with his purpose to entertain the less conventional undertone here. Indeed, this demonstrates again what the later editor affirmed about Qohelet correcting proverbs (12:9). He takes what seems to be an ordinary, orthodox proverb and subverts it. In this way, Qohelet equates conventional wisdom with the "song" and "laughter of fools," which is itself equated with burning kindling (7:5–6).

This matches Qohelet's statement in 7:7, that "extortion turns a wise person into a fool." The word for "extortion" here is the same word Qohelet uses in 5:8[5:7] for economic "oppression" (*'osheq*). Furthermore, the verb that the NIV translates as "turn into a fool" is the word behind Qohelet's discussion of "madness" or, more accurately, "ignorance" in 1:17 and 2:2. Thus, a more literal rendering of 7:7a is "For oppression makes a wise man ignorant." This statement also carries an ambiguity. In the conventional sense, it acknowledges that a wise person can "fall from grace" by engaging in criminal practices that reveal their own folly or ignorance. On the subversive level, it asserts that a world in which oppression is the norm is a world in which conventional

5. Seow, *Ecclesiastes*, 244.

wisdom is rendered useless. In both meanings, wisdom's shortcoming is demonstrated: wisdom does not prevent anyone oppressing others or from being oppressed.

Further subversion occurs in 7:8a: "The end of a matter is better than its beginning." On the surface of it, this expresses conventional wisdom that encourages seeing a task through to completion. But since Qohelet has stated that the day of death is better than the day of birth (7:1), he is again deconstructing wisdom by implying death is better than life.

The second half of the verse (7:8b) has some affinity to the first in that it encourages patience (literally, "length of spirit") over pride (literally, "height of spirit"). This sounds like it is urging the kind of persistence that the conventional understanding of 7:8a describes. The NIV's insertion of "and" at the beginning of 7:8b seems to confirm this, but the conjunction is not present in Hebrew. Instead, 7:8b starts abruptly and picks up the vocabulary of 7:9. Once again, Qohelet is subverting convention. He is encouraging those who would reject his deconstruction of conventional wisdom not to be haughty or rankled by it, for such a response "resides in the lap of fools" (7:9b). In this way, Qohelet continues to align traditional wisdom with folly, both being inadequate for making sense of a mad world.

This brazen caricature of wisdom becomes sardonic and even sarcastic in 7:10–12. The conventional meaning of 7:10 is that it is unwise to pine for the past, since it does not aid in dealing with the present or the future. Yet wisdom itself draws on past experience to provide guidance for the future. Wisdom is tradition: the lingering voice of dead sages. By labeling such backward glancing unwise, Qohelet once again calls into question wisdom's utility. But he is also calling into question all of Israel's orthodoxy. To ask about "the old days" is to ask about Israel's history—about the covenant between Yahweh and the nation at Sinai; about the laws that were to guide his people; about the pledges to David of a permanent dynasty in Jerusalem; and about promises of restoration and regathering to the land. These were all features of Israel's heritage that Qohelet, as a Jew, and, even more so, as a descendant of David, owned. By judging it unwise to pine for them, Qohelet was resigning himself to the probability that they were gone forever. The barbarity of the Ptolemaic world in which Qohelet lived had taken the nation so far from its moorings that Qohelet considered it unwise to ponder them any further. This was not because he deemed God's law or promises to be ill-conceived, but because circumstances had all but drowned any hope of recovering past glories, and it was impossible to know what God was doing in history (cf. 3:11). So, in deconstructing conventional wisdom, Qohelet was also deconstructing prophetic hope.

The sarcasm comes in 7:11, where Qohelet again exploits ambiguities. If we are primed to hear conventional wisdom, we will read this as a proverb: "Wisdom, like an inheritance, is a good thing and benefits those who see the sun." However, this stands at odds with Qohelet's claim that there is nothing new under the sun and that it is all meaningless anyway (1:9, 14). The wording in Hebrew is also unusual, which means the conventional meaning is not an easy fit. It literally reads, "Wisdom is good with property, and a benefit to those who see the sun." "Property" (*nahalah*), which the NIV translates here as "inheritance," refers to an estate—goods and land that can be passed from father to son. As we have seen elsewhere, it was the Ptolemaic elite, like Apollonius, treasurer of Ptolemy II, who owned such estates, and this often came to them by forcible seizure (cf. 5:8, 13–14; 6:1–2). Thus, at one level, Qohelet is sarcastically claiming that wisdom does indeed have value, but only if one is still in possession of their own assets rather than struggling to cope in the face of economic savagery.

On a deeper level, the word *nahalah* picks up all the associations of Israel's life under God—of being Yahweh's covenant nation, being in his land, and sharing in the Davidic dynasty that he had installed over Israel. When we perceive the historic significance of this term, Qohelet's statement falls into line with the previous verse: the past glory is gone. Israel was now scattered across various lands, subject to foreign dynasties, even within the land God had once given them, and no longer in control of their own "property." As such, it could barely retain its own status as God's "property." The term was essentially meaningless now. Perhaps most poignantly for Qohelet, a son of David, the nation no longer had any "share" in the Davidic dynasty. Israel was now lost "property," and Qohelet was part of a lost dynasty. Lamentations 5, penned at the fall of Jerusalem in 586 BC, captures the pain of this loss. "Our inheritance has been turned over to strangers, our homes to foreigners" (Lam 5:2). Qohelet stands with similar pain but expresses it with acerbic sarcasm. Conventional wisdom would be useful to people if Israel was still in possession of its own "property." Alas, it was not, and Qohelet was not their king. This is another subtle jibe at the baffling nature of God's will.

This next verse (7:12) has difficult syntax in Hebrew. To make sense of it, we must leverage the sentiment of Qohelet's previous statements, the parallel connections to 6:10–12 that Seow identifies (mentioned above),[6] and Qohelet's historical context. The NIV translates the first part as "Wisdom is a shelter, as money is a shelter." This conveys the structure of Qohelet's statement, in which he appears to place wisdom on the same level as money

6. Ibid., 241.

(literally, "silver"). This is not, as Fredericks claims, a positive assessment of wisdom and assets in the great Solomonic tradition.[7] On the contrary, it is supremely subversive, since conventional wisdom places the value of wisdom far above silver. Job 28, the great poem on the value of wisdom, concludes, "the price of wisdom is beyond rubies" (Job 28:18). In terms of conventional thought, then, Qohelet is devaluing the price of wisdom. Once again, he has coined an anti-proverb that effectively states, "Like wisdom, like money!" This does not mean he sees wisdom as worthless, but rather as just another commodity, like fine perfume (cf. Eccl 7:1) or, here, silver. He describes the practical "value" (NIV: "advantage") of wisdom in the second half of the verse: "Wisdom preserves those who have it." Once again, this sounds like conventional wisdom, but since Qohelet has just devalued it to the same price as silver, he is highlighting its limitations. The phrase literally reads, "Wisdom keeps its owners alive." In a cruel world like the Ptolemaic kingdom, where money talks, money is the wisdom that can be traded to keep people alive. The prominent citizens who fell afoul of the ruthless tax farmer, Joseph Tobias, failed to keep themselves alive by refusing to hand their money over to him (*Ant.* 12.180–85). As Qohelet has claimed earlier, death is preferable to life in this kind of world, anyway. Wisdom, therefore, is a tradable commodity that should lead its owner to surrender his money to another in order to save his own life. Yet, that is ultimately undesirable anyway. It certainly does nothing to change Qohelet's world. Wisdom would be useful if he (and Israel more broadly) had more control over their world and possessed their own "property" (7:11). Alas, they do not.

Qohelet's discourse throughout this section has been full of dark thoughts, even to the point of championing death over life. However, this is not a satisfactory philosophy on life, and nor is it Qohelet's real purpose. Qohelet does not actually want to esteem death more highly than life. Rather, he is engaging in the classic rhetorical strategy of *reductio ad absurdum*—a means of demonstrating the absurdity of a situation by taking it to its logical extremes. When the extreme is seen to be absurd, the flaws of the original situation are exposed. Qohelet uses it here as a shock tactic. It lets him express his deep dissatisfaction with the world by exposing its depravity, demonstrating the limitations of conventional wisdom, and revealing how little humans know and control in life. Indeed, a situation in which death appears more attractive than life is not an argument for the goodness of death but of the dire and desperate nature of the situation. Thus, amid the depressing claims and anti-proverbs, we must hear Qohelet's pained cry for things to be different.

7. Fredericks and Estes, *Ecclesiastes & the Song of Songs*, 172–73.

Unfortunately, Qohelet concludes that wisdom cannot change the harsh reality of the world in which he lives. In 7:13 he reiterates his claim from 1:15 ("What is crooked cannot be straight" [author's translation]), but he now makes God the overt subject, couching the idea in a rhetorical question: "Consider what God has done: Who can straighten what he has made crooked?" Tellingly, he depicts God as making things crooked—another subtle accusation that God, whose sovereignty is uncontestable, is ultimately responsible for bending the world out of shape. And so Qohelet returns to a form of his advice to enjoy the basics of life. He encourages his readers to enjoy the good times while they last (7:14a). Once again, this is not *carpe diem* optimism but acknowledgement that humans are not in control of their own destinies. God makes both the good times and the bad (7:14b), so no matter what humans might do, or how much wisdom they profess, they cannot "straighten" God's seemingly "crooked" purposes. Rather, humans are better off resigning themselves to whatever God decides to impose on them, and if this includes a fleeting moment of goodness, it should be enjoyed while it lasts.

The Limits of Orthodoxy and Wisdom (7:15–24)

To this point, Qohelet has concluded that, though the rich and the poor live differently, their lives are both ultimately miserable and meaningless. He has also confirmed that there is no practical difference between the wise and the foolish. Thus, economics and wisdom do not provide the meaning Qohelet desires in life, and they certainly do not change anything. This leads him now to turn down another avenue and test whether there is a meaningful difference between another set of people: the righteous and the wicked.

The covenantal dynamic of the law is important for framing Qohelet's words here. God demands that his people actively pursue righteousness and shun evil, which will result in blessing. Wickedness, on the other hand, leads to hardship, judgment, foreign oppression, and exile. When Qohelet looks at his society, however, he sees righteous people perishing and the wicked prospering (7:15). He observes the covenantal dynamic turned upside-down. His observations may reflect the fate of Joseph Tobias's victims, the hardship experienced by so many Jews under the backbreaking tax regime imposed by the Ptolemies, as well as the longevity and lifestyle of the Ptolemies and their lackeys, like the Tobiads.[8] This observation leaves Qohelet in a deep quandary. He knows God demands righteousness, yet righteousness seems to

8. Ptolemy I, the general of Alexander the Great who established the Ptolemaic kingdom, lived to the ripe old age of eighty-four (367–283 BC). Yet, he perpetrated numerous atrocities, including his conquest of Jerusalem in 301 BC. Ptolemy II lived to the age of sixty-three (309–246 BC), which was still a significant lifespan in the ancient world.

attract punishment while wickedness is ostensibly rewarded.[9] Should one be righteous because God demands it, but risk dying young, or should one flout God's demands and risk his punishment, but then perhaps live a long life?

Qohelet evidently feels trapped here, as he discerns a risk in both what the law commands as well as what it condemns. He has burst an orthodox "bubble" through his observations, and yet, as a pious Jew, he does not wish to contravene God's law. In fact, being afraid of God, Qohelet does not want to risk his displeasure. God had exiled his covenant people from their land for wickedness, rendering them subservient to foreign overlords—a situation from which they had not really recovered. Life in Ptolemaic Judea was hard enough for the average person without "poking the bear" through unrighteous behavior. Qohelet's ethical dilemma sees humanity trapped by God's unpredictable behavior, leaving him feeling that it is impossible to win in life. He simply wants to know if there is a safe way to live.

His ensuing advice in 7:16–18 is absurd, and is meant to be understood as such. He says, "Don't be overrighteous" (7:15) and "Don't be overwicked" (7:17). When cast in the light of the law, these statements are farcical, and amount to an anti-proverb. To fully appreciate this, we may state his advice by its corollaries: "Be slightly righteous," and "Be slightly wicked." Qohelet is not cautioning against self-righteousness[10] or hubris.[11] He uses the same word for "righteous" (*tsadiq*) here (7:16) as the one in his initial observation (7:15), so there is no shift in meaning. Fredericks argues that not being overrighteous means "one should not deceive oneself in thinking that a long life can be assured . . . by extending oneself beyond one's means."[12] But this is precisely the dilemma that Qohelet encounters in 7:15. If God demands righteousness through obedience to the law, and yet the righteous perish before their time, what real value does righteousness have? There is "an inversion of justice."[13] Restating the dilemma does not solve the dilemma. Besides, the law urges Israel to "Love the LORD your God with all your heart and with all your soul and with all your strength" (Deut 6:5). Qohelet is proposing that this be scaled back, which says volumes about the problems he perceives with God's ways. Neither is Qohelet talking about moderating one's expectations to avoid being

9. It's impossible to know if Qohelet had this specific example of the righteous suffering unjustly in mind, but it demonstrates the point nonetheless. In Qohelet's day, the righteous suffered terribly at the hands of the wicked.

10. Contra George R. Castellino and Roy B. Zuck, "Qohelet and His Wisdom," in *Reflecting with Solomon*, 39–40; Whybray, *Ecclesiastes*, 120–21.

11. Contra Iain W. Provan, *Ecclesiastes, Song of Songs*, NIV Application Commentary (Grand Rapids: Zondervan, 2001), 152.

12. Fredericks and Estes, *Ecclesiastes & the Song of Songs*, 175.

13. Shields, *The End of Wisdom*, 181.

frustrated or appalled at what one sees.[14] He is advising specific behaviors. In commanding his readers not to be overwicked, Qohelet is not acknowledging that "everyone has an amount of evil within them."[15] Even though he goes on to acknowledge that fact in 7:20, he is issuing a command here, not making an indicative observation. Therefore, we cannot agree with Fredericks' summary that "Qoheleth's presuppositions are consistent, then, with traditional biblical theology: be righteous; be wise; do not be wicked; do not be foolish."[16] On the contrary, traditional biblical theology "implies Israel should use all its energies to be loyal to Yahweh their God. This leaves no room for negligence or half-heartedness."[17] As the great poem on wisdom, Job 28, states, "The fear of the Lord—that is wisdom, and to shun evil is understanding" (Job 28:28). Qohelet's advice here is a far cry from this.[18]

The absurdity of Qohelet's commands is, however, not to be taken literally. Rather, it is another example of *reductio ad absurdum*—taking a situation to its logical extreme to highlight its flaws. Just as he has critiqued conventional wisdom, he is now critiquing orthodoxy. Qohelet's commands assume the validity of the law, but he demonstrates how orthodoxy and conventional wisdom do not map easily onto the world. To think they do is not only simplistic, but sometimes absurd. If one tries to align orthodoxy with the world, as conventional wisdom does, one can only come to the conclusions that Qohelet does here: one should avoid extreme righteousness and extreme wickedness. Instead, one should "hedge bets" by aiming for medium-righteousness and medium-wickedness—a kind of "path of least resistance" (cf. 11:2). This completely unorthodox conclusion is not one that Qohelet intends to stand by. Rather, it demonstrates three points. First, humans should be frightened of a seemingly inconsistent God who demands one thing but ostensibly dishes out another (7:18). This is a position of extreme discomfort, which pitches the orthodox view of God against the observable reality of the world. Second, despite the stipulated covenantal dynamic, "it is impossible for anyone to know what the ultimate outcome of his or her behavior will be" (7:14).[19] Third, if there are no guaranteed outcomes for either righteousness or wickedness, then there is no practical difference between the two, which

---

14. Peter Enns, *Ecclesiastes*, Two Horizons Old Testament Commentary (Grand Rapids: Eerdmans, 2011), 84.

15. Fredericks and Estes, *Ecclesiastes & the Song of Songs*, 175. Cf. Roger N. Whybray, "Qoheleth the Immoralist? (Qoh 7:16–17)," in *Israelite Wisdom: Theological and Literary Essays in Honor of Samuel Terrien*, ed. John G. Gammie (Missoula, MT: Scholars Press, 1978), 197.

16. Fredericks and Estes, *Ecclesiastes & the Song of Songs*, 175.

17. Athas, *Deuteronomy*, 111.

18. Cf. Longman, "The 'Fear of God' in the Book of Ecclesiastes," 17.

19. Shields, *The End of Wisdom*, 182.

renders life unsafe and meaningless (7:15). Qohelet ties orthodoxy in a kind of Gordian Knot.

Having questioned orthodoxy, Qohelet attempts to mitigate the damage in 7:19–22. Indeed, this demonstrates that Qohelet is himself uncomfortable with his own conclusion and that his anti-proverbial advice in the preceding verses is more rhetorical than actual. Qohelet does not wish to jettison wisdom and orthodoxy completely, as he admits here that they have real value. A wise man is potentially stronger than ten rulers in a city (7:19)—an observation he will demonstrate again later (9:13–16). The problem, however, is that the savagery of the world curbs the effectiveness of wisdom, which is what Qohelet points out in 7:20, where he discusses human sinfulness. The NIV translates the initial conjunction of the verse (*ki*) as "Indeed," which gives the impression that 7:20 is reinforcing the idea of 7:19. While this is a standard way to translate the conjunction, it is difficult to see exactly how 7:20 supports 7:19. The conjunction itself, as a marker of positive assertion, can be used to counter or correct a prior statement (cf. 1 Sam 18:25).[20] When taken in this way, we can translate the conjunction as "But," which seems the better option. In that case, Qohelet affirms the value of wisdom (cf. 2:13) but acknowledges that every person is sinful, which makes the world a horrid place in which to live. It means sin often wins out over wisdom and righteousness, which is precisely his observation in 7:16.

The universality of sin leads Qohelet to encourage his readers not to pay attention to every word they hear (7:21a). In the context, this has three functions. First, it cheekily acknowledges that his anti-proverbs in 7:16–17 are not to be taken as actual advice but as demonstration of the absurdity of the world in which he lives. Second, it asserts that the world sometimes defies the constraints of wisdom and orthodoxy. Some things in life are inexplicable and meaningless, like the inversion of justice in 7:15. So not everything conventional wisdom and orthodoxy say can provide benefit or understanding. Third, it means that people must acknowledge the possibility that they are wrong. This comes out in the brief scenario Qohelet entertains in 7:21b–22. Qohelet implies that if one heard their servant cursing them (7:21b), the usual response would be to deem the servant wrong and perhaps even punish him. After all, it would not be the place of a servant to criticize their master. But then one must also admit that they too have cursed others (7:22). If the servant is wrong, then one must acknowledge that one may well be wrong, too. Universal sinfulness means that everyone is flawed; therefore everyone has

20. This is most often the correction of a negative statement containing the particle of negation (*lo'*). However, it is not the presence of the particle of negation that provides the means of correction or contrast, but rather the nature of the conjunction *ki* itself, which is an indicator of positive assertion.

the potential to get it wrong. Thus, of all people, the wisest and most astute should have the Socratic self-awareness to realize their own limitations and ignorance on certain matters. Otherwise, wisdom merely becomes arrogance.

This epistemic humility engenders two further noteworthy points. First, it means that when one sees an inversion of justice like that of 7:15, it may indicate that orthodoxy is wrong or that one is simply not in possession of all the facts. Qohelet seems willing to entertain both possibilities, though he himself cannot make any sense of the situation. He is truly agnostic on the issue. Second, Qohelet's advice here helps explain why he is himself so reticent to curse God openly. He is willing to lay out the evidence that suggests God has made the world "crooked" (7:13), but he is not willing to make a final prosecution. He still holds to the validity of orthodox doctrine (such as the covenantal dynamic of blessing and cursing) and God's sovereignty, but he is not so arrogant as to think that he can explain the crooked shape of the world by it. Thus, Qohelet's epistemic humility is mixed with his very real fear of God.

So, Qohelet comes clean in 7:23–24 by admitting that he "was determined to be wise" but failed. He is open to the idea that life does have a meaning, but "Whatever exists is far off and most profound—who can discover it?" (7:24). Qohelet humbly admits his agnosticism on the meaning of life, but this leaves him dissatisfied, bemoaning the apparent meaninglessness of it all.

The Superficiality of Conventional Wisdom (7:25–8:1)

Nonetheless, Qohelet continues to test the caliber of wisdom and the deficiencies of folly (7:25). In 7:26, he seems to take a sudden tangential turn that has kept commentators confused for centuries. He discusses "the woman who is a snare" to men, and states, "The man who pleases God will escape her, but the sinner she will ensnare." On its own, the relevance of this verse to the preceding context is confusing enough. However, Qohelet goes on in 7:27–29 to discuss how, in his investigations, he found one upright man among a thousand but not a single upright woman, followed by the claim that God made all humanity upright, but humans have "gone in search of many schemes." That is, Qohelet's thought seems to move from discussion of a wicked woman and a good man, to a generic denunciation of all women and most men, and thence to a generic denunciation of all human beings. These statements are almost impossible to reconcile with each other, especially if we insist Qohelet has a positive outlook on the world that is in line with orthodoxy. The apparent misogyny is also disconcerting.[21] Indeed, the puzzling nature of these verses

21. Unfortunately, the misogyny has been reinforced by some commentators. Longman refers to such instances by John Chrysostom and Martin Luther in *Ecclesiastes*, 206.

has led some to propose the woman is purely a metaphor, such as Ogden, who sees her as symbolic of untimely death.[22] None of these options, however, does justice to the context.

We must, therefore, allow the flow of Qohelet's discourse to help us determine the sense of these verses. Crucially, we should notice that these verses follow on from Qohelet's critique of conventional wisdom and orthodoxy. In 7:25 he states that he is continuing to test the merits of wisdom and the flaws of folly. Thus, we should frame 7:26–29 within this evaluative framework. This then leads us to observe that "the woman who is a snare" (7:26) bears a striking resemblance to the adulterous woman of Proverbs (cf. Proverbs 7)—a common motif in conventional wisdom. It seems that Qohelet is once again quoting conventional wisdom here to critique it. When understood as a quote, 7:26 becomes not Qohelet's own view necessarily but rather a proposition he is testing. Interestingly, he does not appear to deny the validity of the proverb. Indeed, the fate of the Seleucid king Antiochus II, who was poisoned by his own estranged wife Laodice, to whom he had returned in 246 BC, may be in Qohelet's mind here.[23]

Nevertheless, the next two verses show that Qohelet finds the proverb does not go far enough. Thus, in 7:27–28a he admits trying to add one thing to another to find a solution, presumably to the meaninglessness of the world, but comes up with nothing. At this point he seems to quote another conventional proverb: "I found one upright man among a thousand, but not one upright woman among them all" (7:28b). It is as though Qohelet is in dialogue here with a proponent of conventional wisdom who, unlike Qohelet, claims to have gotten to the bottom of the problems of the world. This may perhaps reflect some of the debates that Qohelet had with conventional sages, whose views he found too simplistic. The proponent confidently asserts that, while an upright man is hard to find, it can still be done, but it is impossible to find an upright woman. In other words, Qohelet's opposition claims that the biggest problem in the world is the female sex. The reference to searching among a thousand here may be an allusion to the situation of Solomon. Solomon was the singularly wisest man in all Israel, but not one woman in his harem of a thousand wives and concubines was upright. Instead, they drew Solomon into idolatry (1 Kgs 11:1–13), ensnaring him like the sinner in 7:26. For Qohelet, this does not show that women are what is wrong with the world. On the contrary, it demonstrates that everyone—male and female—has sinful tendencies

22. Graham S. Ogden, *Qoheleth*, Readings (Sheffield: JSOT Press, 1987), 120–21.

23. The suggestion is purely speculative, though. Antiochus II is, however, Qohelet's "old but foolish king" of 4:13.

(7:29). Picking up the imagery of Genesis 1, Qohelet affirms the orthodox tenet that God created humanity good (Gen 1:26–31), before affirming that all humans have gone astray. Indeed, his statement in 7:29 is reminiscent of God's observation in Genesis 6:5: "The LORD saw how great the wickedness of the human race had become on the earth, and that every inclination of the thoughts of the human heart was only evil all the time." This simply proves the shortcomings of conventional wisdom, exposing some of its confident conclusions as trite and contradictory. The evils of the world cannot be parsed as the fault of women, for even the wisest of men is flawed. This conclusion aligns completely with Qohelet's earlier statement in 7:20, that there is not a single person on earth who is righteous and without sin. Qohelet is, therefore, not a misogynist.

This causes us to reconsider Qohelet's quotation of conventional wisdom back in 7:26. The proverb there stated that the man who pleases God would escape the wily woman while the sinner would be trapped. Although Qohelet does not disagree with this, he shows thereafter that there is no one who pleases God. Both Jarick and Shields argue that the one who escapes the wily woman is simply the one God chooses to favor, removing the responsibility from the realm of human decision and placing it solely in the divine. Shields claims this shows that "human beings are not masters of their own destiny."[24] However, the Hebrew phrasing describes the one who escapes the wily woman as literally "good before God" and contrasts him with a sinner, suggesting that human action is indeed on view. While Qohelet acknowledges God's ultimate sovereignty over human affairs, he still believes humans have genuine will of their own. Although Qohelet can affirm the conventional wisdom of 7:26, both 7:20 and 7:29 show that no one is ultimately good. The wisdom that the proverb expresses, therefore, is purely moot, demonstrating the limitations of conventional wisdom. Much of it can be affirmed, but much of it does not adequately deal with the reality of a world populated by sinners.

Qohelet's hard realism now gives way to sarcasm in 8:1.[25] His two rhetorical questions place the conventional sage in his sights, implying that no one is really wise, and no one really "knows the explanation of things." He then quotes a proverb about the positive value of wisdom: "A person's wisdom brightens their face and changes its hard appearance." But Qohelet is not agreeing with the original intent of this proverb. Indeed, he has earlier stated that "with much wisdom comes much sorrow; the more knowledge, the more

24. Shields, *The End of Wisdom*, 187; John Jarick, *Gregory Thaumaturgos' Paraphrase of Ecclesiastes*, SBL Septuagint and Cognate Studies 29 (Atlanta, GA: Scholars Press, 1990), 190.

25. Longman, *Ecclesiastes*, 209.

grief" (1:18). Rather, having spent much of his discourse deconstructing the value of wisdom, he now caricatures it as having a mere placebo effect. The conventional sages may think that they have all the answers, which might make them feel like they have a grasp on the world and its workings. For Qohelet, this is not true enlightenment—it merely enlightens the face, not the soul. It is superficial. Thus, Qohelet's sarcasm here preempts his statement in 8:17, that even if the wise claim to comprehend the world, they actually do not.

For Qohelet, the world is a painful puzzle that defies simple explanation. His realism and thorough research beneath the surface have catalogued inversions of justice, the universal depravity of human beings, the limits of conventional wisdom and orthodoxy, and the inscrutability of God. Although there may be meaning in the world somewhere, he simply cannot discover it. Only God can know it, and he has not revealed it to humans (cf. 3:9). While conventional sages may be content with trite wisdom, Qohelet is weighed down by what he knows. Ironically, then, Qohelet's pessimism makes him wiser than the wise, though he ultimately claims this to be of no real value anyway.

LIVE the Story

Injustice and Sin

The inversion of justice causes Qohelet considerable angst. Not only does the state of the world appall him, it also makes him suspicious of God. The natural question that arises from his observations is, "How can a good God let such bad things happen to good people?" It is one of the most important philosophical questions that plagues humanity. Indeed, the elusiveness of an answer has led people to abandon the idea of a good God, or of a God altogether. It is not a purely academic question, for behind it lies the very real pain and suffering of many lives. Qohelet could see this amongst his compatriots in Ptolemaic Judea, and it is something so many of us see or experience ourselves.

Grappling with the question entails dealing with God's law, the nature of righteousness, and sin. God's law was not given to Israel as a means of getting to heaven or of fixing everything that is wrong with the world. Rather, it stipulated customs, standards, regulations, and order to enable Israelites to have a well-functioning society in the land of their "inheritance." It did not deal with the deeper problem of human nature. On the contrary, it only mitigated that deeper problem within Israelite society. That is why God's law had within it provisions for failure—sentences for the guilty as well as protocols for making restitution. If an Israelite followed the relevant protocols, even if they had failed at some point, they could still be considered "righteous"—that is, having the right to remain a member of Israel's covenant society within the land of their "inheritance." Indeed, Paul claims to have been just such a person, saying of himself, "as for righteousness based on the law, faultless" (Phil 3:6).

Yet Israel ultimately failed to attain even this level of legal righteousness. The nation willfully disobeyed God, for which they paid the ultimate price: the downfall of their society and exile from the land of their "inheritance." The law, being external and written "on stone," could not cure the depravity of the human heart.

Qohelet's society lived with the legacy of their own sinfulness. They were no longer an independent society but subservient to foreigners—the Assyrians, Babylonians, Persians, and Alexander in ages past, and now the Ptolemies. Soon they would fall under the Seleucids and later the Romans. They were powerless to enact the kind of society God's law envisioned. Instead, they were suffering oppression and exploitation that had the legal sanction of their Ptolemaic overlords. Yet, even when they could establish an independent Jewish state under the Hasmoneans (142–63 BC), the deeper problem of human sinfulness remained, which the law simply could not cure.

Qohelet perceived the deeper problem within humanity—the inner flaw of sin. Qohelet identified it when he stated, "Indeed, there is no one on earth who is righteous, no one who does what is right and never sins" (Eccl 7:20). His category of righteousness here extends beyond the legal definition of a good citizen. Like Paul, one might be faultless in terms of the righteousness that comes from the law—legally innocent—but everyone was still a sinner in desperate need of a cure for sin. Good citizens were still sinful people. This did not mean it was right for such good citizens to suffer—this was still a reprehensible injustice that demonstrated the excesses of Ptolemaic imperial power. Qohelet was right to decry it. While it is right to express exasperation at this problem and ask, "Why do the righteous suffer?," it would be remiss if we did not also ask, "What can be done about the even deeper problem of human sin?" Qohelet observed people in power using their propensity to sin to make the lives of others miserable, but he also recognized that the cancer of sin lay within everyone.

Once again, we must underline that Qohelet lived in a "BC" world. Having only the law and the Prophets to guide his deliberations, Qohelet was understandably in a quandary over making sense of God and the world. But the coming of Christ reconfigures the way we understand God and the world. Though Qohelet knew God and made right observations about him and the world, he did not have the full revelation of God. The death of Jesus outside the walls of Jerusalem in AD 33 is the key to unlocking the meaning in God's purposes. While it does not provide an answer to all our queries, it does shed the necessary light for trusting God.

When Jesus was arrested, convicted, and executed as a criminal, he was treated as a wicked man even though he was innocent of any crime. Qohelet's inversion of justice—the righteous perishing and the wicked prospering (Eccl 7:15)—is exemplified starkly and tragically in the crucifixion of Jesus. Qohelet would have looked at Jesus's death and cried, "Meaningless!"—for that is ostensibly how it seemed. Yet, reflecting on Jesus's death some decades later, the Apostle Peter picks up the language of Isaiah 53:4–5 and tells his audience, "'He himself bore our sins' in his body on the cross, so that we might die to sins and live for righteousness; 'by his wounds you have been healed'" (1 Pet 2:24). He goes on to say that "Christ also suffered once for sins, the righteous for the unrighteous, to bring you to God" (1 Pet 3:18). In the death of Jesus, the righteous one, we see God working to reconcile sinful people to himself. Human sin is given ultimate expression but also punished and dealt with in the death of Jesus.

Paul echoes Qohelet's sentiments about the universal depravity of human beings in Romans 3:12. He goes on to say that in Christ a new kind of righteousness is revealed—one that goes beyond the legal definition of being a good citizen. It is not a righteousness obtained by one's legal innocence but by trusting in Israel's messiah, Jesus (Rom 3:21–22). This gift is a new kind of righteousness that deals with the inner flaw of human sinfulness, for it comes from Christ, who "was delivered over to death for our sins and was raised to life for our justification" (Rom 4:25). As Paul tells the Corinthians, "God made him who had no sin to be sin for us, so that in him we might become the righteousness of God" (2 Cor 5:21). The result of this righteousness is not the right to be a citizen in the covenantal society of Israel within a Middle Eastern territory, but the right to be a citizen of heaven. In Christ, then, sin is dealt a death blow, and humanity is reconciled to God.

Thus, the suffering of the righteous that Qohelet observed is the very means that God used to save humanity from sinfulness as it was focused on the one person, Jesus Christ. In him, we see the righteous suffering in the most brazen display of human sinfulness, but we also see supreme justice as sentence is passed and carried out on human sin. The two seemingly irreconcilable concepts of innocent suffering and the justice of God find their resolution in the death of Jesus Christ, which brings about the reconciliation of all things to God. The cross of Christ is the focal point of human suffering and justice. Without it, Qohelet's verdict that "Everything is meaningless" is the last word. Thankfully, it is not.

This gospel of reconciliation is revolutionary. It should prompt us to examine ourselves, acknowledge our own sinfulness, repent with faith in Christ, and be reconciled to God. The sign of this reconciliation is the granting of God's Spirit to those who trust in Christ (cf. Eph 1:13–14). As Paul states in Romans 8, the Spirit of God ensures that there is no condemnation for those in Christ and enables people to live in righteousness, in step with the Spirit, rather than in the weakness of human flesh. This also prompts us to address the injustices in our world. Paul's words to Titus are apt in showing that the gospel is the only substantive hope for the world's ills:

> For the grace of God has appeared that offers salvation to all people. It teaches us to say "No" to ungodliness and worldly passions, and to live self-controlled, upright and godly lives in this present age, while we wait for the blessed hope—the appearing of the glory of our great God and Savior, Jesus Christ, who gave himself for us to redeem us from all wickedness and to purify for himself a people that are his very own, eager to do what is good. (Titus 2:11–14)

While we live in the present age, we will still see, suffer, and even perpetrate injustice. Our lives are still scarred by sin. We should never lose the sense of horror and pain that Qohelet had when he saw injustice in his day. The gospel compels us to address injustice, starting with ourselves. The inner transformative work of the Spirit is the only hope we have to accomplish this. Any other means will fall short. While we applaud all human efforts to address wickedness and suffering, we must also acknowledge that only in Christ is human sinfulness ultimately dealt with. Thus, Christ's death reconfigures the way we see and tackle injustice. It does not give us the details of why a particular person suffers in a particular circumstance, but it certainly points us to the solution and encourages us to wait for the blessed hope of final redemption. Our God is one who has known injustice and suffering, perpetrated by our own hand against him, but he has reconciled us to him and in his grace offered us eternal life.

Wisdom and Orthodoxy

Qohelet was troubled by the limits of conventional wisdom and orthodoxy (correct belief about God). This demonstrates two key points. First, it shows once again that Qohelet lived before the final revelation of God in Christ. What God had committed to his people in the Old Testament was true, but it was also incomplete. There were gaps in Qohelet's knowledge that understandably led him to confused despair. Until innocent suffering and justice are brought together in the cross of Christ, they are kept apart in apparent irreconcilability and meaninglessness. The cross of Christ, though, focuses the problem and solves it. The gospel, therefore, expresses the wisdom of God in Christ. To the world, this wisdom is utter folly, but it reveals the genius of God and his grace to save human beings through Christ (1 Cor 1:20–24). The gospel, therefore, also reconfigures wisdom, such that it cannot now be defined without reference to what God has done in Christ. This wisdom is countercultural, as it overturns power and greatness and places love and service at the center of human existence. Living before the definitive enactment of this wisdom, Qohelet's knowledge was incomplete, and therefore his despair was understandable. Had Qohelet lived in the New Testament era, he would undoubtedly have written a very different book.

Nevertheless, this does not mean we today should jettison Qohelet's discourse or deny his angst. His reflections were based on incomplete revelation, but they were still "upright and true," as the Epilogist affirms (Eccl 12:10). Qohelet's recognition of conventional wisdom and orthodoxy's limits helps us see the second point, namely that, while the gospel has reconfigured wisdom, the world is still a messy place. Even with the benefit of the gospel, no single person can claim to have all the answers. Like Qohelet, we need the epistemic humility to recognize that we cannot grasp all things. The gospel gives us the biggest solution in life, but it would be unwise and arrogant to think that we therefore know all the answers to life.

By the same token, we must not reduce God simply to orthodox statements. The gospel of the Lord Jesus Christ is God's ultimate revelation to humanity, and it shapes our belief. As such, it is to be received with thanksgiving as real, true, trustworthy, and essential. Orthodox statements are, therefore, of immense importance. Paul, for example, could issue "trustworthy sayings" that deserved full acceptance (1 Tim 1:15; 3:1; 4:9; 2 Tim 2:11; Titus 3:8). Creeds, like the Nicene Creed, give us wonderful statements that summarize and express the essence of the Christian faith in helpful ways. Nevertheless, while wholeheartedly affirming such orthodox statements, we must also realize that God, humanity, the world, life, and faith are not reducible to just those statements. Orthodoxy is like a passport or driver's license. A person's passport or license is a factual statement of who they are and can be used to determine the person's identity accurately. Despite this, a person is more than the sum of the statements on their identification documents. Hence, we can affirm the factuality of who God is and what he has done in Christ, and we cannot know him apart from this. But God is not just words and acts. He is a being who can be known. When we recite creeds, we are, as it were, holding up God's passport and acknowledging who he is. This is vital for Christians, as it states that we know God factually, but knowing God is more than just facts—it's about relationship.

A significant danger for Christians is nominalism—the idea that we subscribe to certain correct beliefs about God, but we do not actually know God himself. Knowing God entails knowing about him, but it is so much more than possession of facts about him. As Paul argues in Romans 1:18–25, knowledge of God without subsequently honoring and thanking him is useless. It only provokes God's displeasure and opens the door to replacing him with idols of our own manufacture. The angst in Qohelet's reflections reveals not just a man troubled by unsolvable equations, but a soul in agony at being unable to comprehend the God he knew. So, our relationship with God in Christ must be more than knowing facts. It must be about knowing him.

CHAPTER 6

Ecclesiastes 8:2–10:4

LISTEN to the Story

[2]Obey the king's command, I say, because you took an oath before
God. [3]Do not be in a hurry to leave the king's presence. Do not stand up
for a bad cause, for he will do whatever he pleases. [4]Since a king's word is
supreme, who can say to him, "What are you doing?"

> [5]Whoever obeys his command will come to no harm,
> and the wise heart will know the proper time and procedure.
> [6]For there is a proper time and procedure for every matter,
> though a person may be weighed down by misery.
> [7]Since no one knows the future,
> who can tell someone else what is to come?
> [8]As no one has power over the wind to contain it,
> so no one has power over the time of their death.
> As no one is discharged in time of war,
> so wickedness will not release those who practice it.

[9]All this I saw, as I applied my mind to everything done under the sun.
There is a time when a man lords it over others to his own hurt. [10]Then
too, I saw the wicked buried—those who used to come and go from the
holy place and receive praise in the city where they did this. This too is
meaningless.

[11]When the sentence for a crime is not quickly carried out, people's
hearts are filled with schemes to do wrong. [12]Although a wicked person
who commits a hundred crimes may live a long time, I know that it will go
better with those who fear God, who are reverent before him. [13]Yet because
the wicked do not fear God, it will not go well with them, and their days
will not lengthen like a shadow.

[14]There is something else meaningless that occurs on earth: the righ-
teous who get what the wicked deserve, and the wicked who get what the

righteous deserve. This too, I say, is meaningless. 15So I commend the enjoyment of life, because there is nothing better for a person under the sun than to eat and drink and be glad. Then joy will accompany them in their toil all the days of the life God has given them under the sun.

16When I applied my mind to know wisdom and to observe the labor that is done on earth—people getting no sleep day or night—17then I saw all that God has done. No one can comprehend what goes on under the sun. Despite all their efforts to search it out, no one can discover its meaning. Even if the wise claim they know, they cannot really comprehend it.

9:1So I reflected on all this and concluded that the righteous and the wise and what they do are in God's hands, but no one knows whether love or hate awaits them. 2All share a common destiny—the righteous and the wicked, the good and the bad, the clean and the unclean, those who offer sacrifices and those who do not.

As it is with the good,
  so with the sinful;
as it is with those who take oaths,
  so with those who are afraid to take them.

3This is the evil in everything that happens under the sun: The same destiny overtakes all. The hearts of people, moreover, are full of evil and there is madness in their hearts while they live, and afterward they join the dead. 4Anyone who is among the living has hope—even a live dog is better off than a dead lion!

5For the living know that they will die,
  but the dead know nothing;
they have no further reward,
  and even their name is forgotten.
6Their love, their hate
  and their jealousy have long since vanished;
never again will they have a part
  in anything that happens under the sun.

7Go, eat your food with gladness, and drink your wine with a joyful heart, for God has already approved what you do. 8Always be clothed in white, and always anoint your head with oil. 9Enjoy life with your wife,

whom you love, all the days of this meaningless life that God has given
you under the sun—all your meaningless days. For this is your lot in life
and in your toilsome labor under the sun. 10Whatever your hand finds to
do, do it with all your might, for in the realm of the dead, where you are
going, there is neither working nor planning nor knowledge nor wisdom.
11I have seen something else under the sun:

The race is not to the swift
    or the battle to the strong,
nor does food come to the wise
    or wealth to the brilliant
    or favor to the learned;
but time and chance happen to them all.

12Moreover, no one knows when their hour will come:

As fish are caught in a cruel net,
    or birds are taken in a snare,
so people are trapped by evil times
    that fall unexpectedly upon them.

13I also saw under the sun this example of wisdom that greatly
impressed me: 14There was once a small city with only a few people in it.
And a powerful king came against it, surrounded it and built huge siege
works against it. 15Now there lived in that city a man poor but wise, and
he saved the city by his wisdom. But nobody remembered that poor man.
16So I said, "Wisdom is better than strength." But the poor man's wisdom
is despised, and his words are no longer heeded.

17The quiet words of the wise are more to be heeded
    than the shouts of a ruler of fools.
18Wisdom is better than weapons of war,
    but one sinner destroys much good.
10:1As dead flies give perfume a bad smell,
    so a little folly outweighs wisdom and honor.
2The heart of the wise inclines to the right,
    but the heart of the fool to the left.
3Even as fools walk along the road,

they lack sense
and show everyone how stupid they are.
4 If a ruler's anger rises against you,
do not leave your post;
calmness can lay great offenses to rest.

Listening to the Story in the Text: Letter of Rib-Addi (El Amarna, Letter 79); Scenes of the Siege of Lachish from Sennacherib's Palace, Nineveh (now in the British Museum); Sennacherib's Annals (Taylor Prism); 2 Kings 18:13–19:37 (paralleled in Isaiah 36–37; 2 Chr 32:1–22); Isaiah 1:8–9; Jeremiah 7:1–8:3; Josephus *Antiquities* 12.156–86; Epic of Gilgamesh (Meissner Tablet, iii.6–14)

As we turn to this next portion of Qohelet's discourse, it is worth considering the nature of ancient siege warfare, particularly as it affected Jerusalem through the ages. We must also look again at the Ptolemaic administration, taxation, the career of Joseph Tobias, and of his uncle, the high priest Onias II.

Ancient cities were fortified with walls to keep enemies out and citizens safe within. This meant that siege was a standard type of ancient warfare. An enemy army would blockade the city to starve the population. If the citizens did not surrender and, instead, reached the point of desperation, the enemy army would attempt to break into the city. They would build siege towers or earthen ramparts, to give archers better angles of fire and infantry the opportunity to scale walls. They would attempt to break down gates or breach walls with battering rams. The human toll on both sides of siege warfare was high, but the experience was especially terrifying for the citizens trapped within the city, where starvation, thirst, and civil strife festered while violence constantly threatened to burst in. The imagery of being caught like a fish or a bird was widely employed to describe both the helplessness of citizens and siege's dehumanizing effects. For example, Rib-Addi, the ancient king of Byblos, sent a letter to his overlord, Pharaoh Akhenaten (c. 1351–1334 BC),[1] begging for troops to attack the "Habiru" who were besieging him, describing himself "Like a bird that lies in a net, a cage" (EA 79:35–36).[2]

Sennacherib's invasion of Judah during the reign of Hezekiah (701 BC)

1. The letter may have been sent earlier to Akhenaten's father, Amenhotep III.

2. Translation after K. C. Hanson (http://www.kchanson.com/ANCDOCS/meso/amarna79.html), adapted from Samuel A. B. Mercer, *The Tell El-Amarna Tablets*, 2 vols. (Toronto: Macmillan, 1939) and William L. Moran, *The Amarna Letters* (Baltimore: Johns Hopkins University Press, 2000).

is particularly telling. He decorated his palace walls in Nineveh with scenes from his successful siege of the Judean city of Lachish. Not only do these depict archers, infantry, and battering rams, they also portray the wholesale impaling of Judean nobility, dismemberment of Judean soldiers, and the forced deportation of citizens. The terror of the event, captured in still stone relief, is palpable. Sennacherib also left an account (Taylor Prism) of the invasion, including his siege of Jerusalem. In it he boasts, "He himself [Hezekiah], I locked up within Jerusalem, his royal city, like a bird in a cage. I surrounded him with earthworks, and made it unthinkable for him to exit by the city gate" (*COS* 2:119B). Ironically, Sennacherib failed to capture the city—a fact memorialized in biblical texts (2 Kgs 18:13–19:37; Isa 36–37; 2 Chr 32:1–22).[3] The unexpected deliverance of Jerusalem took on epic proportions within the theological psyche of Judeans at the time. It even gave impetus to notions of Jerusalem's invincibility. Jeremiah claimed such braggadocio was misguided (Jer 7:1–8:3), and he was proven tragically correct. The Babylonians besieged Jerusalem twice (597 BC and 586 BC), with the second spelling the city's downfall. Ezekiel portrays some of the last kings of Judah as lion cubs netted and trapped by the nations (Ezek 19:1–9), while Habakkuk depicts Jerusalem's besieged citizens as "fish in the sea," whom the wicked enemy catches in a net and drags away (Hab 1:14–15).

The siege of 586 BC was not the final time Jerusalem was violently taken. Ptolemy I captured the city in 301 BC. Though this may not have been after a protracted siege, it was brutal nonetheless, including the slaughter and deportation of citizens (cf. Zech 13:7–14:2) and the dismantling of the city's defenses.[4] The prophetic image of Jerusalem as a "shelter in a vineyard, like a hut in a cucumber field, like a city under siege" (Isa 1:8) was, therefore, of enduring relevance.

For Palestine more widely, the change from Persian to Hellenistic rule brought considerable cultural, political, and economic change. Palestine was a fruitful land with a thriving economy, producing goods that were valued far and wide. The olive and wine industries were particularly lucrative.[5] However, the nature of trade changed during the third century BC. Under Ptolemy II (283–246 BC), the minting of coins increased almost fivefold.[6] The reason

---

3. Not only did Sennacherib fail to capture Jerusalem, but no archaeological evidence of any siege has ever been found. It seems Sennacherib generously embellished his account.

4. Victor Tcherikover, *Hellenistic Civilization and the Jews* (Grand Rapids: Baker, 1959), 56–58.

5. Ibid., 70.

6. Sneed, *The Politics of Pessimism in Ecclesiastes*, 97–98; Martin Hengel, *Judaism and Hellenism: Studies in Their Encounter in Palestine during the Early Hellenistic Period*, 2 vols. (London: SCM Press, 1974), 43–44.

was not just economic growth, but the replacement of bartering with coinage as the dominant means of exchange. Coinage had been introduced to the region centuries before,[7] but bartering was still the dominant model until Ptolemy II. By monetizing the economy, the Ptolemies made it easier for goods to move in just one direction. That is, goods that went from "A" to "B" were not matched with goods that went from "B" to "A." Instead, they were replaced by money, and all the goods ended up at "B." While this in theory provided more purchasing power and choice for most people, it also meant that the powerful could more easily control the direction and price of goods while maintaining opulent lifestyles. The goods that would ordinarily have circulated within Palestine's local economy were now being exported abroad, mainly to Egypt, where the ruling elite were. There were, therefore, fewer goods left locally for consumers, which would have driven up prices. And this occurred at a time when consumers had less and less money for discretionary spending. On top of that, the Ptolemies then imposed numerous taxes that took even more money from the average consumer. These taxes increased the price of goods even further, which, in turn, drove merchants to demand lower wholesale prices for goods in order to offer competitive prices at resale that still maintained profitable margins. Thus, while retail prices were driven higher, the return for producers and manufacturers—the average person in Judea—was even lower. The taxes applied to all, so the average person was now receiving less for their work, paying more taxes, and having much less purchasing power over an already reduced range of goods. It drove most people to subsistence, poverty, debt, and slavery. It is little wonder that many Jews chose to migrate to Alexandria, the center of political and economic potential, during the third century BC. The city soon boasted the largest Jewish population in the world. Jewish life in Judea was suffocating.

All this was exacerbated by the fact that the elite, like Apollonius (the treasurer of Ptolemy II), were not simply consumers at the final point of trade, but also merchants—the middlemen who bought the goods at the point of production. That is, the elite were often able to bypass the intermediate stage of trade by using their own agents (such as Zenon and his employees) to acquire and ship goods. These agents were ostensibly middlemen and, therefore, could still demand bargains at the point of production to maintain their margins at the point of retail, but they owed their station to the elite. Taxation was also enforced by arms where necessary. All this meant the Ptolemaic elite

7. Coinage was probably invented in the seventh century BC, with Croesus of Lydia being the best exploiter of the new system. Nevertheless, coinage only became widespread during the Persian Era (539–332 BC).

could maintain a stranglehold over the economy and the lives of both the working and middle classes.

Then, in 227 BC, Ptolemy III granted Joseph Tobias the right to double the tax revenues throughout Palestine and neighboring regions. The already considerable strain on the population doubled overnight. The details of Joseph's rise to prominence are discussed in the Introduction (see "Context and Date"), but one particular aspect of it is pertinent to this section of Ecclesiastes. After Joseph's uncle, Onias II, earlier refused to pay Ptolemy the fee for his charge over the Jewish nation, Joseph called a public assembly in the Jerusalem temple and persuaded the people that, though Onias had brought them to peril, he himself would act on their behalf and avert disaster. Joseph extolled his own virtues and received public acclaim as a champion of the people. Armed with this approval, Joseph successfully defused Ptolemy's threat of punitive action against the Jews (*Ant.* 12.164–173). It was at that point that Joseph turned on the people who had acclaimed him as their champion by doubling the region's tax burden. He held the rights to tax the population for twenty-two years (*Ant.* 12.186, 224), earning a massive fortune in the process.

As a prominent citizen in Jerusalem, Qohelet not only knew about these events but experienced them at close quarters. Though the Davidic royal family no longer held any power, they would still have been minor celebrities—a little like today's deposed royal families of Europe (e.g., the "Glücksburgs" of Greece). Yet there was no political possibility of anyone in the family, like Qohelet, attaining real power. On the contrary, Qohelet probably experienced the erosion of any wealth and influence he might have had under the choking deeds of Joseph Tobias on Ptolemy III's behalf. Even the faintest flicker of Davidic hope would thus have been permanently snuffed out at this time and any sense of Davidic celebrity lost. Qohelet's advice to salvage the enjoyment of the basics in life is quite poignant considering these developments. In this next section Qohelet reissues this advice, but in slightly more detail that is reminiscent of ideas found in the ancient Epic of Gilgamesh. In the epic, the protagonist, Gilgamesh, fears that he will succumb to a sickness that has gripped him since the death of his companion, Enkidu. In his travels, he comes by a seaside inn, where he encounters a maiden named Sabitum,[8] to whom he divulges his fears. She says to Gilgamesh:

> O Gilgamesh, where are you wandering?
> The life that you seek you never will find:
> when the gods created mankind,

8. Sabitum is called Šiduri in other versions of the epic.

death they dispensed to mankind,
life they kept for themselves.
But you, Gilgamesh, let your belly be full,
enjoy yourself always by day and by night!
Make merry each day,
dance and play day and night!
Let your clothes be clean,
let your head be washed, may you bathe in water!
Gaze on the child who holds your hand,
let your wife enjoy your repeated embrace!
For such is the destiny [*of mortal men*].[9]

Sabitum's advice places human endeavor in the context of gods who are mean-spirited toward humanity. While she encourages Gilgamesh to make the most of life, as Jastrow rightly notes, her response strikes a sad note, "showing how hopeless it is for man to try to escape death which is in store for all mankind."[10] Thus, all human endeavor, including joy, is tainted by the surety of death imposed by the gods. Although written many centuries before Qohelet (c. 1750 BC), the form of this advice was still current enough in Qohelet's Ptolemaic context to have exerted some influence over how he framed his own advice to his readers (Eccl 9:7–10). Once again, it raises, for Qohelet, serious questions over God's attitude to humanity and the nature of human life under his sovereignty. Qohelet felt he was watching any hope for both himself and his nation slip into meaningless oblivion.

EXPLAIN the Story

The Good, the Bad, the Meaningless (8:2–10:4)

After exposing the limits of conventional wisdom and orthodoxy in the previous section, Qohelet the pessimist now turns pragmatist. For the rest of his discourse, he will address practical matters and make some stinging criticisms of leaders in his day. He will offer some conventional wisdom where he deems it deals adequately with a situation. But, unsurprisingly, he finds it often fails. So, he will continue critiquing wisdom and situations that play meaninglessly on the historical stage while also adding his own earthy brand of wisdom into

9. Andrew George, trans., *The Epic of Gilgamesh* (New York: Barnes & Noble, 1999), 124.

10. Albert Tobias Clay and Morris Jastrow, Jr., eds., *An Old Babylonian Version of the Epic of Gilgamesh*, Pantianos Classics (N. Charleston, SC: CreateSpace Independent Publishing Platform, 1920), 8.

the mix. What this shows is not that Qohelet wished to get of rid of wisdom but rather to sharpen it in some way that might prevent folly and evil from undermining it. The extreme hardships that Jews in Judea faced under poor local leadership and the avarice of the Ptolemies exposed the limits of conventional wisdom, which is more suited to dealing with simple conventional situations. But extreme times call for extreme measures, and Qohelet wishes to offer his own extreme form of wisdom. Once again, we will see him issuing his advice to make the most of the basics in life, but this will continue to expose the harsh realities of life in Ptolemaic Judea.

Defying the King (8:2–15)

In Hebrew, 8:2 begins with an inexplicable first-person pronoun, "I" (*'ani*), which makes no sense whatsoever with anything around it. The NIV has attempted to include it in translation by the phrase, "I say." This suggests that a verb has fallen out of the text, but there is no hint in other manuscripts that this occurred. There are a few possibilities for dealing with this oddity,[11] but whatever the case, the sense of the clause is still clear: "Obey the king's command."

The division of clauses in 8:2–3 is a puzzle, even before we try to determine their meaning.[12] The many readings on offer demonstrate just how problem-

---

11. One possibility of dealing with this is simply to remove the word from the text on the assumption that it was a copying error that crept into the text at some point. The LXX certainly does not include it, but it is impossible to know whether the Greek translator excised the word in translation or read from a Hebrew text that did not have the extraneous word. The only other viable possibility is that the second and third letters of the Hebrew pronoun (*nun* and *yod*) are the result of a scribe's sloppy handwriting and that their respective strokes originally formed a different letter, *taw*. This would make the original word *'et*—the direct definite object marker rather than a pronoun. It would mark the following phrase, which literally reads, "mouth of a king," as a direct definite object. It certainly functions as an object within the sentence, so this makes sense in context. The difficulty with the suggestion is that the phrase does not appear to be grammatically definite (it has no definite article or defining suffix). This is not a significant objection, but the suggestion is purely speculative, since we have no manuscript evidence to give further guidance.

12. There is ambiguity over whether the first clause of 8:3 belongs with the previous clause in 8:2 or with what follows it in 8:3. The LXX reads this first verbal expression in 8:3 as "Do not hurry," which implies a set of vowels (*'al-tebahel*) that differ from those inserted by the Masoretic scribes, who read, "Do not worry" (*'al-tibbahel*). The NIV follows the LXX at this point and is generally preferred. The issue is exacerbated by the further ambiguity over whether the phrase "from him" (8:3) belongs with the clause before it ("Do not hurry") or the clause after it ("you should go"). Some translators try to solve the dilemma by creating a single idea across both clauses here, namely, "Do not be hasty to walk away from him" (so Fredericks and Estes, *Ecclesiastes & the Song of Songs*, 188; cf. ASV). This is quite problematic, though, as the last verb here is not a complementary infinitive that creates a subordinate clause ("to walk") but a finite *yiqtol* verb that creates an independent clause ("you should go"). The LXX rightly renders it with a subjunctive (*poreusē*), recognizing the modal force of the Hebrew *yiqtol* verb. The Masoretes paired the phrase "from him" with the following clause, seemingly to avoid an apparent contradiction ("Do not hurry away from him. You should go. Do not stay in a

atic these clauses are. In determining the clause divisions and their meaning, we should take three factors into account. First, the verses intertwine the concept of obeying the king with taking an oath before God, such that it is difficult to separate the two ideas as mutually exclusive.[13] We need, therefore, to determine a context in which these two ideas function essentially as one. Second, Qohelet combines negative commands (negated jussives in Hebrew) with positive commands (modal *yiqtol* verbs in Hebrew). We should read these as complementary and mutually informing. And third, we must recognize that Qohelet is talking here about coming and going from the king's presence. The average citizen in Judea would never have had opportunity to deal personally with the Ptolemaic king, who was ensconced behind closed doors in Alexandria. Qohelet is, therefore, unlikely to be dispensing generic advice for the masses. It is more probable that he is addressing those who did have access to the king.

Combining these observations, we can translate 8:2–5a as follows:

> Obey the king's command. Because of the oath to God, do not hurry away from him [i.e., the king]. You should go. Do not stay for a bad cause, for he will do whatever he wants, because the word of the king is supreme. Who will say to him, "What are you doing?" He who obeys a command will not experience anything bad.

At first glance, this translation seems enigmatic or even nonsensical. However, Qohelet's immediate Ptolemaic context solves this dilemma. Qohelet is presenting a cutting criticism of the high priest, Onias II. When Ptolemy sent an envoy to Onias to demand the fee for Onias's charge (*prostasia*) over the Jewish nation, Onias refused. In this, he would have broken an oath he had sworn (cf. *Ant.* 12.8), presumably in the temple[14]—a move that brought with it not just the threat of Ptolemy's wrath but also God's (cf. 5:2). Many Jews would have perceived this as a significant error from their high priest, as the disquiet in Jerusalem during this time indicates (*Ant.* 12.160–165). Qohelet takes Onias to task for being quick to go back on his word and for remaining

bad situation"). While the sense of this might seem contradictory, the syntax still works, prompting the question of whether there might be a way of interpreting this that is not contradictory after all (see discussion below).

13. A conjunction *waw* joins the first two clauses together. Shields reads 8:2a as a heading ("Observe the command of a king") for what follows, but this seems motivated by a lack of clarity over how it relates to the next clause, even though they are connected by a conjunction. At any rate, it would be peculiar for a heading to include the specific instruction of an imperative. See Shields, *The End of Wisdom*, 192.

14. See also Krüger, *Qoheleth*, 154.

obstinately in Jerusalem "for a bad cause" rather than going to Alexandria to placate the king. If he had obeyed the king's command in the first place, or sought to patch things up quickly, no one would have feared any reprisals (8:4–5). But Onias was fraternizing with Ptolemy's enemies, the Seleucids in Syria (see discussion of 4:13–16 above). When Seleucus II died in 225 BC, Onias was left in a political cul-de-sac, beholden to his nephew, Joseph Tobias, who had placated the king and risen to the position of chief tax farmer (see "Context and Date" in the Introduction). Onias's recalcitrance had created a crisis that not only imperiled Jerusalem, it also ruined the region's population more broadly through the crushing financial burden that Joseph inflicting upon it. When we see how the context informs Qohelet's words, we realize that what initially appears to be contradictory advice not to hurry away but also to go (8:3) makes perfect sense. Onias should not have hurried away from Ptolemy III to the Seleucids, and he should have gone to Alexandria to placate Ptolemy rather than leave Joseph to do it instead.

Crucially, Qohelet does not name any of the players here. He recognizes the incendiary nature of his words, which could potentially endanger him in a world that did not recognize freedom of speech as a right (cf. 10:20). As such, he "covers his tracks" by screening his specific criticisms behind a veneer of anonymous generalization—a tactic he will employ again (9:17–10:20). All this demonstrates once more that Qohelet is not himself a king. He is not in a position of authority, and he is not offering comfort or protocol lessons. He is spectating and bewailing the damaging mistakes wrought by those in authority.

The NIV understands 8:5 as a single continuous thought, but the first half should be put with the previous verse (see above), and the second half is best taken as a kind of headline—"Time and Judgment"—followed by a statement that runs into the next verse: "The heart of a wise man knows that there is a time and judgment for every purpose." This reflects both conventional wisdom as well as Qohelet's poem cataloguing the times (3:1–8). Indeed, the word Qohelet used for every "activity" under the sun in 3:1 (*hepets*, NIV "matter") is the same word he uses here for every "purpose." But the veracity of this statement here needs to be tempered by what he says next. Though a sage may rightly believe that every action has a proper time and consequence, no one can accurately predict what is going to happen. Humans can make sudden and terrible decisions, as Onias's behavior proves. And yet, humans do not ultimately direct the course of history (8:6b–7). As Qohelet shows through his earlier poem (3:1–8), God controls the time of every activity (cf. 7:14). In other words, Qohelet implies that conventional wisdom may be right in saying that things happen at a particular time for a particular purpose—even Onias's poor decisions and Joseph Tobias's wily schemes—but it cannot say what that timing or purpose actually is. This "pulls the rug out" from under any comfort that conventional wisdom might impart, and once more demonstrates its limits.

Qohelet then extends the unpredictability of the future to the moment of death in 8:8. The four lines here are a pair of couplets that each give an analogy first and the actual point second. Qohelet's purpose here is to show that death ultimately comes to everyone, and no one can control when it occurs (8:8a), let alone avoid it (8:8b). The death of both Seleucid brothers by 225 BC, which left Onias in the lurch, is clear proof of this. By stating that wickedness does not save those who practice it (literally, "its owners"), Qohelet is subtly pointing out that even human kings, be they the Seleucid brothers or the Ptolemies, who preside over state-sponsored corruption, die. So, while obeying Ptolemy might mean bearing considerable cost—even as much as twenty silver talents in Onias's case—the oppressed party can take a small measure of comfort from the fact that the king will one day die and won't be able to take any wealth with him.

This is then reinforced in 8:9. The NIV understands Qohelet to be observing a man who lords it over others only to end up hurting himself. However, the Hebrew reads, "A time when man rules over man for his detriment." This wording permits the implication that harm comes to those who are ruled. Onias may have felt tyrannized by Ptolemy's demands, but he was by no means the only one. Now Onias's defiance had brought greater hardship to others, as Joseph Tobias exploited the situation for his own ends. Onias's own complaint about Ptolemy's damaging behavior had now become a complaint about Onias too.

As Longman notes, the next verse (8:10) "vies for the most difficult in the book."[15] The Hebrew Masoretic Text has numerous difficulties, perhaps because of sloppy scribal copying or a poorly preserved manuscript.[16] Krüger translates the verse, "Then I saw how wicked people were buried and went in to rest; but those who had done right had to leave a holy place and were forgotten in the city. That also is futile."[17] Shields offers, "Thus I saw the wicked brought from the holy place to graves but those who acted justly

15. Longman, *Ecclesiastes*, 218.

16. These problems pertain to suspect or missing letters, unusual verb forms, and perhaps a missing word. This has given rise to multiple theories on the translation and meaning of the verse. The LXX seems to have read the Hebrew *waba'u* ("and they come"—itself an unusual form) as *muba'im* ("brought"). If correct, the Hebrew text has undergone haplography at both the beginning and end of the word. The LXX also reads Hebrew *weyishtakkehu* ("and they would forget themselves"—another unusual form) as *wayyishtabbehu* ("and they praised"), which will be discussed in further detail. There is also ambiguity as to whom exactly the plural verbs in the second half of the verse refer to—the "wicked" or others (the righteous?).

17. Krüger, *Qoheleth*, 158.

were forgotten in the city. This too is senseless."[18] Longman translates, "Thus, I observed the wicked buried and departed. They used to go out of the holy place, and they were praised in the city where they acted in such a way. This too is meaningless."[19] Fox interprets the verse as a contrast between the wicked, who are lauded at their funeral procession through a city, while the burial of honest people is low key or even delayed.[20] The differences between just these four options shows how disputed the meaning of the verse is.

A way forward is to lean again on the flow of Qohelet's discourse, as well as the historical context, but also to try to find clues in what the Greek translator understood by the verse in antiquity. First, immediately before the verse, Qohelet details how not even the powerful who harm others can cheat death (8:9). After it, Qohelet explores the schemes of the wicked (8:11–12). This means that 8:10 is probably also about the powerful or the wicked. This makes Krüger's, Shields's, and Fox's suggestions, which include a statement about the righteous, unlikely in the context. The Hebrew Masoretic Text also reads one of the verbs as *weyishtakkehu*, which places the root of the verb "to forget" (*shkh*) in a stem (*hitpael*) that it otherwise never appears in. This makes the form of this verb highly irregular, which should prompt us to consider other possibilities. The Greek translator read this word with the root *shbh* ("to extol"), which does ordinarily occur in the *hitpael* stem (cf. Ps 106:47; 1 Chr 16:35), and so is a much better fit.[21] Longman's suggestion works with this, and the NIV also reflects it. It should also be noted that the Greek translates the verb as an aorist passive ("they were extolled"). This is certainly possible, and both Longman and the NIV follow suit. However, a reflexive meaning is preferable for a *hitpael* verb. Furthermore, the *yiqtol* mode can be translated as a gnomic present ("they extol themselves") and not just an iterative past ("the used to extol themselves")—a factor that also affects the immediately preceding verb ("they go about"). In any case, these are translational issues to note after just a single minor emendation to the Hebrew text.

With that minor emendation, we can now make sense of the verse within the flow of Qohelet's discourse. In 8:9 Qohelet alluded to the disastrous decisions of Onias and the exploits of Joseph Tobias by talking about bad leadership that causes harm to so many. In 8:10 he counters this, saying,

18. Shields, *The End of Wisdom*, 195.

19. Longman, *Ecclesiastes*, 216.

20. Fox, *A Time to Tear Down*, 283–84.

21. The root in the Masoretic Text can easily be explained as a curtailing of the form of the letter *bet* to (accidentally) produce the letter *kap*. These two letters are very easily confused because of their similar form. The difference between them is a simple "tittle"—a tiny stroke comparable to the difference between our "O" and "Q." In handwriting, it is easy to leave out such a tiny stroke or for it not to register properly on the page.

"But then, I have seen the wicked brought to burial. Though they go about in a holy place and they extol themselves in the city where they have done so, this too is meaningless" (author's translation). This is a curious set of actions that seem like a very specific case, rather than generic behavior of the proverbially wicked. The holy place and city are almost certainly the temple and Jerusalem. This brings the spotlight onto Joseph Tobias, who had walked about the temple and extolled his own virtues above those of Onias, even receiving public acclaim as Jerusalem's potential savior from Onias's folly. But then he sold out the population by promising Ptolemy to double tax revenues acquired from them (*Ant.* 12. 156–86). Qohelet takes clear aim at Joseph's calumny. He would be chief tax farmer of the region for twenty-two years, but Qohelet intimates that no matter what position Joseph held, or what plaudits he received, he would one day die and be buried, too. He critiques Joseph by turning the circumstances surrounding his appointment as tax farmer into a general point. To that end, we also note that Qohelet uses plural verbs in 8:10 for generality. By not naming names, Qohelet "covers his tracks" again (cf. 10:20). Nonetheless, his point is stark: like all other wicked people, Joseph Tobias, too, will one day die, rendering his public career meaningless.

This is little comfort for those who must endure the Josephs of the world, especially when their actions go unchecked or even have state sanction. So, in 8:11 Qohelet reflects on how a delay of justice only encourages criminality. Since everyone has the propensity for sin (7:20), such opportune latitude merely fans the propensity into actual sin, causing damage to untold masses. Again, we must see Joseph in the background here, as Ptolemy's delay in punishing Onias for his breach of trust gave Joseph time to capitalize and become the region's chief tax farmer. While Qohelet is talking overtly about the structures of human justice, he is also questioning why God seems to delay in enacting justice upon the wicked, especially since the covenantal dynamic stipulates that God rewards the righteous and punishes the wicked. Since God is eternal, he is not going to die. With such delays of justice, Qohelet perceives a significant problem with the way the world works.

This comes under further scrutiny in 8:12–13. The NIV translation is contradictory. It entails Qohelet observing the wicked prospering for a long time, but then stating that they will not prosper for a long time and that those who fear God will be better off instead. Not only does this not make internal sense, it contradicts the very next verse (8:14), as well as Qohelet's earlier observation of justice inverted (7:15). Fredericks argues that the wicked here are criminals who have been caught and, even if sentence is delayed, their fate is still secured.[22]

22. Fredericks and Estes, *Ecclesiastes & the Song of Songs*, 195–96.

However, this view falters at several points. First, it fails to account for the logic in 8:11, which laments that the delay of justice leads not to the sure and eventual punishment of the wicked, but to their success. Second, it fails to account for the larger flow of Qohelet's discourse, which finds that society is ill because it does not work according to the covenantal dynamic (cf. 7:15; 8:14). It is, instead, meaningless. Third, it does not appreciate just how dissatisfied Qohelet is with how the world works. Fourth, it does not seem prepared to allow Qohelet to have serious problems with God's apparent unreliability, such that Qohelet feels he has no answers or prospects for change. And fifth, it does not attempt to understand the historical context into which Qohelet spoke. Rather, it tends to treat Qohelet purely as a systematic theologian formulating generic propositions detached from any specific time and place. Fredericks is correct to claim that "[t]he commendation found here is perfectly consistent with what is defined as the beginning of wisdom elsewhere in the wisdom literature, namely the fear of God,"[23] but this does not mean that Qohelet completely agrees with it. Instead, Qohelet appears to be questioning its application. That is, a better way to understand these verses is not as a straight affirmation of how the world *does* work but as a statement of how it *should* work. Qohelet is stating what he knows from tradition rather than experience. He recalls the covenantal dynamic of recompense and says that he knows this is how the world *should* work. The obvious implication is that this is not how it does work, for the wicked evidently get away with their wickedness—Joseph Tobias being the case in point.[24]

With rhetorical sophistication, therefore, Qohelet critiques conventional wisdom. He implies his subscription to the traditional wisdom of the covenantal dynamic because it has just intent. As much as he wants this tradition to be a true reflection of the world, he simply cannot affirm that it is. In fact, he confirms again that justice is all too often inverted (8:14). The NIV gives the impression that the inversion of justice here is "something else" Qohelet observes, but these words are not present in the Hebrew. Qohelet is simply underlining again that his world is an unsafe place in which folly and wickedness make everything "meaningless." So, Qohelet issues his familiar advice to eat, drink, and find whatever joy is possible in life (8:15). Since society is so unjust, Qohelet knows this will be hard to come by. Nonetheless, he still wants people to salvage something good from the days God happens to assign them.

23. Ibid., 195.

24. All that is needed for this understanding to prevail is to translate the *yiqtol* verbs with modal force ("it should go better") rather than indicative force ("it will go better"). This is a standard function of the *yiqtol* verb.

The Same Destiny Overtakes All (8:16–9:6)

Qohelet now takes a step back to survey his deliberations and sum them up. He concludes that no matter how wise a person might be, no one can make sense of the world (8:16–17). He looks at this from both the divine angle ("all that God has done") and the human ("what goes on under the sun"), and finds that God and the world are an impenetrable puzzle that puts meaning beyond reach (8:17).

The inability to discern any sense to the world means that he can perceive no substantive value in righteousness or wisdom (9:1–3a). The righteous and the wise may claim to be "in God's hands," which would be an acknowledgement of his favor according to the covenantal dynamic of recompense. However, as Qohelet has been exploring, the inversion of justice he sees throughout society, as well as colossal acts of folly and wickedness, mean the righteous and the wise are by no means immune from suffering. For most in Ptolemaic Judea, life is a prospect of eating in darkness "with great frustration, affliction and anger" (5:17). Therefore, he states, "no one knows whether love or hate awaits them" (9:1). This statement is not about the serendipitous discovery of diverse experiences in life, but of foreboding. It is about what God in his sovereignty over humans decides to impose on each one. And since no one can possibly know what God wills (8:17; cf. 3:11) or foresee the future (cf. 3:22; 7:14; 8:7; 10:14), being in God's hands is not a guarantee of favor, but a gamble against the odds.

There is, therefore, nothing that really sets the righteous apart from the rest (9:2–3a). Qohelet uses traditional Jewish categories that divide society into sets of opposites: the righteous and the wicked; the good and the bad;[25] the clean and the unclean; those who offer sacrifices and those who refrain; those who take oaths and those who do not (with a finger pointed again at Onias). Regardless of such distinctions, "the same destiny overtakes all" (9:3a). This, for Qohelet, is the "evil" that undermines all human life "under the sun."

In saying this, Qohelet does not go so far as to accuse God of evil. Once again, his Jewish piety will not allow him to do so. But it is what Qohelet does not say here that screams the loudest. The obvious parallel between "all that God has done" and "what goes on under the sun" (8:17) means that his argument certainly heads in that accusatory direction. The fact that he practically charges God with evil, but stops just short of doing so, is evidence of his deep philosophical angst. Qohelet knows God is not evil, even though all the evidence seems to frame him as such. If he could accuse God of evil, then he

25. The Hebrew text is missing "and the bad" (*welara'*) but the sets of opposites within the sentence show that it should be restored. The LXX and other ancient versions rightly restore it.

would have found his meaning. It would mean the world is the plaything of an evil and whimsical deity—a terrible meaning, but meaning nonetheless. But it is his knowledge that God is not such a deity that prevents him from laying that charge directly at God and leads him instead to describe life and destiny "under the sun" as "evil." Thus, Qohelet must live with the unease of balancing precariously on the precipice of commitment to a benign God while staring down dizzily into the dark chasm of an evil deity. It is only his deep bewilderment that prevents him from falling.

Instead of accusing God of evil and falling headlong into the chasm, he states, "The hearts of people, moreover, are full of evil and there is madness [or ignorance] in their hearts while they live" (9:3b). In apportioning blame to human beings, Qohelet is not exonerating God. This is merely another statement of the available evidence that he is willing to declare openly. Ironically, this datum keeps him tethered as he shies away from directly charging God with evil. But it keeps him there at the precipice, struggling to find meaning in a benign God. For despite the wickedness and folly of the human heart, the one fate awaits all—both the wicked and the righteous (9:3a). Along with ignorant Onias, fiendish Joseph Tobias, and predatory Ptolemy, Qohelet and countless innocents will all "join the dead" (9:3b). This is "the evil in everything that happens under the sun" (9:3a).

Verse 4 is another puzzling statement that has caused consternation among commentators. This is due in part to uncertainty over the Hebrew text, as well as the meaning of the verse in the larger context.[26] Seow offers an understanding that does not require any emendation of the consonantal text. He simply reads the interrogative pronoun here more naturally as a genuine interrogative, rather than a problematic relative pronoun (as other versions do), and divides the clauses differently: "Indeed, who is the one who chooses?"[27] He takes this as a rhetorical question that implies no mortal has a choice in their destiny, for God alone decides it. This reading accords well with the statement of 9:7 (see below), as well as earlier assertions of God's determinism (cf. 7:13–14).

This then leaves the statement about "hope" with the next part of the verse. The word for hope (*bittahon*) conveys trust rather than wishful thinking. So, the next statement should be translated, "Among all the living there is a

26. The *ketib* of the Masoretic Text seems to reflect *yibbaher* ("he is chosen") from the root *bhr*, while the *qere* reads the word as *yehubbar* ("he is associated") from the root *hbr*. The latter is also reflected by the ancient Greek translator. The NIV opts for this reading, too, translating the first part of the verse, "Anyone who is among [i.e., associated with] the living has hope." A problem with this reading, however, is that it requires understanding the interrogative pronoun *mi* ("who") to function as a relative pronoun—not impossible, but since the next word (*'asher*) is indisputably a relative pronoun, the syntax becomes irregular.

27. Seow, *Ecclesiastes*, 296, 300.

trust that a live dog is better than the dead lion." In the ancient world, dogs were despised creatures, while lions were treated with awe. The essence of the proverb, then, is that life is better than death, no matter how miserable one's existence might be. Many commentators see Qohelet affirming this as true,[28] but, even as Fox and Brown admit, it runs counter to his earlier assertions that death is better than life (4:2–3; 6:3; 7:1b).[29] Qohelet's persistent pessimism has not suddenly worn off in the space of a couple of verses. He is not confirming the adage but simply pointing out that most people believe it. Indeed, he characterizes it as a popular "trust" (*biṭṭahon*; NIV, "hope") precisely because he wants to prove it untrustworthy. After all, reality is not determined by consensus, especially when ignorance (NIV, "madness") is in people's hearts while they live (9:3). So, he proceeds to debunk the proverb in 9:5–6. In these verses, Qohelet is not proving that "Life is a divine gift to be enjoyed to its maximum as long as there is breath in the nostrils."[30] He is, rather, saying that the only certainty the living have is the knowledge that they will die. Nothing else in life is certain. "No one knows whether love or hate awaits them" (9:1), for life is not determined by one's own choices but by the decisions of others and, chiefly, by God's. For the dead, such considerations are no longer relevant. Their love, hate, and feeling (NIV, "jealousy")[31] are over (9:6). They are no longer living the gamble that is life "under the sun." Thus, with morbid sarcasm, Qohelet implies that the living do not have any actual advantage over the dead, unless one counts knowing that they will die as an advantage.[32] In rather brash fashion, then, Qohelet remains resolute in his pessimism.

Enjoying a Meaningless Life (9:7–12)

Since Qohelet finds no difference between the righteous and the wicked, he returns to his familiar advice to enjoy the basics of life (9:7–10), only this time he goes into a little more detail. His advice is still pessimistic, as he struggles to

---

28. Ardel B. Caneday, "Qoheleth: Enigmatic Pessimist or Godly Sage?," in Zuck, *Reflecting with Solomon*, 112; Roger N. Whybray, "Qoheleth, Preacher of Joy," in Zuck, *Reflecting with Solomon*, 212; Roy B. Zuck, "God and Man in Ecclesiastes," in *Reflecting with Solomon*, 221; Moore and Akin, *Ecclesiastes, Songs of Songs*, 106; Krüger, *Qoheleth*, 170; Fredericks and Estes, *Ecclesiastes & the Song of Songs*, 207–8; Schoors, *Ecclesiastes*, 664.

29. Fox understands Qohelet to be asserting something contrary to 4:3; see *A Time to Tear Down*, 293. Brown sees these words as a pendulum swing for Qohelet away from despair to hope; see *Ecclesiastes*, 92. That Qohelet debunks the adage in the next few verses shows that he has not changed his mind.

30. Caneday, "Qoheleth: Enigmatic Pessimist or Godly Sage?," 112.

31. The word that the NIV translates as "jealousy" (*qin'ah*) does not always denote jealousy in the strict sense. It can indicate zeal or passion—that is, feeling or pathos. When Yahweh is called a "jealous God" (*'el qanna'*, [e.g., Exod 20:5; Deut 4:24]), it marks him as a living deity.

32. Longman, *Ecclesiastes*, 228; Schoors, *Ecclesiastes*, 663; cf. Fox, *A Time to Tear Down*, 292.

salvage something from "all the days of this meaningless life" (9:9). But now he frames his advice with reference to God's will.

Most versions translate 9:7 as a positive command to enjoy life, "for God has already approved what you do," but this understanding is puzzling amidst Qohelet's repeated characterization of life as "all your meaningless days" just two verses later (9:9). What exactly does God approve and how does this lead to eating and drinking with joy? As Longman observes, "It sounds as if he [Qohelet] believes that God gives people unlimited approval for their actions."[33] Tamez argues that Qohelet sees God delighting in human pleasure.[34] This, however, is difficult to reconcile with Qohelet's assertion of life's meaninglessness, as well as the "evil" he consistently observes under God's sovereignty. Fredericks takes "this approval to be of the life and actions of the righteous,"[35] but this would be unusual after Qohelet has denied any difference between the righteous and the wicked (9:2–3) and viewed life as meaningless. Greidanus sees here an allusion to the Genesis creation accounts, in which God gives humanity approval to eat from the trees he created.[36] However, this, too, fails to align with Qohelet's insistence of life's meaninglessness. It also seems to read the restricted conditions of Eden (Gen 2) back into Ecclesiastes and does not account for Qohelet's references to enjoying wine, wearing white, and anointing the head with oil, all of which seem to have nothing to do with Eden.

There is, however, a better way to look at the verse. Instead of translating the Hebrew word *ratsah* as "approved," it should instead be assigned its other nuance, namely "willed" or "determined" (cf. Ps 40:13[40:14]; 1 Chr 28:4). To "approve" of something is to acknowledge it as in line with one's "will." Indeed, the Hebrew noun for "will" (*ratson*) is derived from this same root (cf. Pss 40:8[40:9]; 103:21; 143:10; Ezra 10:11). When understood this way, Qohelet tells his readers to enjoy the basics of life, because "God has already determined your actions." In other words, God shapes history and all the "meaningless days" of a person's life according to his own will (9:9), and it is futile to try to overturn this. Instead, a person should try simply to enjoy the basics if they have the chance: eating, drinking, grooming, and relationship (9:8–9). Even as Qohelet tells his readers, "Whatever your hand finds to do, do it with all your might" (9:10), his advice is weighed down by the heavy melancholy of 9:9 and the inability to guarantee that one's own efforts will yield any positive result,

33. Longman, *Ecclesiastes*, 229.

34. Elsa Tamez, *When the Horizons Close: Rereading Ecclesiastes* (Maryknoll, NY: Orbis, 2000), 116.

35. Fredericks and Estes, *Ecclesiastes & the Song of Songs*, 209.

36. Greidanus, *Preaching Christ from Ecclesiastes*, 233.

for "time and chance happen to them all" (9:11; cf. 1:13; 6:2; 7:13–14). This is not *carpe diem* optimism that sees life as "active and energetic."[37] On the contrary, Qohelet expects most people to be "trapped by evil times," like fish "caught in a cruel net" or birds "taken in a snare" (9:12; cf. 5:17). For Qohelet, humans are God's victims. He is simply advising his readers to make the most of an utterly meaningless situation before they die. In this way, Qohelet adapts the advice that the maiden, Sabitum, gives to Gilgamesh in the ancient Epic of Gilgamesh.[38] The undercurrent here is that God maintains a stranglehold on human existence, putting people in dehumanizing situations with which they struggle to cope. Amid such a harsh "lot" (9:9), Qohelet counsels people to retrieve something of their humanity before the loss of everything at death, if they possibly can.

Folly Outweighs Wisdom (9:13–10:4)

The entrapment of humans that Qohelet depicts in 9:12 also evokes the prophetic images of Jerusalem's experience of siege (cf. Ezek 19:1–9; Hab 1:14–15).[39] In addition to reflecting personal trauma, then, Qohelet's discourse echoes the collective trauma of Israel's national experience. This comes through more overtly in 9:13–16, where Qohelet provides an anecdote of a small city besieged by a great king.[40] As he does throughout the book, Qohelet does not name names in his anecdote, but as Barbour rightly points out, "an allusion without a name can be no less marked."[41] Qohelet tells his anecdote in just such a way that it would "stir up memories of a similar episode" known to his readers.[42] That episode is Sennacherib's siege of Jerusalem (2 Kgs 18:13–19:37). Qohelet creates a mosaic from the biblical narratives and associated prophetic imagery. Thus, Jerusalem is the "small city with only a few people in it" (9:14), evoking the characterization of Jerusalem as "a hut in a cucumber field" and the ensuing reflection, "Unless the Lord Almighty had left us some survivors, we would have become like Sodom, we would have been like Gomorrah" (Isa 1:8–9). Sennacherib is the "great king," as the Rabshakeh calls him in 2 Kings 18:19 and 28, and the wise man who saves the city is the prophet Isaiah, whose advice to Hezekiah is the turning point in the city's

37. Eaton, *Ecclesiastes*, 129.

38. Clay and Jastrow, Jr., *The Epic of Gilgamesh*, 8–9; Seow, *Ecclesiastes*, 305; Brown, *Ecclesiastes*, 94.

39. Barbour, *The Story of Israel in the Book of Qohelet*, 126–29.

40. The word translated "siege works" in 9:14 (*metsodim*) is identical to the word for "net" in 9:12. Translators construe it as "siege works" in 9:14 because it is the object of the verb "build," but this requires an emendation of the word from *metsodim* to *metsorim*. At any rate, the imagery of 9:12 provides a conceptual introduction to the anecdote.

41. Barbour, *The Story of Israel in the Book of Qohelet*, 120.

42. Ibid., 124.

fate. There is an ambiguity in 9:15. The Hebrew wording permits a definitive sense that sees the poor, wise man saving the city but then being forgotten after the event. It also permits a potential sense in which the poor wise man could have saved the city, but no one thought of him, thus leading to the city's demise. The allusions to Sennacherib's campaign favor the former, but the latter cannot be discounted. The anonymous way Qohelet recounts this anecdote lifts it above specifics, making it possible to apply to other situations, also. It may even contain allusions to other incidents in Jerusalem's history (cf. Neh 1:3), which pass us by for lack of sources or collective memory. As Barbour states, "the isolated, nameless event of the siege-tale seems to offer a paradigm for the fortunes of cities, their powers, and their people."[43]

There is also a sense of pining as Qohelet tells this story. It harks back to a time when Jerusalem had been saved from a fearsome foreign oppressor. Now that was but a distant, foggy memory, like the poor, wise man in the story. Qohelet is expressing how different his current circumstances could be—if only there were a truly wise person who could save Jerusalem from the folly of Onias, the threats of Ptolemy, and the schemes of Joseph Tobias, who had sold out the city even as he claimed to be saving it. Not only does this underline Joseph's perfidy, it brings to the fore once again the limits of the sages in Qohelet's day. Their conventional wisdom could not extricate the nation from the recklessness of Onias, the power of the Ptolemies, or the wiles of Joseph, leaving the nation "trapped in evil times" (9:12).

And so, Qohelet quotes conventional wisdom again to critique it (9:17–10:4). Quiet words of wisdom should have been enough to drown out "the shouts of a ruler of fools" (9:17)—an allusion to Onias's loud refusal to pay Ptolemy the twenty talents for his position. As Josephus records, "he was ready, if the thing were practicable, to lay down his high priesthood" (*Ant.* 12.163). Qohelet captures this development, as well as Ptolemy's threatened military action against Jerusalem, in 10:4, where he advises, "If a ruler's anger rises against you, do not leave your post." Shields claims this proverb "bears no obvious relationship to the preceding material," but understanding the specific historical context shows how cogent this saying is.[44] The word for "post" here (*maqom*) is a standard way of referring to the "place" of the temple (cf. Deut 12:5; 1 Kgs 8:21, 29–30), so Qohelet's words relate very much to Onias's willingness to vacate the high priesthood. The verb "leave" is also the same word translated as "lay to rest" in the next clause, which ties the two clauses together. The NIV translates it "calmness can lay great offenses to

43. Ibid., 135.

44. Shields, *The End of Wisdom*, 211.

rest." However, "calmness" does not adequately capture the meaning of the underlying Hebrew word, *marpe'*, which conveys the notion of "healing." In relational contexts, it refers specifically to reconciliation (cf. Jer 14:9; 33:6).[45] Thus, the second clause is better translated as "Reconciliation can lay great offenses to rest." The implication is that if Onias had paid the obligatory fee he was sworn to pay, he would not have brought such adversity upon Jerusalem and Judea. He would have been following Qohelet's sage advice in 7:12: "Wisdom is a shelter, as money is a shelter." Yet, his flagrant obstinacy not only brought the threat of military action, it also opened the door for Joseph Tobias. Though Joseph successfully petitioned Ptolemy for peace, he then treacherously imposed the backbreaking misery of doubled taxes upon the entire region, from which he creamed his own personal fortune. The proverb of 9:18 concisely sums up that development: "Wisdom is better than weapons of war, but one sinner destroys much good." The first half of this proverb was probably a conventional adage that Qohelet counters with his own supplementary observation. In this way, he highlights again the limitations of wisdom. It also brings the earlier anecdote of the little besieged city (9:13–16) to bear on the specific circumstances of his own day. If Onias had done the wise thing, he would have paid Ptolemy his fee, and Jerusalem would have been spared greater hardship. But he refused to listen and acted foolishly instead. "A little folly outweighs wisdom and honor" (10:1).

Qohelet co-opts a proverb in 10:2 to indicate some of the geopolitical ramifications of Onias's decision. The proverb is ostensibly about the divergent paths of wisdom and folly: "The heart of the wise inclines to the right, but the heart of the fool to the left." But this is more than a simple proverb. The "right" (Heb: *yamin*) is a standard way that Hebrew indicates the south, while the "left" (*semo'l*) indicates the north (cf. Gen 13:9; Josh 17:7; Job 23:9). Egypt, the base of the Ptolemies' kingdom, was traditionally viewed as the "south" (or "right"), while the Seleucids who ruled in Syria and Asia Minor were to the "north" (or "left"). The same notion is, in fact, used in Daniel 11, where the "King of the South" is a cipher for the Ptolemies, and the "King of the North" represents the Seleucids.[46] Although Qohelet shows no liking for the Ptolemies, he discerns that it would have been politically more expedient for Onias to have sent his payment "south" to Ptolemy in Egypt, than to have

45. *HALOT* lists two separate entries for the noun *marpe'*, the first derived from the root *rp'* ("to heal"), and the second from the root *rph* ("to grow slack"). However, all instances of this supposed second noun, including Ecclesiastes 10:4, are spelled according to the root *rp'*, not *rph*, and are better understood as conveying a sense of healing or reconciliation.

46. Daniel 11 uses different Hebrew terms for "north" and "south" than those Qohelet uses here. Nonetheless, the conceptuality behind the terms is identical.

leaned toward the Seleucids in the "north." His folly left Jerusalem and Judea vulnerable to the subterfuge and sabotage of Joseph Tobias.

Underlying all this political rhetoric is the inference that Qohelet's Jerusalem needs better and more competent leaders. This brings up the loss of the Davidic dynasty once again—another painful reminder that Qohelet, a son of David, for all his wisdom and piercing intellect, was not a king in power, but a depressed and oppressed citizen who could only conjure up vague memories of his heritage's past glories.

LIVE the Story

More than a Teacher

Qohelet's thinly veiled criticisms of Onias II, Joseph Tobias, and Ptolemy III arise from the anguish of an oppressed soul. He was no mere disinterested observer but one who was directly and adversely affected by the decisions that the powerholders of his world took. This would have been especially galling for Qohelet, who had a legitimate right to rule his people as a descendant of David and who had the intellect to discern the folly and wickedness emanating from the corridors of power, but was powerless to change anything. Qohelet's society was not a democracy in which he could protest, cast a vote, or even run for office. He was utterly disenfranchised and utterly disenchanted.

Qohelet's penetrating discourse exposed both the misdeeds of his day and the little that conventional wisdom could achieve in the circumstances. This was a truly depressing state of affairs, and Qohelet resigned himself to collecting crumbs of joy in the very basics of life. If this were a truly satisfactory philosophy for life, then Qohelet would have been condoning the folly and evil taking place in the upper echelons of society and the damage it was causing to countless lives. Qohelet does not assert his advice as a positive philosophy but as an attempt to salvage something from the dismal reality of his meaningless world. It highlights the need for radical surgery to address the problems in leadership, the deficiencies in the lives of the average person, and the darker self-destructive channels within the human heart. Education and wisdom are valuable, but they cannot solve the world's problems.

This is why Jesus's ministry was not just about dispensing wisdom. When people call Jesus a great, wise teacher, they are paying him a compliment of sorts, but the description sells him far short of who he was and what he did. Though he taught thousands of people, this was not the full extent or essence of his ministry. Though he healed and touched the lives of so many, this was not the substance of his work. Though he prophetically denounced the injustices of the rulers of his day and the spiritual bankruptcy of the religious elite, this too was not the totality of his ministry. Jesus was not just a good teacher. He was God in human flesh (John 1:14), come to serve and give his life as a ransom for many (Mark 10:45). He came to seek and save the lost (Luke 19:10). He came that we might live, and have life to the full (John 10:10). Jesus's life, death, and resurrection bring the love of God into the center of human existence, enabling the forgiveness of our sin and the transformation of our corrupt human hearts by his Spirit. Conventional wisdom may be able to say how things should be, and education may be able to outline options and their consequences. But they can no more convince a rich man to enter the kingdom of God than they can coax a camel to go through the eye of a needle (cf. Luke 18:25). Education and knowledge cannot compel human change. Only the supernatural work of God's Spirit given through the grace of Jesus Christ can perform the radical surgery needed to redeem humanity from itself.

Faith and Doubt

Qohelet's discourse shows a clash of both faith and doubt. His pained, sometimes sarcastic and even cynical tone reveals a man overwhelmed by his world, disgusted by its leaders, and perplexed by his God. In line with classic orthodoxy, he acknowledged the supreme sovereignty of God, but the world he was in depressed him with its misery, folly, and wickedness. It made him question everything, even to the point of doubting the goodness of God. Yet, all he could do was rely on God to effect change. This sounds like a godly strategy powered by faith, but Qohelet was unable to adopt it. The God who had promised so much to Qohelet's ancestors in the past did not seem keen to deliver in the present. For Qohelet, the policy of "let go and let God" merely raised the prospect of a deity who was as heartless as the human rulers who lorded it over their human subjects. The abject misery that Qohelet witnessed in his world, which only seemed to be deepening, was an indictment of both the human rulers who spawned it as well as the God who seemed to sanction it with silence. Qohelet could have all the faith in the world, and still God did not seem to be acting in the interests of the innocent, the righteous, and the oppressed. For us who are removed from Qohelet's context, these are nameless, disembodied figures, but for Qohelet these were real flesh-and-blood people with faces and names, whose lives were being crushed under the folly and sinfulness of the powerful and the apparent inaction of a distant deity.

That Qohelet does not come out and accuse God of folly or evil is astonishing, for that is evidently the endpoint of his deliberations. But this is where we see the element of faith in Qohelet's discourse. He teeters on the brink of blaming all the ills of his world on the God he knows as the omnipotent lord of history but who either seemed to want to do nothing to address the world's problems or who was patently evil. Yet, he never comes out and blames God openly. Instead, he proclaims his own inability to make sense of the world. Qohelet's insistence that all is meaningless is not a fist raised in rebellion against God, though it is certainly a bold cry. It is, rather, a resigned slump of the shoulders whereby, despite the circumstances before him, he would prefer to admit the limits of his own perception and accord God the benefit of the doubt. Faith for Qohelet is not about "letting go and letting God," expressing iron-clad confidence in God, or having all the answers. Rather, it is about admitting, even with utter exasperation and doubt, that he, a mere human, does not have the wherewithal to fathom what God is or is not doing (cf. Eccl 3:11).

What is it that keeps Qohelet from collapsing into the charge that God is foolish or pathologically evil? While he does not say so in direct terms, it is his knowledge of what God has said and done in the past. Qohelet looks with some longing into his own heritage as both a Jewish man and a Davidic descendant, as his many biblical allusions attest. On his own unsteady legs, he leans on these past traditions, even as he questions what some of them might mean now for his own context. It is these inspired traditions that tell him what God is like, and, though the mounting evidence almost contradicts them, Qohelet is unwilling to deny them. This itself might seem foolish, as though Qohelet were trying to lift himself by his own bootstraps, hoping against hope that God is good. But it is also Qohelet's experience that preserves his faith. He is able to evaluate human action and how this contributes to the ills of the world. Qohelet acknowledges God's complete sovereignty over human affairs, but he does not think this absolves humanity of wrongdoing. On the contrary, as this section of his discourse demonstrates, Qohelet sees ignorance in the human heart, as well as recklessness, selfishness, and flagrant injustice. Knowing just how stupid and wicked humans can be, Qohelet will call out folly and evil "under the sun," but refrain from laying the charge overtly against "heaven." He will, instead, attempt to live under the weight of doubt and despair.

Doubt is often a "dirty word" in Christian circles, as it is usually contrasted with faith. Being a Christian is seen to be about the life of victory, certainty, and confidence in God and his goodness. Amid such terms, to doubt is akin to disparaging God and his character and being on the slippery slope to unbelief. Thus, folk who express doubt are sometimes treated as though they have fallen away, are rebelling, or are suffering from an acute spiritual condition. James describes the person who asks for wisdom but doubts as "double-minded and unstable in all they do" (Jas 1:5–8). Unfortunately, these words are sometimes aimed at those who do not or cannot express the utmost confidence that they will receive from God what they ask for. What many do not realize is that James is not condemning lack of confidence, but rather lack of belief that Jesus is the Christ—the Lord who gives godly wisdom. James is telling his Jewish compatriots scattered among the Gentiles (Jas 1:1) that Jesus is Israel's messiah, and this recognition lies at the root of rightly responding to God. If one denies who Jesus is, they will be denying who God is, and so should not expect to receive the benefits of relationship with him. This is not about the amount of confidence one has that they will receive what they ask for. To think that the Christian life is about such confidence is to turn the Christian from a humble, dependent child of God into a spoilt brat with a sense of entitlement to rival Veruca Salt[47] and who cares nothing for their heavenly Father.

For many people, the circumstances of life raise so many unanswerable questions that they cannot but live in doubt and despair. Sickness, grief, loss, depression, persecution, sexuality, relationship breakdown, or simply observing the harsh dynamics of human society or nature can lead many to doubt God and his goodness. Indeed, at times, it seems almost inhuman not to rail against the way things are. As Christians, we must never be quick to condemn those whose cries come from despair, pain, or confusion. Even Jesus himself cried out questioningly, "My God! My God! Why have you forsaken me?" (Mark 15:34). Such cries come not from lack of faith, but from a sense that things are just not right. Qohelet's despondence, as well as Christ's cry from the cross, give us permission to express frustration and pain. To mute them is not only unhelpful, it can be downright destructive.

The Christian life might not be one of exhilaration and ecstasy. It might be strewn with struggles. But it is not rooted in one's own confidence and surety. It is not about one's ability to discern the will of God for the present or the future. Nor is it about unquestioning allegiance, or the ability to come up with all the right answers. It is, rather, rooted in a basic conviction about Jesus—that he is the messiah of Israel; that he died for our sins, and was raised to life for our justification (Rom 4:25).

Qohelet did not have the benefit of knowing Jesus, the son of David who brought to fruition all of God's purposes. Qohelet's discourse bears the hallmarks of doubt and disillusionment. He is sure of the folly and evil in his world, but he is unsure what this means about God. Far from exhibiting unbelief, Qohelet's despondence demonstrates both his commitment to God

47. Veruca Salt is an objectionable character from Roald Dahl's much-loved children's novel, *Charlie and the Chocolate Factory* (1964).

and the softness of his heart. He is not made of spiritual "Teflon," for he is deeply affected by God's seeming inaction and what goes on around him. Nonetheless, he is prepared to live with the frustration of not knowing how to make sense of it all, and even to proclaim this loudly. Indeed, it reveals epistemic and spiritual humility. It is not a comfortable existence, for it troubles him no end. But Qohelet was a smart man whose wisdom and intellect were seen in his readiness to acknowledge not just what he did know, but also that he did not know everything. Though Christians know far more than Qohelet did, because we live in an "AD" world, we would do well to emulate his faith as someone prepared to acknowledge that he did not have all the answers. It will save us from spiritual arrogance and help us depend on God's grace.

Having doubts can be distressing. Understandably, we do not enjoy the threat of having previous beliefs challenged or feeling like we don't have the answers. When others express doubts, we should not "shoot from the hip" to silence them or condemn them, for then we become miserable comforters who lack godly grace. The Christian faith is not about maintaining heroic levels of confidence, having all the answers, or appearing spiritually invincible. To appear like this is either to lie or misconstrue the nature of Christian faith. The Christian faith is, rather, about a person: Jesus Christ. Our security is in him. We are saved by him, which is why we put our faith in him. Just as we might wish to point Qohelet to Jesus, so we must keep pointing ourselves and others to him, for he is our anchor. He is our proof that, despite the world being in its current state, and our lack of answers, God has demonstrated his grace and favor to us.

CHAPTER 7

Ecclesiastes 10:5–12:8

LISTEN to the Story

5There is an evil I have seen under the sun,
the sort of error that arises from a ruler:
6Fools are put in many high positions,
while the rich occupy the low ones.
7I have seen slaves on horseback,
while princes go on foot like slaves.
8Whoever digs a pit may fall into it;
whoever breaks through a wall may be bitten by a snake.
9Whoever quarries stones may be injured by them;
whoever splits logs may be endangered by them.
10If the ax is dull
and its edge unsharpened,
more strength is needed,
but skill will bring success.
11If a snake bites before it is charmed,
the charmer receives no fee.
12Words from the mouth of the wise are gracious,
but fools are consumed by their own lips.
13At the beginning their words are folly;
at the end they are wicked madness—
14and fools multiply words.
No one knows what is coming—
who can tell someone else what will happen after them?
15The toil of fools wearies them;
they do not know the way to town.
16Woe to the land whose king was a servant
and whose princes feast in the morning.
17Blessed is the land whose king is of noble birth
and whose princes eat at a proper time—

for strength and not for drunkenness.
18Through laziness, the rafters sag;
because of idle hands, the house leaks.
19A feast is made for laughter,
wine makes life merry,
and money is the answer for everything.
20Do not revile the king even in your thoughts,
or curse the rich in your bedroom,
because a bird in the sky may carry your words,
and a bird on the wing may report what you say.
11:1Ship your grain across the sea;
after many days you may receive a return.
2Invest in seven ventures, yes, in eight;
you do not know what disaster may come upon the land.
3If clouds are full of water,
they pour rain on the earth.
Whether a tree falls to the south or to the north,
in the place where it falls, there it will lie.
4Whoever watches the wind will not plant;
whoever looks at the clouds will not reap.
5As you do not know the path of the wind,
or how the body is formed in a mother's womb,
so you cannot understand the work of God,
the Maker of all things.
6Sow your seed in the morning,
and at evening let your hands not be idle,
for you do not know which will succeed,
whether this or that,
or whether both will do equally well.
7Light is sweet,
and it pleases the eyes to see the sun.
8However many years anyone may live,
let them enjoy them all.
But let them remember the days of darkness,
for there will be many.
Everything to come is meaningless.
9You who are young, be happy while you are young,
and let your heart give you joy in the days of your youth.

Follow the ways of your heart
    and whatever your eyes see,
but know that for all these things
    God will bring you into judgment.
10 So then, banish anxiety from your heart
    and cast off the troubles of your body,
    for youth and vigor are meaningless.
12:1 Remember your Creator
    in the days of your youth,
before the days of trouble come
    and the years approach when you will say,
    "I find no pleasure in them"—
2 before the sun and the light
    and the moon and the stars grow dark,
    and the clouds return after the rain;
3 when the keepers of the house tremble,
    and the strong men stoop,
when the grinders cease because they are few,
    and those looking through the windows grow dim;
4 when the doors to the street are closed
    and the sound of grinding fades;
when people rise up at the sound of birds,
    but all their songs grow faint;
5 when people are afraid of heights
    and of dangers in the streets;
when the almond tree blossoms
    and the grasshopper drags itself along
    and desire no longer is stirred.
Then people go to their eternal home
    and mourners go about the streets.
6 Remember him—before the silver cord is severed,
    and the golden bowl is broken;
before the pitcher is shattered at the spring,
    and the wheel broken at the well,
7 and the dust returns to the ground it came from,
    and the spirit returns to God who gave it.
8 "Meaningless! Meaningless!" says the Teacher.
    "Everything is meaningless!"

Listening to the Story in the Text: The Instruction of Ankhsheshonq; Josephus, *Antiquities* 12.156–86; Genesis 2–3; 1 Kings 11:1–13; Isaiah 24; Jeremiah 6:22–30; 25:8–11; 49:23–27; Lamentations

Qohelet is keen to dispense his own extreme brand of wisdom in response to the social situation unfolding before him. He challenges convention by exposing its limits and shining a spotlight on the folly and sinfulness of human behavior. He appropriates proverbs to give them edgier nuances that serve his critical purposes.

One piece of writing that seems to have influenced him is a text written originally in Demotic Egyptian called *The Instruction of Ankhsheshonq*. Though the text is arguably older, the surviving papyrus comes from the Ptolemaic Era, so there were copies available during the time of Qohelet.[1] The text tells the story of Ankhsheshonq, a priest of Re at Heliopolis, who visits his friend, Harsiese, at the palace in Memphis to seek advice about a problem. Pharaoh had recently promoted Harsiese to chief physician. It therefore comes as a shock to Ankhsheshonq when Harsiese informs him that he and Pharaoh's entire executive staff are plotting Pharaoh's murder. Ankhsheshonq objects to Harsiese's conspiracy, asking how he could possibly think of such a thing when he owes his position and welfare to Pharaoh, but he fails to dissuade his friend. Unfortunately for both men, a household servant hears their conversation from an inner chamber and subsequently reports the plot to Pharaoh that night. Harsiese and his co-conspirators are executed the following day, while Pharaoh imprisons Ankhsheshonq for failing to report the conspiracy. The irony is that Ankhsheshonq's fate practically justifies Harsiese's conspiracy: Pharaoh is an unreasonable tyrant.

Ankhsheshonq interprets his own fate as a supreme injustice that will incur the wrath of the god, Pre. While in prison, he composes a compendium of proverbs to send to his son, knowing he will now never be able to teach him in person. He begins with a set of statements decrying injustice and the inversion of proper social order around him. Among these statements, he says:

1. We do not know if Qohelet was conversant in Demotic (he probably was not), but under the Ptolemies, the dissemination of literature and its translation increased rapidly throughout the Mediterranean world. Ptolemy II famously sponsored the acquisition and translation of much literature via the Royal Library of Alexandria. The result was a golden age of literary production. Indeed, the translation of the Hebrew Scriptures into Greek may originally have come under his sponsorship. In any case, Qohelet's learning and philosophical prowess demonstrate a man who had evidently read widely. Even if he had not personally read *The Instruction of Ankhsheshonq*, he appears familiar enough with some of its contents that he must have known about it at least in popular oral form.

> When Pre is angry with a land he makes great its humble people and humbles its great people.
> When Pre is angry with a land he sets the fools over the wise.
> When Pre is angry with a land he orders its ruler to mistreat its people.[2]
>
> *(Ankhsheshonq,* 5.9–11*)*

Ankhsheshonq then proceeds to give various proverbs whose morality is "utilitarian, sometimes humorous, and occasionally cynical."[3] As he responds to the injustices in his own situation, Qohelet will borrow the sentiment of these proverbs, as well as others from Ankhsheshonq's instruction, adapting them to provide sophisticated criticism of the leaders of his own society. Once again, Onias II, his nephew, Joseph Tobias, and Ptolemy III will come in for particular attention. Like the anonymous Pharaoh of Ankhsheshonq's tale, Qohelet perceives Ptolemy III to be an unjust tyrant. Like Ankhsheshonq himself, Qohelet perceives both the folly and wickedness of those who owe their positions to the ruler. Thus, Qohelet will continue pressing his criticisms of the high priest Onias II and his nephew, Joseph Tobias. Once again, Onias's refusal to pay Ptolemy the fee for his own position, and Joseph's quick opportunism during the subsequent crisis, form the backdrop for Qohelet's comments. Qohelet seeks to be more cautious than Ankhsheshonq, watching his words carefully, so as to avoid a similar fate.

Also important to the final portion of Qohelet's discourse are prophetic pronouncements and laments about the downfall of cities. The most important of these, but by no means the only one, is the fall of Jerusalem to the Babylonians in the early sixth century BC. It marked the end of the kingdom of Judah and permanently imprinted its trauma on the Judean psyche. The motifs associated with these catastrophes relate especially to the end of urban and agricultural life. People no longer move about freely, but barricade themselves indoors. "Do not go out to the fields or walk on the roads," Jeremiah warns, "for the enemy has a sword, and there is terror on every side" (Jer 6:25). "The ruined city lies desolate; the entrance to every house is barred" (Isa 24:10). The protectors of the city are rendered useless and overcome. "Surely, her young men will fall in the streets," Jeremiah laments, "all her soldiers will be silenced in that day" (Jer 49:26). The normal rhythms and hums of life cease, replaced by eerie silence. Celebration turns to trauma. Mirth fades into misery.

---

2. Miriam Lichtheim, *Ancient Egyptian Literature: A Book of Readings. Volume III: The Late Period* (Berkeley: University of California Press, 1980), 164.

3. Ibid., 9.

Laughter gives way to lament. "I will banish from them the sounds of joy and gladness," Yahweh threatens, "the voices of bride and bridegroom, the sound of millstones and the light of the lamp. This whole country will become a desolate wasteland" (Jer 25:10–11a). The book of Lamentations displays an array of mournful images reflecting on the horror of Jerusalem's plight during and after the Babylonian siege. Some passages relevant to Qohelet's thought include the following:

> How deserted lies the city,
> once so full of people! (Lam 1:1a)
> The Lord has rejected
> all the warriors in my midst;
> he has summoned an army against me
> to crush my young men. (Lam 1:15)
> The elders of Daughter Zion
> sit on the ground in silence;
> they have sprinkled dust on their heads
> and put on sackcloth.
> The young women of Jerusalem
> have bowed their heads to the ground. (Lam 2:10)
> I am the man who has seen affliction
> by the rod of the LORD's wrath.
> He has driven me away and made me walk
> in darkness rather than light;
> indeed, he has turned his hand against me
> again and again, all day long.
> He has made my skin and my flesh grow old
> and has broken my bones.
> He has besieged me and surrounded me
> with bitterness and hardship.
> He has made me dwell in darkness
> like those long dead. (Lam 3:1–6)
> How the gold has lost its luster,
> the fine gold become dull!
> The sacred gems are scattered
> at every street corner.
> How the precious children of Zion,
> once worth their weight in gold,
> are now considered as pots of clay,
> the work of a potter's hands! (Lam 4:1–2)

EXPLAIN the Story

The Approaching End (10:5–12:8)

This is the final section of Qohelet's discourse. Although he continues his critique of conventional wisdom and the leaders of his society, his thoughts fittingly turn to notions of death. As someone who seems well acquainted with old age, he will dispense advice to the proverbial "young man" to make the most of his youth. In doing so, he will not be merely philosophical but also offer social commentary. Qohelet views death not simply as the fate of every human being but also a state that has descended upon his own society through recent events. Qohelet's pessimism continues to soak into even the most positive of his statements here. Thus, he finishes his discourse in the dank darkness of death, devoid of meaning.

The Consequences of Folly (10:5–15)

Having demonstrated the limits of wisdom before the supreme folly of Onias II and the cunning devices of Joseph Tobias in the previous section, Qohelet now discusses the kind of society that results (10:5–20). What ensues is a series of observations and proverbs that resemble some of those found in *The Instruction of Ankhsheshonq*. Again, he does not name anyone, but when read against the backdrop of the machinations in Ptolemaic Jerusalem during the 220s BC, Qohelet's proverbialized statements make for stinging political critique.

His discussion commences with a description of inverted social order brought about by "the sort of error that arises from a ruler" (10:5). These verses (10:5–7) closely resemble the cluster of statements in *The Instruction of Ankhsheshonq* 5.9–11, mentioned in Listen to the Story above. Interestingly, Qohelet avoids using the term "king" here (10:5; cf. *Ankhsheshonq* 5.11). The word for "ruler" (*shallit*) is general enough to apply to many positions of authority. Qohelet's contemporaries would have heard criticism of Ptolemy III at 10:5, and Onias II and Joseph Tobias at 10:6.[4] The NIV begins 10:6 with an indefinite plural ("fools"), but the Hebrew literally says "the fool," which permits the more specific application: "the fool is put in many high positions" (cf. *Ankhsheshonq* 5.10), alluding to Onias's high priestly function as well as his charge (*prostasia*) over the Jewish nation in Jerusalem and Judea.[5] The next

4. Cf. Norbert Lohfink, "*melek*, *shallit* und *moshel* bei Kohelet und die Abfassungszeit des Buches," *Biblica* 62 (1981): 542–43.

5. The high priestly rise to prominence over the Jewish nation is a postexilic development, probably going back to the elevation of Joshua, son of Jehozadak, to leadership over the Jerusalem community in the absence of Zerubbabel, the Davidic descendant, during reconstruction of the temple in c. 519 BC (see Zech 6:9–15). Deborah W. Rooke acknowledges the expansion of Joshua's power

clause literally reads, "and wealthy ones sit in the low place" (cf. *Ankhsheshonq* 5.9). Initially, this seems to classify the wise and the wealthy together, as a contrast to the fool in the previous clause, with the resulting sense: just as the fool is promoted, so the wise/wealthy are demoted.[6] However, it is specifically the wealthy who are demoted here, not the wise. Some commentators take this as evidence that Qohelet "favors the privileged classes of Israel" (cf. 10:17),[7] but Qohelet's view of the wealthy is not always favorable (cf. 5:12; 10:20). A better understanding of Qohelet's meaning arises when we read this in light of Ankhsheshonq's equivalent proverb and Joseph Tobias's terror tactics. *Ankhsheshonq* 5.10 polarizes "the great" (i.e., the wealthy and important) with "the humble" (i.e., the unimportant and lowly), helping explain Qohelet's choice of polarity here. As Josephus notes (*Ant.* 12.181–83), when the cities of Ashkelon and Scythopolis refused to pay him, Joseph rounded up and executed the most prominent citizens, confiscating their wealth. Thus, what Qohelet pictures here is a society whose status quo is turned upside down, because the "ruler" (Ptolemy III) allowed "the fool" (Onias II) to occupy a position of power, paving the way for the likes of Joseph to terrorize innocent people.

Verse 7 also reflects this inversion of social order, as Qohelet observes slaves on horseback and princes (or officials) on foot. Whether he has a specific contemporary event in mind is difficult to know, but the promotion of Joseph Tobias may be in the background here. It might also refer to the similar authority that Ptolemaic agents like Zenon (manager of Apollonius, the treasurer of Ptolemy II) wielded over the local aristocracy in Judea. At any rate, we can hear again Qohelet lamenting that he, a Davidic prince, was but a powerless plebeian. His own heritage now counted for nothing, and, like all other citizens, he presumably suffered considerable losses under Joseph's domination. He was a prince without property (cf. 7:11).

In 10:8–11 Qohelet unpacks some further consequences of societal disorientation. Again, there appear to be affinities with some proverbs from *The Instruction of Ankhsheshonq*.[8] The gist of each proverb he gives is that no one

---

but limits it to the cultic realm (see *Zadok's Heirs: The Role and Development of the High Priesthood in Ancient Israel* [Oxford: Oxford University Press, 2000], 125–51). Yet, this overlooks the likelihood of Joshua's need to fill the breach in civic leadership left by Zerubbabel's (temporary) removal from office. Before the exile, the high priest seems to have been subservient to the Davidic king. After Joshua, there was precedent for the high priest exercising some civic authority. This did not, however, completely eliminate Davidic hope in Jerusalem. Cf. James C. VanderKam, *From Joshua to Caiaphas: High Priests After the Exile* (Minneapolis: Fortress Press, 2004), 23, 42.

6. Cf. Seow, *Ecclesiastes*, 324–25; Longman, *Ecclesiastes*, 242; Fredericks and Estes, *Ecclesiastes & the Song of Songs*, 221, 227; Schoors, *Ecclesiastes*, 719–20.

7. Longman, *Ecclesiastes*, 242; Krüger, *Qoheleth*, 183–84.

8. Ecclesiastes 10:8a resembles the incomplete *Ankhsheshonq* 26.21 ("He who digs a pit . . ."), while Ecclesiastes 10:9a resembles *Ankhsheshonq* 22.5 ("He who shakes the stone will have it fall on his foot").

wins when incompetence and oppression rule the day. Not only do the masses who abide the oppression suffer, but the oppressors will eventually suffer, too. As Jean Baptiste Colbert, finance minister to King Louis XIV of France, once said, "the art of taxation consists in so plucking the goose as to get the most feathers for the least hissing."[9] But Qohelet implies that the Ptolemaic system was so injurious that the Ptolemies risked the "goose" running out of feathers altogether, or taking flight. The oppressed have a fight-or-flight instinct, also.

The fool comes into focus again in 10:12–14a. As earlier, the NIV opts for indefinite plurals ("fools") throughout these verses, but the Hebrew is singular ("the fool"), which allows us again to see Qohelet's proverbial expression as having a specific application, namely to Onias, the fool who wields authority (cf. 10:6). The ancient Greek translator understood the contrast in 10:12 to have repercussions for the fool himself: "Words from the mouth of a wise man are a favor, but the lips of the fool swallow him up." The NIV follows a similar translation. However, the Hebrew can just as legitimately be understood to say, "the lips of the fool swallow us up," so that the fool's words have destructive consequences for both himself and his community.[10] This is particularly significant considering Onias's poor leadership of the Jewish community, which allowed Joseph to fill the kind of power vacuum that Onias had created.

Without knowledge of the historical background, 10:14b–15 seems to change tack quite suddenly with some random proverbial thoughts, but Qohelet continues his reflection here on the delicate situation of Ptolemaic Judea in the 220s BC. He reiterates his earlier claim that no one can predict the future (cf. 7:14; 8:7), which highlights again the volatility of the fool's destructive behavior. The peculiar proverb of 10:15 is not a randomly plucked adage, but another specific criticism of Onias. Josephus reports that when Onias refused to pay the fee for his position, "he did not care for his authority, and . . . he would not go to the king [Ptolemy III], because he troubled not himself at all about such matters" (*Ant.* 12.163). Qohelet captures this attitude in 10:15, which can be literally rendered, "The toil of fools wearies him; he does not know to go to the city." The jarring change from a plural ("fools") to singular ("he")[11] may show that Qohelet has pressed a popular proverb using generic plurals into the service of his pointed criticism of Onias, whose refusal to placate Ptolemy allowed Joseph Tobias to make for the capital city, Alexandria, in his stead, and take advantage of the situation (cf. *Ant.* 12.168).

9. Sneed, *The Politics of Pessimism in Ecclesiastes*, 92.

10. The reason for this is that the pronominal suffix on the verb "swallow" can be taken as either a third masculine singular with energic *nun* ("him") or a first common plural ("us"). The form is identical.

11. The NIV does not reflect this change, since it opts for generic plurals throughout.

Again, Qohelet has not named names, but in this he is quite deliberate. As 10:20 evidences, he is keen to present his comments in generalizing fashion so that he cannot be charged with any misdoing (in contrast to Ankhsheshonq's fate). This would not even be a consideration if his words were purely generic. That he needs to "cover his tracks" proves that his words are politically explosive.[12]

Criticizing the King (10:16–20)

Prudently, Qohelet does not name any kings in his critical discussion at 10:16–18. The NIV has translated the key Hebrew word, *na'ar* (10:16) as "servant," which is certainly plausible (cf. 1 Sam 9:3, 5). However, the term essentially means "youngster" and refers either to young age or inexperience. When connected to notions of kingship, it recalls the self-description of a thirty-year old Solomon when God appeared to him in the dream at Gibeon at the outset of his reign (1 Kgs 3:7). To overcome his inexperience, Solomon asked God for wisdom, which he was granted. Thus, on the one hand, Qohelet is stating that wisdom befits a ruler, as it makes for an orderly society. Wisdom itself, though, is no match for supreme folly and cunning. Even Solomon brought fracture upon the kingdom of Israel by imprudently participating in the idolatry of his many wives (1 Kgs 11:1–13). God told Solomon that this would happen after his death (1 Kgs 11:12), which seems to contradict Qohelet's claim in 10:14. However, the allusion to Solomon in 10:16 simply gives 10:14 the feeling of exasperation: even if you know the consequences that lie ahead, there is no telling them to a foolish king, because he simply will not listen. On the other hand, Qohelet is probably also alluding to the generational change in his own context. On the death of Seleucus II Callinicus in 225 BC, his son, Seleucus III Soter, still in his late teens, succeeded him. After his assassination in 222 BC, his younger brother, eighteen-year-old Antiochus III, took the Seleucid throne. In Egypt, when Ptolemy III also died in 222 BC, his son, Ptolemy IV Philopator, himself about eighteen years of age, succeeded him.[13] Both Seleucid and Ptolemaic power passed into the hands of youngsters. Whether Qohelet was writing before or after the accession of these kings is unclear. Nonetheless, Qohelet implies that, even if the

12. Seow, *Ecclesiastes*, 339–40.

13. Both Krüger (*Qoheleth*, 188) and Schoors (*Ecclesiastes*, 747) consider the possibility that Qohelet is referring to Ptolemy IV's successor, Ptolemy V Epiphanes, who was just five years old when he became king in 205 BC. As appealing as this is, the incidents involving Onias II and Joseph Tobias, which occurred in 227 BC, seem like fresh wounds for Qohelet. So, it is more likely that he is writing not long after them, rather than after 205 BC. It is, however, possible that the Epilogist wrote just after the accession of Ptolemy V.

accessions had not yet occurred, Judea was headed for yet more hardship as immature heads took control of the Ptolemaic and Seleucid realms. Indeed, Ptolemy IV (reigned 222–205 BC) and his "drinking companions and comrades" were known for their "uncounted licentious deeds" (3 Macc 2:25–26). Ptolemy IV very nearly ruined the entire Ptolemaic kingdom through his brattish incompetence and pursuit of luxurious pleasure. When leaders thus prioritize gratification over government (Eccl 10:16b, 17b), disaster is not far behind (cf. Isa 3:4–5; 5:11–12).

Far better is it, Qohelet surmises, when the king is "of noble birth"—literally, a "son of nobles" (*ben horim* [Eccl 10:17]). Longman sees this as evidence that Qohelet "is somewhat of an elitist . . . since he prizes and trusts the upper classes of his society."[14] As we have seen, though, Qohelet is highly suspicious of them. Others see this as a reference not merely to one of noble birth, but of noble character or education.[15] But this is reading the second half of 10:17 into the first. We should, rather, note that the two essential sentiments of 10:17—a son of nobles and eating at the proper time—parallel not each other so much as the two sentiments of 10:16 respectively—a youngster king and feasting in the morning. Thus, we must see the "son of nobles" (10:17a, author's translation) as directly contrasting the youngster king (10:16a). Such a youngster has presumably inherited the throne from his father, rather than usurped power. So, we should assume that such a youngster does indeed have the right to rule and even the right upbringing. Yet Qohelet finds he may still be unsuitable. What, then, is the precise nature of the contrast Qohelet is trying to make?

Qohelet's rhetoric here is most enlightening, for what he says also gives shape to what he does not say but still implies. He does not say the king should be the son of the previous king, for evidently the youngster king could fulfill this, as both Seleucid and Ptolemaic kingdoms demonstrate. Instead, a good king would be "a son of nobles." Qohelet seems to be contemplating an alternative king who has noble pedigree but who is not from the currently ruling dynasty—a potentially seditious idea. His proverb in 10:18 seems to imply this also. Despite its appearance as a traditional proverb about laziness, even a casual reference to a "house" in disrepair amid discussion of royal succession takes on dynastic implications.[16] Furthermore, Qohelet does not say the ideal king should be "the son of a noble" (singular), looking only to the candidate's father, but "a son of nobles" (*horim*), which implies a line of ancestral pedigree

14. Longman, *Ecclesiastes*, 249; cf. Seow, *Ecclesiastes*, 339.
15. Eaton, *Ecclesiastes*, 137; Fredericks and Estes, *Ecclesiastes & the Song of Songs*, 227.
16. Contra Eaton, *Ecclesiastes*, 137.

(a person cannot be the son of multiple contemporary nobles). Furthermore, the NIV translates 10:16–17 in the third person ("Woe to the land. . . . Blessed is the land. . . ."), but Qohelet addresses the land directly in the second person ("Woe to you, O land. . . . Blessed are you, O land. . . ."). When a Jewish man in Jerusalem, under foreign rule, speaks about a better king with ancient pedigree ruling over the land, it is difficult not to hear reference to the land of Israel and its native Davidic dynasty. In a subtle way, then, Qohelet, a son of David (cf. 1:1), is recalling the rule of his own ancestors and claiming that the Jewish nation would better off if it were ruled, not by an ostentatious foreign dynasty but by its own noble dynasty—his own family. Once again, though, Qohelet, who is a son of such nobles, is speaking as a mere plebeian—a disenfranchised subject. This brings to the fore once again the failure of the prophetic hope that God would restore the Davidic dynasty.

The need for caution when speaking against the king (10:20) reveals deep dissatisfaction with his rule. In the first place, Qohelet again probably has Onias's situation in mind—his defiance of Ptolemy III and his flirting with the Seleucids. In that case, the "bird" who would inform on him would be either Ptolemy's ambassador, who had come to Jerusalem seeking payment, or Joseph Tobias, who benefited from Onias's inaction. The terms used for "bird" the second time are literally "lord of wings," providing a metaphor for someone who acts with speed and efficiency. Once again, then, Qohelet offers a criticism of Onias's loud prevarication on flouting his oath to Ptolemy. If Onias had realized that "money is the answer for everything" (10:19) and simply paid up, Judea would not have suffered further.

Yet, Qohelet also provides the reasoning here for his anonymous anecdotes and proverbs. He is aware of just how explosive his criticisms of the current leadership are and how they might land him in hot water. If this were not the case, he would have no need to veil his criticisms behind generalities. The dilemma of the protagonist in *The Instruction of Ankhsheshonq* seems specifically to inform his counsel here. Although Ankhsheshonq was not conspiring to murder Pharaoh, and even tried to dissuade his friend, Harsiese, from carrying out the deed, yet he was still overheard discussing it by a servant, who quickly reported it to Pharaoh that very night. Harsiese, the chief physician, who owed his position to Pharaoh, was subsequently executed, while Ankhsheshonq, despite his innocence, landed in prison for failing to inform Pharaoh. Qohelet adopts the moral of this tragicomic story by advising against reviling the king even in one's thoughts or in one's bedroom, because there is every chance someone might pick up on the discontent and report it before one has a chance to assert their innocence. Onias, who owed his position to the king of Egypt, just like Harsiese, was certainly not innocent in his defiance of the king. Though Qohelet decries the rule of the Ptolemies, he still recognized that discretion would have been the better part of valor for Onias. The high priest should have acquiesced to Ptolemy's demands rather than plotting to switch allegiance to the Seleucids. That he did not lose his life as a result is, ironically, thanks to his upstart nephew, Joseph Tobias. Nevertheless, Harsiese's fate should have made Onias think twice about such flagrant defiance of the king. For his own part, Qohelet seeks to avoid the fate of Ankhsheshonq by not naming names and, indeed, by ostensibly advising against opposing the king. Qohelet is a clever man who perceives the damage being caused to his society, who is unwilling to sit silently by while others espouse ineffective wisdom but who knows he must tread softly. Thus, he dresses his censures in the softer fabrics of the wisdom he is critiquing, thereby avoiding recrimination. Qohelet's strategy lets him say everything by saying very little, and thus avoiding trouble.

Playing it Safe (11:1–6)

As we shall see, the legacy of Ankhsheshonq continues in the next verse (11:1). The NIV has decided that 11:1 refers to maritime trade: "Ship your grain across the sea; after many days you may receive a return." However, the Hebrew text is a little more ambiguous than the NIV suggests, reading, "Let your bread go on the surface of the water, for in many days you may find it." The NIV draws a distinction between what is sent out ("grain") and what comes back (an economic "return"), but in Hebrew there is no such distinction. "Bread" is sent out and "it" is found again later. Even if "bread" is taken metaphorically as one's livelihood, we must question why someone would willingly get rid of their livelihood in the first place. There is also the added difficulty that this advice renders Qohelet's suggestion to enjoy the basics of life practically impossible (cf. Eccl 9:7).

Some argue that this is not about maritime trade at all but about charitable giving, citing two pieces of evidence. First, a mercantile venture seeks profit, but this proverb seems only to describe the recovery of the initial investment. No one sends out bread (or the grain to make it) for trade and expects to get bread in return. Second, the proverb here resembles another proverb in *The Instruction of Ankhsheshonq*. At 19:10, the text reads, "Do a good deed and throw it in the water; when it dries you will find it."[17] The idea is that performing a good deed may initially seem a waste, like discarding something into a river. However, when times get tough, as the metaphorical river dries up, one might receive a helping kindness in return for the initial good deed.

17. Lichtheim, *Ancient Egyptian Literature III*, 174.

In this case, Qohelet would be advising his readers to give charitably to others in the hope of possible reciprocation in future difficulties.[18] This interpretation also has Rabbinic support.[19] Fredericks objects to this view because it evidences an "ulterior motive of getting something in return" for the initial good deed.[20] However, wanting the help of another in a time of need or crisis should hardly be classified as ulterior. At any rate, there are key differences between Ankhsheshonq's proverb and Qohelet's advice here. Ankhsheshonq pictures the good deed as an object to be thrown into the water, where it sinks—to be discovered when the water dries up later. Qohelet advises taking bread and letting it float away on the tide, perhaps to find it again at a later time. The clustering of similar concepts in the two sayings, along with other affinities elsewhere (see discussion above), suggest Qohelet has co-opted the saying from *Ankhsheshonq*. Yet there are obvious differences as well, which mean Qohelet may not be intending to say exactly what Ankhsheshonq was saying in similar words.

When we consider Qohelet's wording, the flow of his argument, and his specific milieu, a more accurate understanding emerges. First, the Hebrew imperative that Qohelet employs (*shallah*) indicates sending something away or letting it go (cf. Gen 8:7). He is compelling the addressee to let bread float away on the water. We see another imperative at the beginning of the next verse (Eccl 11:2), giving the impression that both verses should be taken together. The NIV has decided that 11:2 is also about mercantile endeavors, with its language of investing in ventures. Again, though, the Hebrew is not so specific, reading, "Give a portion to seven, even to eight, for you do not know what evil might occur across the land." Both verses 1 and 2 seem to advise doing something now to guard against possible adverse consequences affecting the land in the future. This advice comes immediately after Qohelet criticizes the ruling regime while counseling against opposition to the king and his lackeys (10:16–20)[21]—effectively chiding Onias for his flagrant defiance of Ptolemy III and his ambassador. When seen in this context, Qohelet's rhetoric in 11:1–2 is aimed at Onias, just as the previous verses are. He is saying that it would have been better for Onias to have paid Ptolemy the fee owed him. Although this would have felt like letting one's own bread float

18. Seow, *Ecclesiastes*, 334–35, 344; Fox, *A Time to Tear Down*, 312–13; Brown, *Ecclesiastes*, 101–2; Krüger, *Qoheleth*, 192; Shields, *The End of Wisdom*, 222–24.

19. Fox (*A Time to Tear Down*, 312) lists the midrash of *Qohelet Rabbah*, the Targum, Rashi, ibn Ezra, and Maimonides (Rambam).

20. Fredericks and Estes, *Ecclesiastes & the Song of Songs*, 234.

21. The chapter division at 11:1 is a late and artificial imposition on the text. Since the original text had no such division, ignoring it gives a better sense of Qohelet's flow of thought.

away on the tide, for while it may have beggared Onias personally, it would have placated the monarch and made for conditions that might have allowed Onias to recover the money at a later time by other means (11:1). As high priest, Onias was head of the lucrative temple cult, presiding over the sacrifices and donations of the masses. It would not have been long before he recouped some, if not all, of his losses in the payment to Ptolemy. Although Qohelet has no fondness for the Ptolemaic regime, he believes it would have been expedient for Onias to invest his political capital in the Ptolemies, even if he desired to switch allegiance to the Seleucids—that is, to have spread his risk, rather than to have put all his "eggs" in the Seleucid "basket" (11:2). His failure to do so brought evil on the land, first with the prospect of punitive military action by Ptolemy, and then, once that threat abated, with the scourge of Joseph Tobias's tax levies, which the entire population of Judea felt. There was now little prospect of Onias recovering any wealth from a beleaguered population. Thus, Qohelet is not dispensing generic advice in 11:1–2, be it about business or charity. Rather, he is continuing to make pragmatic political statements.

This continues over the next few verses (11:3–6). Ostensibly, these are proverbs about humans having no control over the future, and so they flow thematically from the previous two proverbs. Humans cannot control the weather (11:3a) or where and when a tree in the forest falls (11:3b). Waiting for the perfect conditions to sow or reap can paralyze one with inaction, ultimately leaving them with no bread to eat (11:4). God is in control of the world, and his ways are as inscrutable to humans as the way a baby forms in the womb (11:5).[22] Therefore, it is best to play it safe by doing the essential task of sowing seed in the morning while there is light, so that one can eat and survive, while saving the non-essential hobbies for the evening (11:6). Yet, when read against the political climate of Qohelet's day, these verses become a summary of his appraisal of Onias II. The reference to a tree falling either to the north or the south (11:3b) is particularly revealing for, as seen in 10:2, the north is an allusion to the Seleucids in Syria and the south a reference to the Ptolemies in Egypt (cf. Dan 11). Qohelet effectively says that Onias had no way of knowing whether the political advantage would shift from the Ptolemies to the Seleucids, as he seems to have gambled. That decision is ultimately up to God, whose purposes are unfathomable (Eccl 11:5). As a mere subordinate, Onias had no way of influencing the political stakes.

22. Thanks to modern medical research and the invention of ultrasound technology, we now know how a fetus grows in the womb. But the proverb of 11:5 demonstrates the sense of mystery and wonder that the ancients had at the miracle of conceiving life. While the process may have been demystified for us now, the scientific knowledge we have should never abrogate a sense of wonder at God's invention of life.

His prevarication in paying the fee for his position to Ptolemy was akin to watching the wind and failing to plant (Eccl 11:4), and now he was reaping the political and economic consequences. If Onias had wanted to support the Seleucids against the Ptolemies, he would have been better off doing so under cover of nightfall and paying Ptolemy in the light of day, for there was no knowing if the political venture would pay off (cf. 11:6). Instead, Onias openly opposed Ptolemy by flagrantly disregarding his oath to pay for his position. Though his support for the Seleucids ultimately fell through with the deaths of the brothers Seleucus II and Antiochus Hierax by 225 BC, Onias survived in his position because of the intervention of his nephew, Joseph Tobias. But his political mistakes had brought ruin on the lives of countless ordinary folk throughout the country, whose bread now floated away with little prospect of being recovered.

Once again, Qohelet affirms that God is in control of all human activity. His criticisms of the leaders show that he believes humans still have responsibility for the decisions they take, such that people can be legitimately appraised as wise or foolish. Yet, all the variables outside human control are in God's hands. He is the one who determines when the clouds come with rain and whether the tree falls to the north or the south (11:3). The NIV has Qohelet describe God as "the Maker of all things" (11:5) but, in the context, a better rendering is, "God, who is the one who does everything." The idea is not simply that God is the creator of the world but that he is the one who determines the course of events.

Qohelet does not find any comfort in this, though. Events in his day had transpired unexpectedly, with Ptolemy III increasing his control over his kingdom, Onias surviving in his priestly office despite his overt folly, and Joseph Tobias rising to the position of chief tax farmer, bringing untold misery to thousands. On every front, the average Jew in Jerusalem and Judea had lost. This was not a script the conventional sages could have written. Even Qohelet, who could see the limits of such wisdom, could not have predicted it. Indeed, this is his point. This is why he advocates playing it safe by spreading risk rather than gambling one's livelihood, not to mention the livelihood of thousands of others, on a single unpredictable outcome. He is against playing such political roulette when the stakes are people's lives. But the volatility of history once again raises the question of what God, who ultimately controls it, is doing. If it is unwise and damaging for people to take such great risks, why does God permit it? Qohelet's verdict is, "you cannot understand the work of God" (11:5). Once again, Qohelet reaches the brink of a serious charge of callous injustice against God but shrinks back and pleads his own ignorance of what God is up to.

Attempting to Enjoy Life (11:7–8)

Verse 7 begins with a conjunction in Hebrew, showing that this conclusion is integrally linked to what comes before it. The break is, therefore, somewhat artificial, though there is a clear step in Qohelet's thought. Here he gives a philosophical summation to his readers, who must live with the crippling realities of a cruel world.

For all his pessimism, Qohelet still believes life is meant to be pleasant. To see the sun (11:7) is his way of referring to human life "under the sun," as he has described it throughout his discourse. It should be good to see the sun and sweet to experience its light (11:7). Yet he understands that there is something fundamentally wrong with the world, for life also has "days of darkness" (11:8). No one wishes such days upon themselves, but Qohelet sees them as inevitable. The reality of such darkness leads him earlier in his discourse to laud the stillborn baby as the most blessed of humans (6:3). He knows life should not be so frustrating as to make death and non-existence attractive, and this is the closest he comes to stating this overtly. Qohelet is not decreeing hardship for every person in history, as there are undoubtedly people who have lived relatively carefree lives. We must remember that he is not a systematic theologian formulating absolute propositions, but a philosopher reflecting on his own context, which has witnessed folly and eye-watering evil. In this context, the standard expectation for practically every person is to "eat in darkness, with great frustration, affliction and anger" (5:17), and there is little anyone can do to change this.

Since history is beyond the control of any person, Qohelet advises his readers to try to enjoy those aspects of life that lie within their power (11:8). He has no expectation that this will be achievable, since he claims, "Everything to come is meaningless," but he still encourages people to try to make the best of an abysmal situation.

Living in the Shadow of Death (11:9–12:8)

For the rest of the discourse, Qohelet directly addresses a young man in the prime of his life, encapsulated in the Hebrew word *bahur* (11:9)—a classic wisdom motif. From faint encouragement of the young man, he slides into dark pessimism engulfed in thoughts of misery, debilitating age, and death. First, he urges the man to follow the desires of his heart while he is young (11:9). This is not a license for debauchery but a call to live free of the emotional shackles of anxiety (11:10). Qohelet does not mean clinical anxiety, which is a health condition, but a chosen attitude that seeks to control all the variables of human life. As he has affirmed throughout his discourse, Qohelet believes that no human controls all these variables, for the reins of history are firmly in God's hands alone. Since his ways are unfathomable, there is no point trying to guess what God will or will not do. The world is too big to worry about such things. One is far better off with a smaller horizon, paying attention to more immediate concerns, like eating and drinking, personal appearance, and relationships (9:7–10). On a purely philosophical level, this is good advice that seeks to minimize personal stress levels, but in his specific Ptolemaic context, Qohelet is telling the young man to resign himself to living in whatever circumstances God decrees for him—most likely unwanted circumstances ("days of darkness" [11:8; cf. 5:7])—while trying to recover some measure of enjoyment in life's essentials. These act as a coping mechanism, however meager, in a life that feels out of control.

It is precisely because God holds the reins of history that Qohelet also warns the young man that "God might bring you into judgment" (11:9, author's translation). The NIV translates the verb here as an indicative future action that will definitely occur ("God will bring you into judgment"). As we will see, Qohelet is not completely sure about this. We must be careful not to import later biblical notions of judgment back into Qohelet's ideas here but to let him "speak" freely and listen carefully to his argument on his own terms.

Qohelet reasons that God may determine the larger factors of world history, but he is not too distracted to pay attention to the average citizen's life. Therefore, "Remember your Creator in the days of your youth," Qohelet cautions (12:1). Many commentators take the flow of Qohelet's advice here as a positive call to self-controlled godly living, like some statements in the New Testament (cf. 1 Tim 6:6)—a kind of *carpe diem* fueled by piety.[23] However, this is to remove him from his own context and impose ideas from elsewhere in the Bible because they have a similar ring to them.[24] If we remember some of Qohelet's earlier arguments, we will see that this is not what he means. Qohelet's society had witnessed upheaval at the hands of foolish and wicked men, leaving him utterly perplexed at what God might be doing in the world. God's unquestionable sovereignty and the unpredictable nature of life leads Qohelet to be afraid of God (cf. Eccl 3:14). Furthermore, Qohelet is skeptical about any notions of post-mortem judgment. As we have seen earlier, he sees judgment as occurring (at least in theory) during one's own lifetime, in keeping with covenantal orthodoxy whereby God prospers the righteous and punishes the wicked. And yet, Qohelet has observed the righteous suffering while the wicked prosper (7:15). From his admittedly limited perspective, Qohelet does not see a consistency in the notion of divine judgment. He tries to uphold

23. Eaton, *Ecclesiastes*, 145; Fredericks and Estes, *Ecclesiastes & the Song of Songs*, 238, 242; Brown, *Ecclesiastes*, 105; Greidanus, *Preaching Christ from Ecclesiastes*, 281, 287.

24. See brief discussion of this tendency in the Introduction.

the weight of orthodoxy with its insistence on the covenantal principle of just retribution but staggers on the uneven ground of his own observations of the world. Qohelet is not sure that God *will* judge people, but he is willing to affirm that he *can*, and therefore *might*. It is better, therefore, to translate the end of 11:9 with a modal sense as, "but know that for all these things, God might bring you into judgment."[25] Thus, in warning the young man to remember God in his youth, Qohelet is advising him to be afraid of God, who might choose to punish him for any indiscretions (cf. 3:14). It is an affirmation of God's prerogative to judge in accordance with the covenantal dynamic but also an expression of the fearful unpredictability involved in life.

This alters the complexion of 11:10, which advises the banishment of frustration and trouble. While many understand it as another positive encouragement to live free of excessive stress, this grinds against the negative motive given at the end of the verse: "for youth and vigor[26] are meaningless." It also stands at odds with Qohelet's earlier description of his society in 5:7: "All their days they eat in darkness, with great frustration, affliction and anger." While Qohelet does not want such frustration to prevail, he knows it is inevitable in his own context (11:8). So how is it that he can advise the banishment of frustration when he thinks it is inevitable? The conjunctions at the beginning of 11:10 and 12:1 alert us to a progression of thought here.[27] Qohelet is not advising the young man to have a sense of fun and adventure but rather to make his peace with the fact that God is supremely sovereign over his life and may at any time radically alter his circumstances or judge him. There is no point channeling the energy of youth into frustration at God because this will not dethrone him or change his own circumstances. Such youth and vigor are meaningless. Therefore, the young man should remember his creator during his youth and expect days of trouble to arrive (12:1). Qohelet is not, then, advising the young man to forego all stress but to resign himself to God's impenetrable sovereignty over his life.

Even if the young man manages to escape hardship during his youth, as unlikely as that might be in Qohelet's day, he cannot escape his creator (12:1a) or the onset of old age and death (12:1b–7). Qohelet's word choice in 12:1 strikes an alarming note. In calling the young man to remember the deity, Qohelet does not use the word "God," as he has throughout the rest of his discourse. Instead, he urges him to remember "your Creator" (*bor'eyka*). Given the somber nature of Qohelet's thought more broadly, and the pall

---

25. The modal sense is a fundamental meaning of the *yiqtol* verb, which is employed in the clause.

26. The term for "vigor" here is a reference to "black" hair (Heb: *shaharut*), contrasting with the grey hair of old age.

27. In Hebrew, both verses begin with a conjunction *waw*.

of death that hangs over the immediate context, the Hebrew ear could just as easily hear a call to remember "your grave" (*boreka*).[28] Both meanings have virtually identical pronunciation in Hebrew, causing the hearer to do a "double-take." Qohelet exploits this wordplay to bring together the two essential things over which no human has any control—God and death. Death is God's final decree over humanity, which is precisely what Qohelet seeks to explore in this final elegy.

The remainder of Qohelet's discourse describes old age and death as dark days that God will most certainly bring. He likens the shutdown of the body's functions to the end of urban life. It is a most poignant description that blends notions of the weakening human body in old age with the sense of fear and societal decay in Jerusalem under the avaricious oppression of Joseph Tobias and his Ptolemaic backers. With literary sophistication, Qohelet builds multiple layers of symbolism here. The result is a haunting collage of images that poetically captures the heaviness of old age and the disillusionment that he and so many throughout Judea were experiencing in the 220s BC.

The fading celestial luminaries (12:2) portray the eclipse of individual life. They also convey a sense of apocalyptic doom, as death casts its pall across Qohelet's society more broadly. The "keepers of the house" that tremble (12:3a) represent the hands that protect and care for the body, now trembling with age. They also refer to the guards stationed to protect the temple, quaking at the prospect of a military showdown with the Ptolemies, which they can only lose. We see a society disarmed and unable to defend itself. The "strong men," or more literally, "men of force" (12:3b), are the torsos of once agile men, now bent over with age. They are also the "patricians" of society,[29] bent under the humiliating yoke of oppression, like the prominent citizens terrorized by Joseph Tobias. The "grinders" (12:3c) evoke the teeth, many of them lost in old age. They are also women grinding flour at communal mills to produce their bread, now few in number, because the population has dwindled and the wheat has been taken by the king's tax farmers. "Those looking through the windows" (12:3d) are the eyes once again, now weak and without luster. The image also picks up a famous ancient Near Eastern motif of women cowering inside their houses, gazing out of the windows to see if their menfolk will return alive from battle or whether they have fallen to enemy forces who will now come for them (cf. Judg 5:28). This captures the sense of imminent dread and uncertainty that was rife throughout Ptolemaic Jerusalem. Verse 4 depicts fading sounds and loss

28. The Hebrew word *bor* denotes a "pit." Among its uses is as a term for the underworld, to which all the dead go (e.g., Isa 14:15; Ezek 26:20; 31:14; 32:23).

29. I borrow the term from Barbour, *The Story of Israel in the Book of Qohelet*, 149.

of hearing associated with old age but also conveys the idea of people barricading themselves inside their homes against marauding enemies. Verse 5 mentions some of the fears that senior citizens experience—fear of heights (Eccl 12:5a) and travel (12:5b), both sparked by decreased mobility (cf. Jer 6:25). There is a menacing side to this also, as the term for "heights" (Heb: *gaboah*) evokes the term for "tax farmer" (Heb: *gobeh* [cf. Eccl 5:8b]).[30] The parallelism associates the thugs coming to extort taxes with an enemy lying in ambush along a road. The almond tree (12:5c), which blossoms with white foliage, evokes the white hair of old age.[31] The grasshopper dragging itself along (12:5d) suggests the loss of sprightliness and easy movement or, if taken in parallel with the next line, might even be a euphemism for the loss of sexual prowess. The NIV reads the next line as, "desire no longer is stirred" (12:5e). This is paraphrasing the more literal meaning of the Hebrew, which reads, "the caper fails." The flower of the caper bush has a single pistil that protrudes rather prominently from the surrounding stamens. It is evocative of an erect penis, which is perhaps why the caper might have been used as an aphrodisiac in antiquity.[32]

By portraying both old age and the situation of Ptolemaic Jerusalem with these images, Qohelet skillfully achieves several aims. Once again, he undermines conventional wisdom by associating old age not with the attainment of wisdom but with the onset of dotage and disability. It is a subtle jibe that characterizes the sages as ineffective and out of touch with reality. Qohelet also captures the hopelessness that he and so many in his society felt at the turn of events in the 220s BC. There is a sense of foreboding as the previously bustling city falls deathly silent. The normal sounds of urban life, agriculture, and production are muted under the repressive economic policies of the Ptolemies and their greedy grandees, like Joseph Tobias. We get the impression of people's livelihoods being strangled and the death knell sounding across the city. As Barbour rightly notes, Qohelet's melancholic imagery is permeated with echoes of prophetic laments over the fall of Jerusalem to the Babylonians in the sixth century BC.[33] This tragedy became the paradigm of judgment and suffering for the Jewish nation, and, by alluding to it here, Qohelet effectively asserts that the nation was on the verge of another catastrophe. It had never recovered its independence after Jerusalem's fall, and it was now being asphyxiated by

30. Ecclesiastes was originally written without vowel markings. In such a consonantal text, there is no distinction at all between the spelling of "height" and "tax farmer" in Hebrew (*gbh*).

31. The consonantal Hebrew text seems to read the verb as *yena'ets* ("it discards"), but the Masoretes pointed it as *yane'ts* ("it blossoms"). Even with this pointing, though, the spelling is unusual, since it employs an *'aleph* as a *mater lectionis* in the middle of the word. This was common enough in the Second Temple Era but very rare for the Masoretes and their scribal tradition.

32. Seow, *Ecclesiastes*, 380; Longman, *Ecclesiastes*, 266.

33. Barbour, *The Story of Israel in the Book of Qohelet*, 138–67.

the political, economic, and cultural chokehold of the Ptolemies. Thus, with these verses Qohelet utters an elegy for his nation in the tradition of a classic city lament.[34] All this was more salt in Qohelet's wounds, for the already tattered hopes of recovering a Davidic kingdom were rapidly disintegrating into oblivion. As a son of David, who dreamed about building the greatest of all kingdoms at the beginning of his discourse, Qohelet was witnessing not just the decline of his city, but the death and burial of Davidic hope.

So, Qohelet's discourse attains the dark climax of death in 12:5f–7. It represents his reminder to the young man that he should make the most of his youth, if it is indeed possible amid the disintegration of Jewish society in Judea, for old age will permit no pleasure (12:1), and the grave is the "eternal home" (12:5f) from which no return is possible. This reference to the "eternal home" (12:5f) is not to a heavenly afterlife but is a common term used throughout the ancient Near East for the grave.[35]

The symbolism of the four images in 12:6—the severed silver cord, the broken golden bowl, the shattered pitcher at the spring, and the broken pulley wheel at the well—is simple to discern, though the precise signification of the first two is difficult to ascertain. One possibility is that the first two images allude to the *ankh*—the Egyptian symbol of life, sometimes worn as jewelry. According to Gardiner, the Egyptian *ankh* sign was derived from a "tie or strap, especially sandal-strap,"[36] which may account for the "silver cord." Furthermore, the Hebrew word for "bowl" here (*gullah*) is an unusual word that describes the object's round shape more than its function (cf. Judg 15:19; 1 Kgs 7:41; Zech 8:2) and could possibly refer to the loop at the top of the *ankh*. Admittedly, however, the suggestion is speculative.[37] The last two images depict the irretrievable loss of water, the vital fluid of life. All four objects undergo sudden, irreparable damage, symbolizing the moment of death and its finality. The four images could be purely surreal, conveying the dissolution of both being and meaning through a blending of the tangible and the abstract. Seow suggests they may reflect symbolic funerary customs,[38]

34. Ibid., 154–57.

35. For a list of examples, see James L. Crenshaw, "Youth and Old Age in Qoheleth," *HAR* 10 (1986): 9, n.33.

36. Alan Gardiner, *Egyptian Grammar: Being an Introduction to the Study of Hieroglyphs*, Third Edition, Revised (Oxford: Griffith Institute, Ashmolean Museum, 1957), 508; Alan Gardiner, "Life and Death (Egyptian)," ed. James Hastings, *Encyclopædia of Religion and Ethics* (Edinburgh: T & T Clark, 1915), 20.

37. Seow (*Ecclesiastes*, 381) suggests that these first two objects refer to the parts of an "elaborate and resilient lamp," but the connections he draws are also speculative. Cf. Crenshaw, "Youth and Old Age in Qoheleth," 9; Longman, *Ecclesiastes*, 272–73.

38. Seow argues this might explain the number of pottery sherds found in sealed tombs. See *Ecclesiastes*, 381.

but without further evidence it is hard to know if this is correct. Whatever the case, the images pick up two earlier notions. The first is from the immediate context of Qohelet's elegy on urban life. Just as the bustling city falls grimly silent, so these shattered objects typify a shattered people and their declining society. The second notion is from Qohelet's initial theatrical experiment, in which he "amassed silver and gold" as a would-be king (Eccl 2:8), built a thriving society (2:4–9), and denied himself no pleasure (2:10), only to find that it all meant nothing (2:11). Now, as the last act of his drama, we see the dissolution of all that Qohelet imagined, as the silver and gold break and death sweeps everything away to nothingness.

The dissolution of being is captured evocatively in 12:7 as Qohelet refers to human beings as mere "dust" that "returns to the ground it came from"—a clear allusion to God's curse on the man in the garden of Eden (Gen 3:19). As this is God's decree, the allusion underscores God's unchallenged dominion over human life—both individual and communal—confirmed by the claim that the breath (NIV: "spirit") "returns to God who gave it." As we have seen in 3:21 above, this is not about the ascent of the human soul to heaven but God's revocation of the human life force. It marks not a passage to a more blessed existence, but the final oblivion of being. Death lays all low in the dust of the earth, from the patrician to the peasant, the priest to the pauper, the wise to the foolish, the good to the evil. Neither Ptolemy, nor Joseph Tobias, nor Onias, nor Qohelet himself are left. "Generations come and generations go" (Eccl 1:4a). As humanity wastes away in the dust and Qohelet's voice falls silent, he leaves us with the eerie picture of the deity alone, untrammeled in power over the earth, holding the breath of a feeble and fleeting humanity in the grip of his sovereign hands.

One final time, Qohelet's motto resounds (12:8). Along with 1:2, it bookends his entire discourse and has been reiterated in one form or another a further twenty-eight times in between. This is his essential message—the summation of his philosophy and the reflections on human life he has derived from his Ptolemaic context. Now, as it closes his discourse, it functions as a universal epitaph: "Meaningless! Meaningless! Everything is meaningless!"

LIVE the Story

The Death, Resurrection, and Ascension of Jesus

Qohelet's deep pessimism derives from the strange and unforeseen political events of the 220s BC, which had such a calamitous effect on the lives of Judea's ordinary citizens. He felt as though he was witnessing the dying breaths of his nation, for which he held out little hope of recovery. The glory days of David and Solomon were gone, never to be recovered. He, their descendant, could do nothing but watch the decay of his rightful estate as the nation's life ebbed away.

Though Qohelet's assessment was not unfounded, the end did not come perhaps as quickly as he imagined. Through tectonic political shifts, including eight decades as an independent state (142–63 BC), the Jewish nation survived into the first century. By that time, however, it was once again a conquered people struggling under foreign (Roman) domination. The life of the average citizen was one of hardship, and though the temple stood proudly in Jerusalem, God still seemed very distant.

Jesus, however, began his ministry announcing the fulfilment of classic Jewish hopes: the arrival of the kingdom of God. Despite political upheavals, foreign influences, leadership discord, economic misery, uprisings, collusions, and religious divisions, God was coming to the rescue of his people. The God whom Qohelet had perceived to be so puzzling and so distant was finally acting—an eleventh-hour intervention. In response, Jesus urged his compatriots to repent before time ran out and to invest their trust in God's saving action.

Unfortunately, most rejected his calls, failing to believe that Jesus was the long-awaited messiah who would usher in the kingdom of God. According to Jesus, this spelled the end for the nation, as they were rejecting their final hope. He felt what Qohelet had felt a couple of centuries before him: utter despondency. Indeed, shortly before his ultimate rejection, Jesus looked over Jerusalem and lamented, picking up similar sentiments to those that Qohelet expressed in his elegy. "Jerusalem, Jerusalem," he mourned, "you who kill the prophets and stone those sent to you, how often I have longed to gather your children together, as a hen gathers her chicks under her wings, and you were not willing. Look, your house is left to you desolate" (Matt 23:37–38). When his disciples marveled at the temple's architecture, he predicted its tragic demolition, replying, "Truly I tell you, not one stone here will be left on another; every one will be thrown down" (Matt 24:2). As his enemies closed in on him, Jesus experienced complete despair. "My soul is overwhelmed with sorrow to the point of death," he told his disciples in the Garden of Gethsemane (Matt 26:38). Luke tells us that as he was led out to his execution at Golgotha the next morning, he told the lamenting women who followed him,

> Daughters of Jerusalem, do not weep for me; weep for yourselves and for your children. For the time will come when you will say, "Blessed are the childless women, the wombs that never bore and the breasts that never nursed!" Then

> "they will say to the mountains, 'Fall on us!'
> and to the hills, 'Cover us!'"
>
> For if people do these things when the tree is green, what will happen when it is dry? (Luke 23:28–31)

After hoping for God's intervention, when it finally came, the nation rejected it. Jesus could see only a bleak future ahead.

Jesus's words were fulfilled a generation later during the Jewish Revolt of AD 66–70. Much of urban and agricultural life came to a halt as the armies of Rome violently subjugated the nation. Jerusalem was besieged and finally taken. Those who had barricaded themselves in the temple compound were mercilessly slaughtered. The temple itself, the hub of all Jewish life and the means of access to God, was demolished. The nation was dissolved as the events of the Babylonian conquest of Jerusalem in 586 BC were played out anew.

Jesus himself embodied the nation's fate in his own death. As the faithful Israelite, representative of the whole nation, he took onto himself the judgment for its rejection and folly. The Israel of old died in Christ and, because of his innocence, in his resurrection it was transformed into something greater—a new, forgiven people of God. Those who did not heed his call would experience the catastrophe of AD 70—the ultimate dissolution of the nation. But in the new people of God was salvation for the Jew. Surprisingly, there was also salvation for the Greek. Indeed, though this gospel was native to the Jewish nation and the culmination of all its hopes, it spelled salvation for anyone who believed in Jesus, the messiah of Israel, be they Jew or Gentile, wise or foolish (Rom 1:14–16). As lamentable as the rejection of Jesus was, and as awful and tragic as the dissolution of the covenant nation turned out to be, God in his providence had provided the means for the eternal salvation of all people in the death and resurrection of Jesus, the noble son of David (Rom 1:2–4). This signaled not merely freedom from the rigors of political, economic, and cultural oppression, but freedom from their underlying cause: sin itself. In Christ, therefore, there is release from the inner shackles of selfishness and folly that plague every human being, and rebirth into a new reality characterized by forgiveness, love, and reconciliation with God.

Jesus did not take the reins of a human governing system after his resurrection. He did not stage a coup of the Jewish Sanhedrin in Jerusalem that had conspired against him or gather an army to invade Rome. Had this occurred, the people of God would have been limited to very earthly human power structures, requiring the use of force to establish and maintain power—a destructive prospect indeed. Instead, Jesus took the reins of cosmic authority over all creation and conquered every power structure that exists. He broke the tightest of all oppressive grips—not that of Rome over Judea, but of sin over humanity. His authority is characterized not by the wielding of raw power that lays others low but by love that transforms people from the inside out and raises them up to new possibilities—to constructive lives, reconciliation, justice, love, and eternal life itself. No human authority has the power to grant this; only Jesus does. He does not impose this at the point of a sword or the threat of economic subjugation but offers it through the proclamation of the gospel. This is why, at his ascension, Jesus bade his apostles to make disciples of the nations—not through coercion, but by teaching and baptizing them (Matt 28:18–20).

Pleasure and Judgment

In the final part of his discourse, Qohelet counsels the young man to make the most of his youth. We have seen that this was not a call to throw caution to the wind and live with wanton abandon but, in his Ptolemaic context, to do his best to eke out a sliver of satisfaction in a deeply dissatisfying society. Had Qohelet lived in a different time with less adversity, his advice might have been different, cautioning moderation and sobriety. Qohelet's context is, therefore, important for appreciating the ethics we derive from his thought. His reflections were timely—not absolute.

What we may glean from his thought is that life should be enjoyable (Eccl 11:7). As a gift of God, life is good. This does not mean it should be free of challenges, but it does mean it should bring satisfaction. When a person faces suffering and evil to the point where death begins to look attractive, something is horribly wrong. One of the most significant aspects of Jesus's ministry was his healings, in which he conveyed people from the shadow of death into the light of life. These were no mere showpieces to impress people but signposts of the reality he had come to establish. Though God did not design life to be a constant heady thrill, neither did he design it to be a misery. In showing love, compassion, and care, Jesus made a positive impact on the lives of others.

Sadly, there are many of us for whom satisfaction or pleasure is but a distant dream. This might be because of oppressive regimes, war, poverty, financial hardship, physical or mental illness, dysphoria, abuse, or other relationship difficulties. For those of us in such circumstances, life can feel more like the shadow of death than the light of the sun (Eccl 11:7). Jesus's demonstrations of love, including his healings, interactions with various people, and his self-sacrificial death, are the God-given mandate for those of us who can to bring joy closer to those who suffer or have lost hope.

Our temptation today, particularly in the West, is to define satisfaction according to our own individualist standard. Since we are still flawed by sin, sometimes what satisfies us is not what is actually good for us. We selfishly seek only what we want or pursue pleasure in extremes. It is not that extreme pleasure is somehow wrong—it is not! Nor is it that deriving enjoyment from something is bad for us—it is not! But when we see life as being only about ourselves or only about pleasure, we have dangerously blinkered our view and risk careening into dissatisfaction and even destruction.

We may also miss the reality of judgment. While Qohelet was unsure of the concept of eschatological judgment, the New Testament is sure of it. As he talked to the philosophers at the Areopagus in Athens, Paul made the claim that God "has set a day when he will judge the world with justice by the man he has appointed. He has given proof of this to everyone by raising him from the dead" (Acts 17:31). Jesus's resurrection is the first verdict of the final judgment day. As he walked out of his tomb, the eschatological clock struck twelve. It is just that it has not stopped chiming yet. But soon it will. We must not be fooled into thinking our actions have no consequences or that God pays us no heed. Since God created us as a single humanity, our actions inevitably have repercussions for our relationship with him and with each other. God's love for us does not undermine his righteousness and justice, so perfect is his love. Life should be justly enjoyed as God intended. If we do not know God, and Jesus Christ, whom he has sent (John 17:3), we forego true and lasting satisfaction. The prospect of judgment is frightening.

There has been a tendency in recent times, however, for Christians to so emphasize God as the source of satisfaction and pleasure for humans that we end up skewing our view of life and its pleasures. It is sometimes said that all we need is God and that he alone should be our one desire. While the sentiment of focusing our attentions on God is admirable, the collateral damage can be that we repudiate God's many good gifts to humanity. We can unwittingly advocate a kind of ascetic life in which we fail to appreciate fully some of the good things in life as well as some of our responsibilities within society. God did not create life and all its "contents" as mere distractions to be avoided or overcome. When we replace God with other pleasures, we certainly sell ourselves short and lose our compass for life. This does not mean we must deny enjoyment of life or renounce pleasure. "Every good and perfect gift is from above," says James (Jas 1:17). "Everything God created is good," says Paul, "and nothing is to be rejected if it is received with thanksgiving" (1 Tim 4:4).

The key to satisfaction, therefore, is gratitude. It is not that God becomes the only source of satisfaction in our lives, but rather that knowing God through Christ affects every aspect of our lives and overflows into thankfulness. If we can render thanks to God for his kindness to us, whether for the moments of extreme exhilaration or for the humble meal we eat, we will have unlocked the door to satisfaction. This life is not just a test before the next. God created us for this life, and he means us to enjoy it, even as we enjoy him. This is why the age to come is not about a new existence in a different sphere, or about "going to heaven," but about the resurrection of our bodies, the renovation of this creation, and the transformation of society. When Jesus was resurrected, he was raised in his body on this earth—a precursor of what lies ahead for those who are united to him.

CHAPTER 8

Ecclesiastes 12:9–14

LISTEN to the Story

[9]Not only was the Teacher wise, but he also imparted knowledge to the
people. He pondered and searched out and set in order many proverbs.
[10]The Teacher searched to find just the right words, and what he wrote
was upright and true.

[11]The words of the wise are like goads, their collected sayings like
firmly embedded nails—given by one shepherd. [12]Be warned, my son, of
anything in addition to them.

Of making many books there is no end, and much study wearies the body.

[13]Now all has been heard;
  here is the conclusion of the matter:
Fear God and keep his commandments,
  for this is the duty of all mankind.
[14]For God will bring every deed into judgment,
  including every hidden thing,
  whether it is good or evil.

Listening to the Story in the Text: Deuteronomy 5–6; 1 Kings 8; Proverbs 1:7; Hesiod, Theogony 53–62, 915–918; Ovid, Metamorphoses 6.114; Letter of Aristeas 9–10, 28–40; Atheneus, Learned Banqueters 1.3a–b, 22d; Galen, On Hippocrates' on the *Nature of Man*, 109; On Hippocrates' *Epidemics*, Book 3: 239–40

The Jewish nation traced its existence back to the exodus from Egypt and the revelation of God to Israel at Horeb (or Sinai). From these roots, three factors determined the core of Jewish identity and culture: (1) belief in a single deity; (2) adherence to the law of Moses; and (3) connection to the land of Israel, expressed primarily through participation in the sacrificial cult at a single designated site.

The book of Deuteronomy captures all these elements, with chapters 4–6 being particularly important. These chapters describe the revelation of God to Israel and the establishment of the covenant relationship, whereby Yahweh became the suzerain over his subjects, the Israelites. When the people of Israel encountered Yahweh at Horeb, their response was abject fear, prompting them to beg Moses to act as their mediator (Duet 5:24–27). This response of sheer terror was to be cultivated into a genuine reverence and awe to provide the basic rationale for Israelite life and wisdom. The book of Proverbs takes it as the very basis of wisdom: "The fear of the LORD is the beginning of knowledge" (Prov 1:7a). We could say, then, that all three tenets of Jewish identity and culture were summed up in the concept of fearing Yahweh. Moses's words to those who would go on to take the covenantal land are apt in capturing the sentiment:

> These are the commands, decrees and laws the LORD your God directed me to teach you to observe in the land that you are crossing the Jordan to possess, so that you, your children and their children after them may fear the LORD your God as long as you live by keeping all his decrees and commands that I give you, and so that you may enjoy long life. (Deut 6:1–2)

In Qohelet's day, Judaism was by no means monolithic. It was developing in several directions, aided by the diversity of circumstances Jews experienced and the variety of responses to challenges they faced. Under these conditions, the words of Moses in Deuteronomy 4 were critical to the maintenance of Jewish identity in response to foreign influence:

> See, I have taught you decrees and laws as the LORD my God commanded me, so that you may follow them in the land you are entering to take possession of it. Observe them carefully, for this will show your wisdom and understanding to the nations, who will hear about all these decrees and say, 'Surely this great nation is a wise and understanding people.' What other nation is so great as to have their gods near them the way the LORD our God is near us whenever we pray to him? And what other nation is so great as to have such righteous decrees and laws as this body of laws I am setting before you today? (Deut 4:5–8)

Belief in Yahweh was not relegated to the religious sphere. Unlike the modern West, religion in the ancient Near East was not a discrete element of an individual's private life but rather dictated the shape of an entire community's culture and values. It was the whole Jewish nation that was called to fear

Yahweh as its head of state and to observe his laws in his land. This was a national endeavor with political ramifications.

To be a Jew under foreign rule meant, by definition, that true Jewish life was to some extent compromised. This was especially true under Ptolemaic rule, which was based in Egypt, the land from which Israel had been rescued at the exodus. For many Jews in the Second Temple Era, therefore, life felt like a permanent holding pattern, waiting for something to happen that might restore the full form of Jewish life in the land—another act of salvation comparable to the exodus. For some of them, like Qohelet, Judaism could only truly flourish in the land under a Davidic king. After all, Solomon originally established the temple—the central institution of Jewish life—not simply as a place of sacrifice but also as a permanent symbol of the Davidic covenant (1 Kgs 8; cf. 2 Sam 7:11–16). Participation in the Jerusalem temple was, therefore, at least implicitly, an acknowledgement of the Davidic covenant. Many, therefore, longed for God to raise up a scion of the house of David, just as he had promised via the prophets. As much as Qohelet might have wished for such a future, he could only despair at what life had become under the Ptolemies. Indeed, he entered a depressive state of mind that could discern only bleak prospects for the nation.

For some Jews, however, especially the upwardly mobile, the future lay not in recovering the old order but in evolving into new forms. In this regard, Greek culture was an inexorable magnet. One particular aspect is especially relevant to our consideration of the epilogue in Ecclesiastes. As part of his policy to cement the Greek culture of his newly minted Hellenistic kingdom, Ptolemy I (reigned 305–285 BC) founded the Museum (in Greek, *Museion*) in Alexandria, a temple of learning dedicated to the Greek Muses. According to Greek (and, later, Roman) mythology, Zeus disguised himself as a shepherd and seduced the beautiful Mnemosyne (the personification of memory) over the course of nine consecutive nights. The result of their union was the Muses—nine goddesses who inspired the arts and sciences among humanity (Hesiod, *Theogony* 53–62, 915–918; cf. Ovid, *Metamorphoses* 6.114). By setting up an institution in their honor, Ptolemy I thought to promote the arts and sciences under his own patronage. Over subsequent generations, influential thinkers from all over the Greek-speaking world came to Alexandria's Museum to conduct research, analyze sources, hold seminars, argue in debates, and write books. Their housing and living expenses were covered by the royal purse. A contemporary satirist, Timon of Phlius, pokes fun at the endeavors of these thinkers and their royal sponsorship, saying, "Numerous cloistered papyrus-warblers are fattened in Egypt with its many peoples, quarrelling endlessly in the Muses' bird-cage" (quoted in Atheneus,

Learned Banqueters, 1:22d). Despite Timon's condescending tone, his comments reveal an institution keen to promote research and advance knowledge through the maintenance of a community of scholars—a precursor to the modern university. In this growing phenomenon, Jews came under pressure to concede that the beginning of knowledge lay not in the fear of Yahweh but in the acquisition of Greek books.

On that score, an integral part of the Museum in Alexandria was the famed Royal Library. Under the auspices of the Ptolemies, the library grew rapidly to become the largest collection of documents in the ancient world. Indeed, the appetite of the Ptolemaic monarchs for books was voracious. The pseudepigraphical *Letter of Aristeas* was written by a Jew in Alexandria during the mid-second century BC from the perspective of a Ptolemaic court official. Though fictional, and perhaps somewhat exaggerated, it captures something of the scope of the Royal Library's collection during the reign of Ptolemy I in the early third century BC:

> Demetrius of Phalerum, the president of the king's library, received vast sums of money, for the purpose of collecting together, as far as he possibly could, all the books in the world. By means of purchase and transcription, he carried out, to the best of his ability, the purpose of the king. On one occasion when I was present he was asked: "How many thousand books are there in the library?" And he replied: "More than two hundred thousand, O king, and I will make endeavour in the immediate future to gather together the remainder also, so that the total of five hundred thousand may be reached. (*Aristeas* 9–10)

The "bibliomania" of the Ptolemies is also conveyed by a comment and an anecdote told by the second-century physician-cum-philosopher, Galen.[1] Though a few centuries removed from the Ptolemies, Galen was from Pergamum, whose own library, under the auspices of the Attalid kings (contemporaries of the Ptolemies) became the greatest rival to Alexandria's library. Regarding this rivalry, Galen states:

> When the Attalid and Ptolemaic kings were vying with each other in the acquisition of books, a recklessness began to arise with respect to the attribution and preparation of books on the part of those who, for money,

1. Michael W. Handis, "Myth and History: Galen and the Alexandrian Library," in *Ancient Libraries*, ed. Jason König, Katerina Oikonomopoulou, and Greg Woolf (Cambridge: Cambridge University Press, 2013), 366–67.

> brought back to the kings the writings of well-known men. (Galen, On Hippocrates' *Nature of Man*, 109)[2]

This "recklessness" related mainly to copies of texts made hurriedly for quick dispatch to the libraries in order to procure quick payment. It explains why the Ptolemies preferred to acquire the oldest manuscripts available for their collection, and not just fresh copies of them. Thus, Galen elsewhere relates the following incident about the acquisition of Greek plays during the reign of Ptolemy II:

> The interest which the famous Ptolemy took in collecting ancient books is mentioned as not a small sign of interest for the people of Athens, inasmuch as he gave as a deposit 15 silver talents and received the books of Aeschylus, Sophocles and Euripides, but only to copy and return them intact in no time. When he had prepared a magnificent copy on the best of paper, he kept the books which he received from the Athenians and he sent the copies back to them, asking them to keep the 15 talents and accept the new books instead of the old originals which they had given him. Even had he not sent the new books back to the people of Athens and kept the old ones, they could have done nothing since they had accepted the silver on condition that they might keep it if he would keep the books. Therefore they accepted the books, and kept the money. (Galen, On Hippocrates' *Epidemics*, Book 3:239–240)[3]

The cultural colonialism of the Ptolemies brought together a myriad of texts from around the Mediterranean world, sparking a golden age of learning, book production, and the dissemination of ideas. This itself became a vehicle for the proliferation of Greek culture. The *Letter of Aristeas* 28–40 even attributes the translation of the Hebrew Scriptures into Greek to Ptolemy II's patronage of the Royal Library—a creative tale, though not so fanciful as to be completely far-fetched. What it reveals is a brave new world in which ideas were traded back and forth between cultures. While this had always occurred to some extent previously, it reached giddying new heights in the third century BC, with Greek culture becoming the essential medium of exchange. For some fields of knowledge, such as mathematics and medicine, the effect on other cultures was benign. But when it came to such fields as philosophy, religion,

2. Adapted from a translation at http://www.ucl.ac.uk/~ucgajpd/medicina%20antiqua/tr_GNatHom.html.

3. Cited in Handis, "Myth and History," 364.

and ethics, it was a different story. These fields bore the freight of Greek culture and ideals, and therefore struck at people's identity. This challenged cherished notions within Judaism and threatened to subsume traditional Jewish identity, centered as it was on the fear of the Lord—that is, exclusive worship of Yahweh, observance of the law of Moses, and a connection to the land of Israel. These basic tenets of Jewish life were in danger of becoming irrelevant in the brave new Hellenistic world. Learning itself was not the menace, but learning under the influences of Greek culture was. After all, at the heart of this knowledge boom was the great library within Alexandria's Museum—a temple to nine Greek goddesses. Learning was to be commended, but it was a hazardous business for a Jew to disentangle it from pagan Greek culture.

The live question in the late third century BC was how Jews should respond to the cultural tug-of-war they found themselves in. Should they maintain their traditional culture? If so, should this take the form of nationalistic hopes, perhaps in militaristic form, or should this be in the more passive guise of a retreat into quiet piety? Or should Jews move in the opposite direction, abandoning their traditions and embracing Greek ideals fully? Was it time to give up on notions of independence in the land and fall into line with the Greek program coming out of Alexandria, like much of the rest of the world? These were the issues occupying leading Jewish minds at the very time Qohelet bemoaned the fate of the Jewish nation.

EXPLAIN the Story

Epilogue (12:9–14)

As we have already seen, Qohelet held little hope that the Jewish nation would bear up under Ptolemaic pressure. His pessimistic musings finish with his motto: "Meaningless! Meaningless! Everything is meaningless!" (Eccl 12:8). However, this is not the last word in the book. That belongs not to Qohelet but to the Epilogist (sometimes called the "frame narrator").[4] One of the key interpretive issues for understanding Ecclesiastes is the relationship between the Epilogist and Qohelet. Does the Epilogist agree with Qohelet's thought? If so, to what extent does he endorse it? Is he perhaps ambivalent? Or does

4. Michael V. Fox, "Frame-Narrative and Composition in the Book of Qohelet," *HUCA* 48 (1977): 91. Technically speaking, 12:8 sees the Epilogist quoting Qohelet, since he refers to Qohelet (NIV: "the Teacher") in the third person. This leads some, like Longman, to make 12:8 the beginning of the epilogue; see Longman, *Ecclesiastes*, 274. However, we still hear Qohelet's words in 12:8, even if in quoted form. And the reissuing of his motto bookends the beginning of the discourse in 1:2. Therefore, it is best to keep it with the discourse and treat 12:9 as the beginning of the epilogue proper.

he disagree with Qohelet and view his ideas as dangerous and in need of correction?

Wrapped up in these issues is the question of how many hands can be discerned in the writing of the epilogue. Some commentators discern three distinct writers in 12:9–14, others see two, and others perceive just one.[5] Those who argue for more than one hand tend to see the first as sympathetic to Qohelet (12:9–11), while the subsequent writers are openly critical (12:12–14), the result being that Qohelet's thought is exhibited as an exemplar of dangerous and even wrong thinking that the faithful should avoid. This makes Qohelet a bit like Job's companions: seemingly erudite and wise, but nonetheless wrong. Longman, who argues for a single hand in the epilogue, understands the Epilogist as willing to admit that Qohelet had admirable motives but that his contemplations were "inadequate." Accordingly, the Epilogist feels the need to turn his son's attention away from Qohelet toward "the foundational truths of his faith."[6] Fredericks also sees just one hand in the epilogue but argues that the Epilogist endorses Qohelet as "the model of the wise man whom only the extremely dedicated wisdom student should aspire to become."[7] Fox argues that the Epilogist is not another hand at all, but rather that the Epilogist invented the character of Qohelet as a means of teaching his "son" through a story.[8] The lack of consensus demonstrates the complexity of the issues.

To reach a resolution, we must look at the nature of the response to Qohelet within the epilogue, keeping his Ptolemaic context in mind, and how this leads him to detect the weakness of conventional wisdom. As we have seen, Qohelet does not think wisdom is wrong but merely inadequate, since "a little folly outweighs wisdom and honor" (Eccl 10:1). In highlighting such limits, Qohelet demonstrates the vulnerability of Jewish thought in an age attracted to Greek ideas and culture. It is as though he has revealed an exposed flank in Jewish identity, showing how it is susceptible to attack from Greek forces. Though Qohelet accepts the divine revelation on which Jewish identity and orthodoxy is based, he also critiques it through rational thought, empirical observation, and even a bit of playacting—all methods evocative of Greek culture. The epilogue is aware of just how serious the ramifications of Qohelet's contemplations are, so it calls for two responses: "Fear God and keep his commandments" (12:13). As we will see, the first ("Fear God") aligns with Qohelet's observations, while the second ("keep his commandments")

5. For a brief survey of opinions, see Seow, *Ecclesiastes*, 391.
6. Longman, *Ecclesiastes*, 278.
7. Fredericks and Estes, *Ecclesiastes & the Song of Songs*, 244.
8. Fox, "Frame-Narrative."

moves beyond Qohelet's despair to recover a measure of hope. This is not a contradiction of Qohelet, indicative of more than one Epilogist. It is, rather, a signal that one Epilogist views Qohelet's thought as both penetrating and provocative. The Epilogist's endorsement of Qohelet, therefore, is a call to action to prevent the realization of Qohelet's worst fears.

The Work of Qohelet (12:9–10)

The Epilogist refers consistently to Qohelet in the past, which suggests that Qohelet had died by the time the Epilogist was writing. It is noteworthy that the Epilogist feels the need to append this note and not simply issue Qohelet's words without further comment. He begins by describing him as "wise" (12:9), which is not just a generic description of his character but a technical term indicating that Qohelet was among the ranks of Jewish "sages." Thus, he had probably received some kind of formalized schooling. As has been evident throughout his discourse, he was certainly familiar with the Hebrew Scriptures and events in and around the temple in Jerusalem.

The Epilogist also says that Qohelet "imparted knowledge to the people." This simple statement contains a wealth of information. First, it tells us that Qohelet was an educator. Furthermore, he taught not just "people," but "the people." We see in this a notion of Jewish identity. Qohelet was an active teacher of the Jewish people in a world obsessed with knowledge and the proliferation of Greek culture. Thus, he was not just a mild-mannered, wise person but someone on the frontline of the culture wars, with considerable influence in shaping the character of Jewish people. It is this sway that makes Qohelet's discourse such a sharp instrument.

A description of Qohelet's work follows. The NIV translates his three essential tasks as "pondered and searched out and set in order many proverbs." This initially sounds enigmatic, but his discourse demonstrates precisely these tasks. Perhaps a better rendering is that he "weighed, researched, and corrected many proverbs." In other words, he took the wisdom promulgated through conventional proverbs, which were to guide the Jewish people in their current circumstances, evaluated them through his own research, and corrected them to provide more accurate advice. This is, indeed, the kind of thing we have observed throughout his discourse. We could say that the kinds of activities Greek thinkers were conducting over in the Museum of Alexandria, Qohelet was doing for the Jewish people in Jerusalem.

The Epilogist gives an assessment of Qohelet's work in 12:10. The NIV states that Qohelet "searched to find just the right words." The relevant phrase in Hebrew uses the term *hepets*, which, in certain contexts, can mean "joy" or "delight." Thus, if Qohelet sought to find "words of delight," the idea may be that he was primarily concerned with aesthetics, or aimed to please his readers with finely crafted, uplifting literature. But this does not do justice to his discourse, which is sodden with pessimism in every crevice. The word *hepets* is the same word used to denote every "activity" or "purpose" that takes place under the sun (3:1, 17; 8:6). So, a more fitting phrase is that he sought to find "words of purpose." He searched for meaning, but alas, he could not find it. Nevertheless, the Epilogist describes his writing as "upright and true." The term "upright" (*yashar*) can have moral connotations, as well as the more neutral sense of "straight" or "direct." The Epilogist seems to imply both. In other words, though Qohelet's conclusions were unwanted in that he could not find meaning in his context, the words he produced were still purposeful. In that sense, he was successful, composing a discourse that was both forthright and demonstrably correct.

The Epilogist's positive assessment of Qohelet's thought is significant. It means that, for all his pessimism, all his criticism of leadership, his demonstration of conventional wisdom's inadequacies, and even his questioning of God, Qohelet was justified. The Jewish people were in confusing and precarious circumstances, and Qohelet rightly brought this to light. His contemplations were not simply the musings of a cantankerous old man, but the carefully considered conclusions of a highly perceptive individual who felt things deeply. Of course, his conclusion that everything was meaningless is both disturbing and dissatisfying. If humans are fated to die, and the identity of the Jewish nation was in its death throes, what hope could there possibly be? Like Qohelet himself, the Epilogist cared for the fate of his nation. He does not wish to censor Qohelet's provocative wisdom, but neither does he wish Qohelet's motto to leave readers without any hope at all. Therefore, he uses Qohelet's words as a platform from which to make constructive suggestions.

The Words of the Sages (12:11–12)

In these verses the Epilogist extrapolates from Qohelet's activity to the sages more broadly. He describes the words of the sages as "goads" (12:11)—prodding sticks with a sharp, usually curled iron spike near the tip, which herders use to muster and steer their animals. The implication is that Qohelet, like other sages, imparted knowledge and dispensed advice that might initially cause the reader extreme discomfort. A knee-jerk reaction would be to object and discard what he said. However, this would be a mistake, for, though initially disquieting, the purpose of such wisdom is to provide guidance that is ultimately of benefit. Qohelet was a wise man who dispensed such wisdom.

The Epilogist also describes the words of the sages as "planted spikes" (author's translation). The NIV translates the phrase as "firmly embedded nails," following the lead of Jeremiah 10:4, where the relevant noun, "nails," is paired unambiguously with the word "hammer." Some, therefore, understand the reference here in Ecclesiastes as being to spikes nailed into the shaft of a goad. This, however, is doubtful. As 1 Samuel 13:21 intimates, the manufacture or sharpening of a goad required a skilled craftsman, implying it was more than just a nail-studded stick. If the reference here is to additional spikes nailed into the goad's shaft, the implement begins to take on a rather brutal character, resembling something more akin to a war club than a simple cattle prod. In that case, the Epilogist is stretching the metaphor to imply that the words of the sages can sometimes feel more like a bludgeon than a goad. Yet this undermines the purpose of the metaphor in the first place.

An alternative is to see the spikes as another metaphor altogether, independent of the goads. This would imply that the wisdom of the sages is able to fasten things into place like nails do, thus preventing them from moving. In the shifting cultural scene of the Ptolemaic kingdom, this was crucial to maintaining Jewish identity. One final possibility is that the Epilogist is talking not about "nails," but sharpened "stakes" driven into the ground as defensive barriers. This would imply that the wisdom of the sages was meant to protect those within their community by helping them discern limits and make judicious responses, thus preserving their cultural identity and preventing outsiders from posing a threat. Once again, in the culture wars of the Ptolemaic Era, with the phalanx of Greek ideals advancing inexorably, the sages would have been on the frontline of Jewish identity. Qohelet certainly played a sentinel role. His provocative discourse, however, had exposed a gap in Jewish defenses, so the task of the Epilogist, himself a sage, is now to discern the most judicious response—to repair the breach.

The next phrase in 12:11 is literally "masters of collections" (*ba'aley 'asuppot*), which the NIV joins to the previous phrase to yield the translation, "their collected sayings [are] like firmly embedded nails." This option, though, does not deal adequately with the noun "masters" within the construction. As Seow points out, the phrase appears in later Rabbinic literature with the meaning "members of the assemblies"—a technical term for the Sanhedrin, the senate of Jewish elders.[9] If this is the meaning, then the Epilogist counts the sages among Judaism's key advisors and decision makers—the generals and strategists of Jewish identity—along with the chief priests. With his insight into the affairs of leaders, it would come as no surprise if Qohelet had been part of such an august body. However, even if he had been, we simply cannot tell if the term was used this way in Qohelet's day.

9. Seow references the Talmud (b. Sanh. 12a; y. Sanh. 10.28a) and the Targum. See Seow, *Ecclesiastes*, 387; cf. Schoors, *Ecclesiastes*, 838.

A contextually better understanding is to associate "collections" with texts. This would refer to the sages as scholars who studied and produced literature—"experts of the collections,"[10] or even "owners of collections." In this case, the Epilogist pictures the sages as the Jewish equivalent of the Greek thinkers gathered in the Museum of Alexandria, seeking to advance knowledge by collecting texts, pouring over them, editing them, copying them, and even composing new works.

This interpretation has four advantages. First, it implies the kind of activities that the Epilogist describes when profiling Qohelet in the immediately preceding verses (12:9–10). Second, it aligns with the upcoming reference to the making of books (12:12). Third, it explains the otherwise obscure statement that the words of the wise are "given by one shepherd" (12:11). The Greek scholars in Alexandria's Museum could claim to be inspired by the nine Muses—daughters of Zeus who, in the guise of a shepherd, had seduced their mother, Mnemosyne. But the knowledge imparted by Jewish sages, like Qohelet, was "given by one shepherd"—Yahweh, the God of Israel, who tended his people as a true shepherd (cf. Ps 23:1; Ezek 34:12, 16; Zech 9:16). And fourth, it picks up the activity that lay at the heart of the cultural conflict: collecting texts. By referring to the sages effectively as scholars, the Epilogist implies that Judaism has its own army of thinkers who can defend Jewish culture from undue influences and advance knowledge without having to open the gates to Hellenistic ideals. The wisdom inspired by Israel's singular deity, Yahweh, was uniform, unlike the disparate knowledge that might come from nine different Muses, daughters of the capricious and morally questionable Zeus. This does not mean that all knowledge derived by the scholars in Alexandria's Museum was to be discarded as necessarily wrong or incoherent. Any true knowledge must come not from the Muses, but from the one true shepherd, Yahweh, the God of Israel. There is a uniformity to all knowledge, since he is the one who presides over everything that occurs "under the sun." This uniformity also recalls the words of Moses to Israel in Deuteronomy 4:5–8, where he encourages the Israelites to keep Yahweh's commandments, so that all nations would observe the magnificence of their wisdom and justice.

At this point, the Epilogist turns to his "son"—a term that most likely refers to a student rather than actual offspring. He gives him a warning to be wary "of anything in addition" to the words of the sages (12:12).[11] Importantly, the Epilogist does not prohibit his son from engaging with literature that comes

10. Seow, *Ecclesiastes*, 387.

11. Brown sees the Epilogist endorsing Qohelet's discourse as "the final word on all matters pertaining to life and death," and now attempts to dissuade his son from reading anything beyond it. See Brown, *Ecclesiastes*, 117. However, the Epilogist issues a warning, rather than a prohibition, and

from other sources. His attitude is not to censor but to foster critical engagement. Thus, the son should engage critically with literature, but with a sense that recognizes where the critical center of knowledge lies, so as to preserve his own Jewish ideals. He should "plunder the Egyptians" (cf. Exod 12:36), but never walk like them. The preservation of Qohelet's controversial views is the case in point. The Epilogist unashamedly presents Qohelet's discourse in all its bleak and renegade pessimism. He is not afraid of the discomfort that might come from reading his contemplations but welcomes it as growing pains. Thus, the Epilogist here encourages his son in his studies to differentiate between pain that leads to growth and pain that leads to harm.

Part of the Epilogist's warning to his son is the recognition that "[o]f making many books there is no end" (Eccl 12:12). When we understand the context of Ecclesiastes, we realize that the Epilogist is not objecting to book production or education. This would hardly be appropriate, considering he is a sage producing a book to educate his "son." Nor is he bemoaning the never-ending task of learning, being cynical about the benefits of scholarship, or rolling his eyes at the production of tabloid guff. Rather, his statement needs to be read against the background of the bibliomania prevalent in the Hellenistic world at the time. Under the Ptolemies in Alexandria and the Attalids in Pergamum, books were being composed, copied, edited, bought, and transferred all over the Mediterranean. Knowledge was big business, and the business was booming. The Museum of Alexandria with its Royal Library had so much to offer the young, budding scholar: a good, stable living with royal sponsorship, access to thousands upon thousands of books, a community of scholars, prestige, and a thriving metropolis roundabout. This was a far cry from prospects in Judea, where the folly of Onias destabilized Jewish society and the wiles of Joseph Tobias bestowed loss, poverty, and destitution on most of the population. Alexandria, the center of the burgeoning book trade, was a scholar's magnet. But, as we have seen, the book trade was one of the primary means of propagating Greek culture, some of which was at odds with traditional Jewish ideals. In the Ptolemaic Era, the making of many books implied the promulgation of Greek values at the expense of Jewish ones. The Epilogist does not want to keep his son from books, but he does want to guard his Jewish identity. There is, therefore, a double edge to the warning here. The Epilogist is warning his son that not only is there no end to the proliferation of books in Alexandria's veritable book factory, but there is also no telling where participation in it might end. Qohelet had sensed the death of classic Jewish

uses Qohelet as a platform for further advice. The Ptolemaic context also adds considerably more to our understanding than Brown's view allows.

identity. To prevent this from becoming a reality, the Epilogist warns his son not to drink from Alexandria's chalice because it was laced with the hemlock of Greek culture that could poison Jewish ideals. Through this warning, then, the Epilogist issues a caution to his son, which applies the same concerns as Moses's words to the Israelites in Deuteronomy 4:5–8, but in a Ptolemaic context. Jewish identity had to be defended against the Greek ideals being propagated by the Ptolemies.

The last portion of the warning is usually translated, "much study wearies the body" (so NIV). Though many scholars and students can attest to the draining effects of study, the statement here is doing more than pointing this out. The Hebrew noun for study here (*lahag*) is unique in the entire Hebrew Bible. The ancient Greek translator opted for a common word that conveys discipline and devotion (*melete*), which can be used in contexts beyond that of study, such as military training. A cognate Arabic root means to be keen or devoted, while in Syriac it means to glow with fervor. Considering this semantic range, the action on view focuses not so much the acquisition of knowledge through study but on compulsive attachment to something. The ancient sources bear witness to the obsessive bibliomania of the era, and we have flagged the cultural freight that came with it. In this context, the Epilogist is not just warning his son to avoid wearing himself out with study but to avoid a fatal attraction to Greek culture, which would wear away his Jewish identity. Jerusalem was in the grip of Hellenistic kingdoms, so Hellenism was unavoidable, especially for the literati. But if the son was careful, he would be able to negotiate this interaction, successfully guarding his Jewish ideals and not becoming another cultural purveyor of Hellenism. If the sentinels of Jewish identity, the sages, held their ground against the barrage of Hellenism and the ineptitude in their own ranks, then Judaism perhaps stood some chance at a future. It might be possible, in other words, to avoid Qohelet's grim prophetic assessment of the nation's fate.

The Conclusion (12:13–14)

The Epilogist now gets to his conclusion. The NIV softens the tone somewhat ("Now all has been heard; here is the conclusion of the matter"), but the Hebrew is rather forceful and abrupt: "The end of the matter! The whole lot has been heard." This terse tone does not come from displeasure at Qohelet's thought. Rather, the Epilogist agrees with Qohelet, so he now grabs his son by the shoulders, as it were, to steel him for the urgent task at hand, with a view to avoiding Qohelet's worst fears. If the leaders of the Jewish nation were either incompetent or corrupt, it was up to the sages to close ranks and face down the threat of oblivion at the hands of Hellenism. The sage could ill afford to be cavalier.

The Epilogist has two related pieces of advice: "Fear God and keep his commandments" (12:13). These are a call to orthodoxy and orthopraxy, which leads some to conclude that the Epilogist here is correcting Qohelet's unorthodox thought.[12] However, this misconstrues the intent of both Qohelet and the Epilogist. The first imperative ("Fear God") aligns well with Qohelet's own contemplations. In trying to figure out whether there was any rhyme or reason to what takes place under the sun, Qohelet reasoned that God had given humans a sense that there was some kind of purpose, but no human could ever grasp it (3:11). Under those circumstances, God appeared frightening in power and mysteriousness. This led Qohelet to conclude that God does what he does so that humans would be afraid of him (3:14). Now that Judaism appeared to be sinking, all that was left was to salvage a sliver of joy before it slid beneath the cultural waves (3:12–13). The Epilogist, who affirms Qohelet's grim assessment and comprehends the danger Judaism is in, wishes to keep Judaism afloat. Thus, he takes Qohelet's notion and cultivates it in a truly orthodox manner that might make for the nation's survival.[13] God is indeed frightening, as Israel discovered at the foot of Horeb. He is more frightening, in fact, than Joseph Tobias and his tax-collecting thugs, or even the Ptolemies with their armies and cultural juggernauts, not to mention anything of the Seleucids. God is to be feared above all else. Indeed, it is comprehension of just how terrifying God can be that led the Israelites to beg Moses to be their intermediary, so that they could live (Deut 5:24–27). The nation's survival, therefore, lay instinctively in appreciating the frightening immensity of God and cultivating this reflex into a way of life.

This leads seamlessly, then, to the second element of the Epilogist's advice: "keep his commandments." When God saw the Israelites' response to his awesome revelation, the LORD said to Moses, "Oh, that their hearts would be inclined to fear me and keep all my commands always, so that it might go well with them and their children forever" (Deut 5:29). Fear of God leads to observance of God's customs and standards, with the result of social longevity. Such is the dynamic of the national covenant. This is not merely keeping rules to avoid trouble but developing and maintaining a cultural identity based on the revelation of God himself. Thus, the Epilogist advocates a classic orthodox response that is fully in line with traditional wisdom: the fear of the Lord is the beginning of knowledge (Prov 1:7a). Yet, it is not a glib appropriation of

12. Cf. Longman, *Ecclesiastes*, 282; Longman, "The 'Fear of God' in the Book of Ecclesiastes, 19–20.

13. Longman understands the Epilogist to be correcting Qohelet's view of fearing God, whereas I have argued that the Epilogist is showing how Qohelet's view can be incorporated into an orthodox response. See Longman, "The 'Fear of God' in the Book of Ecclesiastes," 13–21.

it but a call to religious and cultural activism in the face of the frightening threat of Hellenism and folly, and the even more frightening God who is sovereign over all.

There is an element of friction here between Qohelet's contemplations and the Epilogist's final advice. Qohelet had observed the righteous—those who fear God and keep his commands—suffering under conditions that, under the terms of the national covenant, would ordinarily be associated with punishment of the wicked. On the flip side, he observed the wicked prospering (Eccl 7:15). Unable to make sense of this situation, Qohelet audaciously proposed being neither too righteous, nor too wicked, thus avoiding direct judgment under the terms of the national covenant and exploitation under the current adverse circumstances (7:16). But Qohelet's brazen advice was not a serious ethic. It was, rather, a demonstration of the dire straits that the Jewish people found themselves in. By highlighting the peril, in which it seemed the faithful Jew simply could not win, it demonstrated that the situation was not sustainable, so something had to give. Qohelet's impertinent advice expressed his own confusion at not being able to figure out what God might be achieving by presiding over such unsustainable circumstances. The Epilogist, however, advises his son to follow the terms of the national covenant and hold station. If God is to be feared above all else, then even if humans cannot determine what he is doing, they must still trust him, and this means obeying him. He advises an ethical approach in keeping with conventional wisdom—orthopraxy that stems from orthodoxy.

Since Qohelet exposes the limits of such conventional thinking, though, the Epilogist does not initially appear to be solving anything. He is not proposing any radical changes, convening a "think tank," or brainstorming for new ideas to alter the nation's current course. One could easily argue that he is, in fact, realizing Qohelet's worst fears and sealing Judaism's fate. It is the human inability to apprehend the magnitude and course of God's purposes fully, as well as the rationale for keeping the commandments, that must guide our understanding of the Epilogist's words. If Judaism's future hung in the balance, and if God was sovereign over all endeavors "under the sun," including Judaism's future, and if he himself had not changed from his previously revealed character but was still committed to the nation and its welfare, then God would act to save them. To this, there was but one response: to hold station by fearing God and keeping his commandments—doing what he had told Israel to do, "that it might go well with them and their children forever" (Deut 5:29). Maintaining this traditional discipline would not ease the economic burdens imposed by Joseph Tobias, nor overthrow the Ptolemies, nor restore a Davidic king to the throne. In fact, Judaism might very well continue to suffer gravely under the exploitation of foreign powers, the volleys of Hellenism, and the infidelity of some of its own. But it was an expression of trust that God had not changed and that he himself would act to make a difference before the nation succumbed to the threats around it. To put it another way, the Epilogist's ethic is shaped by apocalyptic eschatology—that God would personally step into history and alter the fortunes of his people. While they waited for this to occur, the people must remain committed to their God-given identity and standards. This was radical conservativism—radical, because it looked to God for change; conservative, because it relied on past revelation to conserve the nation until salvation arrived.

This apocalyptic eschatology also comes through in the reasoning the Epilogist gives for his commands (Eccl 12:13b–14). The first reason is somewhat ambiguous in Hebrew, because the expression lacks a specific verb. It literally reads, "For this all the human" (12:13b). There are two primary ways of interpreting this. The first is to see it saying, "This is for all humanity." In this case, the Epilogist would be advocating that fearing God and keeping his commandments is the chief end of humanity (cf. NIV). To make this logic work, we would also need to propose that the Epilogist sees a universal purpose to the law of Moses—that it was applicable to all people and not just the Jewish nation. The difficulty with this is that the national covenant was specifically made between Yahweh and Israel. He was their God—their head of state—and they were his people—his subjects. Indeed, the covenant was the factor that distinguished Israel from the other nations (Deut 4:6–8). Despite this difficulty, we must also remember that Qohelet understands the God of Israel to be sovereign over all affairs "under the sun," and this presumes his sovereignty over Gentile nations. Thus, the Epilogist may be advocating a passive proselytism, whereby the wisdom and righteousness of the Jewish nation not only attracts the plaudits of other nations but seeks to win them over and convert them—the inverse of what Hellenism seemed to be doing at the time. The second alternative is to read the clause as saying, "This is everything for the human." In this case, the Epilogist would be arguing that fearing God and keeping his commands is the utmost duty of a person, that person being specifically a Jew. This option has the advantage of maintaining the uniqueness of Israel in the covenant with Yahweh and picking up the logic of Deuteronomy 6, in which the Israelite was to make every effort imaginable to obey God and maintain his customs and standards. Yet, we must recognize that the Epilogist does not overtly narrow "the human" to simply "the Jew." So, while it is plausible, we cannot confirm whether it is probable.

The second reason the Epilogist gives for his advice is that "God will bring every deed into judgment" (Eccl 12:14). The Epilogist does not elaborate on what he understands by the term "judgment." Is he, like Qohelet, advocating the covenantal notion of judgment within history—something akin to the prophetic concept of a Day of the Lord, in which Yahweh moves his agents of judgment to enact a critical day of reckoning that affects the fortunes of his people? Is he, perhaps, arguing for an apocalyptic day of judgment at the end of history, in which God acts directly without any agents and brings about a totally new age that will never end? Or is he asserting the notion of personal post-mortem judgment?

The Epilogist's endorsement of Qohelet's thought and the words he says next are crucial for pointing a way forward. Qohelet formulated his thought within a covenantal framework, whereby God judges actions in an ongoing way through history, blessing the righteous and punishing the wicked. However, his own context showed that this was not always strictly the case, for he observed the righteous suffering and the wicked prospering. Judgment seems to have been, at least temporarily, suspended under foreign occupation, leading to the seemingly unsustainable situation where the faithful were suffering and the nation was at risk of losing its essential identity. Since God was still sovereign over the whole earth, Qohelet advises the young man in 11:9 that God *might* still bring him into judgment within this covenantal framework. The Epilogist, though, goes beyond the possibility of covenantal judgment here. By referring to "every hidden thing, whether it is good or evil," he implies that nothing is beyond the scope of judgment. He also implies that God alone is the scrutineer, making no mention of agents acting on his behalf, as in prophetic theology. He must, therefore, be affirming the certainty of judgment and not just the possibility of it. Since the suffering of the righteous shows no signs of abating under foreign occupation, the Epilogist's certainty of God's judgment must be pinned on a decisive future act of God. This is still within a national covenantal framework, but there is an element of individual judgment here, also (note the singular imperatives in 12:12). In other words, the Epilogist presents the kernel of apocalyptic eschatology, whereby God breaks into history to act directly and decisively on behalf of the faithful in his covenant people.

The Epilogist ends his comments on this sobering note. Qohelet viewed conventional wisdom as insufficient for dealing with the crisis facing the Jewish people in the Ptolemaic Era. The Epilogist does not contradict this but, in fact, commends Qohelet for noting it. If Qohelet was right, then the only thing making the Epilogist's advice sound is apocalyptic eschatology—the certainty that God would intervene. Without it, the Epilogist's counsel is delusional and does nothing to alter the fate of the Jewish nation in its own land. By appealing to the notion of an apocalyptic reckoning, the Epilogist wields the proverbial goad. He strikes a solemn warning for his son to preserve the tenets of Jewish identity as a means of expressing trust in God. The juggernaut of Hellenism may have rammed the broadside of Judaism. Some of Judaism's crew may have scuppered their vessel. Some may even have jumped ship. Others, like Qohelet, may have despaired of their fate. But the Epilogist advises his son to steel his nerves and stay with the sinking vessel in faith that, against all human odds, God would be faithful to his covenant and indeed save the day for them.

LIVE the Story

The Hope of Israel

In Qohelet's day the Ptolemies held sway over Judea. The Jewish nation was not in control of its own land, let alone its own destiny. Many Jews were drawn to Alexandria, the cultural metropolis of Hellenism. Through institutions like the Museum, with its proliferation of books and Greek thinking, and the gymnasium, which created centers of Greek values, training, and education abroad, Hellenism posed a serious threat to the nature and future of Judaism.[14]

The Ptolemies and Seleucids continued brawling throughout the region, until eventually the Seleucids gained control of Judea in 200 BC—barely a generation after Qohelet composed his discourse. Despite initial relief from the heavy tax burdens of the Ptolemies, Judea was soon once more plunged into the turbid waters of hard economic servitude. All the while, Hellenism had grabbed hold of the Jewish hierarchies, who saw that their only chance of survival lay in dressing their biblical heritage and customs in the Greek colors of their conquerors. Classic Jewish hopes, which Qohelet cherished even as he acknowledged their ineffectiveness in the political climate, were being crowded out by the politics of pragmatism. Survival meant capitulation.

This trend had earlier driven Qohelet to despair. Those who still clung to biblical Jewish ideals wondered how much ground they needed to concede to foreign influences just to maintain their national and spiritual ideals. For some, like the Epilogist, the answer lay in not conceding cultural ground at all but in piously maintaining orthodox customs and aspirations in the hope that God himself would soon intervene for the Jewish people and achieve what they themselves could not. This attitude sought to uphold the ideals of Israel's

14. A gymnasium was not built in Jerusalem until c. 170 BC. Nonetheless, gymnasia appeared in other major cities and affected the worldview of their inhabitants, including diaspora Jews who lived in their vicinity. See Athas, *Bridging the Testaments*, forthcoming.

national covenant with Yahweh, which stipulated that faithfulness brought blessing from the deity. It was a call to hold station in no-man's land—to remain immovable even in the face of the enemy's unrelenting cultural volleys, all the while knowing that their enemy was advancing and there was no safe ground to fall back on. This was how the apocalyptic movement in Judaism arose, along with its accompanying mindset open to faithful martyrdom. Some might characterize this as a passive response to cultural and spiritual pressure, but it encouraged active faithfulness to the point of death, if need be. It was conservativism that hoped for radical change. In an environment where nothing felt safe, it clung to the ideals of the past while hoping to God for the future.

There were, however, others who responded not with despair or radical conservativism, but with radical violence. They found that conceding more and more cultural ground left them with not enough ground to stand at all. Rather than wait for God to intervene, they took matters into their own hands and, in 167 BC, lashed out in rebellion against their foreign overlords and those within their own nation who had sold out to Greek culture. The Maccabees—priests who refused to cede any more ground to Hellenism—battled against the Seleucids and eventually founded the Jewish Hasmonean dynasty. But this was not the divine judgment that the Epilogist had imagined might make a decisive change. Though for a time the Jewish nation gained its independence, giving it room to maneuver, the cultural influence of Hellenism was not stemmed. Furthermore, the Hasmoneans were not the Davidic dynasty. In the end, they were powerless to withstand the Romans who took the region in 63 BC. This put the Jewish people right back where they had been—a beleaguered, conquered people, not in control of their own destiny, and wondering when God would intervene.

The apocalyptic mindset that looked to God for salvation, therefore, was widespread in the first century, when Jesus came onto the scene to save "the lost sheep of Israel" (Matt 15:24). Indeed, Jesus was a key proponent of it. He preached that the culmination of all Jewish hopes was imminent. "The time has come," he said. "The kingdom of God has come near. Repent and believe the good news!" (Mark 1:15). God was finally acting on behalf of the Jewish people to establish his rule over them once again—a highly charged political message. Unlike some in his day, Jesus called not for the manufacture and distribution of weapons. Arms would not establish the new kingdom; God himself would do that. The proper response, Jesus said, was repentance—turning back to God and complying with his standards and purposes. Jesus was not overturning the Law and the Prophets but fulfilling them. He was a radical conservative, doing precisely what the Epilogist had advised while fulfilling the Epilogist's apocalyptic eschatological hopes. History had reached its most crucial moment. The day of reckoning had arrived.

The tragedy in Jesus's day was that many of the sages—the Pharisees, scribes, and teachers of the law—had lost sight of the goal of their piety. Ostensibly, they had taken the Epilogist's advice to close ranks and pursue traditional discipline in accordance with the law of Moses, but a critical shift away from the Epilogist's advice had actually occurred. They desired to be so conservative that they lost their radical apocalyptic hope that looked forward to salvation. In letting go of this radical apocalyptic hope, they ironically also relinquished their conservatism. Their theological rudder had broken away from their tiller, leaving them drifting on an open sea while they continued to believe that they were still steering the vessel.

The result of this subtle shift meant that they missed the spirit of the law for the letter of the law. No longer was keeping the law about holding station by facilitating right relationship to God and neighbor until the decisive and transformative act of God for the benefit of his people. Instead, the law became an end in itself—a cultural god of its own, around which they built a religious edifice with their own traditions and regulations. Thus, they elevated their tradition of ritual hand washing above fellowship with the needy and marginalized (Matt 15:1–2; Luke 19:5–7); they promoted the preservation of rules over the preservation of life (Matt 12:9–14; Luke 13:10–17); they sought to exclude and destroy rather than to seek and save the lost (Matt 23:13; Luke 19:10); they looked to condemn rather than to forgive (Luke 6:37; John 8:1–11); they saw humankind as made for the Sabbath rather than the Sabbath as made for humankind (Mark 2:23–28); they sought power and prestige rather than humility and reconciliation with God (Matt 23:1–7; Luke 18:9–14); they sought sacrifice over mercy (Matt 12:7; Mark 12:40–44); they sought to take rather than to give (Mark 7:9–13; Acts 20:35).

When the sages of his day confronted Jesus for not doing as they did, he replied, "You have let go of the commands of God and are holding onto human traditions" (Mark 7:8). They were steering a rudderless vessel. In the process, they had lost the sense of fear and love for God, which should not only have fueled their desire to keep the law but to look forward to and embrace God's salvation when it arrived. But when it did, they missed it, for they were too concerned with their own traditions and regulations. Jesus compared them to children having a tantrum because he (and John the Baptist before him) would not play their games when it was time for wise action rather than trivialities (Matt 11:16–19). He lamented that it would be more bearable for the Gentiles and for Sodom and Gomorrah on the day of judgment than it would be for them (Matt 11:20–24).

True wisdom, Jesus said, lay in listening to him and doing what he said. To illustrate this, he picked the analogy of building a house:

> Therefore everyone who hears these words of mine and puts them into practice is like a wise man who built his house on the rock. The rain came down, the streams rose, and the winds blew and beat against that house; yet it did not fall, because it had its foundation on the rock. But everyone who hears these words of mine and does not put them into practice is like a foolish man who built his house on sand. The rain came down, the streams rose, and the winds blew and beat against that house, and it fell with a great crash. (Matt 7:24–27)

Jesus's use of this analogy was not random. He was not claiming that people should treat him as a philosophical guru for their lives. Rather, he was claiming to be the sole hope for the Jewish nation. The concept of building a "house" was evocative of building the temple—the institution that lay at the center of Jewish life and worship.[15] It was also the most prominent symbol of the Davidic covenant. One of the essential tasks of the son of David was to build the temple, with the permanence of its structure symbolizing the permanence of Davidic rule (2 Sam 7:12–13). The "house," therefore, was not just a concrete symbol for the more abstract concept of life in general. It was, rather, a symbol of the Jewish nation itself and its hope for a renewed Davidic kingdom. Jesus was claiming that the future of the Jewish nation—the future that Qohelet longed for but despaired of and that the Epilogist strived for—lay in the recognition of his own claims to be messiah: the son of David who would fulfill the nation's hopes and usher in the new kingdom of God. To hear Jesus's words and act in accordance with them was to participate in this new kingdom and survive the judgment to come. Failure to recognize and heed Jesus would lead to catastrophe. The storms of recent centuries had not abated, and they were now reaching a climactic moment. Only the apocalyptic intervention of God would save the nation and fulfill their hopes for a new kingdom. Jesus was claiming to be the king of that new kingdom. Without him, Judaism's "house" would come crashing down, temple and all.

The nation's leaders, however, rejected Jesus. They conspired with the Romans and had him condemned to crucifixion. As his dead body hung exposed on the Roman cross, the curtain of the temple—the "house"—was torn violently in two (Matt 27:51). This was not indicative of access to God, but rather that the nation

15. In Hebrew, the standard word for "temple" is the word "house" (*bayit*). This is how the Old Testament refers to the temple in the vast majority of cases.

had sealed its own fate.[16] Its "house" would be left desolate (Matt 23:38)—a catastrophe that was tragically fulfilled in AD 70 when the Roman forces overwhelmed the nation in its bid for independence. In this calamity, the temple was destroyed. The storms that had beaten against the house for centuries now exposed a sandy foundation, and "it fell with a great crash" (Matt 7:27).

While the old order crashed, the new kingdom did not. Before his death, Jesus gathered around him a remnant of Israel, typified by his twelve apostles, who would become the foundation of the new kingdom (cf. Eph 2:19–22; Rev 21:14). Though hidden from the eyes of the wise and the learned, the new kingdom was revealed to "little children" (Matt 11:25). Those who had weathered the pressure of the cultural storms, who craved righteousness despite the persistent battering, who maintained their apocalyptic hope of salvation, and who were willing to lose their lives in order to save them now grasped hold of the kingdom as Jesus offered it. Surprisingly, even Greeks came seeking him (John 12:20–22).

God did intervene for his people by stepping into history in the person of Jesus, establishing the new kingdom by his death and resurrection. This is a kingdom not just for the lost sheep of Israel, but for all people. The gospel is for the Jew first, but it is also for the Greek; it is for the wise, as well as the foolish; it is the power of salvation for all who believe (Rom 1:14–16). The culture wars that had threatened to undo the people of God before the coming of Christ found their resolution in him.

The apostle Paul captures this resolution beautifully in his letter to the Ephesians. Speaking as a saved Jew, he writes to the Gentile Ephesians of the peace and unity between Jew and Gentile that comes from the person and work of Christ:

> For he himself is our peace, who has made the two groups one and has destroyed the barrier, the dividing wall of hostility, by setting aside in his flesh the law with its commands and regulations. His purpose was to create in himself one new humanity out of the two, thus making peace, and in one body to reconcile both of them to God through the cross, by which he put to death their hostility. He came and preached peace to you who were far away and peace to those who were near. For through him we both have access to the Father by one Spirit.

16. The imagery of Heb 6:19–20 and 10:19–22 certainly does claim access to God through the priestly work of Christ. The author explores the work of Christ in the ideal heavenly temple, and contrasts this with the work of the Levitical priesthood in the earthly tabernacle/temple. However, this is not the purpose of the Gospel writers in relating the tearing of the curtain in the earth temple in Jerusalem.

> Consequently, you are no longer foreigners and strangers, but fellow citizens with God's people and also members of his household, built on the foundation of the apostles and prophets, with Christ Jesus himself as the chief cornerstone. In him the whole building is joined together and rises to become a holy temple in the Lord. And in him you too are being built together to become a dwelling in which God lives by his Spirit. (Eph 2:14–22)

The Christian Pursuit of Knowledge

Some of Qohelet's discourse makes for uncomfortable reading. He throws down fierce challenges to traditional notions, frames serious questions about God, and is unafraid to proclaim his inability to find answers. His whole discourse is a fist slammed down in utter frustration and despair. The Epilogist's endorsement of Qohelet carries some important lessons that Christians today would do well to take on board.

First, like Qohelet, Christians should not be afraid to ask and explore difficult questions, even if they challenge cherished ideals. This is, in fact, part of being a radical conservative. Christians are not called to live in ignorance or blind allegiance, but in trust of God. To ask questions is not to disbelieve, but to seek understanding. Our faculties are, of course, not immune from our sinfulness, but they are still God-given and meant for our benefit. Indeed, failure to ask questions and investigate them is an abrogation of our responsibility as Christian human beings living life "under the sun."

Second, like Qohelet, we may not always be successful in finding the answers we seek. Living with such a gap in our knowledge can be disconcerting, because everybody loves certainty, and the gospel leads us to security in Christ. We are also naturally drawn toward solutions that appear simple rather than complex, and we tend to prefer answers proposed by those whom we admire or that confirm our previously held beliefs. However, simplicity does not always equate with correctness. Our admiration does not count as a qualification. Tradition is not always a guarantee of veracity. At times, these can give us a false sense of security, blinker our scope, and even lead us to arrogance. Furthermore, we can often use the Bible in ways that are unwarranted, expressing clear-cut confidence in matters that are actually jagged and messy. Though the Bible is the revelation of God and, therefore, is our authority, it does not answer all our questions in life. It is also an intricate mix of documents. Qohelet's questioning of previous traditions is a demonstration of this intricacy. Though the essential message of Scripture is clear, it is not monochrome. All of Scripture is God-breathed and, therefore, useful for life (2 Tim 3:16–17), but it sings in harmonies—not in monotones.

Furthermore, life is not simple and straightforward. We must, therefore, be prepared to live with unanswered questions or with juggling complexity, however clumsy it may seem. Like Qohelet, we must be honest about the limits of our own knowledge and comprehension. Though we know significantly more about God and his purposes than both Qohelet and the Epilogist, because we live on this side of the cross and empty tomb, we are still meager humans and God is still the deity who is sovereign over all creation. As Isaiah 55:8–9 states:

> "For my thoughts are not your thoughts,
> neither are your ways my ways,"
> declares the LORD.
> "As the heavens are higher than the earth,
> so are my ways higher than your ways
> and my thoughts than your thoughts."

To acknowledge our own limitations is to work within our God-given nature as human beings. Failure to acknowledge them is to put ourselves in the place of God, which is detrimental to all human endeavor. It is called sin. Our pursuit of knowledge, therefore, requires a hefty dose of humility, honesty, and vulnerability.

Third, like the Epilogist, we should extend grace to others. Though he agreed with Qohelet, the Epilogist did not despair as Qohelet did. Nonetheless, he demonstrated charity toward Qohelet. As Christians, we have an unfortunate tendency to be crusaders before we are so charitable, even toward fellow Christians. Showing charity to others does not mean we are compelled to agree with them, but the love of Christ does compel us to display love and understanding. This is not negotiable. It is part of our other-person centered duty as representatives of the Lord Jesus Christ. If we are willing to ask tough questions, if we are willing to put up with uncertainty and complexity, and if we are humble enough to admit our own limits, then it is no great leap to be gracious to others, as Christ was.

Fourth, all knowledge is God's knowledge. In Qohelet's day, a golden age of learning was underway, and the Museum in Alexandria gave it considerable momentum. Yet this sparked a significant challenge to Jewish culture. It was not the advancement of knowledge that posed the threat, but the pagan Greek values with which that knowledge came packaged. To study in the Museum of Alexandria was to partake in the worship of nine Greek goddesses. These values threatened not just the personal integrity of Jewish people but the very relationship between God and his covenant nation and their hopes for salvation. Knowing God is not a subscription to ignorance. On the contrary, knowledge itself is good, for true knowledge is simply the discovery of the structures that God himself has encoded into his creation. But the discovery of knowledge under the auspices of the Ptolemies and their Museum was not a neutral endeavor.

In the modern world, this has changed significantly. The pursuit of knowledge has been secularized, in that it has been taken out of the religious sphere and placed in a kind of neutral zone. Although this poses some challenges for Christians, on aggregate, it has been of significant benefit. It means, at least in theory, that Christians do not have to subscribe to values or ideals that are at odds with Christian belief in order to seek knowledge. It has led to academic freedom that should excite us to explore, seeking to discover more of the world that God has created and over which he presides. Even the removal of God from the sciences is not itself detrimental, for science looks to discover the structures within the natural creation—not the structures of God himself. Only if we mistake God for creation will this become problematic, and such a blurring between the creator and the creation is actually disastrous. The designer of a house is not the house itself, and one may appreciate the engineering that holds the house together even if one does not personally know the designer.

Moreover, if we are confident that this world is indeed the creation of our God, and that all true knowledge is his knowledge, we will pursue it bravely, even when it presents conundrums that may destabilize our confidence. We will not deny these challenges or pretend that we have all the answers but rather continue to pursue knowledge as we continue to fear the Lord. Furthermore, Christians will turn their pursuits of knowledge into doxology. We will take the discoveries we make, the challenges we encounter, and the knowledge we gain and sanctify them by using them to reflect on the one who created us, who is sovereign over us, who loved us, died for us, and rose for us. This is not a call to retreat from the world but to engage it fruitfully in a godly manner.

Fifth, fear of the Lord is indeed the beginning of knowledge. Though all knowledge is God's knowledge, Scripture is still our ultimate authority for knowing God. It was the principle of knowing God through his own revelation that guided the Epilogist in his advice to his son. Scripture, as the self-revelation of God, is sufficient for knowing him and for matters pertaining to salvation. Although the Bible is unique in this regard, it is not hermetically sealed off from the rest of reality. Since all knowledge is God's knowledge, the Bible is connected to the rest of reality. This means that pursuing understanding in other fields may potentially enhance our knowledge of Scripture and aid us in maintaining it as our authority. We have seen, for example, how understanding the Ptolemaic context of Qohelet helps us to interpret his discourse better than if we did not. This does not compromise the authority or sufficiency of Scripture; it enriches our understanding of it. Christians should not be solipsistic. True wisdom is not myopic. It is educative, not propagandistic. If the fear of the Lord is the beginning of knowledge, we will maintain the revelation of God as central and engage with the rest of reality fruitfully.

Finally, our security and hope lie in Christ. Qohelet felt deeply despondent over the fate of the Jewish nation and of human beings more generally. He lived with the awful uncertainty of not knowing what God was doing, even to the point where he practically questioned the goodness of God and the pressure of Hellenism brought him to virtual breaking point. And yet, as the Epilogist hoped, and as Jesus demonstrated, God was trustworthy. He acted in accordance with his own sovereign and divine purposes, which were far loftier than our own limited notions "under the sun." There is nothing "under the sun" that is not "under heaven." Therefore, nothing can separate God's people from the love of Christ (Rom 8:35). Were this not the case, and were God not dependable, the Epilogist's advice would have been worthless. But he was right, and God did act to save. We can take this security and hope into all walks of life, including our pursuit of knowledge. For when it is framed by the redemption we have in Christ, we will understand that our knowledge does not save us. Research, education, technology, and the exchange of ideas are of immense benefit to human life, but these will not save us or yield us everlasting life. Our hope is for the resurrection of our bodies and the transformation of creation. As Paul said to the Corinthians, "If the dead are not raised, 'Let us eat and drink, for tomorrow we die'" (1 Cor 15:32). But the dead are raised (cf. 1 Cor 15:20). As Peter aptly wrote, "Praise be to the God and Father of our Lord Jesus Christ! In his great mercy he has given us new birth into a living hope through the resurrection of Jesus Christ from the dead" (1 Pet 1:3).

Introduction to Song of Songs

On even the most casual reading, the Song of Songs (hereafter, "the Song") is likely to raise eyebrows. This short book of ancient Hebrew love poetry is replete with erotic imagery, sexual innuendo, and risqué metaphors, which, for the average Bible reader, can be quite confronting. A closer reading only heightens the sensation. It is difficult to know what to do with such sensual literature. Rabbi Aqiva (AD 50–135) spoke of those who sang the Song as a bawdy tune in taverns (t. Sanh. 12:10). He condemned such treatment of the Song, for to him, the Song was the holiest piece of Scripture, and all of history was not as worthy as the day on which God gave it to Israel (m. Yad. 3:5). But why is such erotic literature in the biblical canon? What is its purpose and message? What connection does it have to God? These questions, and others like them, challenge us to read this curious book more closely in the pursuit of understanding.

Authorship

Tradition ascribes the Song to Solomon on the basis of the title in the first verse: "The song of songs, which is by Solomon." First Kings 4:32 states that Solomon, in addition to speaking 3,000 proverbs, composed 1,005 songs. It is surmised that the Song is one of this number, and indeed it is the best of them all because of the title's construction, "song of songs," which indicates a superlative in Hebrew: "the best song."

However, as Fox notes, the rabbis never appealed to Solomonic authorship to buttress the claim that the Song was canonical.[1] The book's title can be interpreted differently, and, indeed, the content of the Song demands that we do. The Hebrew preposition *le*, which is attached to Solomon's name in the title, does not have to indicate authorship. It can also be a dedication ("for Solomon") or even subject matter ("about Solomon"). A comparable expression supporting the latter is found in the title of Isaiah's "Song of the Vineyard" (Isa 5:1), where the same preposition (*le*) is attached to "vineyard" as an indication of subject rather than authorship or dedication. Furthermore,

1. Michael V. Fox, *The Song of Songs and the Ancient Egyptian Love Songs* (Madison: University of Wisconsin Press, 1985), 250.

Solomon is not the main character in the Song. He is a background figure, albeit a very important one, as he causes the essential predicament of the Song's drama (see "The Narrative of the Song" below). This means the Song views him rather unfavorably. It is highly unlikely that Solomon composed a piece portraying himself as a villain. But it is entirely plausible that someone composed a Song using Solomon as a character. As will be argued below, the Song conveys a fictitious story that employs Solomon in a secondary, but pivotal, role. The book is, therefore, anonymous, and its title is better rendered, "The Best Song, which concerns Solomon."

Date

If Solomon is not the author of the Song, there is no reason to limit its composition to Solomon's reign in the tenth century BC. This merely gives us the earliest possible date for the book. The mention of Solomon places the setting of the Song during Solomon's reign, but its composition could have been centuries later. Song 6:4 mentions the city of Tirzah, which served as capital of the northern kingdom of Israel in the late tenth and early ninth centuries BC (cf. 1 Kgs 14:17; 15:33). The city was severely damaged in the Assyrian destruction of Israel in 723 BC but was only abandoned about a century later. This, however, does not give us the latest possible date for the Song's composition, for memory of Tirzah as the earliest capital of Israel is preserved in biblical literature and therefore could be recalled at any time afterwards. The manuscript of the Song found at Qumran, 6QCant, dates to the Herodian Era (late first century BC), but the Greek translation of the Song in the LXX is slightly earlier, dating perhaps to the late second century BC.[2] This, therefore, provides the latest possible date for the book.

It is likely that the Song carries some deliberate allusions to themes evident in prophetic literature. For instance, the motif of two lovers whose relationship is in some way troubled intersects with the prophetic metaphor of Yahweh as the husband of Israel (Hos 1–2; Ezek 16). This connection between the woman and Israel also intersects with the prophetic portrayal of Israel as Yahweh's vineyard (Isa 5; Ezek 19:10). Also, the characterization of the "daughters of Jerusalem" provides a link with Lamentations, which personifies the destroyed Judean capital as the once beautiful but now traumatized "Daughter Jerusalem" (Lam 2:15). These allusions seem intentional rather

2. For further discussion of the Hebrew and Greek manuscript evidence, see Roland E. Murphy, *The Song of Songs: A Commentary on the Book of Canticles or The Song of Songs*, Hermeneia (Minneapolis, MN: Fortress, 1990), 8–10.

than accidental, which means the Song's composer lived after the Babylonian destruction of Jerusalem in 586 BC.

The Song is written in what is generally termed "Late Biblical Hebrew," rather than the "Standard Biblical Hebrew" that most books of the Old Testament are written in. While a considerable swathe of scholars still view Late Biblical Hebrew as necessarily postexilic, recent research has shown that the relationship between these two forms of Hebrew is not necessarily one of linear development. This makes dating a biblical book on the basis of the distinction between them unwise.[3] Other data are required to provide a firmer basis for dating.

In addition to the prophetic allusions above, we do have two linguistic data that are reliably tied to historical eras. The first is the Persian loanword *pardes* in Song 4:13, meaning "paradise," "park," or "botanical garden" (NIV, "orchard"), that cannot have entered Hebrew before the Persians exercised hegemony over Hebrew speakers from the late sixth century BC (see discussion in Introduction to Ecclesiastes). The second is the Greek loanword *appiryon* at Song 3:9, derived from the Greek word *phoreion*, meaning "litter" or "sedan chair" (NIV, "carriage"). Greek influence in the Levant pre-dates the arrival of Alexander in the late fourth century BC, but the nature of this word, as a luxury item for transporting royalty and aristocracy, suggests it probably entered Hebrew only after the establishment of the Hellenistic kingdoms that succeeded Alexander. Some commentators have suggested the word derives from Sanskrit *paryanka*, or Persian *upari-yana*,[4] but these are less convincing. Bolstering the Greek connection is the genre of the Song. While not a play, the Song seems influenced by Greek plays with their cast of characters and choruses. We see the same phenomena in the Song (see "Genre" below), though it retains the mechanisms of Hebrew poetry.

In addition, there is scope for interpreting the Song as metaphorical of a broader theological and historical reality that prevailed between the late third and early second century BC. During these decades, Jews suffered economically and socially under the oppression of both the Ptolemies (301–199 BC; see Introduction to Ecclesiastes for further discussion) and the Seleucids (199–164 BC). Hellenism also threatened biblical faith considerably, reaching a critical juncture in the persecution by Antiochus IV between 167–164 BC. During these years, Jews within Palestine were faced with a monumental decision: either they acquiesced to a liberal agenda that was moving the Jewish faith toward pagan Hellenistic ideals that would align them with the rest

3. Young, Rezetko, and Ehrensvärd, *Linguistic Dating of Biblical Texts*; Rezetko and Young, *Historical Linguistics and Biblical Hebrew*.

4. See brief discussion in Murphy, *The Song of Songs*, 149; cf. *HALOT*.

of the progressive Hellenistic world, or else they retained their conservative, traditional (biblical) faith that espoused exclusive devotion to the God of Israel via the Mosaic law, putting them at odds with the Hellenistic world. The latter decision came at great cost, as some faced not just opposition, but death for their decision (cf. 2 Macc 7). In the Song we find the main character, the woman, facing a similar decision: to compromise her ideals by acquiescing to the agenda of her brothers and the king (Solomon), who do not have her best interests at heart, or else to cling tenaciously to the one who truly loves her, the shepherd boy, even if this costs her life (see "The Narrative of the Song" below). If, as is likely, the Song is more than just an exploration of erotic love and conveys something of the relationship between Israel and her God, then it has the greatest resonance with the Antiochene persecution and the subsequent Maccabean Revolt (167–164 BC).[5] From the open-ended nature of the Song's climactic finale (Song 8:5–14), we may deduce that the Song's composer did not yet know of a resolution to Judaism's predicament at the time of composition, though the Song's theological metaphor advocates the passive resistance of embracing martyrdom if necessary—the kind of situation that many Jews faced under the Seleucids. On that basis, it seems most plausible to place the composition of the Song in c. 166 BC, during the heat of the Antiochene persecution and the initial outbreak of the Maccabean Revolt, when Judaism was struggling for survival and how best to respond to the piercing challenge of Hellenism.

Genre

The title of the book identifies it as a "song" (1:1). Whether it was performed with musical accompaniment we cannot know, for the book consists purely of poetry without any further musical direction. As Hebrew poetry, its basic dynamic is parallelism, which rhymes concepts (rather than sounds) in parallel lines. This also means that the Song employs sophisticated poetic devices, some of which cannot be adequately conveyed in English, such as alliteration, assonance, and wordplay. The content of the poetry helps us classify it as love poetry and, as we will see, more specifically a ballad.

Through the ages, interpreters have grappled with whether the book represents a single song or a series of songs. Those who see a single song tend also to see a narrative of sorts that unifies the book,[6] though there are those

5. For a discussion of these events and their significance, see Athas, *Bridging the Testaments*, forthcoming.

6. Calvin Seerveld, *The Greatest Song in Critique of Solomon* (Palos Heights, IL: Trinity Pennyasheet Press, 1967); Provan, *Ecclesiastes, Song of Songs*, 244–45; Michael Goulder, *The Song of Fourteen*

who see a unity but no narrative.[7] Those who see more than one song view the book as a collection of disparate poems that, although they share similar themes, resist a unifying narrative.[8] Some proponents of the latter perspective surmise that the poems developed from originally cultic poetry about Canaanite or Mesopotamian deities. This stems from the similarity of motifs and images known from the literature and iconography of these ancient cultures. Yet, the themes of love and sex are ubiquitous in human societies, representing some of our most primal human drives and emotions, and the most intimate of human relationships. Similarities between the Song and other ancient literature should not surprise us. Indeed, as Fox has demonstrated, the Song bears the strongest affinities to Egyptian love poetry.[9] Yet, similarities should not be confused with dependence. In any case, the desire to connect the Song to ancient precursors from neighboring cultures arises after reaching the conclusion that the book is comprised of several poems.

However, two factors push toward viewing the Song as a unity. First, the title dubs the book a "song" in the singular (1:1), specifically singling it out as "the song of songs." While it is possible that this denotes a song consisting of several songs,[10] this kind of phrasing in Hebrew usually indicates a superlative, which we can render, "the best song." It is not inconceivable that the title conveys both meanings—a song consisting of several songs, and the best song, but a second observation leads only to the superlative interpretation, namely that a consistent set of voices is discernible throughout the whole book. The Hebrew text does not have character headings to show the transition from one voice to another, as many modern English Bibles do. Rather, the speakers must be determined from the grammatical clues in the poetry. Hebrew verbs can be marked for gender (masculine or feminine) as well as number (singular or plural), which aids the task, but there are some ambiguous moments. In any case, these speakers persist throughout the entire book, meaning the poetry is not simply an abstract exploration of themes but a set of poetic interactions between characters who speak to each other. These characters are also consistent for the duration of the book, such that we do not merely have

Songs, JSOTSupp 36 (Sheffield: Sheffield Academic Press, 1986), 2–4.

7. Meik Gerhards, "The Song of Solomon as an Allegory: Historical Considerations," in *Interpreting the Song of Songs—Literal or Allegorical?*, ed. Annette Schellenberg and Ludger Schwienhorst-Schönberger, Biblical Tools and Studies 26 (Leuven: Peeters, 2016), 60–62.

8. Robert Gordis, *The Song of Songs and Lamentations: A Study, Modern Translation and Commentary*, Revised and augmented (New York: KTAV, 1974), 17–18; Marvin H. Pope, *Song of Songs: A New Translation with Introduction and Commentary*, Anchor Yale Bible 7C (New Haven: Yale University Press, 1977), 54; Othmar Keel, *The Song of Songs*, trans. Frederick J. Gaiser, Continental Commentary (Minneapolis: Fortress, 1994), 17.

9. Fox, *The Song of Songs and the Ancient Egyptian Love Songs*, xxii–xxvi.

10. Tremper Longman, *Song of Songs*, NICOT (Grand Rapids: Eerdmans, 2001), 55.

characters in individual vignettes, but a cast. Certain stock phrases are also repeated throughout the book with only minor variation, such as the adjuration of the daughters of Jerusalem (2:7; 3:5; 5:8; 8:4) and the connection between two lovers (2:16; 6:3; 7:10). All this suggests the book is one unified poetic piece, and not merely a pastiche of poems.

The Narrative of the Song

The cast of speaking characters throughout the Song raises the possibility that it presents a coherent narrative or drama. Origen (AD 184–254) was the first known proponent of such a view.[11] Discerning the narrative is, however, a grueling task. The Song lacks distinct narrative prose, with 8:11 being the only verse other than the title that is not poetic dialogue, though even that is uncertain. This leaves us searching the characters' dialogues for evidence of deliberate interconnections that represent narrative developments. It has left many a commentator despairing of finding any narrative thread to hold the Song together. This leads some to suggest that the cast of characters appears in a series of related yet disparate vignettes[12] or a non-narrative unity.[13]

The search for a narrative also runs the risk of reading more into the text than is there. This is a significant caveat, for our understanding of the Song should be constrained by its content and devices rather than our own wishful thinking. It also risks trying to read the Song as a genre other than love poetry. Narrative tends to be presented in prose, whereas the Song is a sophisticated poetic piece. Nonetheless, we would not be doing the Song justice if we did not search for a narrative thread in poetic form, for the consistent cast of characters and their dialogue is a natural foundation for a story of some kind. Hebrew poets are not averse to conveying a narrative through poetry (cf. Exod 15:1–18; Judg 5; Ps 105). It is right, therefore, to identify the characters that the Song presents and search for a predicament that gives rise to their story.

---

11. Origen interpreted the Song allegorically, so his drama theory was not about its surface meaning but its allegorical value as a story of God's love for the church.

12. Morris Hirsch Segal, "The Song of Songs," *VT* 12 (1962): 477–78; Fox, *The Song of Songs and the Ancient Egyptian Love Songs*, 202–9; Tom Gledhill, *The Message of the Song of Songs: The Lyrics of Love*, BST (Leicester: Inter-Varsity Press, 1994), 21–22; G. Lloyd Carr, *The Song of Solomon: An Introduction and Commentary*, TOTC (Leicester: Inter-Varsity Press, 1984), 44–45; Longman, *Song of Songs*, 55–56.

13. J. Cheryl Exum, *Song of Songs: A Commentary*, OTL (Louisville: Westminster John Knox Press, 2005), 37; Richard S. Hess, *Song of Songs*, Baker Commentary on the Old Testament Wisdom and Psalms (Grand Rapids: Baker, 2005), 34.

The Cast

At the center of the Song is a young woman who has fallen in love with a man. Debate rages, however, over who this man is, as his identity carries significant repercussions for our understanding of the Song. There are two theories. The first identifies him as King Solomon. This understands the Song as the story of a budding romance between the Israelite monarch and the young woman, who is never personally named. Some proponents of this view argue that the young woman is the daughter of Pharaoh, whom Solomon married as part of an alliance with Egypt (1 Kgs 3:1) and for whom he built a palace (9:24).[14] Others argue the woman is a simple country girl—a "Shulammite" (Song 6:13) from the town of Shunem (or Shulam), with whom Solomon fell hopelessly in love.[15] In either case, the title of the book (1:1) is used to support the view, since Solomon's name appears in it either as author ("by Solomon") or primary subject ("concerning Solomon").

There are, however, considerable difficulties with this theory. First, as mentioned above, Solomonic authorship is unlikely. Second, even if the title reads "concerning Solomon," it does not necessarily follow that he is the main character; he need only be one of the characters, with his reputation providing the major frame of reference for the whole work. Indeed, Solomon is the only character specifically named in the whole Song, which makes him distinct amongst the *dramatis personae*, and the only one who can provide such a frame of reference. This could reinforce him as the main character, but this is evidently not the case. The young woman is the primary *persona*. She is the first and last to speak (1:2; 8:14), has the most lines, and her character develops through the Song. Third, the relationship between the young woman and the man with whom she has fallen in love seems to be a forbidden romance. In 8:1–2 she pines for different circumstances that might allow them to be seen together in public and show visible signs of affections without attracting opposition. As we will see in the commentary, this is not merely cultural modesty that demands even husbands and wives refrain from public affection. It is not just public affection that is forbidden, but the entire relationship. Solomon hardly befits this situation since, as monarch, he would have had the freedom to fraternize with whomever he wished, and to marry any single girl he liked. His reputation as a prolific polygamist (1 Kgs 11:1–3) makes it hard to see how his romance with this one young woman was forbidden or

14. Victor Sasson, "King Solomon and the Dark Lady in the Song of Songs," *VT* 39.4 (1989): 407–14.

15. John Phillips, *Exploring the Love Song of Solomon: An Expository Commentary* (Grand Rapids: Kregel), 193; Paul J. Griffiths, *Song of Songs*, Brazos Theological Commentary on the Bible (Grand Rapids: Baker, 2011), 146.

even difficult. And fourth, the end of the Song presents Solomon negatively, contrasting him with the Song's heroine (8:11–12).

Writing in eleventh century Spain, the Jewish writer, Abraham ibn Ezra, suggested that that there were two male characters in the Song.[16] This was developed somewhat in the nineteenth century, by Heinrich Ewald, who argued that the main male speaker in the Song was Solomon, who, over the course of five days, tries unsuccessfully to woo a young woman (the "Shulammite") by bringing her into his royal court. She, however, is already in love with a shepherd boy, and thus resists the king's overtures and remains faithful to her true love.[17] Ewald's theory was quite influential, but the portrait of Solomon that emerged from his analysis was somewhat contradictory. On the one hand, Solomon is wise and illustrious, but also wanton and exploitative. He wields power that keeps hundreds of women in his harem, capturing the humble Shulammite in order to marry her, but gives her leeway to sing the praises of her beloved shepherd boy and eventually permits her to return to him unmolested. Though the storyline of the Song does not have to be realistic, Ewald's perspective lacked cohesion.

Despite its shortcomings, Ewald's theory moved in the right direction. Along with ibn Ezra's perspective, we may derive from it a second and more likely theory about the identity of the leading man. He is not Solomon, but the humble young shepherd with whom the young leading lady is in love (Song 1:7). Solomon does feature in the Song (3:6–11; 8:11–12), but he is distinct from the shepherd. Ewald correctly discerned a love triangle of sorts, as both the monarch and the shepherd boy have an interest in the young woman, but Ewald misconstrued the nature and role of the respective characters. Iain Provan is a proponent of this modified love triangle view, arguing that Solomon is presented negatively.[18] This commentary takes a very similar view but differs from Provan's approach in the way it understands the predicament facing the woman (see "The Drama" below).

In addition to these three characters are the daughters of Jerusalem, who function as a background chorus interacting with the woman at certain junctures of the Song. Their exact identity is debated, but it is best to see them as the queens and concubines of Solomon's extensive harem (6:8–9). The woman's brothers are mentioned at the beginning of the Song (1:6) and appear toward its end with a speaking role (8:8–9). Other characters mentioned but without a speaking part are the watchmen of the town (3:3; 5:7) and

16. See Iain W. Provan, *Ecclesiastes, Song of Songs*, 246.

17. Heinrich Ewald, *Die Dichter des Alten Bundes. Vol. II: Die Salomonischen Schriften*. 2nd ed. (Göttingen: Vanderhoek & Ruprecht, 1867), 333–36, 370–415.

18. See Provan, *Ecclesiastes, Song of Songs*, 246.

Solomon's warriors (3:7–8). The woman's mother (1:6; 3:4; 6:9; 8:1–2), Solomon's mother (3:11), and the shepherd's mother (8:5) are also mentioned, but merely in passing, and so they have no "visible" role.

The Drama

A discernible drama does unfold throughout the Song, though a first attempt to see its contours can be difficult. There are several reasons for this difficulty. The Song's poetry is quite sophisticated, with the words often performing artistic feats in Hebrew that open possibilities of meaning and associations difficult to convey in English. Occasionally the meaning of some verses seems opaque. Metaphors also abound, which shield the naked eroticism of the text while inviting deeper consideration of it. We must work hard as readers of the poetry and its devices. Furthermore, the Song does not assert its narrative in a straightforward way as prose does. Rather, the Song moves between subtle hints of its storyline and more overt presentations of it. There is linear development through it, but this is not always simple and straightforward. The first concerted reading of the Song is like doing a jigsaw puzzle without knowing the full picture. It is only after the final piece has been placed that one can stand back and appreciate the whole. This then allows someone to do the puzzle all over again with much more understanding. The Song hides some of its drama until the very final verse. But like most songs, when we have listened to it once, we are invited to listen again, this time with the knowledge of the whole drama. Thus, it is on a second concerted reading that the full drama of the Song becomes apparent and previous ambiguities are dispelled. This commentary will discuss the meaning of this fuller reading of the Song.

One significant objection to the notion of reading the Song as a dramatic narrative is that drama is meant to be performed on a stage. Not only do we have no stage directions in the Song, but it is difficult to conceive of how some aspects of the Song could be performed. For example, how does one perform a metaphor? If it is only by speaking it, then it is not being acted, which undermines the notion of a drama. Furthermore, it is highly unlikely that some of the more sexually explicit content of the Song was or could be performed before a Jewish audience. Stating that the Song is a drama with a narrative is not to claim that it was necessarily an acted drama. The Song is not a play; it is a poem, but a poem conveying a storyline. In that sense, the Song is rightly classified as a ballad. It is lyrical, but not theatrically performative.

The drama of the Song centers around a young woman who has fallen madly in love with a shepherd boy. They are both intensely attracted to each other and long to express their feelings in the intimate sexual union of marriage. However, the woman's older brothers have pledged her in marriage to Solomon, which will benefit them economically and socially, turning the woman's relationship with her beloved shepherd into a forbidden romance. The Song plays on this predicament, exploring the couple's passionate desires for each other and their anxieties over the future, as well as Solomon's reputation as a prolific polygamist. It presents a poetic argument for the place of attraction and consent in marriage, the beauty of sex in the context of love, the superiority of monogamy over polygamy, and the grave injustice that can be perpetrated when people and love are commodified.

As the Song progresses, Solomon's arrival to claim the woman for his harem looms larger. The woman's dreams and actions become more desperate, and her beloved shepherd boy watches longingly and painfully from afar as she is being prepared as a bride—Solomon's bride rather than his. Before her time runs out, the woman decides to take the drastic action of sleeping with her beloved shepherd as a means of dealing with the supreme injustice of being forced into Solomon's bed. This is a shocking action, but one that highlights the monstrous nature of what the woman's brothers are foisting upon her. What many might see as a great blessing and fortune—marriage to the king—is a crime against the woman and the young man who actually loves her. The woman's plan is not an argument for sexual license that might condone sex outside of marriage but rather an argument that sex rightly belongs within a marriage between a man and a woman who are committed to each other in love and attraction. The kind of "marriage" to Solomon, for which the young woman is being prepared, is presented as a travesty and a crime. Thus, the highly unorthodox nature of the woman's plan, reminiscent of the measures taken by Tamar (Gen 38) and Ruth (Ruth 3), demonstrate not her wantonness but the injustice of her circumstances. By sleeping with the shepherd, she will either force her brothers to marry her to the shepherd, or else see her branded as a promiscuous woman and executed. Her statement in 8:6, that "Love is as strong as death, passion as fierce as Sheol" (author's translation), provides both the rationale for her actions and the essential theme of the Song. Yet, after she has been intimate with the shepherd, her brothers decide to try and pass her off as a virgin so they can still gain personally from her marriage to the king. At the climax of the Song, Solomon arrives to claim the woman, but the shepherd also appears. The Song ends with the woman urging her beloved shepherd to flee. It implies a tragic end, but the abrupt finish means we never "see" what happens to the woman or the shepherd. This provides enough ambiguity for the reader to imagine various postscripts that might provide the woman and her shepherd some justice.

Interpretation

Perhaps the most surprising absence from the cast of characters is God. Some suggest that the Hebrew word *shalhebetyah* in Song 8:6 contains an element of the divine name, Yahweh, but this is not straightforward. The word is probably an intensive form meaning "inferno" (see discussion at Song 8:5–7). This puts the Song in the same basket as Esther as the only biblical books that do not overtly mention God. Yet, this fact is somewhat deceptive. The word *shalhebetyah* hides the divine name in plain sight within an unusual word that draws attention to itself. This is an apt literary device when we consider that the Song addresses a situation in which traditional loyalty to Yahweh was outlawed, so that those who wished to remain faithful to Yahweh had to practice their faith surreptitiously (again, see discussion at Song 8:5–7).

Furthermore, down through the ages the Song has been interpreted as an allegory of the love between God and his people. Unlike Esther, a manuscript of the Song (6QCant) was among the texts deposited in the caves at Qumran, suggesting it was probably interpreted with reference to God. The oath formula that the woman uses throughout the Song alludes to God, though it does so in a veiled manner (see discussion at Song 1:12–2:7). More than this, the allegorical interpretation casts God in the role of the male lover and Israel or the church as the woman. It picks up the prophetic motifs of Yahweh as the husband of Israel (Hos 1–3; Ezek 16) and the New Testament imagery of the church as the bride of Christ (John 3:29; Eph 5:25–33; Rev 19:7; 21:2, 9; 22:17). Although this prevailed as the standard interpretation since antiquity, the Enlightenment challenged church tradition, aided by the discoveries of texts from the ancient Near East, which brought to light the poetry of other ancient cultures. Scholarship has since given rise to the plain meaning of the Song as an exposition of human love and sexuality. This leads us to ask whether the allegorical interpretation is a legitimate way of reading the Song at all.

In an allegory, the plain meaning of the work is purely a vehicle for the symbolic meaning that lies within. Accordingly, the plain meaning does not need any coherence of its own—only the symbolic meaning does. It may be that the overt sexuality of the Song led pious ancient readers to seek an alternative meaning that was not so blatantly ribald. Furthermore, the commitment to Solomonic authorship may have led to confusion over the plain meaning of the Song, since it is difficult to discern coherence if one demands Solomon composed the Song and featured in it as one of the main characters. Platonic philosophy, with its notion of reality residing in the ethereal realm of ideas rather than in the physical world, might also have influenced this line of interpretation. Subsequent Neoplatonic philosophy probably also played a part, especially with its notion of the ascent of the soul to higher forms of knowledge and spiritual experience. These philosophical currents easily gave rise to hermeneutical tendencies that sought a purer and more heavenly meaning for the Song. Accordingly, commentators have derived interpretations of the Song that, to the modern reader, sound fanciful and even unhinged. For example, references to the woman's breasts (Song 4:5; 7:3, 7–8) have been variously interpreted as the Old and New Testaments, the church from which the Christian is spiritually nourished, the commands of loving God and loving neighbor, the blood and the water, and even the outer and inner person united in a single sentient being.[19]

The questions arise, however, whether the Song itself permits such allegorical interpretations, and if so, whether controls exist to constrain interpretation. According to Otto Kaiser, the allegorical view contradicts the clear wording of the Song, and it will accordingly disappear before long.[20] Indeed, it is difficult as a modern reader to appreciate how the Song could ever have given rise to an interpretation that totally overlooks the plain sense of the Song. As both Keel and Schwienhorst-Schönberger assert, it is unlikely that we would have ever interpreted the Song allegorically if it were found in isolation rather than in the canon of Scripture.[21] The naked eroticism of the Song might embarrass some into dressing the Song in the modest attire of religiosity, leading to allegorical interpretations. The divine marriage metaphor provides an ostensible cue for this. Yet, the prophets use this metaphor for its legal significance as a depiction of the national covenant rather than its erotic imagery. The Song, however, is overtly erotic and has only slight connection to legal concerns. Since Rabbi Aqiva shows that the Song was read by some in antiquity without allegory, even if he disapproved of it, we should approve of reading the surface meaning of the Song. In other words, the Song is, in the first place, a ballad about human love and sexuality.

Yet, recent studies have reinvigorated the possibility of discerning meaning beneath the surface of the plain sense.[22] Since the Song is poetry, it thrives

19. Dennis F. Kinlaw, "Song of Songs," in *The Expositor's Bible Commentary*, vol. 5 (Grand Rapids: Zondervan, 1991), 1203.

20. Otto Kaiser, *Einleitung In das Alte Testament: eine Einführung in ihre Ergebnisse und Probleme* (Gütersloh: Gerd Mohn, 1969), 361, as cited in Gerhards, "The Song of Solomon as an Allegory," 54–55.

21. Keel, *The Song of Songs*, 1; Ludger Schwienhorst-Schönberger, "The Song of Songs as Allegory: Methodological and Hermeneutical Considerations," in Schellenberg and Schwienhorst-Schönberger, *Interpreting the Song of Songs—Literal or Allegorical?*, 13–14.

22. See the pertinent essays in Annette Schellenberg and Ludger Schwienhorst-Schönberger, eds., *Interpreting the Song of Songs—Literal or Allegorical?*.

on the ability to imagine far more than the words denote. Indeed, the Song's eroticism comes out more through connotation than denotation, being largely couched in metaphor. Given these metaphorical dynamics at work throughout the book, there is no categorical reason to discount the possibility of a more symbolic or even mystical reading of the Song. Yet, such a reading must proceed on the clues of the text itself, be constrained by its themes and literary parameters, and preserve the plain sense of the text. Allegory, which does not invest much in the plain sense of the text, should therefore be left aside.

The Song is not, however, a parable either. A parable presents a coherent story on its surface, but its purpose is to teach a symbolic meaning that lies beneath the story's surface. In other words, the primary meaning of a parable lies beneath the surface of the text rather than above it. It is difficult to sustain this view of the Song, for which the surface meaning is not only coherent but arguably its primary meaning. Parables also tend to be prose narrative, which the Song is not. The Song is ostensibly a ballad about the phenomenal love between two young people who face seemingly insuperable forces threatening to wrench them unnaturally apart. Yet it is replete with symbolism that beckons us to delve deeper for meaning. The oath in Song 2:7, for example, contains veiled reference to the divine, inviting us to probe further and uncover the divine elsewhere in the Song (see discussion of Song 1:12–2:7). The daughters of Jerusalem allude to the personification of conquered Jerusalem, inviting us to consider notions of power, conquest, and loss. At times we find the imagery intersecting with ideas found elsewhere in biblical literature. There is no complete subterranean plot, though, waiting to be unearthed. The Song's primary meaning lies on the surface. Rather, we simply find wells here and there, which tap into themes from the larger story of God and his people. As such, the Song is neither allegory nor parable. It is a ballad, but as we consider its drama and passion, we find occasional opportunity to stop and drink in deep metaphors that remind us of the larger world to which this love story belongs and that speak into a situation of acute theological and cultural crisis in Judaism (the Antiochene persecution of 167 BC). These metaphorical connections to other biblical texts, the mention of Solomon, and their value for addressing that period of crisis were arguably the primary reasons for the book's authoritative status.

The dating of the Song and its intertextual connections to other parts of Scripture allow us to anchor the Song in the context of Second Temple Judaism, especially the Hellenistic Era. Under the largely benevolent rule of the Persians, Judaism thrived and developed, albeit not without challenges. During the Hellenistic Era, the challenges facing Judaism escalated significantly. The threat of Hellenism provides the context for understanding the metaphorical significance of the Song. The presentation of two lovers in the Song does indeed imbibe the prophetic metaphor of the divine marriage between Yahweh and Israel. Solomon, however, is an outsider to this relationship in the Song, threatening to tear the relationship apart by the sheer power behind his claim over the woman.[23] His reputation as a prolific polygamist with his harem of foreign idolatrous women suggests that Solomon is symbolic of outside forces. He is the powerful monarch who does as he pleases and thus represents the imperial and cultural forces of Hellenism that threatened to undo faithful, biblical Judaism during the reign of Antiochus IV Epiphanes. As readers, we desire to see the woman and her beloved shepherd prevail against the threat that Solomon poses. On the metaphorical level, we are drawn to champion the covenant relationship between Israel and Yahweh against the threat of Hellenism.

In the Song, the woman's brothers, who are her guardians, attempt to gain personally from marrying her to Solomon. Metaphorically, they represent the leaders of Judaism in the late third and early second century BC, whose leadership exposed the Jewish nation to the seemingly inexorable pressures of Hellenism, often for personal gain. We are reminded of the likes of the high priest Onias II and his opportunistic nephew, Joseph Tobias, in the 220s BC (see Introduction to Ecclesiastes for further discussion). We are also reminded of the rivalry between Jason and Menelaus for the high priesthood in Jerusalem and their Hellenistic tendencies. In 174 BC Jason wrested the priesthood off his brother, Onias III (who had held the office legitimately) by bribing the Seleucid king, Antiochus IV. Once in office, Jason turned Jerusalem into a fully-fledged Greek polis with all the relevant Hellenistic institutions (2 Macc 4:7–17). Two years later, he lost the priesthood to Menelaus, who paid Antiochus an even larger bribe for the position and who continued an aggressive Helenizing policy. Both Jason and Menelaus were changing the nature of Judaism from its very center in Jerusalem and its temple. Judaism had already felt over a century of Greek undercurrents, and by selling out to Hellenism, Jason and Menelaus turned these into a tidal wave that threatened to subsume it.

This gained yet more force in 167 BC when Antiochus returned from an aborted campaign in Egypt.[24] When he arrived in Judea, he found Jerusalem embroiled in conflict between Jason and Menelaus. Antiochus addressed this is several ways. First, he initiated a massacre in Jerusalem as his forces took strict control of the city. The garrison forces occupied the Seleucid citadel, known

23. Gerhards ("The Song of Solomon as an Allegory") has a similar view of the Song, arguing for its Hellenistic milieu, though he sees a different role for Solomon and is still content to use the classification of "allegory."

24. Our main sources for these developments are the opening chapters of 1 and 2 Maccabees.

as the Acra, which was being constructed in the City of David, south of the temple. Thousands lost their lives, and many survivors fled. Second, Antiochus removed official recognition of the Jewish nation, which had previously allowed them to maintain their traditional beliefs and practices. He turned the temple of Yahweh in Jerusalem into a temple dedicated to Olympian Zeus. He also instituted a royal cult, which enforced the recognition of Seleucid sovereignty through sacrifice offered to a statue of himself placed beside the altar in Jerusalem—an event that Daniel calls "an abomination that causes desolation" (Dan 9:27). This effectively forced those who desired to worship Yahweh via the temple cult into idolatrous worship of Zeus and Antiochus. Thus began an official persecution of those Jews determined to remain exclusively loyal to traditional beliefs in Yahweh. Those who resisted these changes and clung closely to their original faith effectively became outlaws, and many of them lost their lives for their beliefs between 167–164 BC. Judaism was caught between seemingly illegal devotion to Yahweh, and the Jewish leaders who wanted to hand the faith over to the redoubtable forces of Hellenism.[25]

The woman in the Song embodies this struggle. She is resolute in her devotion to her beloved shepherd and is willing to face death rather than capitulate to Solomon. Though the Song finishes on a tragic note, we never witness the final demise of the woman. Metaphorically, this gives us hope that, despite the enormous waves threatening to drown orthodox Judaism, something might still be done to rescue it. The end had not yet come.

The Hellenistic milieu of the Song, therefore, is important. The Song's *meaning* is about human love, sexuality, power, personhood, monogamy, and polygamy. The Song's *significance* is about the struggle of Judaism to retain its orthodox, biblical principles and hopes in the face of poor local leadership and enormous Hellenistic pressure—both imperial and cultural—during the Antiochene persecution of the second century BC. This significance grows with the further revelation of the New Testament, in which God comes to the rescue of his people in a surprising way through Jesus Christ. It is possible, therefore, to extend the allusions organically from Israel to the church, and from Yahweh to Jesus.

Structure

Where some see fourteen,[26] twenty-three,[27] or forty-two songs,[28] I see one song, as the title (Song 1:1) suggests. Discerning units within the Song

25. See Athas, *Bridging the Testaments*, forthcoming.
26. Goulder, *The Song of Fourteen Songs*.
27. Longman, *Song of Songs*, viii.
28. Keel, *The Song of Songs*, v–vi.

is somewhat difficult. There are some key markers of structure, such as the woman's adjuration of the daughters of Jerusalem (2:7; 3:5; 8:4) and the various *wasfs*—sections of descriptive praise of the lovers' bodies (4:1–15; 5:10–16; 6:4–9; 7:1–10), yet even these have some blurry edges. I have attempted to divide the Song up into units that best capture the evolution of its drama and provide what I see as the best units for preaching without the need for too much repetition.

1:1	**Title**
1:2–2:7	**The Lovers**
1:2–6	A Woman in a Dilemma
1:7–11	A Playful Exchange
1:12–2:7	Awakening Love
2:8–5:8	**Desire and Anxiety**
2:8–17	Rendezvous at Night
3:1–5	Dream Scene One: Searching
3:6–11	Dream Scene Two: Solomon
4:1–5:1	Dream Scene Three: Longing
5:2–8	Harsh Reality
5:9–6:10	**Defiant Devotion**
5:9–16	Praising the Beloved
6:1–3	Uncertain Future
6:4–10	Distant Praise
6:11–8:14	**The Finale**
6:11–13	A Moment of Decision
7:1–10	Making Love
7:11–8:4	A Forbidden Relationship
8:5–7	Love as Strong as Death
8:8–10	The Brothers' Deliberations
8:11–14	The Finale

Resources for Teaching and Preaching

There is a huge diversity of books about the Song of Songs because of the lack of consensus in how to read it. Although I did not always agree with them, the ones I found most useful in writing this commentary were those by Exum, Keel, Murphy, Pope, Provan, Seerveld, and the collection of essays in Schelleberg & Schwienhorst-Schönberger. In addition, I recommend the following works for further study.

Athas, George. *Bridging the Testaments*. Grand Rapids: Zondervan (forthcoming).

Davidson, Richard M. *Flame of Yahweh: Sexuality in the Old Testament*. Peabody, MA: Hendrickson, 2007.

Grainger, John D. *The Wars of the Maccabees*. Barnsley: Pen & Sword, 2012.

Smith, Des. *Garden of Love: 4 Interactive Bible Studies for Small Groups and Individuals*. Interactive Bible Studies. Kingsford, NSW: Matthias Media, 2017.

Webb, Barry G. *Five Festal Garments: Christian Reflections on the Song of Songs, Ruth, Lamentations, Ecclesiastes and Esther*. New Studies in Biblical Theology. Leicester: Apollos, 2000.

CHAPTER 9

Song of Songs 1:1–2:7

LISTEN to the Story

1Solomon's Song of Songs.

2Let him kiss me with the kisses of his mouth—
for your love is more delightful than wine.
3Pleasing is the fragrance of your perfumes;
your name is like perfume poured out.
No wonder the young women love you!
4Take me away with you—let us hurry!
Let the king bring me into his chambers.
We rejoice and delight in you;
we will praise your love more than wine.
How right they are to adore you!
5Dark am I, yet lovely,
daughters of Jerusalem,
dark like the tents of Kedar,
like the tent curtains of Solomon.
6Do not stare at me because I am dark,
because I am darkened by the sun.
My mother's sons were angry with me
and made me take care of the vineyards;
my own vineyard I had to neglect.
7Tell me, you whom I love,
where you graze your flock
and where you rest your sheep at midday.
Why should I be like a veiled woman
beside the flocks of your friends?
8If you do not know, most beautiful of women,
follow the tracks of the sheep
and graze your young goats

by the tents of the shepherds.
9 I liken you, my darling, to a mare
among Pharaoh's chariot horses.
10 Your cheeks are beautiful with earrings,
your neck with strings of jewels.
11 We will make you earrings of gold,
studded with silver.
12 While the king was at his table,
my perfume spread its fragrance.
13 My beloved is to me a sachet of myrrh
resting between my breasts.
14 My beloved is to me a cluster of henna blossoms
from the vineyards of En Gedi.
15 How beautiful you are, my darling!
Oh, how beautiful!
Your eyes are doves.
16 How handsome you are, my beloved!
Oh, how charming!
And our bed is verdant.
17 The beams of our house are cedars;
our rafters are firs.
2:1 I am a rose of Sharon,
a lily of the valleys.
2 Like a lily among thorns
is my darling among the young women.
3 Like an apple tree among the trees of the forest
is my beloved among the young men.
I delight to sit in his shade,
and his fruit is sweet to my taste.
4 Let him lead me to the banquet hall,
and let his banner over me be love.
5 Strengthen me with raisins,
refresh me with apples,
for I am faint with love.
6 His left arm is under my head,
and his right arm embraces me.
7 Daughters of Jerusalem, I charge you
by the gazelles and by the does of the field:

Do not arouse or awaken love
until it so desires.

Listening to the Text in the Story: 1 Kings 11:1–13 (daughters of Jerusalem); Isaiah 5:1–7; 62:4–5; Jer 3:6–18; Lamentations 1–2; Ezekiel 16; 19:10; Hosea 1–3

The Song of Songs is associated with Solomon, whose name appears in the title and at various points throughout the Song (1:5; 3:7, 9, 11; 8:11–12). As we will see, Solomon is a minor character in the Song, but his role is nonetheless significant (see discussion of 1:2–6 below). His depiction in 1 Kings 11:1–13 exerts the most influence over his presentation in the Song. There we learn that he "loved many foreign women" (1 Kgs 11:1) and kept a harem of "seven hundred wives of royal birth and three hundred concubines" (11:3). We are also told that he accommodated the worship of his wives' foreign gods, going so far as building altars to these gods in and around Jerusalem (11:4–8). By violating the national covenant in this way, he contributed to the fracture of Israel into a northern and southern kingdom, and the nation's eventual downfall (11:9–13). It is this image of the potentate and serial womanizer, rather than the wise Solomon, that we encounter in the Song.

Solomon's harem also features in the Song as the "daughters of Jerusalem." As we examine the plain meaning of the Song, we see them as a crowd of women without individual identities, who act collectively as a foil for the one woman who is the Song's main character. Their characterization as "daughters of Jerusalem" harks back to the personification of conquered Jerusalem in Lamentations.[1] There we encounter "Daughter Jerusalem" (Lam 2:15) who has been dealt a grievous blow. She is a tragic figure who, once beautiful, has suffered extreme violence. Her world has been turned upside down as her independence has been taken from her. She has witnessed and experienced abuse, and lies forlorn in a hopeless state. She has been conquered. Similarly, as we will see, the "daughters of Jerusalem" are conquered women whose characterization reflects tragedy. Yet, they are also foreign women associated with foreign deities. This aspect of their being, which derives from 1 Kings 11, comes into play when we trace the Song's intersections with other parts

1. The Book of the Twelve (Hos–Mal) contains references to Daughter Jerusalem (cf. Mic 4:8; Zeph 3:14; Zech 9:9), which are generally positive in feel. However, the female figures in the Song all carry an element of tragedy as women who have experienced male domination (specifically from Solomon). As such, the depiction of Daughter Jerusalem in Lamentations has far greater resonance here.

of Scripture. Drawing all these aspects together, the Daughters of Jerusalem represent a city—the hub of Jewish life—that has compromised its biblical ideals, sold out to foreign culture and deities, and thus lost its true self.

Also important to these intersections is the prophetic portrayal of Yahweh's covenant relationship with Israel as a marriage (Isa 62:4–5; Jer 3:6–18; Ezek 16; Hos 1–3). Love is a primary theme in the Song, and it is central to the prophetic metaphor. Hosea 1–3 develops the metaphor extensively through Hosea's marriage to Gomer. The metaphor implies that Yahweh and Israel belong together, but their covenant relationship is troubled by Israel's perpetual unfaithfulness, which symbolizes the nation's worship of foreign deities. The tragic Daughters of Jerusalem are, therefore, a poignant foil for the young woman who would remain faithful to her one true love, the shepherd.

Along similar lines is the "Song of the Vineyard" in Isaiah 5:1–7 (cf. Ezek 19:10). This lyric parable depicts Israel as a vineyard that Yahweh plants on a hillside and goes to great lengths to cultivate. Despite his efforts, the vineyard yields only bad grapes, symbolic of the nation's failure to follow Yahweh's directives. The woman in the Song of Songs refers to her "vineyard" (Song 1:6), which is not only symbolic of her own person but permits us to draw connections between her and Israel in Isaiah's Song of the Vineyard. That song is also composed as a song "for the one I love" (Isa 5:1a), which uses the precise term of endearment (in Hebrew, *dodi*) that the woman in Song of Songs uses for the man she loves. This, then, allows us to infer a further connection between the shepherd in the Song and Yahweh.

EXPLAIN the Story

In this opening section of the Song, we are introduced to the cast of characters who feature throughout it. On center stage, as it were, is a young woman who has fallen in love with a young man, whom we also meet. She has brothers with whom she has a difficult relationship. To one side of the stage are the daughters of Jerusalem, who form a chorus that interacts with the woman. Though we do not meet him personally, we learn of the king, whose existence creates the predicament of the Song's "story."

Title (1:1)

The first verse contains the title of the book, which is literally rendered, "The song of songs, which is to Solomon." The use of a singular noun in construct with its own plural is a standard way that Hebrew uses to express a superlative. We find a comparable expression in the description of the inner temple chamber as "the holy of holies," meaning "the most holy place" (e.g., 1 Kgs 6:16). This superlative sense is easy to glean from an adjective like "holy," but a little harder with a noun like "song." The only viable option is to understand the phrase as an endorsement of the song's quality: "the best song."

The reference to Solomon is traditionally understood as an attribution of authorship (cf. NIV). However, as seen in the Introduction, this is difficult to sustain. It is better to interpret the Hebrew preposition (*le*) attached to Solomon's name as indicating subject matter. In Isaiah's "Song of the Vineyard" (Isa 5:1), the same preposition (*le*) is attached to "vineyard" as an indication of subject. We should, therefore, translate this titular verse as, "The Best Song, which concerns Solomon."

The Lover (1:2–2:7)

A Woman in a Dilemma (1:2–6)

The Song itself begins in 1:2 with the main character, the woman, expressing her yearning to be kissed by a particular man. At this initial point, we do not know who this man is. He is off stage, as it were. Nor do we know how the woman knows him, let alone how she has fallen in love with him. Nonetheless, the deep well of desire comes through in the sensuality of the woman's remarks, with allusions to touch ("kiss"), taste ("wine"), smell ("fragrance"), hearing ("name"), and sight ("poured out"). These intermingle with each other to create an overwhelming physical experience, which sets the tenor for the rest of the Song. This is our first hint at the sensual and erotic nature of this poetry.

The identity of the woman is withheld from us, as is that of the man she desires. This is a poignant reflection of the historical situation of the Antiochene persecution, in which the recognition of the Jews' national identity was revoked and the name of Yahweh was suppressed by turning his temple in Jerusalem into a temple of another god (Olympian Zeus). It is not until 1:5–7 that we are given some details about the woman and the man. Nevertheless, they remain anonymous and, therefore, beyond our full knowledge. The woman refers to the man's "name" (1:3), but we never learn what it actually is. As readers, then, we are kept at a distance from this relationship, though we will have opportunity to observe it, even some of its most intimate expressions. All we learn here is that the man's name is like "perfume poured out" (1:3). In Hebrew, the alliteration poetically reinforces the point, as the word for "your name" (*shemeka*) matches closely the word for "perfume" (*shemen*). This metaphor gives us a way to understand the woman's excitement at the man she loves while allowing her alone to experience the essence of his identity.

There is, therefore, an openness that permits us to view and appreciate this relationship while also preserving its privacy. There is knowledge to which only the two lovers are privy. This dynamic is crucial for our approach to the Song. As we will see, many of the metaphors and similes employed throughout the Song are highly suggestive, filled with innuendo and unmistakable sexual allusions. Yet, by keeping the lovers anonymous to us and veiling (even if thinly) their amorous desires and actions in poetic metaphor, we are given real understanding of this most intimate relationship, even as we are kept at arm's length from it. We comprehend the relationship in all its contours, but we are never allowed to partake of it ourselves. In this way, the Song sanctifies the relationship of the two lovers, openly acknowledging it and its nature while maintaining its special status in a way that enables the lovers alone to experience its essence.

The privileged position of the woman in relation to the man comes out in 1:3–4. The "young women" can see the man's endearing qualities and "love" him. Yet, she is the one who expresses a desire to be kissed by him (1:2) and then speaks to him directly in a way that closely associates herself with him (1:4).

Her call for the man to take her away with him (1:4a) at first sounds like romantic spontaneity. Indeed, there is an urgency in her words, reinforced by the cohortative, "Let's run away!" (NIV: "let us hurry!"), but it is not simply the urgency of desire that drives the woman here. She literally commands the man, "Drag me behind you" (*moshkeni 'ahareyka*). This is not because she has melodramatically swooned with desire, for she can evidently run with him. Keel makes comparison to much older Sumerian poetry, in which a woman describes her lover as a lion and desires him to drag her off like prey,[2] but such animal imagery is lacking here. Rather, the imperative suggests the woman is in a situation from which she wants the man to extricate her. The same verb is used to describe how Joseph's brothers "dragged him" out of the pit of his confinement to sell him to Midianite merchants (Gen 37:28) and how Jeremiah was "dragged out" of a muddy pit where he had been left to die (Jer 38:13). When paired with the desire to run away, we hear a sense of desperation in the woman's voice. Something is wrong.

Her next words bring the problem to light. The NIV translates the next line as an expression of desire: "Let the king bring me into his chambers" (Song 1:4b). However, the Hebrew is a plain statement: "The king brings me into his chambers." Some point to this as deriving from a wedding custom that portrays the groom as a king and the bride as a queen and that what we see here

2. Ibid., 45.

is the groom bringing his new bride into the bridal chamber to consummate their union.[3] While plausible, the suggestion is based largely on Arab folk customs of the nineteenth century.[4] The association between chambers and consummation is, however, strong in this romantic context, so the NIV's translation is understandable. It is not until we read further into the Song and, indeed, reach its climactic finale (8:11–14), that we understand this statement with full clarity. It is not, as our first impression might understand, an innocent expression of fervent desire but a statement of a sinister predicament. The woman is here stating that someone other than the man she loves has laid claim to marry her and wants to bring her into his bed. That someone else is none other than the king, whom we learn later is Solomon (3:7, 9, 11; 8:11–12). At this early stage, we have only the tension in the woman's previous words as a hint that something is wrong, and we gain greater appreciation for her dilemma as we keep reading.

The way the Hebrew states the dilemma here in 1:4b might initially give the impression that this marriage to the king has already occurred. This is possible, but as the drama of the Song unfolds, we read of Solomon's approach to claim the woman as his bride (3:6–11). Thus, if the woman's line here states it as an accomplished event, the rest of the Song must be viewed as a flashback recounting how she came into the king's chambers. More likely, though, the woman states here the king's intention to bring her to his chambers—that is, to marry her and have her enter his harem. She presents this intention as a simple fact (a *qatal* verb), which gives it an urgency that radically alters the situation between her and the man she loves. Their courtship is in danger. She stands to become a royal concubine in a life of luxury (potentially even queen of the realm, bearing royal children), but this will tear her away from the man she loves and confine her within the chambers of another, whom she does not love—the king. Herein lies the essential predicament of the Song.

On the historical reality behind the Song, we see the royal decree of Antiochus in 167 BC revoking the ethnic status of the Jews, thereby dissolving any legal difference between them and all other peoples in the Seleucid kingdom. The Jews were henceforth to be recognized as people belonging to Antiochus, not to Yahweh, sparking the desperate petitions of the faithful to Yahweh to rescue them from this dire circumstance.

No sooner has the woman stated the cause of her angst than we hear a chorus of voices pledging to celebrate and commemorate (1:4c–e). What the

3. Pope, *Song of Songs*, 303; Richard S. Hess, *Song of Songs*, Baker Commentary on the Old Testament Wisdom and Psalms (Grand Rapids: Baker, 2005), 53.

4. See discussion in Pope, *Song of Songs*, 141–45.

NIV translates as "we will praise your love" should more properly be translated as "we will memorialize your love." The original consonantal text of the Hebrew makes it difficult to discern whether the chorus wants to commemorate the woman, the man she loves, the love they share, or even the love they think will blossom between the woman and the king.[5] In any case, the chorus's pledge juxtaposes the future and the past. The love between the woman and the man, filled with joy, desire, and such potential, now faces an empty future of frustration, non-fulfillment, and mere wistful remembrance. The dilemma that threatens to tear the lovers apart highlights themes that the Song takes up elsewhere: the pain of separation (5:6–7), the injustice of love not taking its natural course (7:11–13), the monstrosity of forced affection (2:7; 3:5; 8:4), and the raw tenacity of love (8:6–7). Though well intentioned, the chorus's pledge to commemorate highlights the desperate dilemma of the courting couple.

In 1:5, the woman addresses the chorus directly. Here we learn that the chorus consists of the "daughters of Jerusalem." We might identify these as the "young women" of 1:3 who admire the man. However, in 5:9 the chorus seems ignorant of the man's virtues, making such an identification doubtful. The association of these women with Jerusalem suggests that they are, in fact, the harem of Solomon. Jerusalem is, after all, the royal capital. This produces an interesting dynamic that allows us to evaluate the respective situations of both the woman and the daughters of Jerusalem. The daughters all blend into a single mass as the harem of Solomon. Though the woman is anonymous to us, she always remains distinct from them, just as Israel was to remain distinct from all other nations. This allows us to see the woman as a fully orbed primary character. We can identify her by her own actions and words about herself—her love, her desires, her fears, her vulnerability, and her relationship with the man she loves. By contrast, the daughters of Jerusalem are static and two-dimensional. We never learn about a single one of them. We do not read of their loves, desires, fears, and vulnerabilities. As a harem, they are not permitted the benefits of such distinctives. Rather, we only ever hear them speak as one undifferentiated group. Yet, they are not called the "women of Solomon" but the "daughters of Jerusalem." This allows us to see them as a chorus of individual women, but whose distinct identities have been subsumed by their situation. This, in turn, helps us see the injustice perpetrated against them as well as the injustice about to be foisted upon the woman in the Song. By being pledged to the king, she is about to join the ranks of these

5. The primary Qumran manuscript of Song of Songs (6QCant) also presents a viable but alternative reading that further confuses the picture of who or what exactly is being commemorated.

daughters of Jerusalem and lose her distinct identity, also. The label "daughters of Jerusalem" underscores this injustice. It picks up the personification of Jerusalem as the tragic "daughter" figure of Lamentations, who experiences the overthrow of her previous existence, the loss of her independence, the grief of broken relationships, the hopelessness of dashed dreams, and the pain of physical violence. This is the reality of the daughters of Jerusalem, and soon to be that of the woman as well. Thus, over the course of the Song, we not only feel the panic of the woman in the desperate predicament she faces, but we also feel sympathy for the chorus of women who have already been conquered before her. By keeping the woman distinct from them, we maintain a sense of hope for her and may appreciate the beauty and freedom of the relationship she shares with the young man she loves, with all the potential it holds, while understanding the severity of her predicament by which she stands to lose it all. It is a metaphorical way of depicting how fitting it is for Israel to be devoted to Yahweh, which differentiates her from the other nations.

While she is yet free, the woman has the benefit of distinction and so is able to describe herself in 1:5–6. She is dark, yet lovely (1:5a), which means she has been tanned by the sun (1:6b). This distinguishes her as a commoner who does manual work, unlike the royal harem, which is secluded within chambers (cf. 1:4b). She refers to the black tents of Kedar, an allusion to the desert tribe mentioned in Psalm 120:5–6, where it is associated with warlike activity. She then instantly parallels this with the "tent curtains of Solomon," thereby associating Solomon's quarters with darkness, belligerence, and conquest. It sounds exotic, but a sinister sense lurks within.

In 1:6 the woman mentions her "mother's sons," who seem to have charge of her. The Song never refers to a father figure, so we presume the father is no longer on the scene. Guardianship would thus naturally have passed to her brothers. They will appear again at the end of the Song as the drama reaches its climactic moment (8:8–9). Thus, they bracket the song with their appearance and are therefore pivotal to the "story." In both instances, their appearance is associated with vineyards (cf. 8:11), and there is evident antipathy between them and the woman. This highlights their role in her dilemma. Here in 1:6 the woman claims her brothers were angry with her and made her take care of vineyards. Schwienhorst-Schönberger understands the sequence here to show that the brothers were angry that their sister did not tend her own vineyard and therefore put her to work on other vineyards instead.[6] This is driven, however, by the concerns of an allegorical interpretation. It also seems unwise that the brothers would depend on their sister to work other vineyards if she had not

6. Schwienhorst-Schönberger, "The Song of Songs as Allegory," 41.

cared for her own. Rather, the order presented in the Song itself seems logical enough: the brothers were hostile to their sister, put her to work in vineyards, presumably their own, leading her to neglect her own vineyard.

There is evident symbolism at work here. In the bracketing episode at the end of the Song, the woman claims, "But my own vineyard is mine to give" (8:12a). The vineyard is symbolic of her own person, especially her body. By making her work other vineyards, the brothers dispossess her of the right of self-determination and force her to do their bidding. In terms of the Song's larger drama, this means they are the ones responsible for pledging her in marriage to the king and reaping a handsome reward for it—a fact that is not fully evident at this early point but comes to clearer light at the end of the Song (8:8–12), and therefore clearer here upon a second reading. Her failure to keep her own vineyard is perhaps an indication that her appearance is unkempt. More likely, though, it is a metaphor for the loss of her virginity before marriage. Like the king bringing her into his chambers (1:4b), it is unclear whether this has already occurred at this early stage or is being foreshadowed as inevitable. Since we are at the beginning of the drama, the latter seems more likely, but we cannot discount the former. In any case, the woman is not apologetic but explanatory, insinuating that the loss of her virginity is (or will be) the logical result of her brothers' unreasonable attitude toward her. By dispossessing her of the right to self-determination (cf. Menelaus's agreement to the removal of the Jews' ethnic status in 167 BC), they force her to take matters into her own hands, which entails the drastic measure of losing her virginity. The circumstances surrounding this are not yet known; we have to keep reading further to figure out what they are. On a first reading, suspicion naturally falls on the man she loves as the one to blame for her loss of virginity. When reading the Song for a second time, we know that the woman's brothers are ultimately the ones to blame for driving the woman to desperate measures, but on the first reading we must wait for the drama of the Song to unfold to see this fully. Suffice it to say, the loss of virginity before marriage was potentially punishable by death (Deut 22:13–21). The stakes in this situation are very high.

A Playful Exchange (1:7–11)

These verses depart from the previous "dialogue" between the woman and the daughters of Jerusalem. They represent a playful exchange between the woman and the man she loves, who speaks here for the first time, but there is also continued tension. From the exchange, we learn that the man is a shepherd (1:7). The woman desires to know where he shepherds so that she does not need to keep searching for him and hiding her identity around his companions (1:7). The need to hide her identity stems from the fact that their relationship is forbidden now that the king has laid claim to the woman. He teases her by telling her to graze her young goats around other shepherds. This might mean that the woman is a shepherdess, but as we have already seen, she belongs to a family that keeps vineyards (1:6). It is more likely, then, that the man is simply extending the playfulness of her question by encouraging her to use her charms on others—a game of "hard to get" in reverse—while also acknowledging the tension in their circumstances. They love each other and express playfulness toward each other, but their relationship is still forbidden.

From the exchange we see that the woman has deep feelings for the man and does not love anyone else. He reciprocates here by expressing his feelings for her. He lauds her as the "most beautiful of women" (1:8a) and calls her "my darling" (1:9a). He likens her to "a mare among Pharaoh's chariot horses" (1:9a). This sounds most unusual to a modern, urban reader but is perfectly at home in an ancient, largely rural context. These kinds of similes and metaphors abound throughout the Song. The comparison here gives the woman the airs of royalty and grace. The man can understand that others are attracted to the woman, even the king himself. She is highly desirable, even prized as a potential mother of royalty who would benefit a dynastic house. In saying this, the man hints both at his own desire for her and that she is beyond his reach. This is not because she is "out of his league," but because circumstances are drawing her away from him. He is a lowly shepherd, and a shepherd of higher standing and greater power—the king—has laid claim to her. He can imagine her in jewelry as a bride (1:10). Though he might wish her to be his own bride, the daughters of Jerusalem chime in at this point to say that they will make jewelry of gold and silver for her (1:11), as she will soon join their ranks. This merely highlights the dilemma of the two lovers. The prospect of a royal wedding, which would ordinarily be cause for celebration and praise for the lucky bride, hangs ominously as a dark shadow over the courting couple, for it would tear them apart.

Awakening Love (1:12–2:7)

The woman speaks again in 1:12. Most take her reference to the "king" here as a noble depiction of the man she loves.[7] Such fantasy would not be out of place in an intimate relationship. Yet, the dominant image of the king throughout

7. Carr, *Song of Solomon*, 84; Murphy, *The Song of Songs: A Commentary on the Book of Canticles or The Song of Songs*, 135; Gledhill, *Message of the Song of Songs*, 115; Duane L. Garrett and Paul R. House, *Song of Songs / Lamentations*, WBC 23B (Nashville: Thomas Nelson, 2004), 146; Exum, *Song of Songs*, 110; Hess, *Song of Songs*, 67; Iain M. Duguid, *The Song of Songs*, TOTC 19 (Downers Grove, IL: Inter-Varsity Press, 2015), 87.

the Song is of Solomon, presented as a third party who comes from afar with an entourage of armed men (cf. 3:7–11). Whenever the woman describes the man she loves, she uses an accompanying possessive pronoun that demonstrates the intimate connection between the two lovers. For example, she calls him "my beloved" in the next two verses (1:13–14), or "the one my heart loves" (3:1). The idea is best captured in 2:16, where she says, "My beloved is mine and I am his." The use of possessive pronouns thus intertwines the two lovers. Yet, whenever the king is mentioned, the expression never has a possessive pronoun attached to it (e.g., "my king"), and the shepherd never calls the woman "queen" (or "my queen"). In fact, he distinguishes her from queens and concubines in 6:8–9. This is because the king and his harem of consorts are distant figures and not to be equated with the two lovers. Thus, as the woman speaks about the "king" here in 1:12, she speaks not about the shepherd she loves but about Solomon, the distant monarch, to whom she has been pledged in marriage. It is evocative of Antiochus IV's decree that required Jews to participate in the idolatrous royal Seleucid cult.

The NIV has the woman describe the king as "at his table" (1:12a), which takes its lead from the Greek translation (LXX). However, in other contexts the relevant Hebrew word (*mesab*) denotes "surroundings" (1 Kgs 6:29; 2 Kgs 23:5; Ps 140:9[140:10]). The woman is, therefore, contrasting the distant king "in his own surroundings" with the shepherd she loves, whom she holds close and describes as "a sachet of myrrh resting between my breasts" (1:13). Together the two lovers go on to describe their own surroundings. They are not in the chambers of a distant palace ringed with manicured pleasure gardens. They do not belong in such quarters, for they are not actually royalty. Instead, they are in the lush and wild countryside, where the green grass is their bed, the trees are their palace, and they themselves are each other's pleasure garden (1:12b–2:3). The imagery speaks of their relative poverty in comparison with the distant king while glorifying the wealth of their love. In terms of the larger predicament, it demonstrates that the woman has no need of gold and silver ornaments (1:11). She has all she needs in her shepherd boy, who is like the most luxurious oriental ointments—nard (1:12b [NIV, "perfume"),[8] myrrh (1:13a), and henna (1:14a). Marrying the king might bring riches to others, especially her brothers, but it would impoverish her.

The lovers trade compliments (1:15–16; 2:1–3), which not only proves their feelings for each other but also distinguishes them from others. The

8. I concur with Fox in understanding the woman to be referring to the man when she talks of "my nard," as it provides the best poetic parallelism. See Fox, *The Song of Songs and the Ancient Egyptian Love Songs*, 105.

woman wants none but her shepherd boy, and he wants none but her. She is "Like a lily among thorns," and he is "Like an apple tree among the trees of the forest" (2:2–3). To reinforce the point, the woman imagines the shepherd bringing her into the "house of wine" (NIV, "banquet hall"). In light of the surrounding imagery, this is probably a fantasy imagining a vineyard as an inviting place of nuptial celebration, where the lovers can have their way with each other (2:5–6). It stands in sharp contrast to the king's intention to bring the woman unwilling into his own cold chambers (1:4b).

Sexual connotations pervade this exchange. The "sachet of myrrh" is evocative of the man's genitals and fertility, mentioned together with the woman's breasts (1:13). Her desire to sit and taste his "fruit" (2:3) is suggestive of oral sex. There is mention of a bed (1:16) and passionate embracing (2:6). The reference to raisin cakes (NIV, "raisins") has overtones of female pudenda and aphrodisiacs,[9] while being "refreshed" with apples plays on the description of the man in 2:3. This has connotations of spreading a bed (cf. Prov 7:16) and of aphrodisiacs.[10] The allusions are overtly erotic, designed to express the natural course of the intense romantic love between the woman and the man as they imagine marital bliss together. Yet there is no specific indication at this point that the lovers have let their passion take its course. When the woman describes her lover as an apple tree, she states her "desire" (NIV, "delight") to sit in his shade (2:3c), which implies that she wants to be intimate with him, but not that she has been. The highly charged nature of the imagery makes abundantly clear that these desires are welcome and seek fulfilment in sexual union. That is, they give a sense that it would be just and appropriate for the two lovers to be joined together, not just in a casual sexual encounter that trivializes their passion but in a lifelong union that provides security for the perennial and fertile expression of their love. Together with the lovers, then, we hope to see this union become a reality. Yet, as much as the woman desires to sit in the shade of her lover, it is the shadow of Solomon that is cast over her.

The oath she puts the daughters of Jerusalem under (2:7) helps us understand her dilemma further. The daughters of Jerusalem are, to some extent, a "sounding board" for the woman,[11] which is poignant since they represent the fate that awaits her within the harem of Solomon. They also function as the audience within the Song, observing the relationship of the woman and her shepherd boy. They occupy a similar vantage point to us as readers, who also

9. Raisin cakes were offered or consumed in fertility rites. See Pope, *Song of Songs*, 378–80.

10. Ibid., 380–81; Keel, *The Song of Songs*, 88; Fox, *The Song of Songs and the Ancient Egyptian Love Songs*, 108–9.

11. Fox, *The Song of Songs and the Ancient Egyptian Love Songs*, 110; Gledhill, *Message of the Song of Songs*, 127.

observe the relationship. As the woman directs her warning to them, then, it also flows toward us.

The oath appears in various forms throughout the Song (2:7; 3:5; 5:8; 8:4). Here the woman adjures the daughters of Jerusalem "by the gazelles and by the does of the field" (2:7; cf. 3:5). Various explanations exist for this choice of formulaic witnesses. Keel draws comparison with iconography on seals and jewelry from the ancient Near East, where divine figures sometimes appear in sexually suggestive depictions alongside deers and goats. He argues that the Song here avoids direct appeal to foreign deities but uses these shy and agile creatures, which seem to represent the divine, to maintain the same kind of "sacred aura" as seen in the seals and jewelry.[12] Mitchell argues that gazelles and does only copulate in mating season, so that the woman is stating that people should wait for God's timing to act upon their love.[13] This suggestion is relevant, especially for other aspects of the Song. However, it does not explain fully the formulaic expression here.

As Steinmann observes, the only viable explanation that accounts for all the words in the oath formula is Gordis's suggestion that it is a veiled reference to God.[14] In Hebrew, "by the gazelles" (*bitseba'ot*) sounds identical to the word for "hosts" in the expression "Yahweh of Hosts," and "by the does of the field" (*be'aylot hassadeh*) sounds similar to "by God Almighty" (*be'el shadday*).[15] Thus, the woman makes an appeal to the divine, but modestly avoids direct reference that might be misused in a highly provocative context. It also gives the oath an element of secrecy by using code words for the divine. In line with the metaphorical significance of the Song, and the persecution of conservative Judaism under Antiochus IV's rule, this is a way of portraying true faith in Yahweh as subversive and needing to proceed carefully and almost surreptitiously in a hostile environment (see Live the Story below).

The woman warns the daughters of Jerusalem—and, therefore, us as readers also—against awakening love before it desires. Though the word for love here (*'ahabah*) is generic, in the context of the Song it clearly refers to romantic love—the erotic affection (cf. Greek, *eros*) that awakens between

---

12. Keel, *The Song of Songs*, 90–94.

13. Christopher W. Mitchell, *The Song of Songs*, Concordia Commentary (St Louis: Concordia, 2003), 698.

14. Gordis, *The Song of Songs and Lamentations: A Study, Modern Translation and Commentary*, 27–28; Andrew E. Steinmann, "Gazelles, Does, and Flames: (De)Limiting Love in Song of Songs," *JESOT* 2.1 (2013): 29–33.

15. This kind of circumlocution that veils reference to the divine occurs even in modern contexts today, though usually in exclamations of surprise. One might, for example, say "Jiminy Crickets!" to avoid reference to "Jesus Christ." While the contexts and intent may be different to what we have here in Song of Songs, the device itself is comparable. See further discussion in Steinmann, "Gazelles, Does, and Flames: (De)Limiting Love in Song of Songs," 30–33.

a man and a woman, igniting within them intense desires that draw them inexorably toward each other and fulfilment in sexual union. Indeed, this has been what the lovers have entertained in their exchange. Such love should be left to awaken when it sees fit, as it has with the woman and the shepherd. Their feelings for each other are not forced but have arisen naturally. So, it is entirely fitting for them to be united in an erotic bond.[16] And yet, the charge also highlights the woman's dilemma. She is being forced into a relationship with another—the distant king for whom she has no feelings. In this unwanted circumstance, love is being commanded to awaken, in a manner evocative of Antiochus IV's decree compelling Jews to participate in the royal Seleucid cult. Yet such love cannot truly be compelled. It is an oppressive imposition manufactured by others. By stating all this as an oath with veiled allusions to God, the woman represents such an arranged marriage as both an aberration and a veritable crime. It is further evidence that the woman does not desire marriage to the king, but rather to be united with the man she does love—her shepherd boy. The love she truly bears for him is painful in her dilemma.

LIVE the Story

Metaphorical Significance: God and his People

The oath in 2:7 alludes to the name and titles of God, inviting us to probe further and uncover the divine in the Song. In Deuteronomy, Moses expressly tells the Israelites, "Fear the Lord your God, serve him only and take your oaths in his name" (Deut 6:13; cf. 10:20). So, while he is not overtly mentioned here, God is still made present by this oath. He is a silent witness of the Song's drama, ever watching over the affairs of humanity.

A similar connection exists at 1:3, where the woman describes the man's "name" without explicitly stating it. This concept of "name" appears only here in the Song and specifically focuses on the man rather than the woman.[17] We may infer a symbolic link between the name of the male lover in the Song and the name of Yahweh—an important Deuteronomistic concept (cf. Deut 5:11). Both the man in the Song and Yahweh are shepherd figures (Song 1:7; cf. Ps 23:1; Isa 40:11; Jer 31:10; Ezek 34:11–16). If the male lover is symbolic of Yahweh, we may, in turn, connect the woman with Israel—a connection clinched by the prophetic metaphors that depict Israel as both the wife of Yahweh (Isa 62:4–5; Jer 3:6–18; Ezek 16; Hos 1–3), and his beloved

16. Cf. Exum, *Song of Songs*, 118–19.

17. Schwienhorst-Schönberger, "The Song of Songs as Allegory," 39.

vineyard (Isa 5:1–7; cf. Song 1:6). At the heart of the marriage metaphor is the concept of love, faithfulness, and covenant. Hosea 1–3 develops this in detail through the troubled relationship between Hosea and his wayward wife, Gomer. This living metaphor symbolizes how, during the monarchic era, Israel was unfaithful to the national covenant with Yahweh, like an unfaithful wife. This initially seems to conflict with the picture of the two lovers in the Song, who share a profound mutual love. The woman's dilemma, namely her prospective marriage to the king, injects the notion of the woman's separation from the one with whom she truly belongs. As the woman's brothers, who have charge of her, are responsible for pledging her to the king, so Israel's own guardians—its kings, elders, and priests—were responsible for leading Israel away from Yahweh. First Kings 11:1–13 shows Solomon's part in this, though he was by no means the only one in the history of Israel and Judah. Solomon's role in the Song is not just as the king who threatens to tear the lovers apart but as the conqueror of women, who would add yet another to his harem of women with no identity. Thus, Solomon, the distant king with his harem of foreign wives, comes to represent the foreign empires, like the Seleucid kingdom of Antiochus IV, who conquer and rule over Yahweh's people. As the woman faces the prospect of losing her identity in the king's harem, so Israel faces the prospect of losing its distinctiveness and its connection to Yahweh by becoming just another nation under the sway of a foreign empire. Just as tearing the woman away from her shepherd is a violation of the proper order, so Israel separated from Yahweh its God is also an aberration.

Yet this is precisely what was happening in the author's day (the early second century BC). Antiochus IV revoked the ethnic status of the Jews in his kingdom in 167 BC, officially dissolving their distinctiveness from other nations. This was being reinforced by the aggressive Hellenizing tendencies of the Jewish elite, led by the likes of the high priests, Jason and Menelaus, who vied with each other in compromising the biblical principles of Israel's historic faith and selling out to foreign and liberal Hellenistic ideals. Like the forbidden romance between the young woman and her shepherd boy, the relationship between Israel and her God was being forbidden under the pressure of Hellenism and the decrees of Antiochus IV. In this context, faithfulness to God became a subversive activity. The Song thus portrays the faithful as becoming like the young woman who resorts to veiling herself to avoid detection while trying to express devotion to her true love (Song 1:7). The oath by which she adjures the Daughters of Jerusalem is like an undercover code, which both acknowledges and hides the "name" of the divine (2:7; cf. 1:3). It is suggestive of a hostile environment in which loyalty to Yahweh could only be expressed furtively.

The vineyard imagery (Song 1:6) also reminds us about the breakdown in Israel's relationship with God. This is what Isaiah's "Song of the Vineyard" (Isa 5:1–7) is about. Hosea 2:14–15 depicts Israel's restoration as Yahweh wooing his beloved back to him and giving her back her vineyards. Thus, the combination of the imagery and the dilemma in the Song point to Israel's rocky relationship with God and her struggle under foreign regimes that threaten to keep her from him while encouraging resistance that refuses to capitulate to foreign pressure.

These themes encapsulate the ongoing struggle in God's relationship with humanity, and they extend into the New Testament, where they reach their resolution. In John 2:1–12, Jesus attends a wedding at Cana, at which the supplies of wine run out, threatening to bring festivities to an end. As the woman in the Song adjures the daughters of Jerusalem not to awaken love before its time, Jesus responds to his mother's implied demand that he do something by stating that his time had not yet come (John 2:3–4). Jesus's time comes later in the Gospel (12:23), but at this wedding he gives a glimpse of his glory by performing a miracle: he turns water into wine. This miracle is not merely about a supernatural feat but about the difference Jesus makes to Israel's relationship with God. In the Song, the woman pines for her shepherd to bring her into the "house of wine" where they can consummate their love (Song 2:4). Jesus also, at the right time, brings about the fulfilment of Israel's relationship with God by changing the old order, symbolized by water, into the new order, symbolized by wine. The result is something better, which enables the covenantal partners to continue their celebration and, ultimately, consummate their relationship. The miracle foreshadows the full and final consummation that Jesus enables between God and his people through his death and resurrection. This is a loving union, planned through the ages, and brought inexorably to fruition in the person and work of Jesus and the indwelling of the Spirit (John 14:26; 17:21). He overcomes every hindrance between God and humanity, be it the world, sin, the devil, or anything else (John 1:29; 8:42–47; 16:33; cf. Rom 8:35–39). In Christ, humans are united with God in a union of perfect love. Thus, Paul rightly declares that nothing in all creation can separate God's people from the love of God that is in Christ Jesus their Lord (Rom 8:38–39).

Sex and Marriage

Though dressed in metaphor, there is no mistaking the sexuality that exudes from the two young lovers in the Song. Their affection for each other is depicted as a phenomenon that has awoken between them. To some extent, this means their feelings are beyond their control, as their love seems to have a life of its own. This is not a wild beast of passion that has suddenly been roused in a fury that overcomes them, though their feelings are certainly intense. Rather, it is like a vine that has taken root and sprung forth. Its germination has occurred suddenly, awakening feelings within the couple for each other. Yet, as they reach for imagery to convey these feelings, they give expression to them and exercise control over them. They train the vine, as it were. The vine is such that, by its very nature, it will eventually yield the fruit of intimacy.

Feelings of intense passion and the drive of a couple to experience pleasure together are perfectly normal and, indeed, God-given. God designed sex not simply as a clinical activity for the procreation of the human race, but for the fertile and passionate union of two people in a fervid bond of love. It is the ultimate expression of their union and naturally gives rise to the birth of children who embody it.

The desire of the courting couple in the Song for this intimacy is obvious and good. It helps us see that they belong together. The predicament that threatens to tear them permanently apart is, therefore, a tragic development. In this way, the Song demonstrates that sex is very good, but marriage is its native habitat. Marriage is tailor made for the expression of the deepest affection a man and a woman can have for each other. What the two lovers in the Song share is not merely a desire for quick and casual passion. If that were the case, there would be no real dilemma. It is the permanence of the woman's prospective marriage to the king—a man she does not love—that makes her situation so desperate. Though marriage is an institution for expressing unconditional love toward another person, and the woman could indeed express such unconditional love toward the king, should she marry him, the injustice of this situation demonstrates the central place that personal attraction should occupy within marriage. It is this that gives sex its true pleasure factor. Without it, sex is robbed of its power, love is rendered soulless, and marriage is impoverished. Without love, attraction degrades into lust or bleaches into sterility. All this does not mean that sex makes a marriage; but marriage, as the permanent union of a man and a woman, is the fitting context for sex. Pivotal within this utmost expression of human love is personal attraction.

Polygamy

The daughters of Jerusalem give rise to mixed feelings within us as readers. In the Solomonic tradition, they are the king's harem of foreign women—idolaters who lead the weak-willed king into worship of their foreign gods. On that count, they are culpable of one of the most grievous sins in Israelite society under the national covenant with Yahweh. Yet, as "daughters of

Jerusalem," they are conquered women who have fallen prey to the wiles of a womanizer who wields manifest power. In so doing, they have lost their discrete identities and merged into an amorphous crowd that only ever speaks corporately. On this count, we have considerable sympathy for them as victims of male power.

Their situation raises the issue of polygamy. In Israel, this took the specific form of polygyny—one man marrying many women. Polyandry—one woman marrying many men—was never entertained, because it would engender confusion about the paternity of children. If it had been entertained, there would be no perceivable dilemma for the woman in the Song. It is the reality of polygyny that threatens her relationship with the shepherd whom she loves. Despite having an entire harem, the king desires to marry her also.

In Deuteronomy 17:17, as Moses gives instructions to the Israelites on the conduct expected of an Israelite king, he states, "He must not take many wives, or his heart will be led astray." This advice is more concerned about the national effects of a king committing idolatry than the effect of polygamy on women—a concern that was realized in Solomon's apostasy. Polygamy was, however, permitted in Israel, as Deuteronomy 21:15–17 demonstrates. Though the Bible never gives a detailed rationale for polygamy, we do get some clues that allow us to piece some thoughts together.

First, we must remember that the ancient world was undeveloped. It did not have the benefit of the institutions, social and economic infrastructures, technologies, services, and opportunities that we enjoy today, which allow a person to live and thrive independently. On the contrary, everyone in ancient society was dependent on their clan or tribe for survival. The clan provided mutual protection, a workforce for economic provision, and social interaction—that is, for day-to-day survival. This is why the clan was the basic unit of ancient society, rather than the individual. In such an undeveloped society, "there was little possibility for women within it to live a single life viably on their own. Instead, the physically strong (usually men) were called upon to protect the weak (women, children, and the elderly), and to do so within the context of clear, committed relationships."[18] Through marriage, a woman became integrally attached to a clan and cemented her place within it by contributing children, who could carry on the clan in the next generation and preserve its land. In this way, women (and children) became part of a clan structure whose links of kinship provided them with the social security they needed in a world that could be patently dangerous to live in and enabled them to provide for others also. Outside such a clan structure, a woman was

18. Athas, *Deuteronomy*, 242.

particularly vulnerable to exploitation. Marriage and childbearing were, therefore, not just the major contribution of a woman to her ancient society, but also the fundamental means of her survival in a way that is not quite the case for women in developed societies today.[19] Polygamy was a means by which one man could provide security to more than one woman within an ancient clan structure. The reality and frequency of war also meant that young men's lives were often cut short, which would have led to a disproportionate number of women to men. It was incumbent, therefore, on the surviving men to provide security for the women of a clan as well as replenish the clan's population. Marriage gave this security permanence and ensured the unambiguous identity of children within the clan—something polyandry could not guarantee.

Within ancient Israel, polygamy was not just tolerated but endorsed. Indeed, when God rebukes David through the prophet Nathan for raping Bathsheba and murdering her husband, God says to him, "I gave your master's house to you, and your master's wives into your arms. I gave you all Israel and Judah. And if all this had been too little, I would have given you even more" (2 Sam 12:8). It is not for having multiple wives that God rebukes David, for he affirms that he himself had given those wives to David. Instead, he punishes him for adultery—that is, sleeping with (or, more accurately, raping) another man's wife—and murder. In Ezekiel 23 God issues a parable through the prophet in which he depicts himself as the husband of two sisters (see especially Ezek 23:5, 18, 36–37, 45).

Polygamy was certainly not a perfect system, and with human nature being profoundly flawed, it was open to abuse. Rather than using power for the benefit of others, men could all too easily use power for selfish ends. For example, it could lead a man to neglect his first wife and her children in favor of a second wife. The law in Deuteronomy 21:15–17 stipulates measures to guard against this. For women, polygamy represented a trade-off. It may have provided a measure of social security within a clan structure, but it could also represent a loss of identity. Sharing a husband with at least one other woman was an inevitable compromise that was not ideal. Jacob's marriage to both Leah and Rachel demonstrates this. Having fallen in love with the younger Rachel, Jacob wanted to marry her. He did not offer to marry Leah in addition to Rachel but had to be tricked into it by his father-in-law, Laban (Gen 29:16–30). The arrangement compromised both women. Furthermore, it easily gave rise to situations of interfamilial strife and rivalry, as we see numerous times in biblical narratives (Gen 16:3–6; 30:1–24; 1 Sam 1:1–8).

What the Song shows us is the passionate affection between one young

---

19. Yet, even today, this is still the reality for many women around the world.

woman and one young man, which should lead to their union in marriage, where they can give themselves to each other fully. From this we may infer that monogamy is the best context for the expression of these desires, as it allows two people to give themselves to each other fully in a complete and unencumbered union. Monogamy promotes personhood. Genesis 2 is indicative of this ideal, as it shows God creating one man and one woman, whom he brings together in union and from whose union society grows. Solomon's marriage to many women compromises his ability to experience a meaningful, intimate, and wholehearted union of persons with any of them. In such an arrangement, the women lose their personhood and become mere chattel. True union involves more than just the joining of two bodies in a sexual act—it involves a union of persons in body, heart, mind, and future. In other words, there is a spiritual dimension to marriage that the physical union demonstrates but does not exhaust. The problem with polygamy is not that it is adultery, for it is not, but that it adulterates full union. It fractionalizes and, therefore, compromises the spiritual dimension that exists between a husband and a wife. Within the Song, the woman faces the prospect of not just losing the man she loves but also her own personhood.

The social system that allowed polygamy in ancient society seems foreign to us today, and for good reason. In modern times we have developed societal mechanisms that give women more options and opportunities to thrive independently in society. These empower women to retain their full personhood and express their distinctiveness in various ways that include, but are not limited to, marriage and the bearing of children.

The richness of human society is, in part, due to the manifold types of relationship that exist amongst us. We are siblings, grandparents and grandchildren, friends, neighbors, colleagues, fellow citizens, and the like. Yet, at the heart of the growth of human society is the marriage relationship, which works best when one man and one woman come together in a physical and spiritual union that unassailably bonds them together in love and leads to the engendering of new life as the outworking of that love.

Jesus and Women

One of the many facets of Jesus's ministry was the place he gave to women. He recognized their worth as wives and mothers but did not limit their worth to these roles. He certainly did not see them as the merchandise of men or as chattel for men's pleasure. He saw them as people. He knew their names (John 20:16), understood their stories (John 4:17–18), recognized their strengths and vulnerabilities (Luke 10:38–42), appreciated them (Mark 14:6–9), interacted meaningfully with them (Mark 5:34), and related to them in godly love

(Luke 7:44–48). He embodied in himself the perfect love that existed in the eternal Godhead, and he demonstrated this within human society.

Tragically, the covenant nation rejected Jesus, conspiring against him and bringing about his death. In so doing, the nation set its course firmly toward conquest and destruction—a reality it experienced in AD 70 when the Roman armies rolled through the country. On the way to his crucifixion at Golgotha, he turned in his tortured state to the women who were mourning for him and warned them of the peril to come. "Daughters of Jerusalem," he said, "do not weep for me; weep for yourselves and for your children. For the time will come when you will say, 'Blessed are the childless women, the wombs that never bore and the breasts that never nursed!'" (Luke 23:28–29). Once again, the daughters of Jerusalem faced the trauma of conquest.

Yet, Jesus's ministry was redemptive in so many ways. Not only did he atone for human sin, he created a new people of God and boosted the place of women within society. The way he interacted with them provided a model of relationship that appreciated the particularity of each person, including women. It is no small thing that the risen Jesus asked of the disconsolate Mary Magdalene at the tomb, "Woman, why are you crying?" (John 20:13), and that she was the first bearer of the good news of his resurrection (John 20:17–18). This sanctification of womanhood within the gospel of Jesus Christ is a message our world desperately needs to hear.

CHAPTER 10

Song of Songs 2:8–5:9

LISTEN to the Story

8 Listen! My beloved!
Look! Here he comes,
leaping across the mountains,
bounding over the hills.
9 My beloved is like a gazelle or a young stag.
Look! There he stands behind our wall,
gazing through the windows,
peering through the lattice.
10 My beloved spoke and said to me,
"Arise, my darling,
my beautiful one, come with me.
11 See! The winter is past;
the rains are over and gone.
12 Flowers appear on the earth;
the season of singing has come,
the cooing of doves
is heard in our land.
13 The fig tree forms its early fruit;
the blossoming vines spread their fragrance.
Arise, come, my darling;
my beautiful one, come with me."
14 My dove in the clefts of the rock,
in the hiding places on the mountainside,
show me your face,
let me hear your voice;
for your voice is sweet,
and your face is lovely.
15 Catch for us the foxes,
the little foxes

that ruin the vineyards,
    our vineyards that are in bloom.
16My beloved is mine and I am his;
    he browses among the lilies.
17Until the day breaks
    and the shadows flee,
turn, my beloved,
    and be like a gazelle
or like a young stag
    on the rugged hills.
3:1All night long on my bed
    I looked for the one my heart loves;
    I looked for him but did not find him.
2I will get up now and go about the city,
    through its streets and squares;
I will search for the one my heart loves.
    So I looked for him but did not find him.
3The watchmen found me
    as they made their rounds in the city.
    "Have you seen the one my heart loves?"
4Scarcely had I passed them
    when I found the one my heart loves.
I held him and would not let him go
    till I had brought him to my mother's house,
    to the room of the one who conceived me.
5Daughters of Jerusalem, I charge you
    by the gazelles and by the does of the field:
Do not arouse or awaken love
    until it so desires.
6Who is this coming up from the wilderness
    like a column of smoke,
perfumed with myrrh and incense
    made from all the spices of the merchant?
7Look! It is Solomon's carriage,
    escorted by sixty warriors,
    the noblest of Israel,
8all of them wearing the sword,
    all experienced in battle,

each with his sword at his side,
prepared for the terrors of the night.
9King Solomon made for himself the carriage;
he made it of wood from Lebanon.
10Its posts he made of silver,
its base of gold.
Its seat was upholstered with purple,
its interior inlaid with love.
Daughters of Jerusalem, 11come out,
and look, you daughters of Zion.
Look on King Solomon wearing a crown,
the crown with which his mother crowned him
on the day of his wedding,
the day his heart rejoiced.
4:1How beautiful you are, my darling!
Oh, how beautiful!
Your eyes behind your veil are doves.
Your hair is like a flock of goats
descending from the hills of Gilead.
2Your teeth are like a flock of sheep just shorn,
coming up from the washing.
Each has its twin;
not one of them is alone.
3Your lips are like a scarlet ribbon;
your mouth is lovely.
Your temples behind your veil
are like the halves of a pomegranate.
4Your neck is like the tower of David,
built with courses of stone;
on it hang a thousand shields,
all of them shields of warriors.
5Your breasts are like two fawns,
like twin fawns of a gazelle
that browse among the lilies.
6Until the day breaks
and the shadows flee,
I will go to the mountain of myrrh
and to the hill of incense.

7You are altogether beautiful, my darling;
there is no flaw in you.
8Come with me from Lebanon, my bride,
come with me from Lebanon.
Descend from the crest of Amana,
from the top of Senir, the summit of Hermon,
from the lions' dens
and the mountain haunts of leopards.
9You have stolen my heart, my sister, my bride;
you have stolen my heart
with one glance of your eyes,
with one jewel of your necklace.
10How delightful is your love, my sister, my bride!
How much more pleasing is your love than wine,
and the fragrance of your perfume
more than any spice!
11Your lips drop sweetness as the honeycomb, my bride;
milk and honey are under your tongue.
The fragrance of your garments
is like the fragrance of Lebanon.
12You are a garden locked up, my sister, my bride;
you are a spring enclosed, a sealed fountain.
13Your plants are an orchard of pomegranates
with choice fruits,
with henna and nard,
14nard and saffron,
calamus and cinnamon,
with every kind of incense tree,
with myrrh and aloes
and all the finest spices.
15You are a garden fountain,
a well of flowing water
streaming down from Lebanon.
16Awake, north wind,
and come, south wind!
Blow on my garden,
that its fragrance may spread everywhere.
Let my beloved come into his garden

and taste its choice fruits.
5:1 I have come into my garden, my sister, my bride;
I have gathered my myrrh with my spice.
I have eaten my honeycomb and my honey;
I have drunk my wine and my milk.
Eat, friends, and drink;
drink your fill of love.
2 I slept but my heart was awake.
Listen! My beloved is knocking:
"Open to me, my sister, my darling,
my dove, my flawless one.
My head is drenched with dew,
my hair with the dampness of the night."
3 I have taken off my robe—
must I put it on again?
I have washed my feet—
must I soil them again?
4 My beloved thrust his hand through the latch-opening;
my heart began to pound for him.
5 I arose to open for my beloved,
and my hands dripped with myrrh,
my fingers with flowing myrrh,
on the handles of the bolt.
6 I opened for my beloved,
but my beloved had left; he was gone.
My heart sank at his departure.
I looked for him but did not find him.
I called him but he did not answer.
7 The watchmen found me
as they made their rounds in the city.
They beat me, they bruised me;
they took away my cloak,
those watchmen of the walls!
8 Daughters of Jerusalem, I charge you—
if you find my beloved,
what will you tell him?
Tell him I am faint with love.

Listening to the Story in the Text: "The Stroll" (P. Chester Beatty I, nos. 31–37); "Three Wishes" (P. Chester Beatty I, nos. 38–40); "Nakhtsobek Songs" (P. Chester Beatty I, nos. 41–47); P. Harris 500, Song 7; Turin Erotic Papyrus; 1 Maccabees 1:29–64; 2 Maccabees 5:11–26

In this section of the Song, we see the young shepherd boy come to the woman's house, urging her to come away with him or let him in. This motif, familiar even today in cinematic romance, has a long history stretching back centuries before the composition of the Song. Such scenes demonstrate the motif of confinement placed upon the young woman by her guardians. The house, its doors, and its locks are also symbolic of the woman's body and her sexuality, and therefore have the potential to explore the themes of sexual chemistry, voyeurism, and forbidden love.

Papyrus Chester Beatty I, from twelfth-century BC Egypt (Twentieth Dynasty), contains several love poems. Among them are the "Nakhtsobek Songs" (nos. 41–47), named after the scribe who wrote them. Some of these poems play on the motif of a man seeking a woman at her house. In one of them (no. 47), a man finds the woman's door locked, which prompts him to promise the door sacrifices if it opens, or else he will pay a carpenter to fashion a flimsy door instead:

> I passed by her house in a daze.
> I knocked, but it was not opened to me.
> A fine night for our doorkeeper!
> Bolt, I will open you!
> Door, you are my fate. . . .
> O Door, exert not your strength,
> so that oxen may be sacrificed to your bolt,
> fatlings to your threshold. . . .
> But every choice piece of our ox
> will be saved for the carpenter lad,
> that he may fashion us a bolt of reeds,
> a door of grass.
> Then at any time the brother can come
> and find her house open,
> and find a bed spread with fine linen,
> and a pretty little maidservant too.[1]

1. Translation adapted from Fox, *The Song of Songs and the Ancient Egyptian Love Songs*, 75–76.

The Egyptian Papyrus Harris 500, dated to the thirteenth century BC (Nineteenth Dynasty), also contains several love poems. In one of them (no. 7), a young man desires to be the doorkeeper for a woman he fancies, whom he calls "my sister," just as the shepherd boy in the Song calls his beloved (Song 4:9–10, 12; 5:1–2). He wants this position so that he can spy on her, even if it means attracting her anger:

> The mansion of my sister:
> Her entry is in the middle of her house,
>   her double-doors are open,
> her latch-bolt drawn back,
>   and my sister incensed!
> If only I were appointed doorkeeper,
>   I'd get her angry at me!
> Then I'd hear her voice when she was incensed—
>   As a child in fear of her![2]

A similar scene occurs in this section of the Song (2:8–17), though it is not quite so voyeuristic. Furthermore, the woman in the Song is not angry at the man's arrival, but excited. She sees him "leaping across the mountains, bounding over the hills" (2:8) and likens him to a gazelle. Similar motifs appear in other Egyptian poems, as in the poem, "Three Wishes," from Papyrus Chester Beatty I:

> If only you would come to your sister swiftly,
>   like a gazelle bounding over the desert,
> whose legs are shaky, whose body is weary,
>   for fear has entered his body.
> A hunter, dog with him, pursues him,
>   But they can't even see his dust.[3]

The imagery of the gazelle, therefore, conveys notions of speed and agility as well as skittishness and danger. As we will see, these ideas converge on the man in the Song, too.

In the Song we also find the man praising his beloved's beauty (2:14; 4:1–15; 6:4–9)—a very common theme in all types of romantic literature. This sustained focus on a person's beauty is often called a *wasf*, an Arabic

2. Translation adapted from Ibid., 14.
3. Translation adapted from Ibid., 66–67.

term meaning "description."[4] An ancient Egyptian poem from Chester Beatty I, which Fox calls, "The Stroll" (nos. 31–37), includes a similar focus on the enchanting effect that a woman's physical beauty has over her lover. As in the Song, the man in "The Stroll" calls his beloved, "my sister":

> One alone is my sister, having no peer:
>   more gracious than all other women.
> Behold her, like Sothis rising
>   at the beginning of a good year:
> shining, precious, white of skin,
>   lovely of eyes when gazing.
> Sweet her lips when speaking:
>   she has no excess of words.
> Long of neck, white of breast,
>   her hair true lapis lazuli.
> Her arms surpass gold,
>   her fingers are like lotuses.
> Full her derrière, narrow her waist,
>   her thighs carry on her beauties.
> Lovely of walk when she strides on the ground,
>   she has captured my heart in her embrace.[5]

The Turin Erotic Papyrus, dating from twelfth-century BC Egypt (Twentieth Dynasty), is a long scroll in a poor state of preservation. Nonetheless, part of the papyrus clearly depicts in explicit pictorial form a man having several erotic encounters with a woman. In one vignette, she is on her bed naked, reaching for him while he is either under her bed or beside it.[6] It is difficult to know whether the vignette implies the woman is dreaming of the man or whether he has fallen from her bed. In either case, the notion of her desire is clearly present. In this next section of the Song, we find scenes reminiscent of this (3:1; 5:2–6), though the sophistication of the Song's poetry contrasts with the crass cartooning of the papyrus. The woman's desire for her beloved shepherd boy comes through quite strongly, as she lies in her bed unclothed and dreams of sharing intimacy with him.

Both 1 Maccabees 1:29–64 and 2 Maccabees 5:11–26 were written some decades after the Song, but they give us valuable insight into the course of

---

4. Technically, a *wasf* can have any subject, with the main idea being a sustained descriptive praise of that subject. However, it is often employed in the context of romantic poetry.

5. Translation adapted from Fox, *The Song of Songs and the Ancient Egyptian Love Songs*, 52.

6. Keel, *The Song of Songs*, 123 (fig. 69).

events during the Antiochene persecution, which lie behind the Song. They relate how, in 170 BC, Antiochus IV authorized the construction of a citadel in Jerusalem, known as the Acra. It was built to the immediate south of the temple in the City of David (1 Macc 1:33), and became a Seleucid stronghold by which they could control the city and promote Hellenistic culture. While it was being constructed, Antiochus IV invaded Egypt twice. His second attempt in 167 BC was thwarted by Roman diplomatic intervention. Antiochus retreated through the desert and arrived back in Palestine to infighting between the two claimants of the high priesthood, Jason and Menelaus. Antiochus put the fighting down ruthlessly, which included slaughtering thousands of innocents in the temple courts. He then revoked the ethnic status of the Jews, by which they enjoyed the privilege of worshiping Yahweh. He converted Yahweh's temple into a temple to Olympian Zeus and promoted the worship of his own statue in the temple as a new means of enforcing loyalty to the crown. He also augmented the Acra with further walls, making it a virulent symbol of Hellenistic oppression. All these measures caused conservative Jews to abandon the temple and flee the city, leaving Jerusalem essentially in the hands of an occupying Seleucid force. These events stand in the background of the whole Song but are particularly relevant to this next movement of it.[7]

EXPLAIN the Story

Desire and Anxiety (2:8–5:8)

In this next movement of the Song we find the woman at home at night, where the shepherd boy comes secretly to her. The tension builds as both the sexual energy between the couple intensifies and the threat of Solomon's arrival to claim the woman becomes more real. Fantasy and reality become intertwined in a dream sequence that plays out the lovers' hopes and fears, before a dose of harsh reality demonstrates the grave circumstances the couple face.

Rendezvous at Night (2:8–17)

After the oath in 2:7, the scene changes, and we find the woman inside a house. This seems innocuous enough, but it gives a sense of confinement, reminding us that she is constrained by her predicament: she has been pledged in marriage to the king, even though she has fallen in love with a shepherd boy. We wait, therefore, for the king to come and collect her, and so incorporate her into the daughters of Jerusalem—his harem of women who have lost

7. Athas, *Bridging the Testaments*, forthcoming.

their distinctive personhood. Yet, it is not the king who appears in 2:8, but the man she loves. He comes "leaping" and "bounding" across the surrounding hills "like a gazelle or a young stag" (2:8–9). We catch a sense of his haste and the woman's rising excitement as he approaches.

The young man arrives at the "wall" behind which the woman is located (2:9). She refers to this as "our wall," but it is difficult to know whom she counts in that first-person pronoun ("our"). She might be grouping herself with the daughters of Jerusalem. In that case, this might mean she is physically present with them, though the precise circumstance of that would be unclear. It might simply be a conceptual connection, in that the ethereal chorus of daughters is ever present with the woman, regardless of where she actually is. Alternatively, the woman may be identifying herself with her family, so that "our wall" refers to part of the family home. In 8:9–10 her brothers refer to her as "a wall," as does she, though with a different Hebrew word (*homah*) than the one here at 2:9 (*kotel*). At 3:4, however, she refers to her "mother's house," which makes this option most likely.

The symbolism of the wall works in several directions. On one level, it is the physical barrier that the woman is behind. On another level, it highlights the situational constraint she is under—her unwanted betrothal to the king, which is keeping her from a lifelong relationship with the man she truly loves. It is a barrier that the man is trying to circumvent by urging the woman to come outside and come away with him (2:10–14). To him, she feels inaccessible and beyond reach, like a dove "in the clefts of the rock, in the crannies of the cliff" (2:14). Historically, it evokes the construction of the Acra, the Seleucid citadel built next to the temple in Jerusalem in 170 BC that became the bastion of Hellenistic culture and control in the city (1 Macc 1:33, 36). On yet another level, the wall signifies the woman's virginity. This is the connotation when her brothers refer to her as a wall at 8:9–10, but it is present here, and also in 5:7 (see below).

The man is peeping through the windows and lattices to see the woman (2:9). It is quite provocative, but as the scene unfolds we realize that, unlike the young man in Papyrus Harris 500, song 7, he is not a voyeur. He does not merely wish to spy on the woman and remain hidden in the shadows. On the contrary, he wants her to come out to him so they can be together physically. Many English versions have him entreat the woman, "show me your face," because "your face is lovely" (2:14, NIV; cf. KJV, NRSV, ESV, CSB), but the Hebrew uses a word that refers to physical appearance generally (*mar'eh*).[8]

8. Pope, *Song of Songs*, 401.

He desires to see all of her. His words, then, are taut with sexual tension as he expresses his desire for her body.

This tension is reinforced at 2:15, where the woman responds with a call to "Catch the foxes . . . that spoil the vineyards."[9] The "vineyard" is symbolic of a woman's body (cf. 1:6; 8:12), making this a metaphor for virile young men seducing innocent young women.[10] But there is a saucy playfulness in her response, as she refers endearingly to "little foxes," and proclaims her vineyard to be "in blossom."[11] The beauty of the poetry here is that it allows for two seemingly opposite readings simultaneously. "Catching" the little foxes can be an act of prevention to protect the woman's virginity, yet it also expresses her yearning to "catch" her man in tight embrace.[12] Indeed, the same verbal root (*'ḥz*) is used to describe just that in 3:4. The tension this double entendre creates leads us to see that the courting couple belong together in a lifelong union that allows them to fulfill their desires for each other. The king's claim on the woman is the obstacle to this that returns us once again to the notion of the wall being a constraint.

This makes 2:16a even more significant, for it expresses the essence of the relational expectation in the Song: "My beloved is mine, and I am his." This simple declaration states what is proper in the Song: by virtue of their love and desire for each other, the woman and the shepherd boy belong to each other and, therefore, should rightly be joined together in a permanent union that leads freely to the consummation of their love. The woman describes her shepherd boy as grazing (NIV, "browsing") among the lilies (2:16b). On the one hand this portrays him as a shepherd doing his job, but since shepherds do not ordinarily graze flocks in fields of lilies, there is evident symbolism functioning here. In 2:9 the woman characterized the man as a gazelle or a young stag, and she does so again in 2:17. She may, therefore, be depicting him in 2:16 as a gazelle with an appetite for eating lilies. The woman has also described herself as a lily (2:1), and later in the Song lilies are metaphorical for the pubic region (6:2–3; 7:2). Thus, the woman sees in her shepherd boy a partner with whom she wants to share intimacy. The pair do not desire a casual sexual encounter, nor do they seek to flout propriety. They have waited through their relational "winter" to consummate their love, but, as the shepherd boy declares, "the

9. The verse is spoken in the plural ("our vineyards are in bloom") to plural addressees (the imperative "Catch" is plural in Hebrew), making identifying the parties in the verse difficult. The best fit, however, is that the woman is responding to the man in rhetorical fashion. See Ibid., 403–5; Duguid, *The Song of Songs*, 98–99.

10. Fox, *The Song of Songs and the Ancient Egyptian Love Songs*, 114.

11. Murphy, *The Song of Songs*, 141.

12. Cf. Exum, *Song of Songs*, 130.

winter is past; the rain is over and gone" (2:11). His subsequent hailing of springtime with its burgeoning life (2:12–13) expresses his estimation that they have abstained for long enough and the time is now ripe for their union in marriage. This would be the most fitting and natural thing in the world—as fitting and natural as spring following winter. In this way, the dilemma they face in the woman's betrothal to the king is deemed a cataclysm of nature.

The woman's appeal to the break of day and the fleeing shadows (2:17) tells us that this brief rendezvous between the two lovers has occurred at night. She now bids her shepherd boy depart. Some commentators read this verse as the woman inviting the man to make love to her,[13] but this is innuendo rather than the plain meaning. The Hebrew word she uses in urging him to "turn" (*sob*) ordinarily implies turning around and away from the speaker (cf. 1 Sam 15:27). She thus prompts him to leave and "be like a gazelle or like a young stag"—that is, to run hastily across the hills as he did when he came to her (2:9), but now in the opposite direction. Her instruction thus forms an inclusio with 2:9 and brings this scene to an end. Even though the time for their union is right, circumstances prevent them from enacting it. In the NIV, the woman urges him back across "the rugged hills" (in Hebrew, *harey beter*),[14] understanding the word *beter* as a noun denoting something "cut apart" into pieces (cf. NRSV, ESV, CSB; Gen 15:10), and therefore "rugged." Fox understands it as a reference to the mountains of Bether, a place some eleven kilometers southwest of Jerusalem.[15] Similar refrains appear at 4:6 and 8:14 (the last verse of the Song), but in each case the last phrase differs. Nonetheless, even if we have a place name, Bether, here at 2:17, the root meaning of the Hebrew word captures the circumstance that prevents the lovers from being joined together. They are being "cut apart"—put asunder rather than united.[16] This final phrase, therefore, tinges the scene with the pain of separation. The Song's dilemma is keeping the woman from the man she loves and dictates that, against both their inclinations and the natural order of things, he must flee from her. Though spring has arrived, the winter of their predicament continues. Even as she beckons him to run, she suggestively invites him not to relinquish that wild instinct that brought him to her "leaping" and "bounding over the hills" (2:8). Thus, her words reveal her anxiety, but also a twinkle in her eye.

---

13. Gordis, *The Song of Songs and Lamentations*, 54; Keel, *The Song of Songs*, 114–15.

14. The MT employs a pausal form here, that can be rendered *harey bater*.

15. Fox, *The Song of Songs and the Ancient Egyptian Love Songs*, 116.

16. Duguid takes a different line, arguing that the cleft shape of the landscape alludes to the lovers' future consummation. However, this does not take into full account the woman's dilemma in the Song. See Duguid, *The Song of Songs*, 100.

Dream Scene One: Searching (3:1–5)

We next find the woman alone in her bed at night (3:1a).[17] There is no sign of her lover, which prompts her to search for him (3:1b). This is not sudden regret at bidding him leave, nor is it an actual search. Rather, this is a search conducted while she is on her bed. It is, in other words, a dream sequence. Even her sleep is filled with thoughts of her lover.

Some commentators resist the idea that this is a dream on the basis that the woman appears to be doing real things, even if they are strange. However, this is part of the artistry of the Song, giving us the specific impression that we are watching something real here, before revealing that it had been a dream (5:2). At 3:2 we get the impression that the dream is over and the woman is now awake, for she gets up and begins looking for her lover through the town. We then experience a series of scenes with this arresting reality, taking us through moments of exhilaration in which the lovers' dilemma appears to be joyfully resolved, as well as moments that rein in our excitement and make us question whether fulfilment has indeed occurred. This state of ambiguity continues right up until 5:2, when we finally read that the woman is still asleep. Thus, as is often the case with dreams, reality and fantasy are woven together in a disorienting way that makes it hard to tell them apart, until eventually we wake to the realization that none of it was real. In this way, the Song keeps alive our hope for positive resolution to the dilemma of the lovers while also delaying it and heightening the tension. The gap between fantasy and reality is tantalizing, yet frustrating. The feeling of reality throughout this dream sequence also helps us feel the intensity of the emotions that both the woman and the man experience. And as we will see, in 5:2–8 there is a parallel to this scene, and the woman appears to wake at the beginning of it. The parallel is significant for helping us compare the woman's hopes, as depicted in the dream, with the reality she is actually living.

This extended dream sequence takes place on her bed, which is evocative of her desire for intimacy with her shepherd boy. The first scene in the sequence (3:1–5) sees the woman looking through the town for her beloved shepherd. Since she had told him to flee back to the hills (2:17), we get the sense that she is now trying to chase him down before he even exits the town. She does not desire separation from him but yearns to be with him. Throughout the short scene, she refers to him four times as "the one my heart loves" (3:1–4), reminding us of her affection for him, from which we infer her complete lack

---

17. The Hebrew for "night" is plural (*leylot*), which might indicate something occurring "night after night." The use of an accompanying *qatal* verb, *biqqashti* ("I looked for"), would, in that case, be unusual for a repetitive action. More likely, the plural of "night" is indicative of duration, meaning "during the night (watches)." See Murphy, *The Song of Songs*, 145.

of affection for the king who intends to bring her into his own chambers (1:4b).

In her search, she is found by the town's watchmen (3:3). Interestingly, it is they who find her, not the other way around, which gives us a sense of dread. While she is searching for her lover, the watchmen appear to be searching for her, and here they close in on her. She is being watched—not by her lover, whom she desires, through a window and lattice (2:9), but by guards in the streets. This motif occurs again in 5:7, where we see a rerun of the present scene, though it will have a very different ending there. In both cases, we get the impression that the woman is under guard and, therefore, not free, a situation evocative of the Seleucid occupation of Jerusalem after Antiochus IV revoked the ethnic status of the Jews in 167 BC. Her love of the shepherd boy is forbidden, which puts both of them in jeopardy. Her behavior here is not just irregular, but perilous.

Yet, our sense of dread immediately dissipates, as it is not the watchmen who catch her but she who catches her lover after suddenly finding him (3:4; cf. 2:15). The watchmen vanish, as it were, and rather than telling her lover to flee to the hills (cf. 2:17), she brings him back to her house and into the chamber where her own mother had conceived her (3:4). The reference is highly suggestive and seems to resolve their dilemma. The woman has not been brought into the chambers of the king (cf. 1:4b) but has instead brought the man she truly loves into her own chambers to consummate her love with him and possibly conceive a child by him. The fact that the scene reaches this resolution in a "house" is evocative of the historical desire of conservative Jews in 167 BC for Yahweh to return to his "house," the temple in Jerusalem, and reinstate his cult, thus ending the royal cult of the Seleucids and of Olympian Zeus. All the tension in the "story" thus dissolves. The scene finishes with the woman once more adjuring the daughters of Jerusalem not to awaken love before it so desires (3:5; cf. 2:7). With this we understand that love has indeed awoken and the lovers are now acting upon it. While love has awoken between them, the woman is, in fact, still asleep. As we will soon realize (5:2), the scene is but a dream, and its resolution is unrealized—a pure fantasy.

Dream Scene Two: Solomon (3:6–11)

No sooner has the woman dreamed of being joined intimately with her shepherd boy than reality bites within her dream. Imagined coitus is interrupted by movement from the desert (3:6). The desert is an antagonistic environment from which one expects hostile forces to emerge: harsh, hot winds (cf. Jer 4:11; Hos 13:15), savage creatures (Jer 5:6; Lam 4:3), and belligerent enemies (cf. 2 Kgs 3:8; Isa 21:1; Lam 4:19; 5:9). What arrives is an impressive regal procession emanating with exotic fragrances (3:6–8). This is none other than Solomon, borne on a litter and dressed for nuptial celebrations (3:11), surrounded by trained warriors (3:7–8). That this procession is part of the woman's dream comes from the fact that the warriors are armed "against the terrors of the night" (3:8). The pleasant fragrances and expensive materials from which Solomon's litter is made give the procession an air of inviting opulence. Yet, the warriors are not merely accompanying Solomon but are armed and ready for battle, lending the scene an ominous feel. There is both allure and hostility in this procession, which develops the dilemma of the Song. The woman is dreaming of Solomon arriving to claim her at the very moment in her dream when she is finally with the man she actually loves. The procession's magnificence shows that she recognizes the appeal in the prospect of marrying the king. There is so much to gain. The daughters of Zion (presumably the same as the daughters of Jerusalem) are even called to witness the spectacle and Solomon's joyfulness (3:11). Yet, Solomon arrives as an enemy from the desert with armed soldiers ready to conquer. There is no accompanying description of the woman's joy. Though she can appreciate the spectacle and its enticements, the woman still sees Solomon as a threat. The entire scene recalls the arrival of Antiochus IV in Palestine after aborting his campaign in Egypt and trekking back through the desert (167 BC). He came flexing his military muscle, seeking to consolidate his control over the Jewish nation.

The overwhelming imagery of the procession also gives us a sense of just what the woman and the shepherd boy are up against. They are a simple young couple in love, but they face a will and might they can scarcely imagine. What chance do they really stand at being able to outmaneuver such a juggernaut and stay together? The scene also zeroes in on Solomon's "litter" (3:9; NIV, "carriage"), which focuses our attention on Solomon's intentions. The litter is specifically called a "bed" in 3:7 (NIV, "carriage"), which is suggestive. Its description begins with its expensive materials but finishes by associating its interior with the love of the daughters of Jerusalem.[18] It is not that the daughters of Jerusalem were artisans who constructed a royal palanquin. Rather, the implication is that Solomon has bedded many women in this lavish litter. It therefore stands in contrast with the woman's simple bed (3:1), in which she has been dreaming of sleeping with the only man she really loves (3:4). What began as a dream of sublime fantasy (3:1–5) has been tainted by the woman's anxieties.

18. The NIV separates "daughters of Jerusalem" from this phrase at the end of 3:10 and instead reads it with 3:11 as a vocative in parallel with "daughters of Zion." However, this has to ignore the preposition attached to the word "daughters" in the Hebrew text, which clearly connects it with what precedes it in 3:10.

Dream Scene Three: Longing (4:1–5:1)

The arrival of Solomon in full regalia makes the woman's predicament more urgent. As the royal procession ascends ominously from the desert, the woman's dream takes another sudden turn. Her lover now speaks and praises her beauty. As he lauds her, we realize that he is admiring her beauty as a bride, giving the notion of her marriage to Solomon a sense of inevitability. Her eyes are behind a veil (4:1). Her neck is adorned with jewels (4:9). Over her bust rests a garland of lilies (4:5).[19] Her body and her garments are perfumed (4:10–11). Most poignantly of all, he calls her "bride" (4:8–12; 5:1). Though English versions translate this as "my bride," the possessive pronoun "my" is not present in Hebrew. In fact, the word "bride" occurs six times in the Song, all within this scene, and each time the word is without a possessive pronoun. He calls her "my darling" (4:1) and "my sister" (a term of endearment; 4:9, 10, 12; 5:1), but never "my bride." She is always simply "a bride." This dissonance encapsulates the relational predicament of the Song. The woman and the man belong to each other (2:16a; 7:10) and, therefore, should be joined together in marriage. Though she is rightly his bride, she has become Solomon's trophy. Solomon's procession includes sixty soldiers armed for combat (3:7–8), and now the man describes his beloved's neck as "the tower of David," on which "hang a thousand shields, all of them shields of warriors" (4:4)—a clear historical allusion to the Seleucid Acra in the City of David (1 Macc 1:33). The love of his life has been claimed and conquered by another, and she has become inaccessible to him. The gems on her neck, which promise wealth, luxury, and bridal festivities, are symbols of her captivity and detainment from him.

In 4:6 the shepherd boy declares his intention to escape through the night. As in 2:17, when the woman urged him to flee so as not to get caught, he now echoes the same sentiment in the dream. Since Solomon and his armed warriors have arrived and conquered his beloved, it is no longer safe for him. Thus, he prepares to flee through the dreamscape to the distant "mountain of myrrh, and to the hill of incense" (4:6). Since these exotic commodities originate in southern Arabia and the Horn of Africa, we understand his intention to remove himself far away, which gives us a sense of the danger he now faces. As this is the woman's dream, we also sense her anxiety at potentially losing him forever. Fleeing means the shepherd must tear himself away from the woman he loves and who, by all propriety, should be his bride. Indeed, there is a hint of desire in his statement, as he will soon associate his beloved's charms with incense and myrrh (4:12).

19. Cf. Hobbins' suggestion in Fox, *The Song of Songs and the Ancient Egyptian Love Songs*, 131.

In 4:8 he entreats her to come with him. Alas, she now feels as inaccessible as the summits of Amana, Senir, and Hermon—the highest mountains of Lebanon and Syria.[20] As much as he might call her down from these remote peaks, she is now in the "lion's den and the mountain haunts of leopards" (4:8). She has become Solomon's prey. Though she might desire to escape with him (cf. 1:4a), she is trapped. Since this is the woman's dream, her fears and anxieties come once more to the fore.

Yet, it seems, the shepherd cannot tear himself away. Though she is being stolen from him, he feels that she has stolen his heart (4:9), and he cannot leave her. He is rapt with the woman's beauty and stays to laud her charms (4:10–11), despite the danger to him. His praises become more erotic, with 4:11 evoking the pleasure of passionately kissing her. The heightened sensuality betrays his desperation, as there is an urgency to his desire and, therefore, a frustration of being unable to fulfill it, even though this is but a dream. Solomon's claim has rendered the woman off limits to him. Throughout the Song, garden imagery is evocative of the woman and her body (1:6; 4:16–5:1; 6:2; 8:12), but because of Solomon's claim over her, she has now become "a garden locked up" (4:12). The image of flowing water suggests the welling up of desire and the ability to act freely in satisfying it, as one slaking their thirst. Now the woman has become "a spring enclosed, a sealed fountain" (4:12). Though they both desire intensely to be together and experience sexual intimacy, circumstance has thwarted them.

Nonetheless, desire continues to cascade within as the symbolism becomes overtly erotic. In 4:13–15 the man extends the garden imagery, portraying his beloved as a fantastical "paradise" (NIV, "orchard")—a botanical wonderland of assorted exotic plants. In antiquity, such botanical parks were specifically built as palatial pleasure gardens for royalty. On the one hand, this reminds us that the woman has been specifically earmarked for the pleasure of the king, and the previous scene in the dream shows Solomon on the march to collect her. On the other hand, its sensuality tells us of the shepherd's passion to experience pleasure with his most magnificent beloved. He associates her "erect" nipples (*shelahayik*; 4:13; NIV, "plants") with exotic tastes and fragrances,[21]

20. The exact location of Amana is a matter of conjecture but is probably a peak in the Anti-Lebanon range, perhaps associated with the Abana (or Amana) River. Senir is either a designation for the whole Anti-Lebanon range, of which Mount Hermon is the southernmost peak, or an alternative name for Hermon itself.

21. The enigmatic Hebrew word *shelahayik* has been variously understood as "plants" (NIV), "branches" of trees (CSB), or "channels" of water (cf. NRSV; Keel, *The Song of Songs*, 176), with a further variety of connotations about the woman's body inferred from them. Fox points out that the word in later Mishnaic Hebrew comes to mean an irrigation channel (Fox, *The Song of Songs and the Ancient Egyptian Love Songs*, 137), and we may point to the name of the Siloam Pool as having a

and speaks of her as "a garden fountain, a well of flowing water" (4:15), picking up imagery of moistness associated with feminine arousal.[22]

The woman reciprocates in 4:16 with her own expressions of desire. The NIV interprets the verse as the woman beckoning the "north wind" and "south wind" to blow on her garden, which is certainly a possible interpretation. However, the word "wind" is not present in the Hebrew text, so the NIV infers it on the basis of the nearby verb "blow." An alternative interpretation is that the woman beckons the "north" and the "south" to come at her, perhaps with hostile intent, as a veiled allusion to the coming of Solomon.[23] Her garden, which is symbolic of her body, is what "blows" (or "breathes out"), causing the fragrance of its spices to spread out and attract her lover, the shepherd. In either case, the idea of "blowing" (or "breathing") picks up the Hebrew terminology of 2:17 and 4:6, expressing the arrival of daybreak as the "blowing" of the day. The woman is, therefore, beckoning the arrival of day as a symbol of resolution to their plight—a time of fulfilment when she and her lover can experience passion together—something they cannot experience in the real present, for she is still not his bride. The language also evokes the heavy breathing associated with the throes of sexual ecstasy. Thus, within the dream she invites her beloved to experience this ecstasy with her—to enter "his garden and taste its choice fruits" (4:16). By the end of the verse she has become "his garden," demonstrating her desire to give herself to him in full bodily union. He answers her invitation in 5:1, and the dream comes to a blissful end in passionate intimacy. The daughters of Jerusalem encourage them to satisfy their hunger and thirst for intimacy—to "eat," "drink," and "be drunk on lovemaking" (NIV, "drink your fill of love"). The ethereality of the dream makes us wonder whether the obstacles to their union have been miraculously overcome, or whether they have thrown caution to the wind and come together despite the present predicament.

---

comparable meaning. However, all these options give the word a meaning specifically associated with a botanical park ("paradise"), whereas the man uses botanical imagery as metaphors to describe what these are *like*, rather than to state what these actually *are*. These are features that the woman herself possesses. The underlying word (*shelah*) comes from a root meaning to send or stretch forward and is given in the plural here. These are best understood as bodily protrusions that can erect and extend outwards. One possibility is that it refers to the woman's "limbs" (NJPS). However, the highly erotic nature of these verses, and their focus on taste, suggest the more intimate meaning of the woman's nipples in a state of arousal (cf. Prov 5:19). The comparison to pomegranates within the clause also suggests the shape of the female breast.

22. Israelite culture tended to refer to the female reproductive system with images of springs (Lev 12:7; 20:18; Prov 5:18).

23. Reference to the north and the south are also likely allusions to the Seleucids and the Ptolemies respectively, as they are in Daniel 11, Ecclesiates 1:6, and 11:3. Alternatively, they might allude to the directions from which Antiochus IV approached Judea, namely from the Seleucid heartland in Syria to the north, and from campaigning in Egypt to the south.

Harsh Reality (5:2–8)

In 5:2a we return to reality. The verse signals to us the completion of the dream sequence, as we find the woman asleep on her bed with her mind (literally, "heart") awake. This is where she has been all along since 3:1, and everything since then has been a dream playing out both her desires and fears. Now she is woken by the sound of knocking at her door (5:2b). It is possible that she is still asleep and hears the knocking in her dream, but two factors suggest otherwise. First, she tells us that she has been sleeping in 5:2a, which forms a neat bracket around the intervening content (3:1–5:2a), giving us the impression that the dream sequence is over and we have landed back in reality. Second, in 5:2b she utters the exact same phrase as she did in 2:8 when she heard her lover coming to her house at night: "Listen! My beloved!" This current scene follows a similar sequence to that earlier scene, when her lover came to the house and she urged him to run. She had been awake back then, and she seems to be awake again now. Third, events later in this scene seem to parallel the first scene of her dream (3:1–5), but with a vastly different outcome. We are thus presented with a contrast, suggesting that while 3:1–5 had been a dream, this current scene is not.

While this scene parallels earlier ones (2:8–17 and 3:1–5), there are some key differences. For instance, there is no indication that the shepherd has come bounding across the hills (cf. 2:8). He is simply there at the woman's house. Earlier he had been peeping through the windows and lattices (2:9), but now he tries to lift the latch of the door lock (5:4). These details give us the impression that the shepherd did not actually flee as the woman urged him in 2:17, immediately before her dream began (3:1). As in her dream, it seems the man cannot tear himself away from her. While she has been sleeping, he has remained resolutely close by. Thus, what we have here is not a repeat of the earlier scene, but its completion.

The entire scene presents a crescendo of desire, especially after the suggestiveness of the woman's dream. The man begs her to open for him. Though he is referring to the door, the sexually charged atmosphere fills his instruction with desperation and innuendo. He spouts endearments in rhythmic fashion, one after the other ("Open to me, my sister, my darling, my dove, my flawless one"; 5:2).[24] This is magnified by the woman's own admissions. She is in a state of undress and has washed her "feet"—a common euphemism for genitals (cf. Deut 28:57; Ruth 3:4–8; 2 Kgs 18:27; Isa 7:20),[25] which suggests her own

24. The rhythm is more obvious in Hebrew: *pithi-li 'ahoti ra'yati yonati tammati.*

25. Silvia Schroer and Thomas Staubli, *Body Symbolism in the Bible*, trans. Linda M. Maloney (Collegeville, MN: Liturgical Press, 2001), 182.

sexual desire (cf. 2 Sam 11:8). "Hand" is also a euphemism for the penis (cf. Isa 57:8),[26] which laces the man's gesture of thrusting his hand through the hole of the door with unmistakable sexual allusion. The woman's reaction ("my insides jolted at him" [NIV, "my heart began to pound for him"]) and her fingers dripping with myrrh (5:4–5; cf. 1:13) suggest mutual orgasm. The allusions are highly explicit and erotic, exposing the passion of both partners, even though all we are observing is the man's attempt to gain entry to the house. In this way, the sexual tension of the story rises even more, as we feel the relationship between the woman and the shepherd boy heading inexorably toward its natural goal of sexual union. We understand that if the man succeeds in entering the house, the two lovers will indeed act on their passion.

Yet, the scene does more than this, as it continues to highlight the dilemma of the two lovers in the face of Solomon's approach to claim the woman for himself (cf. 3:6–11). The man's gesture of trying to lift the latch of the door that keeps her inside the house (5:4) is figurative of his desperate desire to unlock the dilemma that threatens to keep them apart. The jolting of her insides (5:4) suggests both sexual ecstasy and panic. In wanting to consummate their love, the young couple are risking their lives, for they are not actually married. Though sex does not make a marriage, sex does belong in marriage. If the two lovers sleep together, as they long to do, they will have implied their lifelong union and potentially conceived a child (cf. 3:4). This could consequently seal the expectation of their marriage, so that their larger social situation corresponds with their personal reality (Exod 22:16). Sex, therefore, is potentially a subversive tool for the young couple—a means by which they can outflank Solomon before he has a chance to take the woman.

This is why Solomon's identity is so pivotal to the Song, and why he is the only character expressly named within it. Solomon is a king. If it were simply another commoner with a claim over the woman, the stakes would not be as high and perhaps the couple might stand a chance at outmaneuvering their rival. But they are up against the monarch who commands sixty armed warriors in his personal retinue alone (3:7–8) and who has conquered scores of women (Song 6:9; 8:11–12; cf. 1 Kgs 11:1–3). Is it even possible for them to outflank Solomon in such circumstances? Their love, which is so intense and so innocent, which yearns for its most natural expression within marriage, is tantamount to a crime against the state. Every passing moment brings them closer to a potentially fateful outcome: their union or Solomon's conquest of the woman. Thus, in addition to the couple's palpable sexual energy, there is desperation, making the entire situation volcanic.

---

26. Ibid., 164–65.

The scene reaches a decisive moment as the woman gets up from her bed to open the door for her lover (5:5). It seems the couple will tempt fate after all. As readers, we are in two minds about this. We want the lovers to consummate their love as would be just, for we feel they belong together, yet we realize how this contravenes standard conventions and puts them in such jeopardy.

In any case, when the woman opens the door, surprisingly she finds her lover gone (5:6). The NIV has her heart sinking at his departure, but the Hebrew is better translated, "My soul went forth as he had spoken." That is, she willingly responded to his pleas. With no explanation for his sudden retreat, the woman heads outside into the night to search for him. What she had dreamed earlier (3:1–5) is now played out in reality. That scene in her dream had a happy ending as, despite being found by the town's watchmen, she suddenly found her lover and brought him into her bedroom—a veiled allusion to the desire of conservative Jews to reinstate Yahweh's cult in the Jerusalem temple. Although the dream has primed us, and perhaps the woman also, to hope for a similar outcome now, harsh reality dispels the fantasy. The watchmen find the woman, perhaps alerted by her calling for her lover (5:6de), and subject her to the abuse of physical violence and humiliation (5:7). She refers to them disdainfully as "those watchmen of the walls," which implies they are guarding her virginity (see discussion of 2:8–17 above). Not only is this brutal outcome appalling in itself, it presents in a graphic way the circumstantial violence being done to the woman by denying her own will to be with the man she loves. She has been dehumanized and commodified as a thing to be given to Solomon. The scene's outcome evokes the tragic reality of the massacre of innocent people in Jerusalem, authorized by Antiochus IV in 167 BC (2 Macc 5:11–14, 24–26).

With no explanation given for the man's departure, we are left pondering. Has the man fled because of the guards? Has he hidden himself elsewhere in the town? Has he dashed back into the hills to emerge later (cf. 2:17)? Or has he changed his mind and found the will to tear himself away from the woman he loves, leaving them both to live with the pain of separation and unfulfilled desire (cf. 4:6)?

Unsure of the situation, the woman turns to the daughters of Jerusalem (5:8)—those women whom Solomon has already conquered before her. She had turned and adjured them at the corresponding moment of her dream sequence (3:6), but back then the watchmen left her unharmed and she found her lover and brought him into her bedroom. Now, she turns to them amid the violence being done to her. The uncertainty of where her lover has gone comes out as she pleads with the daughters, if they should ever find him, to tell him that she is "weakened by love" (NIV, "faint with love"). The implication is not merely that she is lovesick for him but that her love for him has made her weak—weak in her ability to resist the pull of desire and the consequences that creates, weak from the violence that the watchmen have inflicted on her, and weak with inability to exercise her own will. This plea to the daughters of Jerusalem highlights the confinement of her own predicament and the dismal prospects of her future.

LIVE the Story

Metaphorical Significance: God and his People

Once again, the marital themes present in the Song permit us to delve beneath the surface of its story to discern larger biblical currents that converge with other parts of Scripture. In this section of the Song, the woman is being presented as a would-be bride, with the tension focusing on whose bride she will be: the distant and powerful king's, who wishes only to use her, or the nearby shepherd boy's, who loves her intensely and wishes to share his life with her. This tension combines with the motif of her confinement ahead of her imminent marriage to the king. We may extend these concerns as metaphors, as we see the woman representing God's people (Israel in the Old Testament, and the church in the New Testament), the shepherd boy representing God, and Solomon representing external powers like the Seleucid king, Antiochus IV. In so doing, the Song gives us a means of evaluating the relationship between God and his people across history.

Throughout Israel's history we see the inexorable pull of foreign empires and foreign gods upon her. This begins with Israel bound in slavery to Pharaoh in Egypt, until Yahweh comes to release her at the exodus. Yahweh grants Israel her freedom and a land in which she can thrive in covenantal relationship with him. Despite this, throughout her generations Israel is constantly drawn to the worship of foreign deities. While the woman in the Song yearns to be with her beloved shepherd, despite the claims of others over her, Israel, by contrast, is attracted to foreign kingdoms and gods that have no love or concern for her. This fatal attraction leads, generations later, to the nation's exile—separation from Yahweh, their covenant God, and deliverance into the custody of foreign empires and their gods. Transferring affection away from Yahweh to others leads only to Israel's harm. Thus, the woman in the Song represents the antithesis of Israel for so much of her history.

And yet, even in the confines of exile, in bitter separation from him, Yahweh still sought to save his people. The shepherd boy in the Song is somewhat powerless to extricate his beloved from her confines, and for many in exile it would have appeared that Yahweh was likewise impotent against mighty Babylon's stranglehold over them (cf. Ezek 37:11; Lam 1:5–6). For some, Babylon even held the appeal of apparent prosperity, just like Solomon's promise of luxury. Yet, Israel rightly belonged with her God, Yahweh, who loved her and sought her best. She belonged in his land, away from Babylon's grasp. The shepherd boy speaks words of tenderness to his beloved in the Song, as Yahweh did to his exiled people (Isa 40:1). But whereas the shepherd boy flees in this part of the Song, Yahweh comes with power to tend his beloved flock with care and bring it back to himself (Isa 40:10–11).

Even so, God's people continued in the postexilic era to live under foreign rule. In those circumstances, there was always the pressure to weaken devotion to Yahweh and succumb to the charms of foreign cultures. This temptation was particularly strong in the Hellenistic Era under the Ptolemies and Seleucids. Greek culture promised so much in the way of learning, social progress, and even, for some, economic prosperity, but it required the abandonment of traditional biblical ideals. It was a step that many were prepared to take, as they migrated away from Yahweh's covenant land, or sold out to Hellenism within it. Though Israel could only fully embrace its own identity in covenantal relationship with Yahweh, many chose instead to leap into the arms of another, who had no real concern for their true identity and personhood.

This pull became even stronger during the Antiochene persecution. In the lead up to it, the Jewish high priests, Jason and Menelaus, who vied with each other for sway over the Jewish people, had steered the nation directly toward Greek culture in a way that was compromising traditional Jewish belief in Yahweh. For example, they equated Yahweh with Zeus, which utterly transformed the character of God revealed in their prior history and Scriptures. When Antiochus IV returned from his aborted campaign in Egypt in 167 BC, and found Jason and Menelaus squabbling, he revoked the ethnic status of the Jews, which had preserved for them the legal privilege of worshiping Yahweh freely and without the need to participate in the royal cult, which offered sacrifice to Antiochus IV as a symbol of loyalty to his sovereignty. Instead, the Jewish nation lost its distinctiveness and participation in the royal cult became mandatory, as it was for all other peoples in the Seleucid realm. Yahweh's temple was converted into a temple dedicated to Olympian Zeus. Like the woman in the Song, being a faithful Jew during this persecution meant becoming an enemy of the state. Antiochus also augmented the Seleucid citadel, the Acra, built in the City of David, as both a place to house his garrison forces, and a veritable acropolis of Greek culture dedicated to Greek gods. The massacre of so many Jewish people who resisted these changes testifies to just how serious this crisis was—something alluded to in the beating inflicted on the woman in the Song by the watchmen of the city (Song 5:7).

The current and future identity of Judaism was at stake. The will of many Jews was being eroded by the harsh winds of Hellenism and political persecution, while those who clung to traditional faith in Yahweh despaired of a long-term solution. In 167 BC it seemed politically impossible that Judaism could weather so fierce a storm. Even the Maccabees, who did momentarily take the ferocity out of the storm in 164 BC by taking back the temple, did not implement a lasting solution to the woes of Judaism. In fact, they went on to found the Hasmonean dynasty, which ended up looking identical to the reign of the high priests Jason and Menelaus, who had instigated the cultural crisis in Judaism during the reign of Antiochus IV. Faithful Jews needed God himself to intervene and do what they could not do: establish permanent salvation.

And so, God himself leapt into Israel's reality at the incarnation. He became the man, Jesus of Nazareth. In becoming human, God entered Israel's "bedchamber," as it were. He came to her in her predicament as her would-be groom (cf. John 3:29), broke the locks of her confinement, and brought her out from captivity under forces that did not have her interests at heart (cf. Col 1:13–14). He acted in love and gave his life that his covenant people might live. And in this act of salvation, he transformed her into his bride, the church (Eph 5:25–27). He betrothed her to himself by granting the Holy Spirit to the church. In this way, the Spirit is the church's pledge of union with Christ, as she waits for the final day when she will at last be united to Christ, her "husband" (2 Cor 1:22; 5:5; Eph 1:13–14). Thus, the New Testament often depicts God's covenant people, the church, as the bride of Christ. It is a prominent theme in Revelation, where the dawn of the new age at the end of history is depicted as a wedding celebration between Christ and his bride (Rev 19:7; 21:2, 9; 22:17).

As the church now waits for that consummation of the ages, there is still the pressure to conform to the world around it. It is the same pressure Jews faced under the brutal regime of Antiochus IV, though the foreign powers and gods may look superficially different now and the challenge may be more subtle. Today the church faces the allure of rampant materialism, the unrestrained pursuit of pleasure, the economic subjugation of others, apathy, the prosperity gospel, the surrender of biblical authority, the compromise of sexual ethics, the grab for political power, the temptation to silence, or a failure to protect the vulnerable. The church has already seen certain quarters run into the embrace of the world—a lamentable leap away from its betrothed who loved her and gave himself up to make her a bride without blemish. As the day of Christ approaches, the church must not get "cold feet." On the contrary, it must continue its fervent devotion to Christ, her beloved groom. This does not consist in the church holding doggedly to its position of power and privilege, which it has long enjoyed in Western societies, for that is only of peripheral concern. Rather, it consists of the church yearning for union with Christ, being identified with his name, wearing his seal, and seeking his kingdom. It consists of men, women, and children clinging in love to the one who loved them first and demonstrating that love to all. In this way, the passion of the woman in the Song for her beloved, despite the attraction of other suitors, stands as an example for us to emulate in our devotion to Christ.

Sex and Personal Union

There is no doubting the sexual chemistry that exists between the woman and the shepherd boy in the Song. Even in the face of Solomon's threatening approach, they share a passion for each other that draws them both toward the expression of their love in sex. This demonstrates the prominent role that sex has in human relationships. It is the most intimate form of human love, as the complementarity of the male and female body enables a man and woman to give themselves fully to each other and to receive the other completely without any restriction or barrier in the pursuit of mutual gratification. Sex is the bodily union that demonstrates the personal union of the two partners—a union in which a person shares their complete personhood of body, mind, and spirit with another. In ordinary circumstances, this sharing of personhood leads to the creation of a new personhood—not just the union of a man and a woman as a familial unit, but the creation of a new life—a child who shares the personhood of both partners. In this way, sex not only binds two people in the present, it also joins their futures through its potency for life creation. Sex is, therefore, profound in the way it enacts and creates identity, family, and future.

Since sex by its nature involves the whole person and their future, its native context is family life, where a couple share their entire lives together. This is, indeed, why the woman and the shepherd boy in the Song long to be together. When sex is used outside such a marriage context, there is an impairing of personhood. For example, casual sex sees two people unite in body, and perhaps in mind, but not in spirit or in future. In such instances, sex enacts a tearing of personhood that damages the partners. While they might both consent, and the pleasure of sex might mask it, injury to personhood still occurs, since the spiritual aspect of the partners' respective personhood and its future potential are not involved in the act of union.

In the Song, the dilemma the woman faces threatens to inflict a similar kind of damage upon her own person. By being forced to marry a king, whom she does not love, her body would be united with his, but her mind and spirit would not, and her future would be bent into conformity with his. All this would result in a profound wounding of her personhood that effectively tears her asunder. In such circumstances, the woman is conquered as a person and exiled to an imposed living arrangement, while the shepherd boy she loves is left to grieve her loss.

When the body is disconnected from mind, spirit, and future in such radical ways, as it is in casual sex, the results last beyond the act of sex itself. It can lead to lower self-esteem, feelings of guilt, objectification of self and others, and impaired ability to connect with others. In casual sex, a person may feel a sense of deep relief that they do not have to commit to a lifelong partnership with a person they have just slept with, but this ends up compromising the person and their ability to relate properly to others. It is a wholesale giving of self, followed immediately by an attempt to take back the self—an unhealthy contradiction that is the relational equivalent of trying to unscramble an egg. Alternatively, since sex is meant to accompany strong feelings of love toward another, casual sex can create confusion, as one partner finds themselves emotionally attached to the other partner, who does not reciprocate. Sex is enacted with no option for the future. The purpose of sex, which is to demonstrate an ongoing personal union, is therefore thwarted. Then again, casual sex might dupe one into thinking that such an impaired encounter is a proper personal union, which has the potential to sow further relational confusion when one eventually wants to "settle down" and have a family. One can end up approaching a real union with a casual attitude, which can compromise true cohesion and family life.

For some, casual sex leads to a devaluing of sex and its purpose. The feelings of disconnection can lead to disenchantment with sex and relationships, or a desensitizing to the "high" of sex. This last factor often leads people to seek that high with more partners or in different kinds of sex, some of which can be extreme. This mistakes the sensation of pleasure for the experience of gratification. Pleasure wears off easily, since it is a sensation. Gratification, however, is the personal satisfaction that leads to gratitude—an attitude motivated by love and appreciation of another. The more partners a person has, the less attainable real personal union becomes. This is also why the polygamous Solomon is such a notorious figure in the Song. With a vast harem, he can realistically have only casual encounters with his "wives." With so many partners, personhood is fractionalized and, thereby, compromised.

Casual sex is, therefore, an oxymoron. Human life is filled with relationships that are casual by nature and, therefore, not harmful, such as the brief exchange we might have with a shop assistant who serves us at the counter when we buy something. The same cannot be said for a sexual relationship, which is an investment of one's full identity and the reception of another's full identity. Casual sex tampers with the nature of sex, and (unfortunately) this has the potential to backfire on people in profound ways.

Christian churches need to spell this out, both for people within it and for people in the wider world. Casual sex, which is such a common phenomenon in our world now, especially since the invention of easy and cheap contraceptive methods, is profoundly damaging, as it bifurcates a person's being.[27] It is a kind of self-inflicted violence upon one's own personhood. As Christians, motivated by the ethic of love, we need to point this out, not because we are embarrassed by sex, think it "dirty," want to control people, or keep them from pleasure. On the contrary, it is because we value sex so highly and want to see people thrive in good relationships, leading to deep personal fulfilment. Similar motives should lead us to speak out and take action against other ways in which sex is misused, such as in situations of domestic violence, rape, sex trafficking, and pornography. Above all, it should lead us to proclaim the good news of Jesus Christ, who came in love to deal with our flaws, faux pas, and felonies. We can introduce people to the God who created their entire being, who loved them enough to give his life for them in Christ, who cares for them enough to offer them forgiveness and healing, and who desires to share his redemptive and limitless life with them.

This Christian sexual ethic does, of course, raise the issue of the woman and the shepherd boy in the Song, who plan a sexual encounter outside the bounds of marriage as a means of dealing with their dilemma. Hopefully, even at this point of the Song, the duress they are under hints at how their situation differs from what may be considered casual sex and that the issues they face are not altogether straightforward. Further discussion of this important issue comes in the treatment of the Song's finale (Song 6:11–8:14). Suffice it to say now that the ethical question marks over their actions highlight the extreme situation that is being foisted upon them, which is itself a metaphor of the persecution that conservative Jews suffered under Antiochus IV Epiphanes. But, the finale is not yet upon us, and there is more of the drama to unfold.

27. This does not mean that contraception is wrong. It is not. This is merely a statement that easy access to contraception has resulted in changing attitudes toward sex, some of which are not helpful.

CHAPTER 11

Song of Songs 5:9–6:10

LISTEN to the Story

9How is your beloved better than others,
most beautiful of women?
How is your beloved better than others,
that you so charge us?
10My beloved is radiant and ruddy,
outstanding among ten thousand.
11His head is purest gold;
his hair is wavy
and black as a raven.
12His eyes are like doves
by the water streams,
washed in milk,
mounted like jewels.
13His cheeks are like beds of spice
yielding perfume.
His lips are like lilies
dripping with myrrh.
14His arms are rods of gold
set with topaz.
His body is like polished ivory
decorated with lapis lazuli.
15His legs are pillars of marble
set on bases of pure gold.
His appearance is like Lebanon,
choice as its cedars.
16His mouth is sweetness itself;
he is altogether lovely.
This is my beloved, this is my friend,
daughters of Jerusalem.

6:1Where has your beloved gone,
most beautiful of women?
Which way did your beloved turn,
that we may look for him with you?
2My beloved has gone down to his garden,
to the beds of spices,
to browse in the gardens
and to gather lilies.
3I am my beloved's and my beloved is mine;
he browses among the lilies.
4You are as beautiful as Tirzah, my darling,
as lovely as Jerusalem,
as majestic as troops with banners.
5Turn your eyes from me;
they overwhelm me.
Your hair is like a flock of goats
descending from Gilead.
6Your teeth are like a flock of sheep
coming up from the washing.
Each has its twin,
not one of them is missing.
7Your temples behind your veil
are like the halves of a pomegranate.
8Sixty queens there may be,
and eighty concubines,
and virgins beyond number;
9but my dove, my perfect one, is unique,
the only daughter of her mother,
the favorite of the one who bore her.
The young women saw her and called her blessed;
the queens and concubines praised her.
10Who is this that appears like the dawn,
fair as the moon, bright as the sun,
majestic as the stars in procession?

Listening to the Story in the Text: 1 Kings 11:1–3; 2 Chronicles 11:21; Esther 2:1–18; P. Harris 500, Song 4; Sennacherib's Prism; "Tavern Sketch" (Sumerian Love Song), lines 27–32

The relationship between the woman of the Song and her beloved shepherd boy is under threat throughout the Song. The end of the previous section saw the woman experience abuse for seeking out her darling shepherd boy (5:1–8). An ancient Egyptian love poem (P. Harris 500, song 4) has similar sentiments. The voice in the poem belongs to a woman who does not wish to be separated from her lover, whom she calls "my little wolf cub." In so doing, she declares her rejection of her unnamed guardians' demands that she abandon him:

> My heart is not yet done with your lovemaking,
> my little wolf cub!
> Your liquor is your lovemaking.
> I will not abandon it
> until blows drive me away
> to spend my days in the marshes;
> until blows banish me
> to the land of Syria with sticks and rods,
> to the land of Nubia with palms,
> to the highlands with switches,
> to the lowlands with cudgels.
> I will not listen to their advice
> to abandon the one I desire.[1]

The woman in this Egyptian poem faces opposition to her relationship, which she is willing to resist despite the possibility of violence directed at her as a result. This ugly prospect has already become a development in the Song, as the woman runs into trouble with those who guard her (5:7). The repugnance of such violence in the Song helps us to see the violence involved in tearing the woman and the shepherd boy whom she loves apart. Her prospective marriage to the king is a brutal act rather than a loving one.

This is further exacerbated by the grand scale of the king's harem, which at Song 6:8 is enumerated as sixty queens, eighty concubines, and countless other girls. These figures differ from the configuration of Solomon's harem in 1 Kings 11:1–3, resembling something closer to the scale of his son Rehoboam's harem of eighteen wives and sixty concubines (2 Chr 11:21).[2] The point, however, is not to provide exact numbers, but rather a poetic sense of the abundance of women who already belong to the king. This contrasts with the lone couple at the heart of the Song: a simple young woman and her beloved shepherd

1. Translation adapted from Fox, *The Song of Songs and the Ancient Egyptian Love Songs*, 10.
2. 2 Chronicles 11:21 also mentions sixty daughters (along with twenty-eight sons).

boy, who rightly belong to each other. For Solomon in the Song, women are just a commodity to be seized—something the woman has already begun to experience at the hands of the watchmen who beat and detain her (Song 5:7). This kind of attitude is also observed in Esther 2, as numerous young women are taken into the harem of King Xerxes for his pleasure. We see it also on Sennacherib's Prism, on which he recounts his invasion of Judah. He boasts of taking a hefty tribute from Hezekiah, which included "his palace women" among a hoard of valuable commodities (*COS* 2.119B). The attitude is characteristic of brute power and disregard for others—the use of force and sex in violent conquest of another. It is the institutionalization of rape.

All this highlights the fortitude of the woman here in the Song for wanting to stand up to this, and the deep regard she has for her shepherd boy. She declares openly the intensity of her desire for him. Like the woman in the poem from Papyrus Harris 500, there is no shyness on her part but rather a defiant celebration of her sexual attraction to her lover (Song 5:10–16). Her choice of words is comparable to those found in a Sumerian love song that Jacobsen titles, "Tavern Sketch."[3] In this song, the serving girl of a tavern expresses her attraction toward an inebriated customer who seems to have had a long crush on her. She brims with desire for him:

> O my budding one, my budding one,
> sweet are your charms!
> My budding garden of the apple tree,
> sweet are your charms!
> My fruiting garden of the apple tree,
> sweet are your charms!
> Dumuzi-Apsû himself,
> Sweet are your charms!
> O my pure pillar, my pure pillar
> sweet are your charms!
> Pillar of alabaster set in lapis lazuli
> sweet are your charms!

Such appeal to plants and precious commodities demonstrates the sensuousness of attraction and the value of the beloved. He is most precious to her, and even godlike, Dumuzi-Apsû being a fertility deity. The woman of the Song also uses similar expressions as she celebrates the body of her beloved shepherd boy.

3. Thorkild Jacobsen, *The Harps that Once . . . : Sumerian Poetry in Translation* (New Haven: Yale University Press, 1987), 97–98.

EXPLAIN the Story

Defiant Devotion (5:9–6:10)

At the end of the previous section of the Song, the woman had awoken from a series of dream sequences to find her beloved shepherd boy gone and herself captured and assaulted by the watchmen of the town (5:1–7). In desperation, she charged the daughters of Jerusalem to pass a message to her beloved (5:8). This waking reality now continues in this next section, as she describes to the daughters of Jerusalem the alluring physique of her beloved with clear erotic overtones (5:9–16). The woman is still confined and being prepared to become Solomon's bride, heightening the tension of the predicament. Yet, her beloved shepherd boy is still nearby observing her (6:1–9). He remains committed to her, just as she remains committed to him.

Praising the Beloved (5:9–16)

While the change of speaker in 5:9 creates a literary "seam," this section is not really a break in the scene. The woman has been captured and abused by the watchmen and desires the daughters of Jerusalem to pass a message to her beloved shepherd boy (5:7–8). The daughters of Jerusalem now respond to the woman with a question: "How is your beloved better than others?" (5:9). This is a pointed question that invites the woman to explain the merits of her beloved shepherd boy. The question implies several further questions, perhaps subtler in nature. How can the simple shepherd boy possibly be better than the majestic Solomon? Is the woman not personally better off marrying Solomon? Does the woman not want a life of comfort and privilege? In light of the historical reality behind the Song, these implied questions demonstrate the allure of Hellenism and capitulation to Antiochus IV's policies. The question also betrays a naivety on the part of the daughters of Jerusalem. By asking about the shepherd boy's qualities, they reveal that they, as a harem, do not share the kind of relationship with Solomon, their husband, as the woman does with the shepherd boy.

The woman responds with a *wasf*—a poetic celebration of her beloved's qualities (5:10–16). The description focuses on his physical characteristics, which makes us wonder why she never mentions any of his personality traits. This might be because she is giving a physical description so that the daughters of Jerusalem can find him (cf. 5:8). She describes him from head to toe, comparing the parts of his body to gemstones, precious metals, exotic substances, flora, and fauna. We learn some intriguing details about him here. Unsurprisingly for a shepherd, he is tanned (NIV, "ruddy" [5:10]), just as

David was when still a shepherd boy (cf. 1 Sam 16:12),[4] and he has black hair (Song 5:11). The description is also suffused with the woman's desire. She describes his lips as "lilies dripping with myrrh" (5:13), which seems suggestive of oral pleasures.[5] After describing his entire body, she returns to focus on "His mouth" (5:16). The word she uses (*hikko*) specifically denotes the inside of the mouth, which she describes as "sweetness itself" (5:16)—an allusion to passionate kissing. The sensuality of these descriptions, though, does not necessarily mark the shepherd boy out as better than anyone else. It is possible that the daughters of Jerusalem could offer similar baroque praises of Solomon. But the way the woman finishes her *wasf* makes all the difference: "This is my beloved, this is my friend, daughters of Jerusalem" (5:16; cf. 5:1). The woman aims this comment especially at the daughters of Jerusalem. While it is possible that these women of Solomon's prolific harem each had genuine affection and desire for their royal husband, it is doubtful they could sincerely say they shared a deep love and friendship with him. Polygamy does not lend itself to such depth of relationship, especially on the grand scale at which Solomon practiced it. It is this depth of love and friendship that the woman shares with the shepherd boy that marks him out from all others and proves why the woman is much better off with him than with Solomon. Love and friendship outshine the wealth, prestige, and comfort of Solomon.

Uncertain Future (6:1–3)

The woman's description of her shepherd boy convinces the daughters of Jerusalem of his merits. Not only is he an impressive male specimen, but, more importantly, he is the woman's "beloved" and "friend." Since this qualifies him to be the woman's rightful partner, the daughters of Jerusalem are now willing to search for him (6:1). They can see now that she belongs with him and not with Solomon. Interestingly, this also hints that they themselves do not share the same depth of relationship with Solomon. If they thought the woman could find such love and friendship with the distant monarch, they would not volunteer to search with the woman for her beloved. Their willingness to help her in her plight gives us a sense that the daughters of Jerusalem long for the kind of relationship that the woman and the shepherd boy share, because they

4. At 1 Sam 16:12, the NIV describes David as "glowing with health," but the word used is the diminutive of the same word used here in Song 5:10 (*'adom*). Though its meaning has shifted slightly in Modern Hebrew to indicate "red," in biblical Hebrew it indicates an "earthy" color of reddish-brown. It does not indicate hair color, for in Song 5:11, we learn that the shepherd has black hair.

5. Cf. Pope, *Song of Songs*, 541.

do not have it. Searching with her for her beloved is the closest they can come to experiencing it. They are pitifully immured in marriage without genuine love and friendship, and they wish to spare the woman that fate.

The daughters of Jerusalem ask the woman where her beloved has gone (6:1), to which she replies that he has gone down to his garden to graze (NIV, "browse") and pick lilies (6:2). While this states the simple fact that the shepherd boy has fled back to his regular abode in the countryside (cf. 5:6), it is also filled with both pressing desire and anguish from the woman. On the one hand, it hints at her desire for intimacy with him. Elsewhere the woman is described as a garden (4:12, 16; 5:1; cf. 1:6), and here she speaks of "his garden" (6:2). We are thereby meant to understand that the woman herself is "his garden." The mention of "lilies" is elsewhere evocative of pubic hair (7:2), which makes his "going down" to the garden to "graze" among the lilies a highly erotic notion. On the other hand, the man has fled to his regular haunts, leaving the woman unsure whether he will return. She faces the crushing possibility that he has gone forever and that he might now find someone else—another "lily" among the many in the valleys (cf. 2:1). Even as she states this, she rails against it, declaring adamantly, "I am my beloved's and my beloved is mine" (6:3), which expresses in emphatic reverse order what she had previously declared in 2:16. Though she belongs to the shepherd boy, and he belongs to her, she fears she might lose him. The double entendre of the woman's words here calls attention to their uncertain future.

Distant Praise (6:4–10)

No sooner has the woman expressed her desire and fear than we hear the shepherd boy speak (6:4–9). Though he had fled earlier (5:6), he has evidently not abandoned his beloved or gone in search of someone else. True to the relational dynamic that the woman declares in the previous verse (6:3; cf. 2:16), the two lovers belong to each other. In this scene, the man appears to be at a slight distance from the woman. He is close enough to see and praise her beauty directly to her, but he finishes speaking about her in the third person (6:8–9), which gives a sense of remoteness. Furthermore, she can see him, but he urges her to turn her eyes away from him (6:5). There is an air of danger in the scene that means his presence must remain unacknowledged. So, he is not really speaking to her so much as giving voice to his own feelings about her—a soliloquy expressing both praise and pain. This also explains why she never responds to him directly within the scene. Though she can see him, she cannot hear him. Thus, we have the impression that in this scene the man is following his beloved at a distance, but close enough to reassure her that he is there. He had come to her previously under cover of night (5:2), but now he comes incognito, as it were, and must remain at a distance. This configuration captures the nature of the predicament the two lovers face. They are so intimately close, and desire to be more intimate still, but circumstance is keeping them apart.

The shepherd boy lauds the woman for being "as beautiful as Tirzah" and "as lovely as Jerusalem" (6:4). This parallelism prompts us to identify Tirzah as the city in the central highlands, which became one of the capitals of the northern kingdom of Israel in the generations after Solomon (1 Kgs 15:33; cf. 14:17).[6] It seems unusual for the man to compare his beloved's beauty to two cities, but there is a third element to the poetic parallelism we must account for, though it has long baffled interpreters. The NIV translates this parallel, "as majestic as troops with banners" (Song 6:4; cf. most English versions), on the understanding that the key Hebrew word (*nidgalot*) indicates the organized divisions of an army marked out by their standards or banners.[7] While semantically plausible, this interpretation breaks the parallelism with Tirzah and Jerusalem in the first two lines. The same word (*nidgalot*) appears in 6:10, where the parallelism with "moon" and "sun" means it should be translated as "constellations" (i.e., organized clusters of stars). Applying this same meaning to 6:4 still breaks the parallelism of the verse, so we must find another solution that preserves the poetic dynamic. Pope translates *nidgalot* in 6:4 as "trophies," understanding it as a reference to the skulls and severed hands of vanquished enemies that the goddess Anat wears around her neck and waist in Ugaritic mythology.[8] Not only is this fanciful, it still breaks the poetic parallelism and is semantically and contextually questionable. Garrett attempts to preserve the parallelism by translating the line, "awesome, as panoplied cities,"[9] but we must still grapple with the oddity of comparing the woman to cities. Keel argues that the Old Testament "sometimes presents cities as virgins," such as "Virgin Daughter Zion" and "Daughter Jerusalem" (Isa 37:22), and what we have here in the Song is just a reversal of this imagery.[10] Whereas depicting cities as female figures is a common personifying motif, the reverse represents a depersonalization, which does not work in this context. Despite this doubt over Keel's theory, he seems on the right track in connecting the imagery here to female figures. Within the Song itself, Jerusalem is predominantly

6. Tirzah was also the name of one of the five daughters of Zelophehad, who inherited his estate because he had no sons (Num 27:1–11), but the parallelism here necessitates the identification of Tirzah as a city.

7. The Hebrew word for "banner" or "division" of troops (*degel*) is derived from the same root as the key word here.

8. Pope, *Song of Songs*, 551, 560–63.

9. Garrett and House, *Song of Songs / Lamentations*, 225, 228.

10. Keel, *The Song of Songs*, 212–13.

associated with the "daughters of Jerusalem," and the ambiguous word *nidgalot* is a feminine participle. This raises the possibility that Tirzah and Jerusalem are metonyms for "organized ranks of women" (*nidgalot*) from these two cities—that is, the cities represent clusters of Solomon's harem. The idea of the threefold parallelism in 6:4, then, is that the man deems his beloved more precious and beautiful than all the women of Solomon's harem.[11] Support for this suggestion comes a few verses later when the man uses a second threefold parallelism to compare his beloved to "sixty queens," "eighty concubines," and "girls [NIV, "virgins"] beyond number" (Song 6:8). Through this mirroring of threefold parallels, references to Solomon's women form an inclusio around the man's *wasf* to his beloved. This poetic structure serves two functions. First, it focuses attention on the woman, giving us a sense of the man's captivation with her. Second, it demonstrates her imminent fate: captivity within Solomon's harem. The shepherd boy observes this from a distance, powerless to do anything about it.

The reference to queens and concubines, therefore, gives us greater understanding of the scene. The man is watching his beloved amid the ranks of Solomon's harem, being prepared for her wedding to the king. It parallels one of the scenes in the woman's dream, when the man lauded her as a bride (4:1–15). Even though the scene here feels quite abstract (it is not a straightforward narrative), it is not a dream. The woman's fate is starting to become a reality. This is, therefore, a difficult scene for the man to watch from his distant vantage point. His *wasf* in praise of her beauty parallels his earlier *wasf* during the woman's dream (4:1–15), but this one is much simpler. It overflows with quaint images drawn from the life of a shepherd (6:5–6). Its simplicity contrasts with the ranks of sophisticated queens and concubines around the woman who also celebrate her, though seemingly in anticipation of her marriage to the king. Amidst all the swirling ranks, though, the man sees his beloved as unique (6:9). For him, she is distinct and more beautiful than all the women in the scene combined.

Evidently, the woman's eyes catch sight of her beloved shepherd boy through all the activity around her (6:5). We are not told what emotion her glance conveys, but the man wills her to turn her eyes away from him, because they "compel" him (NIV, "overwhelm"). Is she urging him to flight so as not to be caught, just as she has urged before (2:17)? Or is she spurring him to action, to save her from her plight, as she also has previously (1:4)? In either case, if she continues looking at him she risks exposing him or pushing him into an action that would see him lose everything. His plea for her to look

11. Cf. Provan, *Ecclesiastes, Song of Songs*, 339.

away, then, reveals the powerlessness of his situation. He is so close, and yet so far from her.

It is difficult to know exactly who speaks in 6:10. Numerous interpreters argue that it is the queens and concubines praising the woman, as mentioned in the previous line (6:9).[12] However, we cannot rule out that it is still the man speaking, or possibly an anonymous generic voice, or even all the characters except the woman. Regardless of the speaker's identity, the verse focuses on the woman's stellar beauty, having been prepared to become Solomon's bride. The rhetorical question that forms the verse follows the same structure as that which introduced the armed procession of Solomon during the woman's dream (3:6). In this way, the woman is seen in parallel with Solomon, he with his ranks of armed soldiers (3:7–8) and she with ranks of queens and concubines (6:8–9). This time it is not a dream, and we feel the imminence of the woman's fate. The NIV says she "appears like the dawn," but the Hebrew indicates that she is "peering down" (*nishqapah*) from above like the celestial bodies. This gives a sense of the high and noble position that awaits her as a bride of the king but also of her remoteness from the man. She is as stunning as the sun, moon, and stars, but just as out of reach as they are.

LIVE the Story

Metaphorical Significance: God and his People

Once more, as the romantic drama of the Song unfolds, we hear echoes of Israel's relationship with Yahweh. Just as the woman is under confinement and being prepared for her perilous marriage to the distant king, so Israel during the postexilic era lay confined under foreign empires who all in some way impaired her relationship with her covenant deity, Yahweh. During the Hellenistic Era this impairment reached a critical breaking point, as Jewish leaders began adopting liberal Hellenistic values to the abandonment of their classic Jewish faith. As the writer of 1 Maccabees puts it:

> In those days certain renegades came out from Israel and misled many, saying, "Let us go and make a covenant with the Gentiles around us, for since we separated from them many disasters have come upon us." This proposal pleased them, and some of the people eagerly went to the king, who authorized them to observe the ordinances of the Gentiles.

12. Gledhill, *Message of the Song of Songs*, 196; Fox, *The Song of Songs and the Ancient Egyptian Love Songs*, 153; Longman, *Song of Songs*, 182; Provan, *Ecclesiastes, Song of Songs*, 340.

> So they built a gymnasium in Jerusalem, according to Gentile custom, and removed the marks of circumcision, and abandoned the holy covenant. They joined with the Gentiles and sold themselves to do evil. (1 Macc 1:11–15)

In recounting the pilfering of the Jerusalem temple under Antiochus IV Epiphanes, the same writer describes the anguish of the faithful: "Every bridegroom took up the lament; she who sat in the bridal chamber was mourning" (1 Macc 1:27). This was followed by Antiochus's fateful decree that effectively outlawed conservative Judaism:

> Then the king wrote to his whole kingdom that all should be one people, and that all should give up their particular customs. All the Gentiles accepted the command of the king. Many even from Israel gladly adopted his religion; they sacrificed to idols and profaned the sabbath. And the king sent letters by messengers to Jerusalem and the towns of Judah; he directed them to follow customs strange to the land, to forbid burnt offerings and sacrifices and drink offerings in the sanctuary, to profane sabbaths and festivals, to defile the sanctuary and the priests, to build altars and sacred precincts and shrines for idols, to sacrifice swine and other unclean animals, and to leave their sons uncircumcised. They were to make themselves abominable by everything unclean and profane, so that they would forget the law and change all the ordinances. He added, "And whoever does not obey the command of the king shall die." (1 Macc 1:41–50)

It is difficult to capture how close conservative Judaism came to complete collapse at this time. Both the internal cultural pressure of progressively minded Hellenists and the external legal pressure of the ruling authority subjected faithful conservative Jews to a virtually impossible decision: abandon conservative commitment to Yahweh or die. There were many social and economic advantages in such compromise. Just as a life of wealth and prestige awaits the woman in the Song if she marries the king, so survival and progress awaited conservative Jews if they adopted Hellenistic values and fell into line with Antiochus's decrees. Just as the woman in the Song protests her situation and declares that she belongs to her shepherd boy (Song 6:3), so Israel rightly belonged to Yahweh her God. The demands placed on conservative Jews in the Seleucid Era were brutal and unreasonable. And yet, as the Song portrays the shepherd never abandoning his beloved, so Yahweh did not abandon Israel. As the woman desires to draw near to her beloved shepherd in intimate union as the most natural act in celebration of their bond, so Israel and Yahweh should be drawn together and not forced apart. The proper response to such imposed separation was not capitulation but resistance—a dogged persistence in maintaining Yahweh's laws and customs, despite the mortal threat. In the Song, this persistence will entail the extreme measure of the woman and the shepherd joining together in sexual union. In Jewish history, it entailed faithful Jews going to their deaths for adhering to their faith and others taking up arms to overthrow the oppressive colonial forces.

In 164 BC the Jews momentarily extricated themselves from the Hellenistic vice that held them. For some decades, the Hasmoneans ruled Judea and neighboring territories. Yet, it was not to last, as the Romans arrived in 63 BC and impressed their imperial rule over the region. While the Romans were more beneficent than Antiochus IV had been, the relationship between the Jewish people and Yahweh suffered impairment, as they were not rightly ruled by their own Davidic king.

This changed, however, in the first century, when Israel's God arrived to rescue his people in the person of Jesus of Nazareth, a descendant of David. God had not only come near, he had become one of them and lived among them (cf. John 1:14). John the Baptist recognized this when he saw Jesus, expressing the notion that Israel belonged to Jesus by saying, "The bride belongs to the bridegroom" (John 3:29). The tragedy is that the Jewish leaders rejected Jesus and had him killed for his claims over them. Yet, in God's foresight and genius, Jesus's death and resurrection were the very means by which God redeemed people. The subsequent granting of the Spirit to all who have faith in Jesus is the means by which any person, Jew or Gentile, male or female, may not just know God, but be united to him in an intimate union. The Christian belongs to Christ as a member of his body (1 Cor 12:27; Eph 1:22–23), as his bride who is joined to him (Eph 5:29–32). As 2 Peter 1:3–4 states, the Christian participates in the divine nature and escapes the corruption in the world caused by evil desires by believing in the great and precious promises that Jesus imparted to his apostles.

Belonging to Jesus

The woman in the Song praises the shepherd boy to the daughters of Jerusalem (Song 5:9–16). He is her beloved and her friend, who far outshines Solomon and anything he has to offer her. In extolling her beloved's virtues, the woman convinces the daughters of Jerusalem of just how special the shepherd boy is. In a metaphorical way, this is precisely what Israel was to do before the nations. Moses urges Israel in Deuteronomy 4:5–8 to follow Yahweh's laws and customs as a demonstration to the nations of how good Israel's God was.

When we come to the Hellenistic Era, with its erosion of Jewish ideals and official persecution, such adherence became a weighty challenge. In this context, in which the Song was written, the message of the Song was that faithfulness to Yahweh, his laws, and customs was worth far more than anything Hellenism had to offer. Yahweh was worth the cost of deprivation and opposition that faithful, conservative Jews faced.

In the New Testament, Paul builds on this sentiment in light of the revelation of Christ. In Philippians 3:1–11 Paul describes all the benefits he enjoyed by being part of Israel, before concluding that even these good things he now considered "loss" and "garbage" for "the surpassing worth of knowing Christ Jesus my Lord, for whose sake I have lost all things." Paul suffered tremendously at the hands of both Gentiles and Jewish compatriots who rejected his message that Jesus was Israel's messiah. Yet he was willing to endure this, because he knew that the righteousness of Christ was now his, and this qualified him for resurrection to eternal life. Belonging to Jesus was worth it.

For some Christians today, the cost of following Jesus is very high. It entails rejection by family, eviction from homeland, financial loss, discrimination, physical harm, and even the prospect of martyrdom. One cannot but recall the bravery of twenty-one Coptic Christians in 2015 lined up in orange jumpsuits on a Libyan beach, muttering the name of Jesus before their extremist captors beheaded them in cold blood. For others, the cost is far lower, but no less real. It involves ridicule, social ostracism, or political embarrassment. Wearing the cost of being a follower of Jesus is something Christians must be prepared to do. Jesus himself urged his disciples, who were literally following him to Jerusalem, to be prepared to take up their cross (Luke 14:27), for the prospect of death at the hands of the authorities was very real. It was, after all, what befell him. Christians today are called to take up their cross in a figurative sense. We are not literally following Jesus to Jerusalem, but we are figuratively bearing his name, for we belong to him, and he to us. This means remaining faithful to Christ and his ideals in both the major and minor decisions of life.

A temptation Christians face today is to give in to what the world offers, just as the woman was being tempted to give into marrying Solomon rather than resisting and remaining true to her beloved shepherd boy. The world offers much: popularity, prestige, ease, comfort, wealth, pleasure, and seeming fulfillment. Even these cannot top the quality of Jesus, though the world does not understand this. Like the woman in the Song, Christians must remain steadfastly devoted to Jesus while demonstrating how magnificent he truly is.

A further temptation is to mistake Jesus for the world—to misplace our trust and equate Jesus with religious movements (even other religions), political institutions or parties, national identity, or even seemingly benign concepts like human rights. Some of these might have good elements within them, but they are not and cannot be Jesus. Christians must be prepared to reevaluate and give them up for the sake of belonging to him. Christians are called to wisdom, being in the world but not of it. James warns his readers that "friendship with the world means enmity against God" (Jas 4:4). Our desire must be the same as that which shaped Paul, when he wrote, "I want to know Christ—yes, to know the power of his resurrection and participation in his sufferings, becoming like him in his death, and so, somehow, attaining to the resurrection from the dead" (Phil 3:10–11).

Pornography

Throughout the Song, metaphor veils the expression of sexual desire and sexual acts. Nonetheless, at times the metaphors become unmistakably explicit. This raises the issue of pornography, which the *Oxford English Dictionary* defines as "printed or visual material containing the explicit description or display of sexual organs or activity, intended to stimulate sexual excitement." The candid content of the Song might lead some to classify it as literary porn. However, the intention of the Song is not to "stimulate sexual excitement." It is, rather, didactic: to explore the place of sexual desire in the context of relationship and to advocate cultural and religious resistance in a climate of social, religious, and political persecution. In other words, the Song is not written to titillate but to teach about human relationships and commitment to God. It does not shy away from addressing the very real concepts involved in sex, but it presents them artfully, not clinically.

Pornography exploits what is sometimes a fine line between it and art. Indeed, some try to pass pornography off as art. However, pornography is by its nature exploitative, whereas art is about the expression of meaning and the appreciation of aesthetics. For instance, we may consider Michelangelo's renowned statue, *David*, which presents a complete male nude form. The purpose of the statue is not to incite sexual arousal but to study and celebrate the human body as a marvelous phenomenon. Anyone who has seen the statue in real life cannot help but be awed by the statue's craftsmanship and swayed by its purpose. The Song is similar. It uses poetic literature to teach about the expression and place of sexual desire in human relationships and uses this as a metaphor for God's relationship with his people.

Pornography, by contrast, is about exploiting people's bodies for the sexual arousal of others. It turns sex, which is about the wholesale union of persons, into a commodity to be consumed. This tampers with the fundamentally relational nature of sex, for there is no union that occurs in consuming pornography. Such a notion is impossible and means that there is no mutual self-giving, thus hijacking the purpose of sex. Pornography is anti-relational.

It creates a fundamental distortion by inviting the consumer to "participate" in sex by mere observation or even by proxy, in which one's own person is replaced by another's. In either case, the nature of sex is distorted. Though people involved in making pornography might do so willingly—and some do not—all the issues relating to casual sex explored in the previous chapter affect them. Pornography warps sex, which is a God-given gift to humanity, by trivializing it, degrading the people in it as mere objects to be looked at for the entertainment of others. Furthermore, consuming pornography leads, in many cases, to an addiction that, in our online age, has reached epidemic proportions. The rapid pornification of our world has ruined our personhood, rewired our brains in harmful ways, and damaged our relationships. Ironically, and also tragically, it has devalued sex.

The message of the Song, that sexual desire is good and should be given free expression within the personal union of marriage, is redemptive. This is what the woman and her beloved shepherd seek in defiance of the abusive dilemma foisted upon them. This message seeks to retrieve sex as one of God's good gifts to humanity and see its value for human relationships. Understanding this didactic purpose enables us to comprehend the theology of the Song, as well as admire its artistry in a manner that is not just clinical. It allows us to take the more explicit aspects of its content and, with maturity, appreciate how they capture human emotion and beautifully convey human sexuality. When we understand this message, we can appreciate how the New Testament uses the idea of marriage as a metaphor for the joyous and redemptive union between Christ and the church (Eph 5:31–32).

CHAPTER 12

Song of Songs 6:11–8:14

LISTEN to the Story

11I went down to the grove of nut trees
to look at the new growth in the valley,
to see if the vines had budded
or the pomegranates were in bloom.
12Before I realized it,
my desire set me among the royal chariots of my people.
13Come back, come back, O Shulammite;
come back, come back, that we may gaze on you!
Why would you gaze on the Shulammite
as on the dance of Mahanaim?
7:1How beautiful your sandaled feet,
O prince's daughter!
Your graceful legs are like jewels,
the work of an artist's hands.
2Your navel is a rounded goblet
that never lacks blended wine.
Your waist is a mound of wheat
encircled by lilies.
3Your breasts are like two fawns,
like twin fawns of a gazelle.
4Your neck is like an ivory tower.
Your eyes are the pools of Heshbon
by the gate of Bath Rabbim.
Your nose is like the tower of Lebanon
looking toward Damascus.
5Your head crowns you like Mount Carmel.
Your hair is like royal tapestry;
the king is held captive by its tresses.
6How beautiful you are and how pleasing,

my love, with your delights!
7Your stature is like that of the palm,
and your breasts like clusters of fruit.
8I said, "I will climb the palm tree;
I will take hold of its fruit."
May your breasts be like clusters of grapes on the vine,
the fragrance of your breath like apples,
9and your mouth like the best wine.
May the wine go straight to my beloved,
flowing gently over lips and teeth.
10I belong to my beloved,
and his desire is for me.
11Come, my beloved, let us go to the countryside,
let us spend the night in the villages.
12Let us go early to the vineyards
to see if the vines have budded,
if their blossoms have opened,
and if the pomegranates are in bloom—
there I will give you my love.
13The mandrakes send out their fragrance,
and at our door is every delicacy,
both new and old,
that I have stored up for you, my beloved.
8:1If only you were to me like a brother,
who was nursed at my mother's breasts!
Then, if I found you outside,
I would kiss you,
and no one would despise me.
2I would lead you
and bring you to my mother's house—
she who has taught me.
I would give you spiced wine to drink,
the nectar of my pomegranates.
3His left arm is under my head
and his right arm embraces me.
4Daughters of Jerusalem, I charge you:
Do not arouse or awaken love
until it so desires.

[5]Who is this coming up from the wilderness
leaning on her beloved?
Under the apple tree I roused you;
there your mother conceived you,
there she who was in labor gave you birth.
[6]Place me like a seal over your heart,
like a seal on your arm;
for love is as strong as death,
its jealousy unyielding as the grave.
It burns like blazing fire,
like a mighty flame.
[7]Many waters cannot quench love;
rivers cannot sweep it away.
If one were to give
all the wealth of one's house for love,
it would be utterly scorned.
[8]We have a little sister,
and her breasts are not yet grown.
What shall we do for our sister
on the day she is spoken for?
[9]If she is a wall,
we will build towers of silver on her.
If she is a door,
we will enclose her with panels of cedar.
[10]I am a wall,
and my breasts are like towers.
Thus I have become in his eyes
like one bringing contentment.
[11]Solomon had a vineyard in Baal Hamon;
he let out his vineyard to tenants.
Each was to bring for its fruit
a thousand shekels of silver.
[12]But my own vineyard is mine to give;
the thousand shekels are for you, Solomon,
and two hundred are for those who tend its fruit.
[13]You who dwell in the gardens
with friends in attendance,
let me hear your voice!

[14]Come away, my beloved,
and be like a gazelle
or like a young stag
on the spice-laden mountains.

Listening to the Story in the Text: Genesis 38; Exodus 22:16–17; Deuteronomy 22:13–29; Ruth 3

The predicament of the Song is that the woman loves a shepherd boy but has been pledged in marriage to Solomon. Now in the finale to the Song, the woman resorts to drastic measures. To appreciate her desperation and the implications of her actions, we must understand the social and legal customs surrounding the sexual taboos of ancient Israel. For this we must consider some of the "casuistic" laws in the Pentateuch. These provide "case" studies rather than exhaustive legislation. They "do not describe the totality of things that can happen, nor do they express the only course of action that should be taken."[1] Instead, they exemplify how principles of justice could be applied in particular scenarios, leaving readers to extrapolate how principles might be applied in other scenarios.

Israel recognized that sex was native to marriage and that children had to be born within an unambiguous marriage covenant. Therefore, sex outside of a marriage covenant posed certain problems. The scenario in Exodus 22:16–17 is especially relevant for framing our consideration of the woman's predicament in the Song:

> If a man seduces a virgin who is not pledged to be married and sleeps with her, he must pay the bride-price, and she shall be his wife. If her father absolutely refuses to give her to him, he must still pay the bride-price for virgins.

Although sex occurs outside a marriage covenant in this scenario, there is no question over the paternity of any child that might be born to the woman. Consequently, the law stipulates that the relationship of the couple must be formalized as a marriage. The man is obliged to wed the woman and thereby establish a formal familial unit that locates their sexual union within a permanent marriage covenant. The initial situation of the scenario is regarded as less than ideal, which is why the man must pay a "bride price," presumably

1. Athas, *Deuteronomy*, 183.

to the woman's father. The situation is retrieved by the ensuing marriage and the granting of the title of "wife" to the woman, rather than "concubine."[2]

The scenario is also interesting for what it does and does not say. For example, it sees the man as responsible for the situation, since he is said to seduce the virgin. It does not state whether the sexual encounter is spontaneous or planned, or whether the man and the virgin were courting or just involved in a casual fling. While the case has considerable ambiguity, the two major principles that may be derived from it are clear: (1) sex carries social responsibilities and consequences; and (2) sex rightly belongs in the context of a permanent marriage union.

These principles and the inherent ambiguity of the casuistic law raise an interesting possibility that has a direct bearing on the drama of the Song: is it possible in ancient Israelite society for a courting couple, whose relationship is strongly opposed by others, to sleep together and thus forcibly bring about their marriage as a necessary concession? The spirit of the law suggests that using sex for this kind of social outflanking would be deemed an abuse of the law's principles. The contingency in the law that gives the woman's father the right to veto any ensuing nuptials (Exod 22:17) evidently presents a case in which the father disapproves of his daughter's relationship to the man and provides a means of preventing such social outflanking. However, in the Song the woman's father is never mentioned—only her mother and brothers are. It seems the woman has no father figure (he has presumably died), which is why her brothers appear to have guardianship of her (Song 1:6; 8:8–9). Yet, they are her brothers and do not stand in paternal relationship to her. Since the law does not deal with a circumstance where there is no father figure, a morally grey area emerges. Is the guardianship of brothers over a sister as morally authoritative as that of a father? Does this grant the woman more say in her circumstances, or do the brothers have a full right of veto over her?

Of further relevance to the Song are the casuistic laws pertaining to sex in Deuteronomy 22:13–29. This passage presents a series of similar scenarios, each with a slightly different variable. The case most pertinent to the situation of the two lovers in the Song is Deuteronomy 22:23–24:

---

2. The distinction between a wife and a concubine is never overtly detailed in the Bible, leaving us to make educated guesses from the data. On the surface, a "wife" appears to have had primary ranking as a free woman, while a "concubine" seems to have had secondary ranking as a servant wife. Sometimes a woman brought a dowry (payment to the husband or his family) with her to a marriage, which most likely guaranteed her the status as a "wife" with personal freedom. However, it was also possible for a man to pay his bride's father for the privilege of marriage, which might have given him the right to confer on her the status of "concubine" (a servant wife). This was not a necessity, as the example of Jacob and Rachel demonstrates; Jacob paid for Rachel with his labor, but she was regarded as his wife, not a servant (Gen 29:28–30). While this is the best explanation of the data, the lack of overt biblical definitions for the terms means we cannot be completely sure it is correct.

> If a man happens to meet in a town a virgin pledged to be married and he sleeps with her, you shall take both of them to the gate of that town and stone them to death—the young woman because she was in a town and did not scream for help, and the man because he violated another man's wife. You must purge the evil from among you.[3]

This case differs from Exodus 22:16–17 in one significant way: in Deuteronomy, the virgin is pledged in marriage to someone, while in Exodus she is not.[4] This key difference renders the situation in Deuteronomy a capital offense. In this next section of the Song, the woman is being prepared for marriage to Solomon, yet she does not love him; she loves the shepherd boy. The law in Deuteronomy does not mention the feelings of the virgin toward the man to whom she is pledged, nor does it mention that man's marital status—whether he is unmarried or, like Solomon, already has other wives. Nonetheless, the verdict of the law is quite stark: the woman and the man she sleeps with are worthy of death for their complicity in subverting a marriage covenant.

Yet there are still morally and legally grey areas here, as the predicaments of both Tamar in Genesis 38 and Ruth in Ruth 3 demonstrate. In Genesis 38, Tamar marries Er, the son of Judah, but he dies before he and Tamar have children. Consequently, Judah urges his next son, Onan, to sleep with Tamar so as to give her children and, thereby, ensure her security within the clan structure. Onan subverts this purpose and dies also, leaving Tamar still without children. At this point, Judah pledges Tamar in marriage to his remaining son, Shelah. Yet, since Shelah is still a minor, Tamar needs to wait some years before the marriage is enacted. Judah, however, fears his remaining son might also die and therefore never makes good on his pledge, leaving Tamar without children and in a perilous social situation. Tamar takes the drastic action of disguising herself as a prostitute to trick Judah himself into sleeping with her. Not knowing what he has done, Judah condemns Tamar to death when he finds out that she has become pregnant. Yet, when she reveals that she is carrying his child, Judah is humbled and calls Tamar a righteous woman for having undertaken such an extreme action, risking so much to expose his own folly and rectify her own situation (Gen 38:26).

Similarly, Ruth is a widow without children. She and her mother-in-law, Naomi, are extremely vulnerable as women with no standing in a clan

---

3. The Bible defines this situation as adultery. Polygamy is never equated with adultery, since the paternity of children within a polygamous situation was not in question. Polygamy was, rather, a situation in which one man had more than one marriage covenant.

4. For a discussion on the implications of this casuistic law for a scenario in which a woman does not consent to sex and yet is unable to scream for help, see Athas, *Deuteronomy*, 265–66.

structure. At Naomi's encouragement, Ruth attempts to sleep with Boaz, a kind and generous local benefactor, while he is inebriated one night on the threshing floor (Ruth 3). By sleeping with him, Ruth would be aligning her entire life with his and potentially falling pregnant to him. This would put moral pressure on Boaz to recognize his union with Ruth and take her as a wife, thereby securing her welfare, as well as that of her mother-in-law.[5] The narrative is ambiguous about whether Ruth actually sleeps with Boaz or whether he interrupts her before she can. In any case, the intent is most certainly there, and Boaz recognizes Ruth as a kind, faithful, and noble woman for it, as unconventional as her tactics are (Ruth 3:10–11). Soon after their nocturnal encounter, Boaz successfully negotiates to marry Ruth, thus ensuring her ongoing security and Naomi's.

Tamar's case demonstrates that the laws in Exodus and Deuteronomy are not exhaustive in their scope but present very specific scenarios. Ethical principles must be applied with sensitivity to a scenario's variables rather than applied without consideration of particularity. Tamar was pledged in marriage, and she slept with someone else. Yet, instead of being condemned to death as Deuteronomy 22:23–24 stipulates, she was acclaimed as righteous. This was not a perversion of justice but an enactment of it, though the situation was exceptional and, therefore, not normative. The extreme nature of her circumstances justified the extreme measures she took. Ruth's case demonstrates that laws should protect people, especially the vulnerable. Her furtive attempts to force the recognition of her union to Boaz are interpreted as problematic but noble—not immoral. When seen against the laws of Exodus and Deuteronomy, the cases of these two women demonstrate that there are occasions when what seems to be an ethically questionable action actually upholds the spirit of the law rather than violates it. This social and legal paradox is pivotal to understanding the desperate measures that the woman in the Song takes in the Song's finale, as she attempts to gain control over her circumstances and enact justice.

EXPLAIN the Story

The Finale (6:11–8:14)

With her marriage to Solomon fast approaching, the woman decides on an extreme course of action. Her aim is to preserve the loving relationship she

5. Interestingly, Boaz's marital status before marrying Ruth is never mentioned. It is entirely possible that, as a very influential landowner, he was already married and that Ruth became his second wife.

enjoys with the shepherd boy and avoid being taken into Solomon's harem against her will. Being highly unconventional, the woman's plan is perilous, as it puts her own life, and potentially the life of the shepherd, at risk. It is a chance she is willing to take. After acting on her plans together with her beloved shepherd, the drama of the Song reaches its final crescendo. The woman's brothers appear, as does Solomon, and the fate of the woman hangs in the balance.

A Moment of Decision (6:11–13)

These few verses are perhaps the most obscure of the entire Song. Ambiguities and difficult poetic constructions complicate our understanding of their meaning. Nevertheless, there are ways of unraveling the puzzle that make good contextual sense.

Pope states that there is no way to tell the gender of the speaker in 6:11.[6] Keel argues that the speaker is the man, since he mentions going to the garden (NIV, "grove"), which elsewhere is symbolic of the woman (cf. 1:6; 4:12, 16).[7] However, as Fox notes, 6:11 speaks of a person going down to a garden, and what occurs in 6:12 is a direct consequence of this. Also, the call for the woman to return in 6:13[7:1] only makes sense if she is the one who departed in 6:11.[8] Therefore, it is best to view the woman as the speaker in 6:11–12.[9] Furthermore, the description of the garden in 6:11 is suggestive of the man, rather than the woman. The imagery of stout walnut trees, budding grapevines, and blooming pomegranates are all evocative of male erection and genitalia.[10] Thus, on one level, the woman is stating that she is simply going down to the valley to check if the plant life has burgeoned, but, on another level, she is suggesting what sounds like a sexual encounter with her lover. At this stage of the scene, it is unclear whether the woman is just voicing her

6. Pope, *Song of Songs*, 579.

7. Keel, *The Song of Songs*, 222.

8. Fox, *The Song of Songs and the Ancient Egyptian Love Songs*, 155. cf. Provan, *Ecclesiastes, Song of Songs*, 349.

9. The LXX adds an extra line to 6:11: "There I will give you my breasts." This line also appears at the end of 7:12[7:13]. Whether the Greek translator worked with a Hebrew manuscript that had the extra line in 6:11, or whether he accidentally transposed this line from 7:12[7:13] to 6:11 is a matter of debate. Codex Sinaiticus overtly attributes 6:11 to the man. See Exum, *Song of Songs*, 223.

10. Pope has an extensive study on the sexual symbolism of the walnut, showing how the encased nut was associated with the male glans and the exposed nut with the female vulva. See Pope, *Song of Songs*, 574–83. As Longman (*Song of Songs*, 184) also notes, this kind of association is still evident in English slang today. While Pope's study shows that reference to the walnut can evoke both male and female sexuality, the immediate context views the walnut as a whole tree and, therefore, the encased nut. This is all suggestive of male erection. Furthermore, while the imagery of the pomegranate at 4:13 is evocative of the female breast, here in 6:11 the pomegranate is viewed as part of a tree in bloom, which, with the surrounding imagery, is suggestive of male genitalia.

continued desire for intimacy with her shepherd boy or whether she intends to act upon it. A few verses later (7:1[7:2]), though, it becomes clear that she does act upon it. The predicament of the Song thus heads quickly toward its climactic moment as the woman, pledged in marriage to Solomon, seeks out the shepherd boy whom she loves with the intent of sleeping with him.

The syntax of 6:12 is highly enigmatic in Hebrew and has troubled translators since ancient times. Ancient manuscripts do not make things any clearer. For example, the key manuscript from the Dead Sea Scrolls (4Q106) is almost completely damaged at this point. The LXX has some slight differences to the MT and reads the last part of the verse as a personal name: "My soul did not know; he/she/it set me as [or on] chariots of Aminadab" (cf. KJV, NJPS). Who "Aminadab" is, and what the verse might mean, is impenetrable. Keel argues that the name Amminadab [sic] means "my uncle is a nobleman," and the poem is here playing on that meaning to portray the male figure as "something of a braggart, a dandy like the ambitious Absalom."[11] This argument seems tendentious. Fox suggests minor emendations to the Hebrew text to yield the translation, "I do not know myself—you've placed me in a chariot with a nobleman." He interprets this as the woman being so excited about the encounter with her beloved that she compares it to being paired with a nobleman in a chariot.[12] This is, however, rather oblique. The NIV reads, "Before I realized it, my desire set me among the royal chariots of my people." This reads the first two Hebrew words as a circumstantial clause and runs the rest of the verse together. But again, what this means is elusive.

There are two observations that may shed some light on the obscurity. First, the phrase, "The chariots and horsemen of Israel!" was an exclamation that Israelites used. The prophet Elisha exclaims it in 2 Kings 2:12 as a fiery chariot with fiery horses whisks his master, Elijah, into the sky, never to be seen again. We might think that Elisha was merely blurting out a description of the astonishing event he was witnessing. However, in 2 Kings 13:14, King Jehoash of Israel uses the same exclamation when he sees Elisha on his deathbed. Common to both these episodes is the sudden or imminent departure of someone and consequent feelings of turmoil. Here in Song 6:12 we find a phrase that, while not identical, contains synonymous content and bears the same structure: "The chariots of my noble people." Second, in the next verse (6:13[7:1]) the woman has evidently departed, leaving a group of people to

11. At this point, Keel relies on his theory that the Song is a collection of disparate love poems rather than a single coherent composition, thus obviating the need to connect the meaning of 6:12 to the previous verse. See Keel, *The Song of Songs*, 225–28.

12. Fox, *The Song of Songs and the Ancient Egyptian Love Songs*, 154, 156.

plead for her to come back. It seems plausible, therefore, to read the second half of 6:12 as an exclamation signaling the woman's sudden departure.[13]

This means the first part of the verse (6:12a), which consists of four Hebrew words (*lo' yada'ti napshi samatni*), sits somewhat separately to the exclamation. Two of these four words are verbs ("I knew" and "it set me"), thus forming two distinct but related clauses. As Garrett points out, the first three words ("I did not know myself") are practically identical to an expression in Job 9:21b (*lo' 'eda' napshi*),[14] where it is paralleled with the phrase, "I despise my own life." To not know one's self, then, is to no longer care about one's own life or personal safety.

This leaves us to account for the verb *samatni* ("it set me"). As Exum has suggested, the preceding noun *napshi* ("myself") does double duty as both the object of the first clause ("I did not know myself") and the subject of the second ("my own self set me. . . .").[15] While Exum interprets the thrust of the verse differently, her proposal has syntactical merit, as it logically connects the feminine singular subject of the verb with the feminine singular noun, *napshi* ("myself"). This sees the woman divulge to the reader that her inner person was fixed and resolute. She was determined to embark on a course of action that might imperil her life. We might paraphrase her as saying, "I no longer care for my life. My mind is made up."

Putting all the data together, a coherent picture emerges from 6:11–12. The woman leaves her confines where she is being prepared for marriage to Solomon, whom she does not love. She ostensibly leaves to check on the state of the gardens in the valley (cf. 1:6). Yet, the innuendo in her words reveals that she is seeking a sexual liaison with the shepherd boy whom she loves so dearly. This is not a sudden lapse in judgment or loss of self-control through unbridled passion. It is, rather, a calculated maneuver to force the issue of their romance to a resolution of some kind. In sleeping with her beloved shepherd boy, she is joining herself in a tangible way to him, rather than to Solomon. She also runs the possibility of falling pregnant to the shepherd, thus producing a child that embodies their union, further cementing their relationship and undermining Solomon's claim over her. Like Tamar (Gen 38) and Ruth (Ruth 3), then, the woman is attempting to gain control over her own circumstances and avoid what she sees as an unjust outcome; she does not wish to become one more of Solomon's prolific (and meaningless) sexual conquests.

---

13. A comparable interjection in English is "Good heavens!"

14. Garrett and House, *Song of Songs / Lamentations*, 232. The only difference between the relevant phrases of Job 9:21b and Song 6:12 is the mode of the verb (a *yiqtol* in Job 9:21b, a *qatal* in Song 6:12).

15. Exum, *Song of Songs*, 211, 224.

By embarking on this course of action, the woman is guaranteeing that such an outcome will not occur. She is forcing her brothers either to recognize her union with the shepherd boy and affirm that she belongs to him (cf. Song 2:16; 6:3; 7:10) or uphold Solomon's claim and thus render her liaison with the shepherd boy a capital offense. She is determined either to be with her shepherd boy permanently or be martyred for the love she has for him. Even if tragedy strikes, though, there is still triumph for the woman, for she will have avoided Solomon's harem and experienced intimate union with her beloved shepherd.

Her brothers who, as we shall see, are pivotal in the arrangement with Solomon (8:8–9), stand to lose much if their sister is not presented to Solomon as a virgin. Would they try passing her off as a virgin and risk incurring the king's wrath if he realizes that she has already been with another man? Would they rather openly admit that she has slept with someone else and so risk the execution of their sister and the king's displeasure at their failure to keep her for him? Or would they back out of the arrangement with Solomon and marry her instead to the shepherd as the only legal means for staving off their sister's death? This would then cast Solomon as an outsider with no legal means of interfering in the woman's marriage to the shepherd, though he might make life difficult for them and the woman's brothers. The woman's plan depends on the weight of the law and the disposition of her brothers. Hitherto they have not acted kindly toward her (1:6), but the extreme nature of her circumstances leads her to play this gambit as the only way she might be exonerated, as was the case with Tamar and Ruth. If her plan fails, she would prefer death over repudiating her shepherd boy and marrying Solomon. She expresses this sentiment in 6:12, and it is echoed in 8:6. This is a do-or-die, all-or-nothing attempt to prevent what she feels is the fierce injustice of marrying a man she does not love against her will. Justice demands she marry the one to whom she belongs—her beloved shepherd boy. Aware of the danger, she utters an exclamation that reveals her inner turmoil. Without care for her own life, then, the woman crosses her own Rubicon and seeks out her shepherd boy.

The plea for the woman to return (6:13a[7:1a])[16] substantiates this reconstruction. The fourfold repetition of the imperative, "Come back," gives the sense of a sudden emergency, highlighting the extreme nature and urgency of the woman's sudden action. Exactly who calls her to come back is not immediately apparent. A counter voice later in the verse addresses those calling the woman with a masculine plural verb (*tehezu*), but the daughters of Jerusalem

16. The Hebrew text enumerates Song 6:13 as 7:1, meaning all the verses of chapter 7 differ by one between English and Hebrew.

have been previously addressed with masculine plural verbs and pronouns (e.g., 2:7). The most likely speakers are indeed the daughters of Jerusalem—the queens and concubines who had lauded the woman earlier (6:8–9) and now plead for her to turn back, so they might continue to gaze upon her within their own ranks. However, we cannot discount the town's watchmen, who had earlier caught and abused the woman (5:7), calling after her now to catch and abuse her in voyeuristic fashion once again. In any case, the plea indicates that the woman has fled.[17]

Interestingly, the speakers label the woman as "the Shulammite" (Heb: *shulammit*). This could be an alternative for "Shunammite," marking the woman as a resident of Shunem, a town at the foot of the Galilean hills on the northern edge of the Jezreel Valley (cf. Josh 19:18; 2 Kgs 4:8).[18] Abishag, the young woman who warmed an old and senile David, was a Shunammite (cf. 1 Kgs 1:3), so the term here might indicate an attractive woman destined for the bed of a king. Some point to the root of the name (*shlm*), which denotes peace and wholeness, to surmise that Shulammite means "the perfect one." Comparison is made to Song 6:9, where the man refers to the woman as "my perfect one" (*tammati*), and 8:10 where the woman describes herself as one who brings peace or contentment.[19] Yet, this does not adequately account for the unusual form of the term here. Others have suggested that it is the feminine form of the name Solomon (Heb: *shelomoh*).[20] This is possible, though the expected form of that would be Shelomith (Heb: *shelomit*; cf. Lev 24:11; 1 Chr 3:19). The presence of the definite article also precludes this, even though the article can be translated vocatively ("O Shulammite").

The similarity to Solomon's name is, nevertheless, noteworthy.[21] The term's vowel pattern resembles a passive substantive,[22] which turns the term into a tag indicating Solomon's claim over the woman. She is one who is being

17. Pope (*Song of Songs*, 595) argues that the woman is not being called to return but to "leap," on the basis of a cognate Arabic word and the reference to a dance later in the verse. However, the LXX translates the word as "return" (Greek: *epistrephe*). Furthermore, the root of the word Pope sees here (Heb: *shebi*, from root *yshb*) is used elsewhere in the Song (2:3; 5:12; 8:13) without the meaning of the Arabic cognate. Pope's suggestion is, therefore, unlikely.

18. Goulder, *The Song of Fourteen Songs*, 55. Though "Shulammite" is spelled differently to "Shunammite," they are linguistically similar, as demonstrated by the Arabic name of the town today: Sulam. See Keel, *The Song of Songs*, 228.

19. Fox, *The Song of Songs and the Ancient Egyptian Love Songs*, 157–58; Exum, *Song of Songs*, 227–28.

20. Pope, *Song of Songs*, 596–97; Longman, *Song of Songs*, 192.

21. Cf. Serge Frolov, "No Return for Shulammite: Reflections of Cant 7,1," *ZAW* 110.2 (1998), 257. Frolov surmises that "Shulammite" is indeed a name, but for Bathsheba, the mother of Solomon, rather than for a woman he was marrying.

22. Cf. Robert's suggestion, cited in Fox, *The Song of Songs and the Ancient Egyptian Love Songs*, 157.

"Solomonized." It is more forceful and objectifying than the modern equivalent of "Mrs. Solomon." It characterizes the woman as almost a commodity belonging to Solomon—one of the many women who no longer bear their own name, for their identity has been subsumed under Solomon's. Since the term appears for the first time here,[23] it indicates that the time of the woman's marriage to the king has essentially arrived. The presence of queens and concubines, the woman's decision to sleep with the shepherd boy, her upcoming proposal of spending the night with him in the villages (Song 7:11), and the climax of the Song in chapter 8, all suggest that the woman has taken drastic action on the day before the wedding. The term "Shulammite," therefore, reinforces the notion that she is pledged to Solomon and that she is undertaking an eleventh-hour mission to avoid winding up in the king's harem. After undertaking her mission, she will defiantly declare, "I belong to my beloved" (7:10).

A voice counters the call for the woman to return by asking why they want to gaze upon the Shulammite (6:13b[7:1b]). It is not entirely clear whose voice it is, but the most reasonable candidate is the shepherd. He speaks in the following verse, so he is probably speaking up here to defend the woman he loves. Oddly, he refers to the woman by the term "Shulammite" also—a tag indicating Solomon's (rather than his) claim over her. However, we have already seen the shepherd referring to the woman as a bride even though she was being viewed as Solomon's bride rather than his own (4:8–12; 5:1). This would not, therefore, be an endorsement of Solomon's claim so much as an acknowledgement that he stands little chance of countering it. He might also simply be mirroring the term that the queens and concubines had used of the woman.

The nature of his countering question is puzzling (6:13b[7:1b]). The NIV represents a fairly literal rendering: "Why would you gaze on the Shulammite as on the dance of Mahanaim?" Mahanaim was located just to the east of the central Jordan River, though its significance in this context is unknown. Some view the term not as a toponym but as a common noun signifying "two camps." This might refer to army "camps," which is how the LXX understood it. If so, there is a military image here, which might reflect the historical background of the Song in the military movements of Antiochus IV. The question might even compare gazing at the woman to troops watching a lewd dance for entertainment. The only possibility in which this latter interpretation makes sense is if those calling for the woman's return are the town's watchmen (cf. 5:7). However, "camps" need not refer to army camps in the surface meaning

23. The term appears twice, but both instances are in this verse (6:13[7:1]).

of the Song (cf. Gen 32:7–8; Exod 29:14). The dance in view might be a wedding or even pre-wedding dance, and the "camps" could simply be groups of wedding guests. If so, reference to historical armies would lie beneath the surface meaning of the Song in its metaphorical significance. Whatever the case, the question is obscure enough to prevent absolute certainty about its significance.

Making Love (7:1–10)

In these verses, the woman's planned sexual encounter with her beloved shepherd boy becomes a reality. Numerous commentators understand the passage differently, viewing the ensuing *wasf* as praise of the woman while she is dancing.[24] This interpretation uses the reference to a dance in 6:13 to set the scene for the *wasf*. However, several factors count against this. First, the suggestion requires a very different interpretation of the Song as a whole. Second, it must overlook the protesting voice in 6:13, whose tenor implies it is wrong to gaze at the woman dancing. It is, therefore, unlikely that, after protesting this, we are now indeed gawking at the woman as she dances. Third, if this is a dance, it is a very lewd dance, for it quickly becomes apparent that the man is praising aspects of the woman's body that he could only appreciate if she were unclothed (see below). Fourth, the sexually explicit content of the *wasf* hints that the man is not just looking at the woman but interacting physically with her (7:2, 8–9). It seems more than just his imagination taking liberties here. All this suggests that the woman is not merely dancing but is rather engaging in sexual contact with the man. This is not just innuendo or the expression of sexual energy, but intimacy of the most erotic kind.

The man calls the woman, "noble daughter" (NIV, "prince's daughter"), which means she is either the daughter of a prominent man or, more likely, that her upcoming marriage to the king bestows nobility on her and her wider family.

The man describes the woman's body, ascending from her feet to her head. The sensuality escalates from 7:1b, as he celebrates the curve of her thighs (NIV, "graceful legs"). The NIV translates 7:2a as, "Your navel is a rounded goblet that never lacks blended wine." As Longman points out, though, the navel is not associated with moistness.[25] Indeed, the idea seems somewhat farcical in such an erotic context. The order of praise the man follows also implies that he has not yet reached the woman's actual navel at this point, for

24. Goulder, *The Song of Fourteen Songs*, 55; Carr, *Song of Solomon*, 156; Provan, *Ecclesiastes, Song of Songs*, 352.

25. Longman, *Song of Songs*, 194–95; cf. Pope, *Song of Songs*, 615–16.

in 7:2b, he praises her "belly" (NIV, "waist"), which is "bordered by lilies" (NIV, "encircled by lilies")—a clear allusion to pubic hair at the base of the belly. The "navel," therefore, is more likely an allusion to the vulva.[26] The imagery of a goblet is evocative of cunnilingus, while "blended wine" evokes either vaginal moistness, especially during sexual arousal, or even semen. From there, he adores her pubic region (7:2b), her breasts (7:3), her neck (7:4a), and finally her face and head (7:4b–5). Particularly poignant is the royal imagery he employs. He describes the woman's hair as "thread" of "purple" (NIV, "royal tapestry"), alluding not to its actual color, but to majesty associated with the color, before concluding, "the king is held captive by its tresses" (7:5). While the man is enjoying the sexual delights of the woman he loves, we are reminded that, in reality, the woman is still pledged to the king. His comment casts the woman as Solomon's conqueror, upending the whole predicament of the Song. The enactment of love between the woman and the shepherd has effectively checked Solomon's game of conquest, which makes an historical statement that Antiochus IV's decrees outlawing traditional worship of Yahweh are defeated by Yahweh's people continuing to devote themselves to their true God and his laws. It provides a glimmer of hope that the woman might escape Solomon's clutches. But the story is not yet at an end, so we cannot yet call this a "checkmate." In the midst of sexual passion, therefore, the comment in 7:5 focuses our attention on the Song's dilemma and heightens the tension.

The factuality of this sexual encounter between the lovers comes through most strongly in 7:6–9, as the man adores the woman's beauty, praises the pleasure she induces by her lovemaking, fondles her breasts, and kisses her passionately. In 7:9b the NIV marks a clear break between the man's words and the woman's response, but in Hebrew, the words of the two lovers run seamlessly together, so that she completes his sentence. This poetic device demonstrates the complete intimate union of the two, leading the woman to declare defiantly and triumphantly, "I belong to my beloved, and his desire is for me." The word "desire" here is the same word used in Genesis 3:16 when God curses the woman, and Genesis 4:7 to describe sin's desire for Cain. The word is not overtly sexual. Rather, it denotes a kind of animal instinct—the desire that a predator has for its prey, which is why it occurs in negative contexts in Genesis. Here in the Song, the word indicates two things. First, it indicates the man is wildly in love with the woman, which has led them to share a primal instinct of passion together. The same could not be said for the distant Solomon who does not know the woman and, at best, can only

26. Pope (*Song of Songs*, 615) suggests a connection between the Hebrew word used here, *shor* (from root *shrr*), and an Arabic cognate, *sirr*, meaning "secret," "pudenda," "coition," and "fornication."

be "in lust" with her. More than this, though, the woman is declaring that her beloved shepherd has had his way with her. She has become his conquest, so she rightly belongs to him, not to Solomon. This does not imply that the shepherd has treated her as a commodity or object of lust, but that they have shared sexual intimacy. Behind it lies the essential description of the covenantal relationship, that Yahweh chose Israel to be his people, and so Yahweh is Israel's God (cf. Lev 26:12; Deut 7:6; 14:2; 1 Chr 17:22).

A Forbidden Relationship (7:11–8:4)

In Song 7:11–13, the woman desires to escape with her beloved shepherd to the countryside and spend the night with him there, and the next morning go to the vineyards with him. There is a sense of urgency and longing in her speech and the compressed timeframe. The lovers have finally enjoyed each other's bodies, but this only breeds yearning for yet further intimacy. Thus, the woman's words still exude sensuality and innuendo, recycling some of the imagery used earlier in the Song. She also appeals to the fragrance of mandrakes, which were a common aphrodisiac and fertility drug in the ancient world (cf. Gen 30:14–17), and encourages her lover with the delicacies she has stored up for him (Song 7:13). She is not simply suggesting a pleasant picnic, but further opportunity for sexual intimacy in the small time remaining to them.

Despite their time together, the relationship of the woman and her beloved shepherd remains forbidden, for she is still pledged to marry Solomon. This leads her to pine for different circumstances in which their relationship could be conducted more openly, even if still incognito (8:1–2).[27] Thus, she wishes she could pass her beloved shepherd off as her brother, so that they might interact more freely, show each other signs of affection in public, and even come to the same house together without raising suspicion. She would then be able to give him "spiced wine to drink," and "the nectar of my pomegranates" (8:2)—another thinly veiled allusion to intercourse. The historical circumstance behind the imagery is the desire to bring the rightful sacrificial cult of Yahweh back to his house in Jerusalem, overturning the decree of Antiochus IV, which had turned it into a temple to Olympian Zeus. For now, though, the lovers are together for just a night, expressing their affection for each other in lovemaking (8:3) and enacting their attempt to subvert the claim of Solomon over the woman (8:4).

Verses 3–4 essentially repeat the sentiment of 2:6–7, but whereas the

27. This also demonstrates why the woman's lover cannot be Solomon. If the lover were Solomon, who is a king, there would be no need to hide the relationship.

woman had earlier imagined the man's embrace (2:6), now it is real (8:3). She had earlier charged the daughters of Jerusalem not to awaken love before it desired (2:7), and she does so again here (8:4), though this time with slightly different phrasing. The previous instances of the adjuration (2:7; 3:5) used the Hebrew conjunction *'im* (literally, "if"), which is a standard way that Hebrew expresses oaths. Here, though, the woman uses the interrogative word *mah*, which usually asks "what?" but which in the Hebrew dialect of the Song also expresses the question "how?" (cf. 4:10; 5:9; 6:13–7:1[7:1–2]). This effectively gives the adjuration a more accusatory feel: "How could you arouse, and how could you awaken love before it desires!" The adjuration has thus become a charge. The woman also omits the reference to the gazelles and does of the field, which were present in the previous expressions of the adjuration. This makes the charge brief and urgent. Now that she has slept with her beloved shepherd, the charge carries greater significance. Before this point, the charge (2:7; 3:5) simply provided a positive evaluation of the woman's love for the shepherd and a negative evaluation of Solomon's claim over her. Love has awakened between the woman and the shepherd boy, so their union in marriage would be natural and just. It would be a travesty to prevent it. Yet, love has never awakened between her and the king; therefore, her prospective marriage to him is against her will, against love itself, and a miscarriage of justice. Now, the charge highlights how unjust it is that the woman has had to take matters into her own hands and pursue what would ordinarily be an improper course of action—sleeping with a man out of wedlock—to enable justice to prevail. She has acted under extreme duress to prevent her own rape. The charge, therefore, now conveys the sentiment that it should never have come to this, but it has. The woman has been unjustly driven to take this extreme action. This is not a case of mistakenly thinking that two wrongs make a right, but rather that, as in Tamar's situation, drastic measures must be taken to stop those who hold power over the woman.

Love as Strong as Death (8:5–7)

After spending the night together, the lovers have crossed their personal Rubicon and now emerge on the other side to see what will come of their actions. Will their relationship be affirmed, allowing them to marry? Or will they be condemned for immorality and face death as a consequence?

Their arrival is announced with the rhetorical question, "Who is this coming up from the wilderness leaning on her beloved?" (8:5a). In 3:6 a similar rhetorical question announced the ominous arrival of Solomon and his armed procession in the woman's dream—an allusion to the perilous arrival of Antiochus IV's armies from the desert in 167 BC. In 6:10 it announced the woman had been prepared to become Solomon's bride, again with undertones of Antiochus's movements. Now, a similar question is asked. Once again, the speaker is not identified; as we will see, it is most likely the woman's brothers speaking here. The lovers' time together has been characterized as a nut grove and a valley (6:11), villages in the countryside (7:11), and a vineyard (7:12). It seems incongruous, then, that they are now seen coming from the "wilderness" (8:5). This is symbolic, even as the more fertile locations are, too. The lovers may feel they are emerging from blissful, romantic surrounds, but to others, they are emerging from the hostile desert. As in 3:6, the reference to the "wilderness" (8:5) evokes the arrival of an enemy. Though there is no overtly condemning word here, the tone is ominous. Those witnessing the couple's arrival see them in negative light, suggesting that the speakers here are probably the woman's brothers, who will respond to their sister's actions in 8:8. Beneath the surface, the imagery harkens back to the classic motif that Yahweh brought Israel out of the desert and into his land (cf. Deut 2:7; 8:15; 29:5).

The woman then speaks to her beloved shepherd in Song 8:5b–7. It is not clear whether the other characters can hear this conversation, but her words are emblazoned with defiance and tinged with deep sadness. Her first words, "Under the apple tree I roused you" (8:5b), are an admission that she has slept with him. In 2:3 she had declared her desire for intimacy with him by comparing him to an apple tree, whose fruit she desired to taste, and now it is the location of her "rousing" him. The Hebrew verb used for the expression "I roused you" (*ʿorartika*) can also mean "I stripped you" (cf. Isa 32:11), suggesting the removal of clothes. The sexual connotations are also reinforced by the reference to conception. Moreover, her word choice picks up the language of the adjuration in the previous verse (8:4). Love has indeed been "roused" between the two lovers. The situation preventing their union has necessitated the controversial and premature "rousing" of their intimacy and sparked the accusatory tone of the charge to the daughter of Jerusalem in 8:4.

The pathos of 8:6–7 is palpable. These are arguably the most important verses of the entire Song. In them, the woman prepares her beloved shepherd for the very real possibility of their separation and perhaps even her death. The two have risked everything to be together, but they have no guarantee that they will succeed. Moreover, the question of 8:5 has been ominous. She thus asks him to place her like a seal over his heart and on his arm (8:6). The idea of her being permanently stamped on him carries different significance depending on how their future unfolds. If they are permitted to remain together, the idea conveys their permanent union in marriage. If they are not so permitted, the idea becomes a way of the shepherd remembering her when she's gone—of imprinting her on his memory. It highlights the prospect that the woman may not survive the ensuing fracas over their actions, but he stands the possibility of escaping. Whatever occurs, the plea captures the desperation of their situation and the unyielding love they have for each other.

This is further captured in the reason she gives for asking him: "for love is as strong as death, passion as fierce as Sheol" (8:6b; NIV, "its jealousy unyielding as the grave").[28] Though death may separate them, yet his gesture of setting her as a seal on his heart will be a permanent testament to their love and passion. The Hebrew at this point is replete with sophisticated devices. The second colon reads *qashah kishe'ol qin'ah* ("passion as fierce as Sheol" [author's translation]), containing alliteration and rhyme. The word for "fierce" (NIV, "unyielding"), *qashah*, has the sense of something firm and tenacious, as well as harsh and cruel. The woman's words, therefore, carry a double entendre that conveys both the tenacity of their love as well as the cruelty of the situation that would tear them apart and even kill them. The poetry thus beautifully captures the emotional upheaval of the two lovers.

The woman continues to describe the effects of love in 8:6c. The NIV translates this, "It burns like blazing fire, like a mighty flame." The first part of this couplet is better rendered, "Its arrows are flaming arrows," with the word for "arrow" (*reshep*) related to Resheph, the Canaanite god of death, plague, and the underworld.[29] Resheph is often depicted as an archer inflicting destruction with his fiery darts.[30] Modern audiences would be familiar with the parallel of a baby-like cupid playfully firing arrows at unsuspecting individuals who suddenly find themselves inexplicably falling in love. However, this is a development of the Roman mythology of the boyish deity, Cupid, whose arrows infected his victims with uncontrollable feelings of either love or revulsion, which changed their destiny. The imagery here in the Song is more austere than mischievous. Though not a plain reference to Resheph, the imagery portrays love as a series of unquenchable volleys aimed at the two lovers, changing their destinies. It conveys both the fervency of their undying affection, as well as the destructiveness of their predicament. Behind the destructive imagery is probably an allusion to the Seleucid massacre of faithful Jews in Jerusalem in 167 BC (2 Macc 5:11–14, 24–26).

The second part of the couplet has generated significant discussion. What the NIV translates as "like a mighty flame" is a single word in Hebrew, *shalhebetyah*. It is quite irregular in form and appears only here in the entire

28. Sheol is the name of the underworld in the Hebrew mindset, where all departed persons go.

29. Resheph is attested throughout Syria, Phoenicia, Egypt, and is even depicted in Habakkuk 3:5 as an employed attendant of Yahweh. In Mesopotamia, the deity Nergal had a similar function to Resheph.

30. Pope, *Song of Songs*, 670.

Bible. Debate rages over whether the *-yah* element is a contraction of the divine name, Yahweh, and if so, what this could mean, or what the word means otherwise. The Hebrew root of the word (*lhb*) denotes a "flame," which makes sense of the parallelism to "flaming arrows." If the *-yah* element refers to Yahweh, then the woman would be describing love as a flaming arrow fired by Yahweh, thus portraying the deity as a wreaker of havoc upon the lives of unsuspecting victims. The primary idea, then, is that love surprises people, but turns them into victims of divine mischief. While not impossible, this depiction of Yahweh is difficult to sustain in a canonical context. The LXX understood the *-yah* element as a pronominal suffix (*-eyha*), translating the whole word as "its flames," but this makes little contextual sense.

The best option for understanding *shalhebetyah* is as an intensive form that indicates not just a "mighty flame," but an "inferno." This disconnects the word from any reference to Yahweh but captures the theme of the Song at this point. The imagery plays on both the utility and destructiveness of fire. Love and passion can ignite suddenly and bring people together in a bright and fervid union. But they can also be utterly destructive if the circumstances surrounding the lovers are "flammable," igniting an inferno that can destroy lives. Since love is an unquenchable fire, nothing can put it out or sweep it away—not even many waters or rivers (Song 8:7a). It will burn either for the good of the lovers or for their destruction.

Furthermore, the auditory quality of the word *shalhebetyah* produces an unmistakable allusion to the *bet yah*—the "house of Yahweh"—as it is pronounced. That is, although the word itself simply means "inferno," the Hebrew ear cannot help but detect a surreptitious allusion to the "house of Yahweh" within it. Once again, this picks up the historical milieu behind the Song, in which the temple of Yahweh had been turned into a temple dedicated to Olympian Zeus, thus outlawing the traditional worship of Yahweh (2 Macc 6:1–2). Here, then is a sly, coded reference to Yahweh's temple, which the faithful Jewish reader could not overlook. By hiding this reference to the "house of Yahweh" in plain sight, we see the subversive nature of the Song. Part of its message, then, is that the faithful Jew will still be devoted to Yahweh and his temple, even if that devotion is outlawed and driven by necessity underground.

In Song 8:7b the woman completes her speech with a proverbial statement on how society values wealth above love. If someone chose love over wealth, society would scorn them. In saying this, the woman makes a contrast between the inestimable value of love and relationship above all things, and the impoverishment of a society that devalues love in favor of riches. This provides a justification for her own actions, for by throwing her lot in with the humble shepherd boy whom she loves, she is foregoing the fabulous wealth of

Solomon. In her estimation, this is a worthwhile exchange. Yet, this proverbial statement also sounds the ominous note that the woman could lose everything for the sake of love. If society scorns someone giving away their wealth in the name of love, then how much more would they scorn a person who would give away their life for love?

Once again, there is also a veiled allusion to the circumstances of the Antiochene persecution. The overt reference to a "house" in 8:7b is highly suggestive of the temple in Jerusalem, especially after the ear of the faithful Jew picks up the coded reference to the "house of Yahweh" in the previous verse. We see in 8:7b the skillful allusion to two things. The first, in line with the previous verse, is that faithful Jews would be devoted to Yahweh and his temple, no matter the cost. They would be willing to give up all their earthly goods to remain faithful to Yahweh. The second is an allusion to the high priest Menelaus. In order to get and maintain his position as high priest, he had to pilfer the treasury and paraphernalia of the temple and deliver it to the Seleucid authorities (2 Macc 4:23–32, 45). It was one of many things that made Menelaus so despised in the eyes of faithful Jews. It played directly into the desire of Antiochus, who seems to have been in the habit of plundering temples to fund his ambitions (cf. 2 Macc 5:15–16, 21). The proverbial quality of 8:7b, then, captures both the cost of faithfulness to Yahweh and the despicable quality of the Jewish leaders like Menelaus, who had charge of the nation.

The Brothers' Deliberations (8:8–10)

The proverbial statement of 8:7b prepares us for the response of the woman's brothers (Song 8:8–9) and the climactic finale (8:11–14), in which wealth and love are juxtaposed. Some interpreters view the brothers' words here as playful banter,[31] but the severity of the woman's actions and the gravity of her immediately preceding words demand otherwise. The woman has given her virginity to her beloved shepherd, throwing the arrangement to marry her to Solomon into jeopardy. The spotlight now falls on her guardian brothers to see how they respond.

The brothers seem to be speaking amongst themselves, though this is not entirely certain. They refer to their sister as "young," noting that "her breasts are not yet grown" (8:8). Some commentators surmise that these verses are a flashback or quote from the time of the woman's preadolescence,[32] but this

31. Segal, "The Song of Songs," 480–81; Fox, *The Song of Songs and the Ancient Egyptian Love Songs*, 172–73; Longman, *Song of Songs*, 215.

32. Gledhill, *Message of the Song of Songs*, 235; Longman, *Song of Songs*, 216.

is not necessary. The Hebrew expression "young" is just as easily rendered "younger," and the woman counters her brothers' claims that she has no breasts by declaring boldly, "my breasts are like towers" (8:10). It seems, then, that the brothers are trying to downplay their sister's maturity. They might also be subtly alluding to the fact that, even though she has now slept with a man, her breasts have not yet swelled in confirmation of a pregnancy, giving them leeway to pass her off as still virginal. Hence, their question, "What shall we do about [NIV, "for"] our sister on the day she is spoken for?"

The phrase, "on the day she is spoken for," has a double meaning. The Song's storyline has primed us for the more obvious nuance that this refers to the day she is married to a suitor (cf. 1 Sam 25:39), but the syntax of the Hebrew expression can also mean, "the day she is spoken against" (cf. Num 12:1; Ps 50:20). The woman has exposed herself to accusations of adultery by sleeping with the shepherd boy whilst she is pledged to Solomon, and her brothers now acknowledge this. Several commentators interpret their words as a discussion of how to protect their sister's chastity in the years before she marries, but they are not discussing what to do *before* she marries, but what to do *when* she marries. In other words, their problem does not consist of how to preserve their sister's virginity, but of what to do now that she is no longer a virgin. It is about damage control, not damage prevention.

The brothers entertain two scenarios, each expressed as an "If . . . , then . . ." proposition. In the first scenario (Song 8:9a), they consider the possibility that their sister is a "wall." This characterizes her as chaste and virginal, having resisted all sexual advances. It also characterizes any would-be sexual partners as invading enemies. The brothers seem to be the ones who saw their sister emerging "from the wilderness leaning on her beloved" (8:5), so they know she is not a "wall" (i.e., a virgin). It is probable, therefore, that they are discussing how others (especially the king) might perceive their sister on the day of her wedding. That is, after all, the more pressing question at this point. If others think their sister is a "wall" (i.e., chaste), then the brothers will build "a battlement of silver upon her" (NIV, "towers of silver on her"). A battlement was a defensive parapet at the top of a city wall that provided soldiers with a pathway for patrolling the wall as well as a shield from enemy fire below.[33] These were made of either stone or wood. A silver battlement would have been strategically pointless—an ostentatious waste of resources. The metaphor, then, is not about what the brothers can do for their sister, but what she can

33. The Hebrew word for "battlement" here (*tirah*) can also denote an enclosed encampment, kraal, or even a ledge. The context here in the Song, which places it on top of a wall, demands the meaning "battlement."

do for them. It implies that if their sister is perceived as a chaste virgin when she marries the king, they stand to make a fortune (cf. the reference to silver in 8:11b) that will elevate them in society and put them in the clear. Their rise to wealth and status will be built on perceptions of her chastity, which only need to last until her wedding night. This would have been the outcome they were hoping for, but their sister's radical actions have now jeopardized this.

Thus, they consider a second scenario (8:9b), in which they characterize their sister as a "door." In contrast to the wall, this imagery portrays the sister as sexually active—someone who has opened her body to a man (cf. 5:5). It also implies her sexual partner, the shepherd boy, is an invading enemy who has penetrated her. If she is perceived this way, the brothers state they will need to "enclose her with panels of cedar." Since cedars only grew at altitude in the mountains of Lebanon, cedar wood was hard to come by, but it was strong and durable. Only monarchs and the fabulously rich could afford to use it. The implication here is that the brothers will need to go to herculean lengths to counteract their sister's sexual activity and maintain the king's interest in her. They may not be able to undo the fact that their sister's "door" has been opened (i.e., she has lost her virginity), and others might suspect this of her, too. In this case, the brothers will need to convince others, especially the king, that they have ensured her "door" has not been opened. They do not elaborate on how they might achieve this, as they speak only in metaphors, but they signal their intention to try.

Both scenarios that the brothers entertain show that they do not intend to give their sister in marriage to the shepherd. They also imply the shepherd is an unwanted outsider who must be repelled. At the same time, they also do not want their sister put to death for promiscuity. Yet, nothing in their speech suggests they want to avoid her death out of concern for her. In fact, the characterization of the brothers in Song 1:6 as, in some way, hostile to their sister, means we read their words here as self-serving rather than caring. It seems, then, that the brothers are intent on marrying their sister to the king, despite her extreme actions to prevent this.

The brothers' deliberations spell disaster for the woman. In 8:10 she protests, asserting that she is not a "door" but a "wall" (8:10a), the implication being that she has been chaste. We might be tempted to think that she is lying, since she has evidently slept with the shepherd. However, she is using her brothers' metaphor to show them that, while it might appear that she has acted improperly, she has acted as properly as the injustice of her extreme situation demanded, just as Tamar and Ruth did. She rightly belongs to the shepherd, and her adverse circumstances have forced her to make this a reality. She has been chaste toward him, for she belongs to him.

She also turns the tables on who the real invading enemy is that should be kept out; it is not the shepherd, but Solomon. The woman has acted appropriately to defend herself like a wall against the king's "invasion." In this regard, the imagery of Solomon's entourage from her dream takes on new significance. The king was pictured there arriving from the wilderness with armed warriors ready for battle (3:6–8), but the woman has acted to repel his attack. By preventing her own rape, she has acted as a "wall," not a door. And she refuses to treat her beloved shepherd as an enemy. On the contrary, in his eyes she has brought him peace, not hostility (8:10b). The Hebrew word for peace, *shalom*, is similar to "Solomon" (Heb: *shelomoh*), yet discernibly different, which poetically reinforces her own will: she chooses peace (*shalom*) with her shepherd, even if that means hostility with Solomon (*shelomoh*). Her words radiate defiance against her brothers' intentions, setting the scene for a fretful finale.

The Finale (8:11–14)

The finale begins with a short narrative about Solomon owning a vineyard in Baal Hamon (8:11). All the pieces of the Song's puzzle now fall into place, allowing us to re-read the whole Song with renewed clarity. The most likely speaker is the woman, since she speaks in 8:12 where she continues the theme of the vineyard from 8:11. But the content of 8:11 is more pivotal than the speaker's identity. Throughout the Song, Solomon has been a distant figure, whose existence has only been inferred (1:4, 12; 6:8–9; 7:5) and who has been seen only in a dream (3:6–11). Now, his presence is felt more substantively. Solomon has arrived, and with him the moment of doom that the couple have been dreading.

The Apocryphal book of Judith mentions a place near Dothan in the northern foothills of Ephraim called Balamon (Judith 8:3), which seems to be a Greek rendering of Hebrew's Baal Hamon.[34] This was a well-known wine growing region, so we may have here a historical reminiscence of Solomon's local holdings. More important than the factuality of such a place is the significance of its name. It means both "owner of plenty" and "husband of a throng." Furthermore, throughout the Song the vineyard motif is metaphorical of the woman's body and her sexuality (1:6; 2:15), as well as a place of intimacy (7:12). Solomon is being depicted as a polygamous plutocrat. He has unfettered access to female sexuality, and yet he seeks to add another female to his fold—the woman of the Song.

34. The LXX transliterates the toponym as *Beelamon*, which is different to the form in Judith 8:3, but linguistically similar enough to facilitate a match.

The claim that Solomon let out his vineyard to tenants emphasizes the prolific scale of his harem. It could mean, as Longman argues, that Solomon could not handle the size of his harem alone and therefore needed subordinate guards to manage it.[35] It could also signify that he hired agents to stock his harem with more women, like gardeners tending a productive vineyard. The NIV assumes that it is the "tenants" who "bring for its fruit a thousand shekels of silver" (8:11b), but this would be an odd situation, both for the plain meaning and its metaphorical significance. On the surface, no one would pay such an exorbitant price for fruit or wine. The figure is, in any case, a hyperbole for a grand sum. On the metaphorical level, it is not clear why the guards of the harem are paying, or even what they are paying for. Instead, there is an ambiguity in the Hebrew phrasing that permits the more likely interpretation that the vineyards' keepers received payments from others, rather than made payments themselves. The nature of these payments is also vague, due to the inherent flexibility in the generic Hebrew preposition (*be-*) attached to the word for "fruit." The NIV views the payment as an exchange: a thousand silver shekels "for" the fruit of the vineyard. However, it is grammatically more likely, and contextually more plausible, that a person would bring a thousand silver shekels "in" fruit to the keepers of the vineyard. This is how the LXX understood the phrase. Putting all the data together, the surface meaning is that Solomon had a vineyard, which he put into the charge of keepers, and the workers of the vineyard would produce up to a thousand silver shekels worth of fruit, which they would give to the keepers, and which ultimately went to Solomon for his consumption. In terms of the storyline of the Song, it implies that Solomon used agents to acquire women for his harem, and the right woman could fetch up to a thousand silver shekels for the man who presented her for the king's pleasure.

This reconstruction of the text intersects with several themes and motifs. First, the reference to a "thousand" shekels is evocative of Solomon's one thousand women (1 Kgs 11:3). Second, it illuminates the brothers' deliberations. Their hope was to build a "silver battlement" (NIV, "towers of silver") on their sister's "wall" (Song 8:9), which is now explained as their hope to fetch up to a thousand shekels of "silver" for presenting their sister for marriage to the king. Third, in 1:6 the woman stated that her brothers made her tend the vineyards to the neglect of her own. We see more fully now how this early statement depicts the brothers as scheming to place their obstreperous sister in the king's harem ("vineyard") for their own personal gain. They have no thought for her feelings or how this violates her relationship with her beloved shepherd.

35. Longman, *Song of Songs*, 219.

The brothers consider their sister a commodity to be traded (cf. 8:9) rather than a person to be respected. And fourth, we see how the king's intention to bring the woman into his chambers (1:4) is about Solomon acquiring yet another woman for his harem and how the brothers hope to gain from his royal sexual appetite.

In 8:12 the woman addresses Solomon directly. There is no indication here that Solomon or his agents know anything is amiss, for we never hear their voices. Indeed, at this final climactic moment, the Song gives us just two voices: the woman's and the shepherd's. All others fall mute, though we know the characters must be there, for the woman here addresses Solomon, and the next verse alludes to some male company (NIV, "friends"). Her words also give the impression that she is about to be traded in marriage, as her brothers' have planned. Yet she is openly intransigent, refusing to cooperate with them and yield herself to the clutches of the king and his henchmen. She dissents, "My own vineyard is before me" (NIV, "But my own vineyard is mine to give"), whereas Solomon has his thousand shekels worth of fruit, and his vineyard keepers have their cut of two hundred shekels (8:12b). Her words contrast her own humble circumstances and desires toward her lone shepherd with the wanton proclivities of the polygamous plutocrat, Solomon. With this bold statement, the woman denies Solomon's claim over her, as well as her brothers' plot to give her to him. She is strictly off-limits to the king, who already has a prolific harem for his own indulgence. None but she has the right to determine what happens to her own "vineyard"—that is, her own person. As we have already seen, she has shared her "vineyard" with her beloved shepherd.

The woman's brave recalcitrance leads us to ponder how her brothers and Solomon will react. Though we never hear Solomon speak, the woman's forthright rhetoric has told him that he cannot have his way with her as previously surmised, but the woman has not specifically alluded to her beloved shepherd either. Thus, we are still unsure as to what outcome awaits her. Will Solomon see only a truculent young lass who does not wish to marry him, or will he perceive a lascivious and promiscuous woman who, despite his claim over her, has already given herself to another man?

At this tense moment, the shepherd speaks up (8:13). Though it is not immediately clear that it is he speaking, the woman's response to him in the next verse confirms it. He does not refer to her as his "darling," as he has nine times before (1:9, 15; 2:2, 10, 13; 4:1, 7; 5:2; 6:4), but more distantly as "You who dwell in the gardens." Though not openly endearing, this appellation picks up imagery that portrays the woman as ready to offer her personal delights to a suitor. Given the intensity of the situation surrounding the woman, the shepherd's presence is somewhat surprising. There are male "companions listening attentively" to her voice (NIV, "friends in attendance")—an indication that the woman's brothers, Solomon, and presumably his agents are around the woman at this very moment. It paints a threatening picture, and yet we find the shepherd there also, evidently within earshot of his beloved. If he were not present, there would be no chance at all of him being able to marry the woman he loves, for she would presumably be given to Solomon against her will. But his presence ensures a different outcome, for in speaking up he effectively identifies himself as the man whom the woman loves. With all around her listening attentively to what she will say next, he urges her, "let me hear your voice!" It is a call for her to acknowledge him openly as the one she wishes to marry. His words raise the stakes, for either Solomon will relent and accede to the woman marrying the shepherd, with whom she has already been, or they will both be branded adulterers and put to death.

We might think the shepherd's intrusion at this critical moment is suicidal. Surely at this stage it is wishful thinking to hope he could still marry his beloved. His presence puts both himself and the woman at grave risk. Yet, as the woman has already stated, "Love is as strong as death, passion as fierce as Sheol" (8:6, author's translation). If the couple cannot be together, then they will die together. Even though his presence exposes them both to mortal danger, the shepherd is here being true to his love and commitment to his beloved. She belongs to him, and he belongs to her (2:16; 6:3; 7:10), and so they will not be parted, even at this unpromising moment. Furthermore, in speaking up, the shepherd expresses what we as readers hope for. We have seen the romance of this humble couple, witnessed the intensity of their passion, and observed the tenacity of their love in the face of adversity. We therefore hope, along with the shepherd, that he hears the voice of his beloved, and that against all odds, they might somehow triumph together. With this small but glowing hope, all attention now focuses on what the woman says.

So the Song reaches its dramatic final moment (8:14). The woman turns to her beloved shepherd and utters words that are similar to what she told him when he had come to her at night (2:17). Back then, for fear of being found out, she had urged him to "turn" (*sob*) and head back to the hills. Now, she is even more insistent, beseeching him to "Run away" (*berah*). The NIV translates this as "Come away, my beloved," which sounds like an invitation for the shepherd to join her in departing together. She bids him to flee and "be like a gazelle or like a young stag on the spice-laden mountains." Provan dubs this "an immediate invitation to sexual consummation," reading the spice-laden mountains as a reference to the woman's breasts,[36] but this depends on

36. Provan, *Ecclesiastes, Song of Songs*, 372.

a sudden change of tone and must overcome the plain meaning of the Hebrew imperative *berah* ("run away"). Provan's interpretation, however, highlights the effect the verse has on us as readers. We want the woman to quit the scene with her beloved shepherd and live happily ever after with him, and so we want to interpret the imperative *berah* as the NIV has. Unfortunately, the woman uses a singular imperative ("run away") rather than a plural cohortative ("let us run away"). She wants the shepherd to make good his escape to some faraway land. As he has wished, he has heard her voice (8:13), but her words, full of concern for him, imply her own doom.

The Song finishes abruptly at this doleful point. It is both a tragic and ambiguous ending, for while it hints at the woman's piteous demise, we never actually see it. Nor are we permitted to hear the shepherd's response or see the actions of those surrounding the woman. This leaves us to imagine what happens as the woman's words fade from our ears. As readers, we hope for a happy ending and so imagine the shepherd valiantly plucking her from the clutches of those who surround her and escaping with her to a distant land, there to live out their days together in blissful isolation. In our minds, this would provide them with poetic justice. But the Song's tragic trajectory also has us imagining less favorable outcomes. We might imagine the woman's words triggering action from those around her, leading to the capture of her beloved shepherd, and his demise also. Or we might imagine him escaping lunging hands and brandished weapons and setting off into the distance to live out the rest of his life in lonely, broken misery, his beloved ever set as a seal over his heart (8:6).

Whatever postscript we might imagine, the finale gives clarity to the entire Song, inviting us to listen to it again with greater understanding. As we return to its beginning, we encounter the name of Solomon in the title (1:1) and cannot but hear echoes of a villainous playboy king who ruins the lives of two innocent young people sharing a beautiful romance. We come across the brothers (1:6) and feel contempt for the way they treat their sister as a commodity. We once more find a young woman who has fallen fatefully in love with a simple shepherd boy (1:2–3). Thus, along with the daughters of Jerusalem, we celebrate her and memorialize him (1:4).

LIVE the Story

Metaphorical Significance: God and his People

Jews would have read the Song in its original Hellenistic milieu and seen in the Song's meaning a deeper significance. They would have compared the woman's fate to their situation under the Ptolemies and the Seleucids, especially Antiochus IV. Like the woman, who wanted nothing more than to be with her beloved shepherd, so faithful Jews wanted nothing more than to live under the rule of their true shepherd, Yahweh—to live securely in the land, to worship unhindered at Yahweh's temple in Jerusalem, and to be under the authority of a legitimate Jewish ruler, namely, a Davidic king. Yet, like the brothers in the Song, who did not care for their sister adequately and were motivated by ambition to offer her up to Solomon for the sake of financial gain and higher standing in society, so the leaders of Judaism in the Hellenistic Era sold out many of their countrymen. They sought economic benefit at the expense of the welfare of their compatriots, compromising biblical principles and hopes for the sake of higher standing in society. The poor decisions of Onias II and the opportunism of Joseph Tobias in the 220s BC come to mind (see Introduction to Ecclesiastes for further discussion), as does the competition between Jason and Menelaus over the high priesthood in the lead up to the Antiochene persecution and the Maccabean Revolt in 167 BC. Under the Ptolemies, thousands of Jews emigrated from Judea to Alexandria, the hub of the Ptolemies. This represented a compromise of stout biblical hope and concession to Hellenistic ideals that changed the complexion of much of Judaism.

The inexorable cultural and economic pressure that Hellenism inflicted on Jewish identity and hopes was so strong during this time that it led many to despair of Judaism's future, as Qohelet demonstrates. In the years after 174 BC, Jason and Menelaus undertook a policy that turned Jerusalem into a fully-fledged Greek polis, paving the way for Antiochus IV to pursue his policies that so damaged the Jewish nation. His persecution of Judaism (167 BC) exploited the Hellenistic leanings among many Jews at the time to such an extent that it threatened the very life of biblical faith and its adherents. Indeed, he outlawed exclusive devotion to Yahweh, which meant that Jews determined to be exclusively loyal to the God of Israel had to engage in officially illegal activities. The plan of the woman in the Song to follow a course of action that others would perceive as immoral, and her willingness to face death rather than capitulate to Solomon captures this dilemma. If love is as strong as death (8:6), then biblical faith in God was worth dying for. Indeed, many did die for it during the Antiochene persecution (cf. 2 Macc 7). Yet, by ending abruptly without us witnessing the woman's fate, the Song leaves some room for hope that God might act in an unexpected way to save his people. The woman's final words (Song 8:14) for her shepherd to act as a "gazelle" (*tsebi*) and a "young stag" (*'oper ha'ayyalim*) evokes the oath by which she adjures the daughters of Jerusalem (2:7), with its veiled allusion to the similar sounding

"God" (*'elohim*) of "Hosts" (*tsebaot*). These words are thus transformed into a prayer for God to act.[37]

In the person of Jesus, this is precisely what God did. Becoming incarnate as a human, God entered the fray of Judaism's plight and rescued his faithful. He overcame all other claims over them, purchasing them with his own blood, and transforming them into his new people, the church.

From the Song to the Gospel

The Song ends on an abrupt and somewhat dissatisfying note that leaves us imagining what happens next. In one sense, this spares us witnessing a grim fate for the woman and having all our hopes for her and the shepherd dashed completely. It bequeaths to us the faintest flicker of hope, which effectively invites us to write our own postscript. By engaging our imagination, the Song appeals to our sense of justice and bids us to put things right, not just for the drama within the Song but with other issues, too. It asks us to evaluate the woman's situation, weighing what does happen against what should happen. The difference between the two spurs us to critique Solomon's system, which ostensibly bestowed on certain women the status of queen or royal concubine, but in this particular case fundamentally violated the relationship between a woman and the man she loved. Rather than achieve and maintain justice, the system made victims of innocent people. Identifying the gap between what does happen and what should happen, in turn, helps us develop a critical ethic to apply in our own situations.

Jesus presents a perfect example of this. Like the woman in the Song, who emerged from the wilderness with her beloved and walked into a hostile situation (Song 8:5), so Jesus emerged from the wilderness into a nation riddled with systemic problems and that ultimately refused to hear his call to repentance (Matt 4:1–11, 17; 8:10; 11:20). For the woman in the Song, marriage had been hijacked away from its good and proper purpose and used instead as a weapon against her. Jesus likewise found a people who had turned the means of God's care for them into instruments of oppression. Like the woman in the Song, Jesus became a victim of it. Once, as he walked through grain fields with his disciples on a Sabbath, they picked some of the heads of grain to staunch their hunger (Matt 12:1). They engaged in activity that effectively produced food on a day that demanded no work be done. The Pharisees confronted Jesus over the matter, but he took them to task for their criticism. The Sabbath system had been developed to provide rest and a weekly celebration of freedom (Deut 5:12–15), but it was now being wielded as an

37. Cf. Gerhards, "The Song of Solomon as an Allegory," 74–75.

instrument of oppression. They even questioned whether it was right to heal someone on the Sabbath. In response, Jesus put things right and healed (Matt 12:9–14). To some, he was a lawbreaker who contravened the Sabbath, when in fact he was fulfilling its purpose. He demonstrated that, by the first century, God's covenant nation was not just suffering under foreign oppression, but the very mechanisms that God had given his people to benefit them were being misused, leaving people captive to destitution, sickness, hunger, and poverty. When Jesus walked into the Jerusalem temple, he did not encounter a house of prayer, but a money exchange that fleeced the public and benefited only the powerbrokers of Judaism (Matt 21:12–13). As he watched people donating to the temple coffers, he witnessed a widow drop in the last two coins she had to live on. Though he commended the widow's costly devotion in giving all that was left of her earthly wealth (Matt 12:41–44), he criticized the teachers of the law for developing a system that devoured widow's houses (Matt 12:40). The house of Yahweh, whose purpose was to bring humans to an experience of the mercy of God, had become "a den of robbers" (Matt 21:13).

So endemic had the problem become that Jesus himself was branded a dangerous maverick when he was actually trying to fulfill righteousness. The system's upholders eliminated him in a most barbarous way, executing him by crucifixion. While the Song leaves us imagining the ultimate fate of the woman, the Gospels tell us that Jesus was publicly crucified. And yet, a few days later, he emerged from the darkness of his tomb alive. This was no lucky eleventh-hour escape, for he had certainly died and been interred. This was nothing less than the conquest of death. In the midst of tragedy came the triumph. Jesus had allowed the upholders of the system to vent their worst against him, "and having disarmed the powers and authorities, he made a public spectacle of them, triumphing over them by the cross" (Col 2:15). Jesus transformed this most heinous expression of sin into the means of universal forgiveness. By emerging from the tomb, he provided hope that, in him, humans could be reconciled to God, systems of oppression could be overturned, and love could prevail.

The gospel, as the fulfilment and resolution of the issues raised in the Song, gives us the paradigm for our own ethics. It allows us to look at our own thinking, behaviors, and systems, measure them against what is good and just, and move us to action. This is not a means for implementing what we personally wish for, as the gospel exposes our selfishness and the untrustworthiness of our own desires due to our own sin. We so easily become like the brothers in the Song, or like Solomon, using the systems around us for personal gain to the disadvantage of others and the perversion of justice. Rather, the gospel commits us to an ethic of love that reconciles God and humans, promotes what is good and right for people, and overturns oppression. It seeks justice rather than legalism; understanding rather than assumptions; mercy rather than authoritarianism; protection rather than exploitation; love rather than rights. The gospel call to repentance obliges us to critique our systems and work together for the genuine good of all people, whether this be in government, judiciary, or military; business, industry, or education; familial, social, or church life.

The difficulty of the task lies in the inertia that systems, both formal and informal, produce. Systems tend to frame our lives in such a way that we often operate without an awareness of them, whether that be a daily routine we follow or the cultural and societal institutions within which we function. Often, it is only when an issue personally accosts us that we are moved to correct the perceived injustice, but Christians are called to a more proactive expression of love that seeks justice more widely, rather than just around our own person. This is not about seeking positions of power to impose our views on others, but it does commit those in power to vigilance. Neither is it about assenting to democratically confirmed views, though it calls us to speak out if we are able. It is not even about changing things for change's sake, though it does commit us to reflection, review, and willingness to change. When Paul encouraged Timothy to pray "for kings and all those in authority, that we may live peaceful and quiet lives in all godliness and holiness" (1 Tim 2:2), he was not encouraging disengagement from the world. In Paul's day, Christians possessed little to no power to change society because they lived under the system of imperial Rome. He was, rather, encouraging the Christian ethic of love in that specific situation. Today, many of us live with greater freedoms, which should embolden us to action. The gospel compels us to engage with our world and bring the love of Christ to bear in our interpersonal relationships and our systems so that persons are loved and respected in the way Christ loved and respected persons, thus enhancing our spoken proclamation of the gospel.

This encouragement to engagement does not guarantee that we will always get things right. We might make mistakes or wrongly perceive our own preferences as justice. Or, like the woman and her beloved shepherd, we may still suffer unjustly, be compelled to unconventional action, and even fall afoul of the systems we are in. In any case, we are called to love. As the woman says to her beloved shepherd, "Love is as strong as death, passion as fierce as Sheol" (Song 8:6b, author's translation). Her willingness to die for the sake of what was right was not unwise. She could have chosen to compromise and acquiesce to the system and her brothers' plans for her, but she did not. She loved fiercely. Though unconventional and ordinarily questionable, her actions were not those of a renegade but represented a principled stand for what was right and sought to retrieve as much good as was possible (see "A Retrieval Ethic" below). A similar but more recent example of this is German theologian and pastor, Dietrich Bonhoeffer, who was implicated in the plot to assassinate Adolf Hitler in 1943. Though some understandably take issue with Bonhoeffer's actions, for we would ordinarily deplore such extreme measures, the enormity of evil in the Nazi system, which facilitated atrocities and the murder of untold millions, called for extreme measures. Bonhoeffer acted on the basis of his Christian principles. He and his co-conspirators failed, and they paid with their lives in 1945. But both Bonhoeffer and the woman of the Song embody the biblical principle of being willing to sacrifice all for the sake of others. As Jesus said and demonstrated, "Greater love has no one than this: to lay down one's life for one's friends" (John 15:13).

A Retrieval Ethic

There is no avoiding the fact that the woman and her beloved shepherd boy take a problematic course of action by sleeping together. They seem to have flouted what is ethically normative. Yet, we must bear in mind that they have not simply given in to their passion or decided that they do not care for convention or social mores. On the contrary, their interactions throughout the Song demonstrate that they desire to follow the normative ethical course that would see them marry before having sex. Yet, they are being unjustly prevented from doing this and face an outcome that effectively forces the woman to be unfaithful to the man she loves as a permanent eventuality. This is even more problematic than their course of action to deal with it. As such, their unorthodox action should not be seen as a nod toward sexual license but as a retrieval ethic in a moral dilemma. The purpose of a retrieval ethic is "to retrieve as much good as one can in the situation, and limit as much harm as is possible."[38] It is needed when a dilemma has no perfect way in which it can be solved. The only suitable solution is to opt for the least morally questionable course. In this way, the best ethical outcome is retrieved from a morally ambiguous situation, even though that outcome is not ideal.

There are further parameters to consider in such a situation, though. First, one needs to be sure that there is no unambiguous way to solve the ethical dilemma. It is easy to appeal to a retrieval ethic as a cover for human license, for human nature is, after all, marred by sin and will often look for excuses to permit it. In the case of the woman and the shepherd boy, the power of those in authority over them (the king and the woman's brothers),

38. Michael Hill, *The How and Why of Love: And Introduction to Evangelical Ethics* (Kingsford, NSW: Matthias Media, 2002), 133.

the imminence and permanence of the woman's prospective marriage to the king, and the forcing of the woman to be unfaithful to the man she loves mean all other options have been exhausted. The couple must act and do so immediately, even though there is no ideal way to resolve their ethical dilemma. They do what would normally be considered wrong, but this seeks to retrieve the most good and do the least harm—just as Tamar and Ruth did in their respective situations and were lauded as righteous for doing so (Gen 38; Ruth 3).

Second, one must determine an order of ethical priorities to know what the best ethical outcome is and the least morally questionable way to achieve it. The metaphor that stands behind the drama of the Song is a case in point. Conservative Jews under Seleucid rule faced the prospect of either abandoning devotion to the God of Israel or being branded lawbreakers and face death. Neither outcome was favorable, but the ethical priority lay in devotion to Yahweh over being a law-abiding citizen under the Seleucids. Similar modern ethical dilemmas occur, with a popular test scenario coming from World War II: should one hide Jews from Nazis and lie about it, or tell the truth about the location of Jews and see the Nazis kill them? The competing demands are telling the truth and saving lives, but only one of these outcomes can be achieved. Most would argue that more good is retrieved and less harm is done by saving lives over telling the truth to Nazis.

Third, the definition of "good" and "harm" are critical for a proper retrieval ethic. Again, this is where human sinfulness can undermine good intentions or seek license. Sexual ethics in today's world are fraught with such pitfalls. What guides many people in their decisions and policies about sex today is prizing radical individualism far above collective society; the exercise of personal freedom as the greatest good; a perceived harm if one does not have sex; and the separation of sex from the notion of personhood. This is why sex outside of marriage has become normative in many societies, and divorce so prevalent also. Yet, what drives a truly Christian retrieval ethic is love as the Triune God demonstrates it within himself and as it comes to us in the person of Jesus Christ. In other words, God is the starting point for our ethics, not humanity. This means that a Christian retrieval ethic will be marked by other-person centeredness, and promotion of personhood, for the good of all. In the Song, the ethical dilemma of the woman's forced marriage to the king does not bid her to be other-person centered but rather seeks to tear her personhood apart by conquering and commodifying her through institutionalized rape. It would join her body and her future to a man she does not love (and who does not seem to love her), while her mind and spirit remain joined to the man she does love and to whom she should be married. By sleeping with the shepherd boy, she enacts the integrity of her personhood, joining her body, mind, spirit, and future to him, as is fitting for a marriage.

Three further points are worth considering in appraising the ethics of the woman and the shepherd in the Song. First, sex does not make a marriage, though there is no normative marriage without sex. Thus, there is no possibility for the woman to marry the king and yet not sleep with him. Similarly, the woman sleeping with the shepherd boy does not make them married, but it certainly implies that they should be.

Second, a wedding ceremony does not itself make a marriage. Rather, the public mutual consent of a man and a woman to a permanent sexual relationship is what makes a marriage. In the Song, the woman does not consent to marrying the king, which means that his taking of her does not actually constitute a marriage. This is why many marriage ceremonies today ask whether any in attendance know any reason why the bride and groom should not be joined together, for those who marry unlawfully are not actually joined together in the sight of God. For the woman in the Song, it is as though she is screaming out such a reason, and everyone but her beloved shepherd boy refuses to hear her. As such, they attempt to enact their own marriage, which should result in their permanent union, but her brothers refuse to acknowledge it.

Finally, of critical importance here is the fact that the woman never marries the king at any point in the Song. She is not railing against an unhappy marriage that she is already in by entertaining an adulterous affair with another man. Adultery is not a retrieval ethic, but the woman is not engaging in adultery, even if others might think she is. On the contrary, she is advocating that she should rightly marry the shepherd, to whom she has been faithful—not the king who would effectively rape her. While she remains unwed, there is still hope for retrieving the situation, which helps explain their unorthodox course of action. It is not normative, but it does aim to retrieve some good out of a dire circumstance.

Consent and Objectification

The dilemma of the woman in the Song turns largely on the issue of consent. She was a victim of her brothers' plot to marry her to Solomon against her will, thus rending the relationship she had developed with the shepherd boy and treating her as a mere commodity. Due to its sexual aspect, marriage is an intimate endeavor that involves the whole person in a profound union with another. It is, therefore, just and right to require the mutual consent of both partners—something that was lacking in the brothers' scheme toward their sister.

In some cultures today, arranged marriages occur and are even the norm. In some instances, this involves parents determining a marriage partner for their son or daughter, though ultimately the son or daughter must give consent to the match. In these circumstances, there is usually cultural pressure on the son or daughter to accept the parental choice, which means consent might only be given under duress. In other cultures, young women are simply expected to marry a man that her senior relatives, usually male, choose for her. Little thought is given to the young woman's consent. These kinds of arrangements are predicated on the fact that marriage does not simply bring two individuals together, but also two families with all their historical, socio-economic, and idiosyncratic "baggage." As such, the families are involved in determining the match. Indeed, history is littered with examples of people who have used marriage for social, political, and economic advancement, be it through their own marriage or that of a close relative, like a son or daughter.

The larger familial aspect of marriage is undeniable, as is the collateral social benefit or cost that it engenders. In many Western cultures today, where individualism is the primary societal model, this aspect is often underplayed. In the USA, for example, the comedy film series, *Meet the Parents*, lampoons the possibilities of bringing vastly different groups of people together through a marriage. Yet, it cannot deny the fact that, as persons who are integrally connected to other persons, marriage connects a network of people, not just two individuals.

Nonetheless, we cannot overlook the fact that, at its core, marriage is a union between one man and one woman. While marriage connects families, it does not unite them. Rather, it creates a new family, and this inevitably involves a reconfiguration of relationships. Genesis 2:24 captures this when it says, "That is why a man leaves his father and mother and is united to his wife, and they become one flesh." A marriage union joins the bodies, minds, spirits, and futures of two people. The union of minds is an integral part of this, which is why the consent of the marriage partners must always be sought. If it is not, the union that marriage is designed to engender is compromised, and the marriage partners suffer as a result. Indeed, without consent, a marriage union cannot be properly realized. Instead, what is meant to be a joyful, beautiful, and promising union is turned into a prison of oppression.

This is not to say that arranged marriages are, by definition, wrong or doomed to failure. Oftentimes, marriages brokered by other family members turn out to be successful relationships as the married couple learn to love each other genuinely. Yet, this is a gamble, because genuine affection is not a guaranteed outcome, and it can only occur when real consent is involved. Whenever consent is compromised, either through the pressure of cultural expectation, threat, or the brazen disregard of a bride's or groom's will, a crime of violence occurs against a person. A so-called marriage forged without the consent of both partners is practically the same as rape—sex without a person's consent. Moreover, because it is not a singular event, a so-called marriage without consent is prolonged institutionalized abuse. As in the case of rape, the vast majority of victims in such so-called marriages are women, usually forced into the situation by more powerful male kin. These situations must be called out for the abuse of power that they are, and Christians should do what they are able to prevent them.

We should note that this issue is different to the notion of a person "settling" for a marriage partner. In such cases, a person might not marry the kind of person they initially hoped for, but they still retain the full capacity of their consent to enter what they feel might be a marriage of compromise. Such a situation might have other setbacks, such as little affection or "chemistry" between the partners, but this is separate from the exercise of consent. As in the case of couples brought together by an arranged marriage, but who learn to love each other, there is still hope for such relationships, but there is no certainty that genuine attraction and affection might be kindled.

We can view sex trafficking along similar lines to forced marriage. These are instances where people, usually (though not exclusively) young women, are lured, captured, and transferred to a distant place, where they are held against their will and forced into performing sexual acts either for their captors or for clients, usually to earn money for their captors. Victims are treated as sex objects and forced into dependency on their captors, often reinforced or exploited through drug addiction. While this form of sexual violence has unfortunately been with us for centuries, modern globalization and the blight of internet pornography has made it even more prevalent. People trapped in these situations suffer terribly, are robbed of dignity and personhood, and are treated as mere commodities for the pleasure of others.

In a similar vein is domestic abuse, in which one partner, usually the woman, suffers harm at the hand of the other partner. This might occur through physical violence, intimidation, emotional or psychological abuse, financial control, social isolation, dependency, blackmail, or deprivation of basic needs. All cases of domestic abuse are deplorable, as they imprison a person under the noxious power of their spouse. While Christians rightly want to uphold the sanctity of marriage, we must also rightly apply the ethic of love, which seeks to protect and rescue the vulnerable. In situations of domestic abuse, the marriage has disintegrated and is no longer a union, but a form of slavery in which genuine consent and wellbeing are lacking. As Christians, we not only need to speak against domestic abuse, but also seek to provide help to its victims and enact a retrieval ethic by extracting them from the prison of oppression in which they are trapped. To expect a battered wife to remain with her abusive husband as a Christian witness to him, as a way of upholding marriage, or even as an example of suffering for the sake of the gospel, is an ungodly participation in the abuse perpetrated against her. It resembles the attitude of those Pharisees who criticized Jesus for healing on the Sabbath. The gospel of Christ calls us to act on behalf of the vulnerable and overturn structures that harm them. Providing a means for victims to escape their abusers is not an attack on marriage, but an attempt to uphold the ideal of marriage and retrieve some good for a victim. The attack on marriage occurs the moment a person inflicts violence on their spouse. The defense of marriage occurs when victims of domestic abuse are rescued from their abusers, for this recognizes that, even if the marriage still exists in law, it no longer exists in reality. Just as it was appropriate for the woman in the Song to take extreme measures that, under ordinary circumstances, would have been plainly wrong; and just as it was right for Jesus's disciples to pick grain on the Sabbath and for him to heal; so it is right to extricate an abused person from a so-called marriage.

Sexual harassment is also far too prevalent in our world. At some point in their lives, most woman experience an unwanted sexual advance from men. The sad reality is that, in most cases, this occurs not once but frequently. Men often view the advances they make toward women as complimentary behavior or innocent flirting. It is anything but. Too often, men take objections to these advances as misunderstandings or women overreacting. In some cases, men blame the woman for prompting the advance in the first place. This reveals the depth of the problem, namely that treating women as objects for sexual amusement or gratification derives from a latent attitude in men that they are often not conscious of. Few men would identify themselves as harassers, but such lack of self-awareness is as much part of the problem as the objectification of women is. In the Song, the woman's brothers seem practically unaware that they are treating their sister as a commodity, for they are so focused on what she can bring them that they fail to focus on her as her own person. Although in their case it is economic and social benefit, rather than sexual gratification, they are nonetheless brokering the sexual exploitation of their sister for their own benefit. Such lack of self-awareness comes from an innate selfishness that does not seek the good of another person. It must not be fobbed off as locker room talk. Our modern cultures, which are so steeped in the overt sexualization of the advertising, entertainment, and pornographic industries, are not making it any easier. This is no excuse. All sexual harassment, be it in the form of suggestive comments, unwanted physical contact, or exploitative photography is wrong, and men must desist from it and be held accountable. Christians must not only desist from it, but they must also act against it. As Jesus did, so Christians, especially men, must act in the genuine interests of others that promote their personhood and well-being, rather than exploit it.

The End of the Song

Having come to the end of the Song, it seems appropriate to turn to another song that captures something of its enduring themes and their expression in the gospel of Christ. In the version of the Christmas carol "O Holy Night" by John Sullivan Dwight, the significance of Jesus's ministry, death, and resurrection is captured beautifully in the final verse:

> Surely, he taught us to love one another.
> His law is love, and his gospel is peace.
> Chains shall he break, for the slave is our brother,
> and in his name all oppression shall cease.
> Sweet hymns of joy in grateful chorus raise we.
> Let all within us praise his holy name.
> Christ is the Lord! O praise his name forever.
> His power and glory evermore proclaim.
> His power and glory evermore proclaim.

Scripture Index

Genesis

1 . . . 160
1:26–31 . . . 160
2 . . . 185, 287
2–3 . . . 74, 197
2:8, 15 . . . 74
2:24 . . . 366
3:16 . . . 345
3:17–19 . . . 74
3:19 . . . 216
4:7 . . . 345
6:5 . . . 160
8:7 . . . 207
8:21 . . . 74
9:20–21 . . . 74
13:9 . . . 188
15:10 . . . 300
16:3–6 . . . 286
29:16–30 . . . 286
29:28–30 . . . 335
30:1–24 . . . 286
32:7–8 . . . 344
37:28 . . . 272
38 . . . 258, 334, 336, 340, 364
38:26 . . . 336

Exodus

12:36 . . . 233
15:1–18 . . . 254
20:5 . . . 184
22:16 . . . 308
22:16–17 . . . 334, 336
22:17 . . . 335
29:14 . . . 344

Leviticus

12:7 . . . 306
20:18 . . . 306
23:40 . . . 76
24:11 . . . 342
26:12 . . . 346

Numbers

12:1 . . . 352
16:30–33 . . . 57
27:1–11 . . . 323

Deuteronomy

2:7 . . . 348
4 . . . 223
4–6 . . . 223
4:5–8 . . . 223, 232, 234, 327
4:6–8 . . . 237
4:20 . . . 144
4:21 . . . 144
4:24 . . . 184
5–6 . . . 222
5:5 . . . 102
5:11 . . . 281
5:23–37 . . . 102
5:24–27 . . . 223, 235
5:29 . . . 235–36
6 . . . 237
6:1–2 . . . 223
6:5 . . . 99, 155
6:13 . . . 281
7:6 . . . 346
8:15 . . . 348
9:29 . . . 144
10:20 . . . 281
12:5 . . . 187
12:9 . . . 144
14:2 . . . 346
17:17 . . . 285
21:15–17 . . . 285, 286
22:13–21 . . . 276
22:13–29 . . . 334, 335
22:23–24 . . . 335–36, 337
23:1–8 . . . 51
23:21 . . . 125
25:4 . . . 129
26:7 . . . 55
27–28 . . . 143

28:30 .88
28:33 .132
28:57 .307
29:5 .348
30:19 .27

Joshua

17:7 .188
19:18 .342
19:38 .120

Judges

1:33 .120
5. .254
5:28 .213
9:29 .108
15:19 .215

Ruth

1–4. .20
3. .258, 334, 336, 340, 364
3:4–8 .307
3:10–11 .337

1 Samuel

1:1–8 .286
9:3, 5 .203
13:21 .231
15:22 .93, 127
15:27 .300
15:28 .98
16. .46
16:12 .321
17:40, 49 .98
18:25 .157
19–20. .111
24:15 .104
25:39 .352
28:11–19 .57
30:24 .77

2 Samuel

5:9–11 .21
7. .46, 81
7:1–16 .88–89
7:9 .60
7:10 .95
7:11–16 .224
7:11b–16 .51
7:12–13 .96, 118, 242
7:16 .46
11:8 .308
12:4 .108
12:8 .286
12:9–10 .111
14:1–24 .111
14:25–19:8. .111
20:1 .144
24:10 .111

1 Kings

1:1–2:25. .111
1:3 .342
3–11. .67
3:1 .255
3:1–12:19. .66
3:4 .118
3:4–28 .118
3:7 .203
3:9 .118
4:32 .74, 249
5:10 .93
6:16 .271
6:29 .278
7:41 .215
8. .222, 224
8:1 .52
8:1–9:9. .118
8:5 .118
8:21, 29–30 .187
8:32 .104
8:51, 53 .144
8:63 .118
9:1–9 .118
9:24 .255
10:8–9 .67
11. .76, 143, 269
11:1 .269
11:1–3 .255, 308, 317, 318
11:1–13 .159, 197, 203, 269, 282
11:3 .67, 269, 355
11:4–8 .269
11:9–13 .88, 269
11:12 .203
11:26–39 .89
11:26–12:19. .88
11:29–33 .98
11:40 .111

12:16 . . . 144
12:20 . . . 111
14:17 . . . 250, 323
15:13 . . . 108
15:33 . . . 250, 323
20:24 . . . 108
21:1–16 . . . 66, 68

2 Kings

2:12 . . . 339
3:8 . . . 302
3:9–25 . . . 88
3:19, 25 . . . 98
4:8 . . . 342
9:10 . . . 77
13:14 . . . 339
14:21 . . . 68
15:1–7 . . . 68
17:15 . . . 53
18:13–19:37 . . . 170–71, 186
18:19, 28 . . . 186
18:27 . . . 307
20:20 . . . 66, 68
21:18, 26 . . . 66, 68
23:5 . . . 278
25:1–10 . . . 88, 96

1 Chronicles

3:17–24 . . . 24
3:19 . . . 342
3:19–24 . . . 46–47
7:22 . . . 346
15:16 . . . 76
16:35 . . . 179
22:14 . . . 66, 68
27:25–31 . . . 66, 68
28:4 . . . 185

2 Chronicles

1–9 . . . 67
1:1–10:19 . . . 66
1:7–12 . . . 67, 74
1:14–17 . . . 67
1:15 . . . 67
9:5–8 . . . 76
9:13 . . . 67
9:15–28 . . . 67
9:22 . . . 67
9:27 . . . 67
10 . . . 78
11:21 . . . 317, 318
17:5 . . . 66, 68
26:9–10 . . . 66, 68
32:1–22 . . . 170–71
32:27–28 . . . 68
32:27–30 . . . 66
32:29–30 . . . 68
35:7 . . . 66, 68

Ezra

2:60 . . . 119
4:12–16 . . . 97
4:16 . . . 97
4:18–23 . . . 97
9:9 . . . 119
10:11 . . . 185
10:43 . . . 120

Nehemiah

1:1–4 . . . 97
1:3 . . . 187
1:4–5 . . . 92
2:3–6 . . . 97
2:19 . . . 119
7:62 . . . 119
8 . . . 123
8:18 . . . 92

Esther

1–2 . . . 66, 71
1–10 . . . 20
1:1–8 . . . 70
2 . . . 319
2:1–18 . . . 317

Job

1–42 . . . 20
7:16 . . . 53
9:21b . . . 340
9:29 . . . 53
23:9 . . . 188
27:12 . . . 53
28 . . . 143, 145, 153, 156
28:12 . . . 145
28:15 . . . 145
28:28 . . . 145, 153, 156
35:16 . . . 53

Psalms

1–150 . . . 20
2 . . . 104
2:7–8 . . . 112
6:5 . . . 57
23:1 . . . 232, 281
39:5–6, 11 . . . 53
40:8 . . . 185
40:13 . . . 185
50:20 . . . 352
62:8 . . . 93
62:10 . . . 53
78:33 . . . 53
89 . . . 46–47, 59
89:19–51 . . . 59
89:39 . . . 46
89:46–48 . . . 47
89:48 . . . 57, 59
94:11 . . . 53
103:21 . . . 185
105 . . . 254
106:47 . . . 179
120:5–6 . . . 275
126 . . . 88, 90, 97
126:1–2 . . . 97
137:1 . . . 97
140:9 . . . 278
143:10 . . . 185
144:4 . . . 53

Proverbs

1–31 . . . 20
1:1 . . . 22, 74
1:1–7 . . . 76
1:7 . . . 39, 101, 145, 222
1:7a . . . 66, 223, 235
3:5–18 . . . 145
5:18 . . . 306
6:10 . . . 106
7 . . . 143, 145, 159
7:16 . . . 279
7:27 . . . 145
8:1–36 . . . 66
13:11 . . . 53
13:18 . . . 150
13:22 . . . 80
15:31–32 . . . 150
21:6 . . . 53
22:1 . . . 149
25:1 . . . 66, 74
29:4 . . . 128–29
31:30 . . . 53

Ecclesiastes

1:1 . . 19–20, 22–23, 40, 42, 46, 50, 61, 72, 205
1:1–11 . . . 42, 45, 49–50
1:2 . . . 20, 34, 36, 42, 50, 52, 56, 72, 79, 92, 216, 227
1:2–11 . . . 146
1:2–12:8 . . . 20, 40
1:3 . . . 52, 54–55, 92, 99
1:3–11 . . . 40, 42, 50, 54
1:3–12:7 . . . 50
1:4 . . . 57–58
1:4a . . . 216
1:5–7 . . . 58, 147
1:6 . . . 306
1:8 . . . 59
1:8a . . . 59
1:9 . . . 73, 112, 147, 152
1:10 . . . 47, 57
1:10a, b . . . 59
1:10c, d . . . 59
1:11 . . . 59–60, 73, 112
1:12 . . . 19, 72
1:12–18 . . . 42, 74, 76
1:12–2:26 . . . 40, 42, 52, 60, 64, 72
1:13 . . . 27, 38, 53, 74, 79, 92, 149, 186
1:14 . . . 75–76, 152
1:15 . . . 38, 75, 154
1:16 . . . 19, 21, 60
1:17 . . . 150
1:17a . . . 76
1:18 . . . 76, 160–61
2:1 . . . 76
2:1–11 . . . 76
2:1–16 . . . 42, 76
2:2 . . . 150
2:3 . . . 76
2:4–9 . . . 216
2:5 . . . 70
2:7, 9 . . . 19, 21, 60
2:8 . . . 84, 216
2:10 . . . 77–78, 80, 216
2:11 . . . 40, 216
2:12 . . . 77, 110
2:13 . . . 157
2:13–14a . . . 78
2:14b, 16 . . . 78

2:15 . . . 56
2:15–16 . . . 78
2:16 . . . 80
2:17–18 . . . 78
2:17–23 . . . 42, 78
2:18 . . . 78, 131
2:18–21 . . . 78
2:19 . . . 78, 80
2:20 . . . 78
2:23 . . . 79, 131
2:24 . . . 37, 40, 150
2:24–25 . . . 80, 131
2:24–26 . . . 42, 53, 79
2:24–26a . . . 79
2:26 . . . 80, 92
2:26b . . . 79
3:1 . . . 92–93, 177, 230
3:1–8 . . . 40–42, 91, 99–100, 110, 177
3:1–11 . . . 38
3:1–4:16 . . . 42, 85, 91
3:2 . . . 92
3:2–3 . . . 22
3:2a . . . 95
3:2b . . . 95
3:3a . . . 96
3:3b . . . 96
3:4 . . . 97
3:5 . . . 97
3:5a . . . 97
3:5b . . . 97
3:6 . . . 98
3:6b . . . 98
3:7 . . . 98
3:8a . . . 99
3:8b . . . 99
3:9 . . . 92, 99, 161
3:9–10 . . . 94
3:9–15 . . . 42, 99
3:9–22 . . . 41
3:10 . . . 38, 53, 56, 92, 99
3:11 . . . 39, 91, 99, 112, 151, 182, 191, 235
3:11b . . . 100–1
3:12–13 . . . 37, 102, 105, 235
3:13 . . . 131, 150
3:13b . . . 102
3:14 . . . 38–39, 101, 125, 211–12, 235
3:14–16 . . . 27
3:14a . . . 101
3:14b . . . 101
3:15 . . . 112
3:16 . . . 21, 27, 34, 103
3:16–21 . . . 57
3:16–22 . . . 42, 102
3:17 . . . 103–4, 230
3:18 . . . 53, 104
3:19 . . . 92, 103
3:19b . . . 105
3:21 . . . 36, 57, 103–4, 216
3:22 . . . 38, 104–5, 110, 182
4:1 . . . 40, 105
4:1–3 . . . 42, 101, 105
4:2 . . . 105–6
4:2–3 . . . 184
4:3 . . . 106, 184
4:4 . . . 92, 106
4:4–6 . . . 42, 105–6
4:5 . . . 106
4:6 . . . 106
4:7–8 . . . 92, 106
4:7–12 . . . 42, 105–6
4:8 . . . 107
4:9–12 . . . 107
4:11 . . . 107
4:12 . . . 107
4:13 . . . 22, 108–9, 123, 159
4:13–16 . . . 31, 34, 42, 105, 107, 109–10, 123, 177
4:14 . . . 108, 111
4:15 . . . 32, 109
4:15–16 . . . 109
4:16 . . . 92, 110
4:17 . . . 123
5:1 . . . 123, 125
5:1–3 . . . 123
5:1–6 . . . 25, 27
5:1–7 . . . 22, 42, 123
5:1–9 . . . 93
5:1–6:6 . . . 42, 116, 123
5:1b . . . 123
5:2 . . . 53, 56, 125, 176
5:3 . . . 126
5:4 . . . 125
5:4–6 . . . 125
5:4–7 . . . 123
5:6 . . . 32, 125–26
5:7 . . . 126–27, 211–12
5:8 . . . 127, 129, 150, 152
5:8–12 . . . 42, 127
5:8a . . . 127
5:8b . . . 127, 214

5:9 . . . . . 21, 128–29
5:10 129
5:10–12 129
5:11 . . . . . 129–30, 133, 147
5:12 . . . . . 126, 130, 201
5:13–14 152
5:13–15 130–31
5:13–6:6. . . . . 42, 130
5:13b 130
5:13–14 132
5:13b–14 132
5:14 130
5:15 131
5:16 36
5:16–17 130–31
5:17 . . . . . 34, 131, 146, 182, 186, 210
5:18 . . . . . 37, 150
5:18–19 38
5:18–20 . . . . . 102, 130–31
6:1 132
6:1–2 . . . . . 130, 132, 152
6:2 . . . . . 53, 132, 186
6:3 . . . . . 132–33, 184, 210
6:3–5 38
6:3–6 . . . . . 130, 132, 146, 149–50
6:4 133
6:5a 133
6:5b 133
6:6 132
6:7 . . . . . 129, 146–47
6:7–12 . . . . . 42, 146, 148
6:7–8:1. . . . . 42, 140, 145
6:8 147
6:9 147–48
6:9b 147
6:10 147–48
6:10–12 . . . . . 148, 152
6:10–7:14. 148
6:11 148
6:12 148
7:1 . . . . . 148–49, 151, 153
7:1–14 . . . . . 42, 148
7:1a 149
7:1b 149, 184
7:2 148–50
7:3 . . . . . 148, 150
7:4 149–50
7:5 . . . . . 148, 150
7:5–6 150
7:5–12 150
7:6 150
7:7 150
7:7a 150
7:8 149
7:8a 151
7:8b 151
7:9 151
7:9b 151
7:10 . . . . . 148, 151
7:10–11 22
7:10–12 151
7:11 . . . . . 24, 148, 152–53, 201
7:12 . . . . . 148, 152, 188
7:13 . . . . . 27, 75, 148, 154, 158
7:13–14 . . . . . 38, 41, 53, 183, 186
7:14 . . . . . 148, 156, 177, 182, 202
7:14a 154
7:14b 154
7:15 . . . . . 27, 34, 154–55, 157–58, 163, 180–81, 211, 236
7:15–17 80
7:15–18 41
7:15–22 40
7:15–24 . . . . . 42, 154
7:16 . . . . . 155, 157, 236, 306
7:16–17 157
7:16–18 155
7:17 155
7:18 156
7:19 157
7:19–20 41
7:19–22 157
7:20 . . . . . 156, 160, 162, 180
7:21a 157
7:21b 157
7:21b–22 157
7:22 157
7:23 145
7:23–24 158
7:24 158
7:25 158–59
7:25–8:1. . . . . 42, 158
7:26 . . . . . 145, 158–60
7:26–29 159
7:27 . . . . . 20, 24, 40
7:27–28 22
7:27–28a 159
7:27–29 158

7:28b 159
7:29 159–60
8:1 160
8:2 175–76
8:2a 176
8:2–3 175
8:2–4 21
8:2–5a 176
8:2–15 . . . . . 42, 110, 123, 175
8:2–10:4. . . . . 42, 167, 174
8:3 . . . . . 175, 177
8:4–5 177
8:5 177
8:6 230
8:6b–7 177
8:7 . . . . . 182, 202
8:8 178
8:8a 178
8:8b 178
8:9 178–79
8:10 . . . . . 33–34, 178–80
8:11 180–81
8:11–12 179
8:12–13 . . . . . 41, 180
8:14 . . . . . 80, 180–81
8:15 . . . . . 37, 181
8:16–17 182
8:16–9:6. . . . . 27, 42, 182
8:17 . . . . . 53, 161, 182
9:1 . . . . . 182, 184
9:1–3a 182
9:1–6 36
9:2–3 185
9:2–3a 182
9:3 184
9:3a 182–83
9:3b 183
9:5–6 184
9:6 184
9:7 . . . . . 183, 185, 206
9:7–10 . . . . . 37, 174, 184, 211
9:7–12 . . . . . 42, 184
9:8–9 185
9:9 . . . . . 53, 185–86
9:10 . . . . . 57, 185
9:11 . . . . . 38, 186
9:11–12 40
9:12 186–87
9:13–16 . . . . . 22, 157, 186, 188
9:13–10:4. . . . . 42, 186
9:14 186
9:15 187
9:17 187
9:17–10:3. 40
9:17–10:4. 187
9:17–10:20. 177
9:18 188
10:1 . . . . . 37, 188, 228
10:2 . . . . . 188, 208
10:4 187–88
10:5 200
10:5–7 200
10:5–15 . . . . . 42, 200
10:5–20 200
10:5–12:8. . . . . 42, 194, 200
10:6 . . . . . 200, 202
10:7 201
10:8–11 201
10:8a 201
10:12 202
10:12–14a 202
10:14 . . . . . 182, 203
10:14–16 22
10:14b–15 201
10:15 . . . . . 34, 202
10:16 203–4
10:16–17 . . . . . 24, 205
10:16–18 203
10:16–20 . . . . . 42, 203, 207
10:16a 204
10:16b 204
10:17 . . . . . 201, 204
10:17a 204
10:17b 204
10:18 204
10:19 205
10:20 . . . 21, 25, 111, 177, 180, 201, 203, 205
11:1 206–8
11:1–2 207–8
11:1–6 . . . . . 42, 206
11:2 . . . . . 156, 207–8
11:3 209
11:3–6 208
11:3a 208
11:3b 208
11:4 208–9
11:5 208–9
11:6 208–9

11:7 . . . 210, 219
11:7–8 . . . 42, 210
11:8 . . . 37, 210–12
11:9 . . . 210–12, 238
11:9–12:8 . . . 42, 210
11:10 . . . 210, 212
12:1 . . . 211–12, 215
12:1–7 . . . 25
12:1a . . . 212
12:1b–7 . . . 212
12:2 . . . 213
12:2–7 . . . 22, 41
12:3a . . . 213
12:3b . . . 213
12:3c . . . 213
12:3d . . . 213
12:4 . . . 213–14
12:5 . . . 214
12:5a . . . 214
12:5b . . . 214
12:5c . . . 214
12:5d . . . 214
12:5e . . . 214
12:5f . . . 215
12:5f–7 . . . 215
12:6 . . . 215
12:7 . . . 57, 103, 216
12:8 . . . 20, 24, 36, 50–52, 79, 216, 227
12:9 . . . 21, 25, 146, 150, 229
12:9–10 . . . 25, 42, 81, 229, 232
12:9–11 . . . 228
12:9–14 . . . 19, 35, 39–40, 42, 50, 52, 56, 222, 227–28
12:10 . . . 165, 229
12:11 . . . 25, 230–32
12:11–12 . . . 42, 230
12:12 . . . 232–33, 238
12:12–14 . . . 228
12:13 . . . 39, 228, 235
12:13–14 . . . 42, 49, 234
12:13b . . . 237
12:13b–14 . . . 237
12:14 . . . 237

Song of Songs

1:1 . . . 252, 253, 255, 263, 264, 270–271, 358
1:1–2:7 . . . 264, 267–88
1:2 . . . 255, 271, 272
1:2–3 . . . 358
1:2–6 . . . 264, 271–76
1:3 . . . 149, 271, 281, 282
1:3–4 . . . 271
1:4 . . . 272, 324, 354, 356, 358
1:4a . . . 305
1:4b . . . 275, 276, 279, 302
1:4c–e . . . 273
1:5 . . . 269, 274
1:5–6 . . . 275
1:5–7 . . . 271
1:5a . . . 275
1:6 . . . 256, 257, 270, 275, 277, 282, 283, 299, 305, 322, 335, 338, 340, 341, 353, 354, 355, 358
1:6b . . . 275
1:7 . . . 256, 276, 277, 281, 282
1:7–11 . . . 264, 276–77
1:8a . . . 277
1:9 . . . 356
1:9a . . . 277
1:10 . . . 277
1:11 . . . 277, 278
1:12 . . . 277, 278, 354
1:12–2:7 . . . 164
1:12a . . . 278
1:12b . . . 278
1:12b-2:3 . . . 278
1:13 . . . 278, 279, 308
1:13–14 . . . 278
1:13a . . . 278
1:14a . . . 278
1:15 . . . 356
1:15–16 . . . 278
1:16 . . . 279
2:1 . . . 299, 322
2:1–3 . . . 278
2:2 . . . 356
2:2–3 . . . 279
2:3 . . . 279, 342, 348
2:3c . . . 279
2:4 . . . 283
2:5–6 . . . 279
2:6 . . . 279
2:7 . . . 254, 261, 264, 274, 279, 280, 281, 282, 302, 342, 359
2:8 . . . 298, 300, 307
2:8–9 . . . 298
2:8–17 . . . 264, 295, 297, 307
2:8–5:8 . . . 264, 297

2:9 . . . . . 298, 299, 300, 302, 307
2:10 356
2:10–14 298
2:11 300
2:12–13 300
2:13 356
2:14 . . . . . 295, 298
2:15 . . . . . 299, 302, 354
2:16 . . . . . 254, 278, 299, 322, 341, 357
2:16a 299, 304
2:16b 299
2:17 . . 299, 300, 301, 304, 306, 307, 309, 357
3:1 . . . . . 278, 296, 303, 307, 324
3:1–4 301
3:1–5 . . . . . 264, 301–2, 303, 307, 309
3:1–5:2a 307
3:1a 301
3:1b 301
3:2 301
3:3 . . . . . 256, 302
3:4 . . . . . 257, 298, 302, 303, 308
3:5 . . . . . 254, 264, 274, 280, 302
3:6 . . . . . 302, 309, 325, 347, 348
3:6–8 . . . . . 303, 354
3:6–11 . . . . . 256, 264, 302–3, 308
3:7 . . . . . 269, 273, 303
3:7–8 . . . . . 257, 303, 304, 308, 325
3:7–11 278
3:8 303
3:9 . . . . . 251, 269, 273, 303
3:11 . . . . . 257, 269, 273, 303
4:1 . . . . . 304, 356
4:1–5 295
4:1–15 . . . . . 264, 324
4:1–5:1 164
4:4 304
4:5 . . . . . 260, 304
4:6 . . . . . 300, 304, 306, 309
4:7 356
4:8–12 . . . . . 304, 305, 343
4:9 . . . . . 304, 305
4:9–10 295
4:10 304
4:10–11 . . . . . 304, 305
4:11 305
4:12 . . . . . 295, 304, 322, 338
4:13 . . . . . 251, 305, 338
4:13–15 305
4:15 306
4:16 . . . . . 306, 322, 338
4:16–5:1 305
5:1 . . . . . 304, 306, 321, 322, 343
5:1–2 295
5:1–7 320
5:1–8 318
5:2 . . . . . 301, 302, 307, 322, 356
5:2–6 296
5:2–8 . . . . . 264, 301, 307
5:2a 307
5:2b 307
5:4 . . . . . 307, 308
5:4–5 308
5:5 . . . . . 309, 353
5:6 . . . . . 309, 322
5:6–7 274
5:6e 309
5:7 . . . . . 256, 298, 302, 309, 311, 318, 319, 342, 343
5:7–8 320
5:8 . . . . . 254, 280, 309, 320
5:9 320
5:9–16 . . . . . 264, 320–21, 327
5:9–6:10 . . . . . 264, 320
5:10 320
5:10–16 . . . . . 264, 319, 320
5:11 321
5:12 342
5:16 321
6:1 . . . . . 321, 322
6:1–3 . . . . . 264, 321–22
6:1–9 320
6:2 . . . . . 305, 322
6:2–3 299
6:3 . . . . . 254, 322, 326, 341, 357
6:4 . . . . . 250, 323, 356
6:4–9 . . . . . 264, 295, 322
6:4–10 . . . . . 264, 322–25
6:5 . . . . . 322, 324
6:5–6 324
6:8 . . . . . 318, 323
6:8–9 . . . . . 256, 278, 322, 325, 342, 354
6:9 . . . . . 257, 308, 325, 342
6:10 . . . . . 323, 325, 347
6:11 . . . . . 338, 348
6:11–12 . . . . . 338, 340
6:11–13 . . . . . 264, 338
6:11–8:14 . . . . . 264, 337–38
6:12 . . . . . 338, 339, 341

6:12a 340
6:13 . . . . . . 255, 338, 339, 344
6:13a 341
6:13b 343
7:1 339
7:1–10 . . . . . . 264, 344–46
7:1b 344
7:2 . . . . . . 299, 322, 344
7:2a 344
7:2b 345
7:3 . . . . . . 260, 345
7:4a 345
7:4b–5 345
7:5 . . . . . . 345, 354
7:6–9 345
7:7–8 260
7:8–9 344
7:9b 345
7:10 . . . . . . 254, 304, 341, 343, 357
7:11 . . . . . . 343, 348
7:11–13 274
7:11–8:4. . . . . . 264, 346–47
7:12 . . . . . . 338, 348, 354
8:1–2 . . . . . . 255, 257
8:4 . . . . . . 254, 264, 274, 280, 348
8:5 . . . . . . 257, 348, 352, 360
8:5–7 . . . . . . 264, 347
8:5–14 252
8:5a 347
8:5b 348
8:5b–7 348
8:6 . . . . . . 258, 341, 348, 357, 358, 359
8:6–7 . . . . . . 274, 348
8:6b 349, 362
8:6c 349
8:7a 350
8:7b 350, 351
8:8 . . . . . . 348, 351
8:8–9 . . . . . . 256, 275, 335, 341, 351
8:8–10 . . . . . . 264, 351–54
8:9 355
8:9–10 298
8:9a 352
8:9b 353
8:10 . . . . . . 342, 352, 353
8:10b 354
8:11 . . . . . . 254, 275, 354
8:11–12 . . . . . . 256, 269, 273, 308
8:11–14 . . . . . . 264, 273, 351, 354–58
8:11b 353, 354
8:12 . . . . . . 299, 305, 354, 356
8:12a 176
8:12b 356
8:13 . . . . . . 342, 356, 358
8:14 . . . . . . 255, 300, 357, 359

Isaiah

1:8 171
1:8–9 . . . . . . 170, 186
3:4–5 204
5. 250
5:1 . . . . . . 249, 271
5:1a 270
5:1–7 . . . . . . 269, 270, 282, 283
5:2 98
5:11–12 204
7:20 307
9:6–7 . . . . . . 99, 112
14:9 57
14:9–11 57
14:15 213
21:1 302
24. 197
24:10 197
26:12 99
30:7 53
30:20 50
32:11 348
36–37. 170–71
37:22 323
40:1 311
40:10–11 311
40:11 281
42:9 59
43:19 59
49:4 53
53:4–5 163
55:8–9 245
57:8 308
57:13 53
57:14–21 . . . . . . 88, 105
57:18 105
57:21 105
62:4–5 . . . . . . 269, 270, 281
65:17 . . . . . . 46, 60, 63

Jeremiah

1:1–10 88–89
1:10 95
3:6–18 . . . . . . 269, 270, 281

4:11 302
5:6 302
6:22–30 197
6:25 . . . . . . 197, 214
7:1–8:3 170–71
10:3 53
10:4 230–31
10:8 53
10:15 53
12:14–17 . . . . . . 88–89, 95
12:15 95
14:9 188
23:1–5 . . . . . . 88–89, 98
25:8–11 197
25:10–11a 199
31:10 281
31:10–14 88–89
31:13 97
33:6 188
38:13 272
41:13 76
49:23–27 197
49:26 197
51:33 93

Lamentations

1–2 269
1–5 . . . . . . 20, 197
1:5–6 311
1:1a 199
1:2–4 97
1:15 199
2:10 199
2:15 . . . . . . 250, 269
3:1–6 199
4:1–2 199
4:3 302
4:17 53
4:19 302
5 143–44
5:2 . . . . . . 144, 152
5:4, 6–8 144
5:6–22 144
5:9 302

Ezekiel

16 . . . . . . 250, 259, 269, 270, 281
19:1–9 . . . . . . 171, 186
19:10 . . . . . . 250, 269, 270
23 286
23:5 286
23:18 286
23:36–37 286
23:45 286
26:20 213
31:14 213
32:23 213
34 98
34:1–31 . . . . . . 88, 90
34:11–16 281
34:12 232
34:15–16 98
34:16 232
34:23–24 98
36:33–38 88
37:9 96
37:11 311

Daniel

1–12 20
1:2 92
4:29–30 . . . . . . 66, 68
9:27 263
11 . . . . . . 58, 188, 208, 306
12:1–3 104

Hosea

1–2 250
1–3 . . . . . . 259, 269, 270, 281
2:14–15 283
6:1 96
6:1–3 88
12:1 75
13:14 57
13:15 302

Amos

9:11–15 . . . . . . 88, 90

Jonah

3:7 103
4:6 76
4:11 103

Micah

2:13 96
4:8 269

Habakkuk

1:14–15 . . . . . . 171, 186

Zephaniah

3:14 269

Haggai

2:20–23 47

Zechariah

1:1 120
2:1–5 96
4:1–14 47
6:9–15 . . . . 47, 200
6:10 119
7:1–3 97
7:1–7 88
8:2 215
8:18–19 . . . . 88, 97
9:9 269
9:16 232
10:2 53
13:7–14:2. . . . . 50, 171

Malachi

1:2–3 99

Matthew

2:13–15 30
3:2 92
4:1–11 360
4:17 360
5:3 . . . . 84, 122
5:3–4, 10 114
6:19–21 84
6:24 122
6:33 84
7:24–25 63
7:24–27 242
7:27 243
8:10 360
9:9–13 136
11:15 34
11:16–19 241
11:19 82
11:20 360
11:20–24 241
11:25 243
11:27–28 112
12:1 360
12:7 241
12:9–14 . . . . 241, 361
12:40 361
12:41–44 361
15:1–2 . . . .
241. . . .
15:24 . . . . 39, 240
18:23–25 122
21:9 135
21:12 123
21:12–13 361
21:13 361
21:33–46 . . . . 115, 122
22:1–14 115
22:15–20 122
22:17 135
22:21 135
23:1–7 241
23:13 241
23:37–38 217
23:38 243
24:2 217
26:38 217
26:53 137
27:46 82
27:51 242
28:18 82
28:18–20 219

Mark

1:15 . . . . 92, 134, 240
2:23–28 241
5:34 287
7:8 241
7:9–13 241
8:36 84
10:45 190
12:40–44 . . . . 122, 136, 241
14:6–9 287
15:34 192

Luke

2:1–3 134
2:3 134
2:4–5 134
4:18 114
4:43 92
6:37 241
7:44–48 288
8:2–3 137
10:38–42 287
12:57–59 122

13:10–17 . . . 241
14:27 . . . 328
15:11–32 . . . 115
16:1–13, 19–31 . . . 122
17:20–21 . . . 138
18:9–14 . . . 241
18:18–25 . . . 136
18:25 . . . 190
19:1–10 . . . 122, 137
19:5–7 . . . 241
19:10 . . . 39, 190, 241
23:28–29 . . . 288
23:28–31 . . . 217–18
24:5–7, 25–27 . . . 62

John

1:11 . . . 81–82
1:12 . . . 82
1:14 . . . 190, 327
1:29 . . . 283
2:1–12 . . . 283
2:3–4 . . . 283
3:29 . . . 259, 312, 327
4:17–18 . . . 287
8:1–11 . . . 241
8:42–47 . . . 283
10:10 . . . 190
12:20–22 . . . 243
12:23 . . . 283
14:26 . . . 283
15:13 . . . 363
16:33 . . . 136, 283
17:3 . . . 62, 82, 84, 220
17:21 . . . 283
18:36 . . . 136–37
20:13 . . . 288
20:16 . . . 287
20:17–18 . . . 288

Acts

1–8. . . . 82
2:23 . . . 115
4:12 . . . 63
4:27–28 . . . 115
9:1–20 . . . 62
17:31 . . . 113, 220
20:35 . . . 84, 241

Romans

1:2–4 . . . 218
1:3 . . . 81
1:14–16 . . . 218, 243
1:18–25 . . . 166
3:12 . . . 163
3:21–22 . . . 163
4:25 . . . 163, 192
5:16 . . . 113
8. . . . 164
8:11 . . . 63
8:28 . . . 100
8:35 . . . 247
8:35–39 . . . 283
8:38–39 . . . 283

1 Corinthians

1:20–24 . . . 165
12:27 . . . 327
15:20 . . . 247
15:32 . . . 247
15:54–55 . . . 62
15:55 . . . 83

2 Corinthians

1:20 . . . 82
1:22 . . . 312
5:5 . . . 312
5:21 . . . 163

Ephesians

1:8–10 . . . 112
1:9–10 . . . 62
1:13–14 . . . 164, 312
1:22–23 . . . 327
2:10 . . . 83
2:14–22 . . . 243–44
2:19–22 . . . 243
5:25–27 . . . 312
5:25–33 . . . 259
5:29–32 . . . 327
5:31–32 . . . 330

Philippians

1:21 . . . 62
2:6–11 . . . 136
2:9 . . . 62
3:1–11 . . . 328
3:4–6 . . . 62
3:6 . . . 162

3:8a 62
3:10–11 . . . . . 62, 329
4:12 84

Colossians

1:13–14 312
1:15–19 113
1:18 113
2:15 . . . . . 136, 361

1 Timothy

1:15 165
2:2 362
3:1 165
4:9 165
4:3–4 83
4:4 220
6:6 211

2 Timothy

2:11 165
3:16–17 244

Titus

2:11–14 164
3:8 165

Hebrews

6:19–20 243
10:19–22 . . . . .
243. . . . .

James

1:1 192
1:5 84
1:5–8 192
1:17 . . . . . 84, 220
4:4 329

1 Peter

1:3 247
2:24 163
3:18 163

2 Peter

1:3–4 327

Revelation

19:7 . . . . . 259, 312
21:2 . . . . . 259, 312
21:9 312
21:14 243
22:17 . . . . . 259, 312

Extrabiblical Literature Index

Judith

8:3 . . . 354

Wisdom of Solomon

2:1–5 . . . 104

Ben Sira (Sirach/Ecclesiasticus)

Prologue 33 . . . 25
1–51 . . . 40
13:3–7, 19 . . . 91
36:1–22 . . . 28
50:1–24 . . .
28 . . .

1 Maccabees

1:11–15 . . . 325–326
1:27 . . . 326
1:29–64 . . . 294, 296
1:33 . . . 304
1:41–50 . . . 326

2 Maccabees

3 . . . 40
4:23–32 . . . 351
4:45 . . . 351
5:11–14 . . . 309, 349
5:11–26 . . . 294, 296
5:15–16 . . . 351
5:21 . . . 351
5:24–26 . . . 309, 349
6:1–2 . . . 350
7 . . . 252, 359

3 Maccabees

1–7 . . . 40
2:25–26 . . . 204

Letter of Aristeas

9–10 . . . 222, 224
28–40 . . . 222, 226

Dead Sea Scrolls

4Q106 . . . 339
4QQoh (4Q109) . . . 26
6QCant (6Q6) . . . 250, 259, 274

Josephus
Jewish Antiquities

12.8 . . . 123, 176
12.143–44 . . . 133
12.154–66 . . . 126
12.154–85 . . . 88
12.156–85 . . . 32, 118
12.156–86 . . . 170, 180, 197
12.158 . . . 90
12.160–65 . . . 176
12.160–85 . . . 119, 143
12.163 . . . 187, 202
12.164–65 . . . 33
12.164–73 . . . 173
12.168 . . . 202
12.169–85 . . . 33
12.180–85 . . . 121–22, 131, 153
12.181–83 . . . 201
12.184 . . . 122
12.186, 224 . . . 173
12.224 . . . 122

Rabbinic Literature
Mishnah, Yadayim

3:5 . . . 249

Tosefta, Sanhedrin

12:10 . . . 249

Babylonian Talmud, Sanhedrin

12a . . . 231

Jerusalem Talmud, Sanhedrin

10.28a . . . 231

Qohelet Rabbah

3:5 . . . 97

Greco-Roman Literature

Arrian, *Expedition of Alexander (Anabasis)*
6.29 66
6.29.4–5. 70

Atheneus, *Learned Banqueters (Deipnosophistae)*
1.3a–b 222
1.22d 222–24
5.196a–203b 71
5.196a–203d 66
5.203cd 71
12.536e 66, 71

Galen
On Hippocrates' *Nat. hom.*, 109 .222, 224–25
On Hippocrates' *Epid.*, 3:239–40. . . .222, 225

Herodotus, *Histories*
1.27–28 69
1.27–32 66
1.50–52 . . . . . 66, 69
1.75–88 66
1.86–88 70
4.166 . . . . . 66, 70

Hesiod, *Theogony*
53–62, 915–918. . . . . 222, 224

Ovid, *Metamorphoses*
6.114 . . . . . 222, 224

Phylarchus, *History*
Book 22 71

Polybius, *Histories*
21.42 133

Strabo, *Geography (Geographica)*
15.3.7. . . . . 70, 72

Xenophon, *Agesilaus*
8.6 . . . . . 66, 71

Subject Index

Abel, 61
Absalom, 111
Acra, 263, 297–98, 304, 311
Adonijah, 111
adjuration, 254, 264, 347
adultery, 286, 287, 336, 352, 365
Aegean Sea, 28, 120
Aeschylus, 226
Africa, 304
afterlife, 36, 48, 57, 62, 82–83, 103–4, 106, 113, 164, 196, 211, 215, 219, 221, 238, 328
Ahab, 68
Ahasuerus, 71
Ahijah, 89, 98
Akhenaton, 170
Alexander (Governor of Lydia), 109
Alexander the Great, 24, 28–29, 47, 49, 70, 124, 154, 162
Alexandria, 28–33, 50, 71, 77, 122, 176–77, 197, 202, 224–25, 227, 229, 232–34, 239, 245
Alexandros, 120
allegorical interpretation, allegory, 254, 259–61, 262, 275
alliteration, 252, 271, 349
allusion
- literary, 27, 31, 34, 74, 89, 94, 96, 112, 118, 126, 132, 145, 159, 185–87, 191, 203, 214–16, 250, 263, 271, 275, 279, 281, 306, 321, 359
- historical, 22–24, 28, 31, 34, 50, 106, 109, 118, 126, 145, 148, 159, 179, 186–87, 200, 203, 208, 214, 304, 309, 347, 349, 350–51

Amarna, el, 170
ambiguity, 31, 107, 110, 150, 152, 187, 237
Ammanitis, Ammonites, 119
Amon, 58, 73, 76
Amun, 66, 68
Ancyra, 110
Andrew (apostle), 136
animal, 57, 67, 69, 86, 103–5, 136, 230
ankh, 215
Ankhsheshonq, Instruction of, 197–98, 200–1, 203, 205–7
anonymity, 28, 108, 112, 187, 203, 205
anti-proverb. *See* proverb
Antiochene persecution, 252, 262–63, 271, 280, 297, 311, 326, 351, 359
Antiochus II Theos, 31, 109, 111
Antiochus III (the Great), 40, 110, 122, 133, 203
Antiochus IV Epiphanes, 101, 251, 262–63, 273, 278, 280–82, 297, 302–3, 306, 309, 310–12, 315, 320, 326–27, 343, 345–48, 351, 359
Antiochus Hierax, 31–32, 109–11, 178, 209
Apadana Hall of Darius I, 66, 70
Apamea, 133
aphrodisiacs, 279
apocalyptic, apocalypticism, 39, 49, 237–43
Apollo, 69
Apollonius, 90, 105, 119–20, 127, 129–30, 132, 152, 172, 201
apostasy, 285
Aqiva, Rabbi, 249, 260
Arabia, 304
Aramaic, Aramaism, 55, 108
Areopagus, 220
Aristobulus of Cassandreia, 70
Artaxerxes I, 71, 97
Artaxerxes II, 71, 77
ascension, 62, 82–83, 113, 216, 219
Ashkelon, 119, 201
Asia Minor, 28, 32, 69, 109–10, 119
assonance, 252
Assyria, Assyrians, 49, 89, 95, 144, 162, 250
Athens, 67, 69, 220, 226
Attalids, 225, 233
attraction, 258, 284, 310, 319, 367
Augustus (Caesar), 134
authorship
- Ecclesiastes, 20–25
- Song of Songs, 249–50, 259, 271

Babylon, Babylonians, 22, 26, 28, 46–49, 68, 70, 89–90, 95–97, 119, 144, 162, 171, 198–99, 214, 218, 251, 311
ballad, 252, 257, 260–61
Ben Sira, Jesus, 26, 28
Berenice, 31, 109
Beth Anath, 120
Bethlehem, 134
Bias of Priene, 69
birth, 92–93, 95, 134, 140, 149, 151
blessing, 24, 27, 37–38, 48, 57, 80, 84, 114, 143, 158, 164, 194, 205, 216–17, 240, 258, 288, 317
Bonhoeffer, Dietrich, 363
Book of the Twelve, 96
books, 222, 224–26, 232–34
Booths. *See Sukkot*
breast, 217, 260, 268, 278–79, 288, 291, 296, 306, 331–33, 338, 345, 351–52, 257
bride, 258, 272–73, 277, 304, 310, 320, 324–25, 343
bride of Christ, 259, 312, 327, 330
bride-price, 334
brothers, 252, 256, 258, 262, 270, 275–76, 278, 282, 298, 335, 338, 341, 351–59, 362–63, 365, 368
burial, tomb, 28–29, 46, 48–49, 57, 61, 63, 66, 68, 71–72, 82, 84, 118, 133, 167, 178–79, 215, 220
Byblos, 170
Caesar, 134–35, 137
Callixeinus of Rhodes, 71
canonicity
  Ecclesiastes, 20
  Song of Songs, 249
Canopus Decree, 46, 49
carpe diem, 37, 154, 186, 211
casuistic laws, 334–36
cedar, 48, 67
census, 134
characters in the Song of Songs, 250, 251, 253–54, 255–57, 269, 270
children, childbearing, 61, 69, 82, 114, 117–18, 121, 138, 143, 146, 149–50, 174, 192, 217, 223, 235–36, 241, 243, 273, 284, 285–86, 287, 302, 308, 313, 334, 336, 340. See also birth
Christian, Christianity, 30, 62–63, 83, 112, 138, 165–66, 191–92, 220, 244, 246–47
Chronicler, 68, 76
citadel. *See* Acra
City of David, 263, 297, 304, 311
cleruchy, 30, 119, 127
coin, coinage, 31, 49, 69, 136, 171–72
Colbert, Jean Baptiste, 202
concubine, 67, 335. *See also* harem; queens and concubines
conquered women, 269, 275, 282, 285, 288, 303, 308–9, 314, 340
conquest, 24, 26, 28, 47, 60, 69–70, 82–83, 99, 133, 136, 154, 217–19, 239–40, 261, 269, 275, 282, 285, 288, 303–4, 308–9, 314, 319, 340, 345–46, 361, 364
consent, 258, 313, 336, 365–67
contentment. *See* satisfaction
contradiction, 39, 41, 146, 155–57, 160, 180, 191, 236
Coptic, 30
corruption, 118–21, 124, 127–29, 135, 137, 147, 150, 152, 178, 180, 189, 234
Cos, 120
covenant, 27, 37–39, 46–47, 51, 80–81, 89–90, 95–96, 118, 143, 145, 151–52, 154, 156, 158, 161, 180–82, 211–12, 223–24, 235–40, 242, 245, 260, 262, 269, 270, 282, 284, 310, 311, 312, 325–26, 334, 336, 346
Croesus of Lydia, 69–70, 73, 76, 172
curse, 74, 80, 143, 157–58, 216, 345
Cyprus, 119
Cyrus the Great, 47, 66, 70–72, 77, 84
Damascus, 61–62
damnatio memoriae, 73, 112
Darius I, 47, 66, 70, 77
Darius III (Codomanus), 28
date and context
  Ecclesiastes, 25–34
  Song of Songs, 250–52
"Daughter Jerusalem," 250, 269, 323
daughters of Jerusalem, 217, 250, 254, 256, 261, 264, 269–70, 274–75, 277, 279, 280, 282, 283, 284–85, 288, 297, 298, 302, 303, 306, 309, 310, 320, 321, 322, 324, 327, 341–42, 347, 358, 359
daughters of Zion, 199, 303
David, 19–23, 45–46, 51, 57–58, 60–62, 68, 72, 76, 81, 89–90, 95, 98, 100, 111–12, 118, 126, 134, 145, 151,

189, 192, 205, 215, 217–18, 224, 286, 321, 329
Davidic descent/dynasty/rule, 23–25, 34, 37–38, 46–47, 49, 51–52, 54, 56–60, 62, 72–73, 76, 78, 89–90, 96–98, 100–1, 103, 112, 134–35, 144–45, 151–52, 173, 189, 191–92, 200–1, 205, 215, 217–18, 224, 236, 240, 242, 327, 359
Dead Sea Scrolls, 108
death, 27, 31, 36–38, 41–42, 48–50, 53, 55, 57–63, 72, 77–78, 80, 82–86, 92–93, 95–96, 103–6, 109–10, 113, 115, 118, 121, 131, 136, 138, 140, 149–51, 153–55, 162–64, 167–69, 174, 178, 183–84, 186, 190, 192, 199–201, 203, 205, 210, 212–13, 215–20, 230, 240, 242–43, 245–47, 252, 258, 263, 276, 283, 288, 327, 328, 336, 341, 347–49, 353, 357, 359, 361–62, 364
defense, 107
Delphi, 69
Demetrius of Phalerum, 225
democracy, 67, 139, 189
Demotic Egyptian, 197
desire, 271, 272–73, 279, 281, 296, 297, 299, 305, 306, 307, 319, 321, 322, 329, 330, 345
despair. *See* pessimism
dilemma, 271, 273, 274, 275, 277, 279, 281, 282, 283, 300, 301, 303, 308, 313, 315, 345, 359, 363–64, 365
disappointment, 60, 63, 91, 101–2, 104, 112–13, 128, 149, 154, 158
dodi, 270
domestic abuse/violence, 315, 367–68
double entendre, 299, 322, 349
doubt. *See* skepticism
dream, dream sequence, fantasy, 97, 116, 118, 126–27, 203, 215, 219, 258, 264, 275, 296–97, 301–07, 309, 324, 325, 354
drachma, 121
drama, 257–58
economics, economy, 31–32, 37, 54–55, 66, 80, 90–91, 119–22, 124, 129, 132–34, 136–39, 149, 152, 154, 171–73, 206–8, 214–15, 217–19, 236
Eden, 61, 74, 185, 216
Edict of Caracalla, 51
editor. *See* Epilogist
education, 62, 138, 189–90, 204, 224–27, 229, 232–34, 246–47
Egypt, Egyptians 28, 30, 48–49, 58, 71, 73, 77, 84, 89–90, 95, 111, 119–20, 144, 172, 188, 197, 203, 205, 208, 222, 224, 233, 255, 262, 297, 303, 306, 310–11
Egyptian love poems, 253, 294, 296, 318
election, 99
Enkidu, 48, 107, 173
Epilogist (editor), 20–21, 23, 25–26, 35–36, 39–40, 50, 52, 56, 81, 150, 165, 203, 227–30, 232–42, 244–47
Esau, 99
eschatology, 39, 49, 103–4, 113, 220, 237–38, 241
Esther (Greek version), 71
eternity, 62, 82–83, 85, 100, 104, 113, 164, 196, 215, 219, 328
ethnic status of the Jews, 273, 276, 282, 297, 302, 311
euphemism, 97, 214, 307–8
Euripides, 226
evil, 37–38, 42, 61, 74, 81, 86, 102, 114, 117, 123, 130–32, 145–46, 154, 156, 160, 168–69, 175, 182–83, 189, 191–92, 194, 210, 216, 219, 222, 238, 326–27, 336, 363
exile, 59, 89–90, 92, 95–98, 107–9, 111, 119, 132, 143–45, 154, 162, 201, 310–11, 314
experience, 56, 89, 94, 96–97, 99, 101–2, 114, 131–33, 150, 186, 210, 228, 260, 269, 271–72, 275, 284, 287, 301, 305–6, 314, 318–19, 341, 361, 368
experiment, 56, 60, 72, 75–77, 79, 82, 216
Ezra, 47
faith, 28, 63, 82–83, 115, 164–65, 190–93, 218, 228, 240, 244, 251–52, 259, 262–63, 273, 280, 282, 311–12, 325–28, 349–51, 359
family, 107, 118, 130, 132–33, 143, 236
Fayyum Oasis, 120
fee, 32–33, 90, 110, 122, 124–26, 129–32, 173, 176, 188, 194, 198, 202, 207–9
festival, 20, 51
folly, fool, foolishness, 14, 31, 33, 37–38, 42, 64–66, 70, 76, 78, 80, 84, 86–87,

89, 107, 109–11, 116, 123–27, 131, 141–42, 147, 150–51, 156, 158–59, 165, 169, 175, 182, 188–92, 194, 198, 200–3, 209, 211, 216, 218, 236, 243, 336
forbidden love, forbidden relationship, 255, 258, 277, 282, 294, 302, 346
foreign women, 269, 282, 284
forgiveness, 82–83, 136, 190, 218, 241
frame narrator. *See* Epilogist
free will, 93–95, 107, 115, 153, 160, 185, 208–9
frustration, 37, 42, 55, 59, 78, 83, 117, 131, 146, 150, 154, 156, 191, 193, 210, 212, 244, 274, 301, 305
Fry, Stephen, 114
fulfilment of prophecy/promises, 59, 78, 80–82, 90, 98, 100–1, 103, 112, 114, 134, 205, 217–18, 240–41
Galatia, Galatians, 109
Galilee, 47, 62, 120, 342
garden, 58, 74, 278, 305–6, 322, 338. *See also* grove
Gaul, 109
Gaza, 50
gazelle, 280, 295, 298, 299, 300, 357, 359
gem, 68
Genesis narratives, 61
genitals, 214, 279, 307–8, 338, 345
genre
  Ecclesiastes, 40–41
  Song of Songs, 252–54
Gethsemane, 217
Gezer Calendar, 88, 91, 95
Gibeon, 118, 126, 203
Gihon Spring, 68
Gilgamesh, 46, 48, 55, 58, 60, 88, 107, 170, 173–74, 186
God
  character, 57, 73–75, 77, 80, 82, 90, 94, 99–100, 102–3, 113–14, 132, 148, 154–56, 174, 180–84, 190–92, 209, 217, 230, 237, 239, 247, 327
  creator, 47, 56, 60, 101, 103, 113–15, 143, 158, 160–61, 195–96, 208–9, 211–13, 219–21, 246
  faithfulness, 51, 81, 90, 98, 114, 126, 237, 239, 247
  Father, 62, 112, 115, 137, 192, 243, 247
  fear of, 39, 85, 101–2, 112–13, 116, 125–27, 142, 145, 155–56, 158, 181, 211–12, 222–25, 228, 235–37, 241, 246–47
  kingdom, 81, 84, 92, 133, 136–38, 190, 217, 240, 242–43, 313
  promises, 23, 38, 47, 59, 81–82, 90–91, 95, 98, 100, 102–3, 126, 134, 151, 190, 224
  Son, 62, 114–15, 137, 190
  Spirit, 62–63, 81, 115, 137–39, 164, 190, 243–44
  sovereignty, power, will 35, 38–39, 42, 76, 80–83, 85, 89, 91–94, 96–102, 104–5, 107, 110, 112–15, 123, 125, 132, 135, 137–38, 148, 152, 154, 158, 160–61, 168, 177, 181–85, 190–91, 208–13, 216, 220, 235–36, 238, 245–47
  Trinity, 115, 137, 243, 246, 288
gods (other), 48, 55, 67, 77, 89, 126, 173–74, 223, 253, 269–70, 280, 284, 310–12
gold, 49, 65, 67–69, 71, 136, 145, 216
Golgotha, 217, 218, 288
Goliath, 98
good, goodness, 38, 42, 64, 79–80, 99–100, 113–14, 130, 132, 146, 148, 150, 153, 160–61, 164, 169, 181–82, 191, 206–7, 216, 219–20, 222, 246–47, 284, 315, 330, 350, 360–65, 368
grace, 135, 137, 164–65, 192, 245
gratitude, 220–21, 314
grave. *See* Sheol
Greece, Greeks, 27, 29, 69, 69–71, 78, 243
Greek. *See also* Greece, Greeks; Hellenism, Hellenization; Septuagint
  culture, 26–30, 90, 104, 171, 224, 226–29, 231–34, 239–40, 251, 262, 311, 359
  language, 20–21, 26, 30, 32, 70, 92, 107, 121, 123, 128, 134
grove, 68, 331, 338, 348. *See also* garden
Habiru, 170
happiness. *See* joy, enjoyment, happiness
Hardedef, 49
harem, 256, 258, 269, 273, 274, 278, 279, 282, 297, 318, 321, 323
Harper's Song, 46, 48–49, 57–58
Harsiese, 197, 205–6
Hasmoneans. *See* Maccabees
hebel, 36, 53–54, 61, 78, 80, 124, 133, 148

Hellenism, Hellenization, 30–32, 34, 37, 52, 90–91, 98, 101, 104, 119–20, 171, 227–29, 231–37, 239–40, 247, 251–52, 261–63, 282, 297–98, 311–12, 320, 325–28, 358–59
Hermon, Mount, 292, 305
Herodians, 135
Hezekiah, 51, 68, 73, 76, 170, 186, 319
hope, 38–39, 60, 62, 75, 78–79, 81–83, 100, 112–13, 134–35, 151, 164, 168, 173–74, 183–84, 205, 217–19, 227, 229, 239–43, 245, 247, 263, 275, 301, 309, 345, 357–61, 367
human(ity), 36–39, 41–42, 48–50, 55–63, 69, 72, 74–76, 79–82, 84–86, 88, 91–95, 99–101, 103–5, 107, 113–15, 117, 123, 125, 128, 132, 138, 140, 145, 147–49, 157, 160–65, 173–74, 177, 180, 182–83, 185–86, 189–91, 197, 200, 208–10, 213, 216, 218–20, 222, 224, 230, 236–37, 241, 243–45, 247, 253, 259–60, 263, 281, 283–84, 286–88, 309, 312–14, 329–30, 360–61, 363–64
humility, 158, 165, 192–93, 198, 221, 241, 245
Huwawa/Humbaba, 48, 107
ibn Ezra, 207, 256
identity, 165, 271, 275, 282, 286, 311, 312, 313, 315, 343, 359
ignorance, 53, 59–60, 76–77, 80, 133, 150, 158, 183–84, 191, 193, 209, 236, 244–45, 274
Imhotep, 49
incarnation, 114, 190, 312, 360
inheritance, 24, 65–66, 78 117, 141, 144, 152–53, 161–62
injustice. *See* justice
innuendo. *See* sexual innuendo/allusion/connotation
Intef I, 46, 48, 57
Isaiah (prophet), 186
Israel, 20, 24, 27, 36–37, 39, 46, 50–52, 56, 59, 61, 64, 67–68, 72–73, 78, 80–82, 89, 94–100, 102, 104–5, 111–13, 127, 132, 136, 143–45, 151–53, 159, 161–63, 192, 201, 203, 205, 218, 222–23, 232, 234–37, 239–40, 243, 250, 252, 259, 262, 270, 281, 282–83, 310–12, 325–28, 346
Israel Stele, 49
Jacob, 99
James (apostle), 136
Jason, 262, 282, 297, 311, 312, 359
Jebusites, 21
Jeddous, 120–21, 131
Jehoshaphat, 68, 72, 76
Jericho, 136
Jeroboam I, 98, 111
Jerusalem, 19–21, 23–29, 32–34, 37–39, 45, 47, 49–52, 56, 60–61, 64, 65–68, 72–73, 76–77, 89–90, 96–98, 110, 118–19, 122–26, 133, 135–36, 144–45, 151–52, 154, 162, 170–71, 173, 176–77, 180, 186–89, 198–200, 205, 209, 213–14, 217–18, 224, 229, 234, 239, 250–51, 261–63, 269, 274–75, 297, 302, 309, 323–24, 326, 328, 359. See also Acra; City of David.
Jesus Christ, 30, 34, 39, 61–63, 81–84, 101, 112–15, 122, 134–38, 162–66, 189–90, 192–93, 216–21, 240–47, 263, 283, 287–88, 312, 327–29, 360–61, 363, 364, 368–69
Jews, Judeans, Jewish nation, 24, 27, 29–30, 32–35, 38–39, 41, 47, 50–51, 57, 59, 62, 73, 77, 80, 82, 90–92, 95–97, 101, 103–4, 110, 112, 114, 119–21, 124–27, 133–35, 145, 151, 154, 162, 171–73, 175–76, 191, 198, 200, 202, 205, 208–9, 214–18, 222–25, 227, 229–34, 236–40, 242–43, 245, 247, 251–52, 262–63, 271, 273, 276, 278, 281–82, 297, 302, 309, 311–12, 315, 326–28, 349–51, 358–59, 364
Joanna, 137
Job's friends, 228
John (apostle), 136
John Chrysostom, 158
John the Baptist, 241
Jonathan (son of Saul), 111
Joseph (husband of Mary), 134
Joseph Tobias, 33–34, 37–38, 40, 91, 105–6, 110, 119, 121–22, 127, 129–33, 148, 153–54, 170, 173, 177–81, 183, 187–89, 198, 200–1, 203, 205–6, 208–9, 213–14, 216, 233, 235–36, 262, 359
Joshua (son of Jehozadak), 200–1

Josiah, 51, 68, 73, 76
joy, enjoyment, happiness, 37–38, 40, 42, 55, 65–67, 69–70, 76–81, 83–86, 97, 102, 105, 107, 113, 117–18, 132, 154, 168, 173–74, 181, 192, 195–96, 198–99, 206, 210–11, 219–21, 229, 235, 274, 301, 303, 330, 338, 345–46, 366, 369
Judah, Judea, 22, 29–34, 36–38, 46, 50, 57–59, 67–68, 71–72, 77, 81, 89–90, 95, 101, 110, 122, 124, 127, 130–35, 155, 161–62, 170, 172–73, 175–76, 188–89, 198, 200–2, 204, 208–9, 215–16, 219, 233, 239, 262, 282, 319, 326–27, 336, 359
Judaism, 20, 23, 30, 32, 34, 39, 52–53, 55–56, 77, 90, 97, 101, 104, 134, 182, 191, 215, 217, 222–25, 227–40, 242–43, 252, 261–63, 270, 280, 312, 326, 359–60
judgment, 36, 85–86, 103–4, 113, 125, 143, 154, 163, 177, 196, 211–12, 218–20, 222, 237–38, 241
justice, injustice, 37–38, 67, 86, 91, 103–5, 113–14, 116, 118, 123, 127, 133, 136–39, 145, 147, 157–58, 161–64, 180, 182, 190–91, 197–98, 212, 220, 238, 258, 274–75, 284, 334, 337, 341, 347, 353, 360–62
Karnak, 66, 68
king, 20–23, 30–32, 40, 42, 47, 51–52, 54, 65–67, 71–73, 76–78, 82, 84, 86, 89, 96, 100, 103, 107–9, 111–12, 114, 116, 118, 128–29, 133, 145, 152, 167, 169, 175–78, 189, 194–95, 200, 203–6, 216, 242, 272–73, 277–78, 281–82, 284–85, 308, 325–26, 354–56
kiss, kissing, 271, 305, 321, 345
Kurdi, Aylan, 61
knowledge, 22, 39, 56, 63–64, 66, 74, 82–84, 114, 141, 151, 153, 160–61, 164, 166, 168–69, 177, 183, 190, 192, 220–25, 229, 232–35, 244–47, 260, 271–72, 276, 327–29, 336, 339–40, 345, 356, 365
labor. *See* work
Lachish. *See* Sennacherib, Palace Reliefs of
land, 31, 310–11, 348, 359
Laodice I, 31, 109
law, 89, 123, 134, 136, 143, 151, 155–56, 161, 163, 222–24, 227–28, 234–37, 240–41, 243
leader, leadership, 20, 25, 50–52, 89, 98, 114, 127, 131, 136, 174–75, 179, 189–90, 198, 200–2, 204–5, 209, 217, 230–31, 234, 242, 262, 263, 282, 325, 326, 351, 359
Lebanon, 67, 120, 291–92, 305, 316, 331, 353
Levite, 124
Library of Alexandria, 29, 197, 225–27, 233
life, 35–42, 52–56, 58–62, 69, 72, 75, 78–82, 84–85, 88–89, 91, 93–97, 100, 102–5, 107, 112–13, 117–18, 131–33, 137–38, 144, 146–47, 149–55, 157–58, 164–65, 167–69, 173, 175, 183–86, 189, 192, 195, 210, 212–13, 216, 218–21, 223–24, 227, 235, 241–42, 244–45, 247, 252, 270, 273, 279, 285, 287, 298–300, 308, 310, 312–15, 320, 324, 326, 328, 337–38, 340–41, 351, 358, 362–63
lily, lilies, 299, 304, 321, 322, 345
loanword, 26–27, 251
Louis XIV of France, 202
love, 67, 99–100, 113, 115, 137–38, 165, 168–69, 190, 218–20, 241, 245–47, 258–59, 261, 263, 270, 274, 278, 280–84, 287–88, 299, 302–3, 309–10, 313, 315, 321, 347–51, 357, 361–63, 367, 369
love triangle, 256
Luther, Martin, 158
LXX. *See* Septuagint
Maccabees, Maccabean Revolt, 34, 90, 134, 162, 217, 240, 252, 296, 312, 327, 359
Maimonides, 207
Manasseh, 68, 73, 76
Marcion, 113
marriage, union, 107, 250, 258–59, 262, 270, 276, 281–87, 300, 304, 308, 330, 334–37, 347, 348, 360, 365–68. *See also* bride of Christ; wedding
martyrdom, 240, 252, 328, 341, 359
Mary (mother of Jesus), 134
Mary Magdalene, 137
Masoretic Text, 71, 79, 128, 175, 178, 183, 214

materialism. *See* wealth
Matthew (apostle), 136, 138
meaning, meaninglessness, 19, 24, 27, 34–37, 39, 41–42, 45, 50, 52–56, 60, 62–66, 75, 77–84, 86–87, 91–92, 105–7, 109, 112, 116, 123, 130, 132–33, 137, 140–41, 146–48, 150, 152, 154, 157–59, 162–63, 165, 167–69, 174, 179–85, 189, 195–96, 200, 210, 216, 227, 230, 287, 340
Media, 70
Mediterranean, 77, 88, 226, 233
Megabyzus, 97
Megiddo, 68
Megillot, 20
Memphis, 28, 197
Menelaus, 262, 276, 282, 297, 311, 351, 359
Merneptah, 49
Mesha Stele, 66, 68
Mesopotamia, 28, 58
metaphor, 159, 205–6, 231, 249, 250, 251, 252, 257, 260, 261–62, 270, 272, 276, 277, 280, 281–82, 283, 299, 310, 329, 353, 354–55
misery. *See* suffering
Misogyny, 158, 160
Mithridates of Pontus, 109
Mnemosyne, 224, 232
Moab, 68
money. *See* wealth
monogamy, 258, 263, 287
Moses, 27, 222–23, 227, 232, 234, 237, 241, 281, 285, 327
motto, 27, 36, 38, 40–42, 50, 52–54, 56, 72, 74–75, 79, 92, 216, 227, 230
mourning, 58, 84–85, 90, 96–97, 105, 114, 140–41, 149, 196, 199, 214–15, 217, 241, 288, 326
Museum of Alexandria, 29–30, 224–25, 227, 229, 232–33, 239, 245–46
Muses, 224, 232, 245
Nabonidus, 70
Nakhtsobek Songs (P. Chester Beatty I), 294
name, naming, 19–21, 24–25, 30, 33, 47–48, 51–52, 60, 62–63, 69, 72–73, 82, 92, 118–21, 124–25, 135–36, 140, 149, 168, 177, 180, 186–87, 190, 200, 203, 206, 259, 271, 281, 282, 313, 328, 342, 343, 369. *See also* anonymity
narrative in the Song of Songs, 252–58
Nathan, 46, 286
Nazareth, 61, 112, 134
Nazis, 363–64
Nebuchadnezzar, 68
Nehemiah, 47, 96–97
Nicene Creed, 165
Nineveh, 70, 170–71
Noah, 74
nominalism, 166
Nubia, 318
oath, vow 27, 32, 116, 123–26, 129, 168, 176, 182, 188, 205, 259, 261, 279–81, 282, 347, 359
old age, 41, 210, 212–14
Olympian Zeus. *See* Zeus
Omri, 68
Onias II, 32–34, 37–38, 40, 50, 58, 90–91, 106, 110–11, 122, 124–27, 129–32, 170, 176–80, 182–83, 187–89, 198, 200–3, 205–9, 216, 233, 262, 359
Onias III, 262
oppression, 42, 58, 74, 80, 83, 86, 91, 95, 99, 105, 112, 114, 116, 119–22, 127–32, 134–39, 146–48, 150–52, 154, 162, 173, 179–80, 189–90, 198, 202, 213–14, 219, 233, 251, 281, 297, 327, 360–62, 366, 367, 369
optimism, 37, 79, 154, 158, 186, 211–12
Origen, 254
orthodoxy, 27, 38, 41–42, 53, 56, 73, 81, 101–3, 123, 143, 145, 150–51, 154–61, 164–65, 174, 190, 211–12, 228, 235, 239, 263
Oryas, 120
Panias, 29
Papyrus Harris 500, 294–95, 298, 317–19
parable, 34, 93, 115
paradise (*pardes*), park, 26, 64, 70–72, 77, 84, 251, 305–6
parallelism, 182, 204, 214, 252, 275, 278, 323, 324, 350
Pasargadae, 66, 70–72
Passover, 51, 68
Paul (apostle), 62–63, 112–13, 136, 162, 164–66, 220, 243, 247, 283, 328–29, 362
penis. *See* genitals
Pergamum, 225, 233
Persepolis, 66, 70

Persia, Persians, 26–30, 47, 49, 70–73, 77, 90, 95–96, 162, 171–72, 251, 261
personhood, 263, 287, 298, 311, 313–15, 330, 364–65, 367, 369
pessimism, despair 36, 38–39, 41, 48, 54, 59, 62, 74–75, 79–80, 83, 92, 100, 102, 106–7, 112, 123, 149–50, 153, 160–61, 164–65, 174, 184–86, 189–92, 198, 200, 210, 212–13, 216–17, 224, 227, 233–34, 239, 244
Peter (apostle), 136, 163
pharaoh, 48–49, 84, 170, 197–98, 205, 255, 310
Pharisees, 134–35, 137, 241, 360, 368
Philadelphia (Amman), 119
Philadelphia (Egypt), 120
Philippi, Philippians, 62
philosophy, 27–28, 34–36, 39, 52, 79, 81, 91, 149, 153, 161, 182, 189, 197, 200, 210–11, 216, 226, 242, 259–60
Phoenicia, Phoenicians, 88, 90, 119, 121, 349
Phylarchus, *History*, 71
Pithom Stele, 46, 49
Pittakos of Mytilene, 69
pleasure, 64, 73, 76–78, 141, 149–50, 185, 192, 196, 204, 216, 219–20
poetry, 37, 40–41, 88, 91–95, 98–101, 104, 144–45, 153, 156, 177, 213, 149, 251–54, 257, 259–60, 271–72, 278, 294–96, 299, 318–20, 323–24, 329, 338–39, 345, 349, 354
polis, 30, 119, 239, 262, 359
polygamy, 255, 258, 262, 263, 284–87, 314, 321, 336, 354
pornography, 315, 329–330, 367
portmanteau, 128
possessions, property, 29–31, 69, 77–78, 84, 117, 125, 131–34, 152–53
postexilic era, 26, 200, 311, 325
poverty, poor, 31, 86, 106–9, 112, 114, 116, 121–22, 128–32, 136, 140, 154, 169, 187, 233
power, 21, 29, 31–34, 38–39, 47, 50–51, 53, 58–59, 62–63, 66–68, 72, 75, 82, 86–87, 100–3, 105–6, 108, 112–13, 115, 119, 123, 125, 127–32, 135–38, 142–45, 162, 165, 167, 169, 172–73, 179, 187, 189, 200–4, 210, 216, 218–19, 235, 237, 240–41, 243, 256, 261–63, 277, 284–87, 310–13, 319, 324–25, 329, 347, 361–63, 367, 369. See also God, sovereignty, power, will
pragmatism, 174, 239
preexilic era, 26
predicament, 250, 252, 254, 258, 270, 273, 275, 284, 297, 300, 304, 306, 310, 312, 320, 323, 334, 336, 339, 345, 349
pregnancy, 336, 337, 340, 352
priest, high priest, 32, 40, 50, 58, 90, 106, 110, 124, 170, 176, 187, 197, 200–1, 206, 208–9, 216, 231, 240, 262, 282, 297, 311, 351, 359
profit, 36, 54–55, 77, 131, 140, 206
prosper(ity), 37, 69–70, 80, 118, 132, 143, 154, 167, 180, 211, 216, 238
proverb, anti-proverb, 34, 37, 40–41, 74, 129, 146–50, 152–53, 155, 157, 159–60, 184, 188, 198, 200–2, 204–6, 222, 229
Ptolemies, Ptolemaic Kingdom, 28–32, 36–37, 39, 49–50, 57–58, 73, 77, 90, 95, 97, 99, 101, 105, 119–22, 124, 127, 130, 132–33, 147, 151–55, 161–62, 170–71, 174–78, 187–88, 197, 200, 202–4, 206, 208–9, 211, 213–16, 219, 224–27, 230, 233–36, 238–39, 246, 251, 306, 311, 359
Ptolemy I, 28–29, 46–47, 49–50, 97, 154, 171, 224–25
Ptolemy II (Philadelphus), 31, 46, 49, 71, 73, 77, 90, 109, 118–21, 127, 129, 152, 154, 171–72, 197, 201, 226
Ptolemy III (Euergetes), 27, 32–34, 38, 40, 46, 49, 73, 90–91, 105–6, 110–11, 121–22, 125–26, 130–32, 173, 177–78, 180, 183, 187–89, 198, 200–3, 205–9, 216
Ptolemy IV (Philopator), 40, 203–4
Ptolemy V Epiphanes, 203
pubic region, 299, 322, 345
Qohelet, 20–21, 24–28, 30–41, 51–63, 67, 70, 72–84, 88–108, 110–15, 118–19, 122–38, 143–66, 170, 173–93, 197–217, 219–20, 223–24, 227–30, 233–39, 242, 244–47, 359
queen, 67, 272–73, 278
queens and concubines, 256, 278, 318, 324, 325, 342, 343

Qumran, 26, 250, 259, 274
rape, 315, 319, 347, 354, 364, 365, 367
Raphia, 40
Rashi, 207
reason, logic, 56, 76, 146, 150, 153, 228
reconciliation, 82, 97, 113, 136, 138, 163, 188, 218, 241
reductio ad absurdum, 41, 153
Rehoboam, 78, 89, 95, 111, 318
repentance, 114, 134, 138, 164, 362, 217, 240, 360, 362
resurrection, 39, 61–63, 82–84, 104, 113, 190, 192, 216, 218, 220–21, 243, 245–47, 283, 288, 327, 328–29, 369
restoration, return, 23, 37–38, 47, 51, 59–60, 78, 81–82, 90, 95, 97–98, 145, 151, 205
retribution, recompense, 37, 103, 181–82, 212
revelation, 46, 56, 62, 81, 102, 114, 161–62, 164–65, 223, 228, 235, 237, 244, 246
retrieval ethic, 363–65, 367
rhetoric of subversion, 150–53, 157
Rib-Addi, Letter of 170
righteousness, righteous, 27, 37, 57, 67, 80, 82, 86, 103–5, 141–43, 154–57, 160–64, 167–68, 180, 182–85, 190, 211, 220, 236–38, 243, 328, 336–37, 361–62, 364
Rome, Romans, 51, 66, 72, 113–14, 133–35, 162, 217–19, 240, 242–43, 288, 297, 327
royal cult of the Seleucids, 263, 278, 281, 302, 311, 326
Royal Library. See Library of Alexandria
Ruth, 258, 336–37, 340–41, 353, 364
Sabitum (Šiduri), 173–74, 186
sacrifice, 69, 118, 123–27, 134, 168, 219, 222, 224, 241, 263, 294, 311, 326, 363
Sadducees, 134
sage (wise person), 21, 25, 34–35, 42, 54, 78, 150–51, 157–61, 169, 177, 187–88, 194, 209, 222, 228–34, 241
salvation, 39, 63, 164–65, 217–18, 236–37, 240–43, 245, 247, 312
Samaritans, 82, 101
Samuel, 98, 127
Sanhedrin, 218, 231
sarcasm, 60, 152, 160–61, 184, 190
Sardis, 69–70
satisfaction, contentment, 22, 37, 41, 54, 66, 76, 79–80, 83–84, 93, 117, 128–29, 131–33, 140–41, 146–47, 153, 168–69, 174, 189, 219–21, 314. *See also* joy, enjoyment, happiness
Satrap Stele, 46, 49
Saul, 46, 89, 98, 111, 127
Scripture(s), 19, 30, 35, 56, 226, 229, 244, 246–47
Scythopolis, 201
Septuagint (LXX), Greek translation, 20–21, 26, 30, 71, 108, 123, 128, 175, 178–79, 182–83, 197, 202, 226, 250, 278, 338–39, 342–43, 350, 354–55
Seleucids, Seleucid Kingdom, 29, 31–34, 50, 58, 90–91, 95, 101, 109–11, 122, 124, 130, 133, 162, 177–78, 188, 203–6, 208–9, 235, 239, 251–52, 262, 273, 282, 297–98, 302, 304, 306, 310–11, 326, 349, 351, 359, 364. *See also* royal cult
Seleucus I, 28
Seleucus II Callinicus, 31–32, 34, 109–10, 177–78, 203, 209
Seleucus III Soter, 203
Sennacherib
  King, 22, 70, 170–71, 186–87
  Annals of (Taylor Prism), 170–71, 317, 319
  Palace Reliefs of, 170–71
separation, 274, 282, 300, 301, 309, 310, 327, 348
sex, sexuality, 97, 214, 258–60, 263, 272, 279–81, 283–84, 287, 294, 305–6, 308, 313–15, 319, 327, 329–30, 334–36, 338, 340, 344–46, 352–53, 354, 356–57, 363–65, 367–68
sexual harassment, 368
sexual innuendo/allusion/connotation, 249, 272, 279, 300, 305–8, 340, 344–46, 348
sexual tension, 297, 299, 308
sex trafficking, 367
shalhebetyah, 259, 349–50
Sheba, 67
shepherd, shepherd boy, 75, 98, 224, 232, 256, 257–58, 270, 276–78, 281, 297, 299, 301–2, 310–11, 320–22, 326–27, 341, 346, 353–54, 356–59, 365
Sheol (underworld) 47, 57, 103, 169, 213, 215, 258, 349, 357, 362

Shulammite, 255, 256, 342–343
Shunem, 255, 342
Siege. *See* war, warfare
Siloam Pool, 305–6
Siloam Tunnel Inscription, 66, 68
silver, 32, 65, 67–68, 71, 145, 153, 216, 226, 352, 355
Simon II, 40
sin, sinner, 61, 74, 80, 82–84, 113, 116, 136, 142, 157, 159–64, 168–69, 180, 192, 197, 219–20, 245, 283–84, 288, 345, 361, 363–64
Sinai/Horeb, 89, 102, 151, 222–23, 235
skepticism, doubt, 27, 56–57, 59–60, 63, 73, 103–4, 146, 190–93, 220
slave, slavery, 31, 90, 93, 99, 115, 120–21, 144, 194, 201, 310, 367, 369
Solomon, 20–23, 25, 46, 51–52, 57, 67–68, 72, 74, 76, 78, 89, 98–99, 111, 118, 126–27, 143, 153, 159, 203, 217, 224, 249–50, 255–56, 258, 262, 269, 282, 303–4, 308, 320–21, 354
Solon, 69, 78
song of the vineyard, 249, 270, 271, 283
Sophocles, 226
soul, spirit, 57, 84, 86, 103–4, 196, 216
spice(s), 67–68, 290, 292–93, 306, 316–17, 332, 334, 346, 357
stillborn child, 38, 118, 133, 146, 149–50, 210
Straton, 120
Stroll, The (P. Chester Beatty I), 294, 296
structure
  Ecclesiastes, 40–42
  Song of Songs, 263–64
Sukkot, 20
suffering, misery 37, 61–62, 80, 101–2, 114–15, 122, 133, 136, 143, 147, 149, 154–55, 161–64, 167, 170, 172, 178, 186, 188, 190, 192, 195–96, 198–99, 202, 204, 210, 212, 217, 219, 233, 236, 238, 251, 269, 315, 328–29, 361–62, 366–68
Sumerian Love Song. See Tavern Sketch
sun disk, 49, 57
Susa, 70
Susanna, 137
Syria, 28, 31, 33, 50, 61, 90, 110, 119–22, 177, 188, 208, 305–6, 318, 349
Syriac, 234
Syrian War(s), 29, 31, 50, 90, 99, 109, 133, 297, 303, 306, 311, 343, 347
talents, 32, 67–68, 133, 226
Tamar, 258, 336, 337, 340, 341, 353, 364
Targum, 207
Tavern Sketch, 317, 319
tax, taxation, tax farming, 31, 33, 90–91, 106, 110, 114, 118–22, 128–31, 133–34, 136–38, 153, 172–73, 177, 180, 188, 202, 208–9, 213–14, 235, 239
Tax Edicts of Ptolemy II, 118, 121
teacher, 20–21, 45, 50, 64, 142, 189, 196, 222, 229
temple, 21, 25–27, 33, 47, 55, 66–68, 89–90, 96, 116, 118, 123–26, 134, 136, 167, 173, 176, 179–80, 187, 208, 213, 217–18, 222, 224, 242–44, 262–63, 271, 297–98, 302, 309, 311–12, 326, 346, 350–51, 359, 361
theater, 22–23, 30, 40, 42, 72, 76, 78, 82, 84, 216, 226, 228
Thrace, 110
Three Wishes (P. Chester Beatty I), 294, 296
Thutmose III, Annals of, 66, 68
time, 61, 85, 91–101, 115, 130, 141, 147, 154, 169, 177, 186, 240
Timon of Phlius, 224–25
Tirzah, 250, 323–24
Tobiah "the Ammonite" (ancestor of Tobias), 119
Tobias (father of Joseph Tobias), 33, 91, 119–21, 154
toddler, 61
toil. *See* work
tomb. *See* burial
Tomb of Cyrus. *See* Cyrus the Great
tower of David, 304. *See also* City of David
Trans-Euphrates (satrapy), 97
Transjordan, 33, 90, 119
Turin Erotic Papyrus, 294, 296
unity of the Song of Songs, 253–54
uraeus, 49
Urartu, 70
Uzziah (Azariah), 68, 73, 76
vagina, vulva. *See* genitals
versification, 46, 123, 207
Veruca Salt, 192
vineyard, 68, 74, 120, 171, 249–50, 270, 275–76, 279, 283, 299, 348, 354–56

violence, 91, 96, 106, 114, 121, 131, 170–71, 218, 240, 275, 309–10, 315, 318, 367–68
virginity, 276, 298–99, 309, 341, 351–53
vow. *See* oath
wall, 298–99, 309, 352–54
war, warfare, 61, 77, 85, 96–97, 99, 125, 133, 167, 169–70, 186–88, 198–99, 213–14
warriors, 303–4
wasf, 295–96, 320–24, 344–45
watchmen, 256, 302, 309, 311, 319
wealth, money, 20–22, 24, 31, 67, 69–71, 73, 76–78, 80, 84, 86, 116, 119–22, 128–32, 134, 136–38, 147, 152, 154, 169, 188, 201, 205, 208, 216, 278, 321, 333, 350–51, 353, 361
wedding, 115, 199, 277, 283, 312, 324, 343–44
wickedness, 21, 27, 37, 40, 61, 80, 84, 86, 95, 103–5, 141–43, 154–56, 158, 160, 163–64, 167, 179–81, 183–84, 189–90, 198, 211, 236, 238
wife, wives, 67–68, 143, 159, 168, 174, 203
wilderness, desert, 302–3, 347–48, 360
wind, 45, 48, 58, 64–66, 75–76, 78, 83, 87, 92, 96, 106, 109, 117, 140, 147, 150
wine, 64, 68, 120, 168, 171, 185, 195, 167, 271, 279, 283, 292–93, 331–32, 344–46, 354–55
wisdom, 19–22, 25, 27–28, 34–35, 37–42, 56, 64–65, 67, 73–76, 78, 80, 84, 89, 98, 107–9, 110, 112, 114, 118, 126–27, 141–43, 145–54, 156–61, 164–65, 168–69, 174–75, 177–78, 181–82, 186–90, 192, 194, 197, 200–1, 203, 206, 209–10, 216, 218, 222–23, 228–32, 235–37, 241–43, 247, 256, 269, 329
women, 97, 137, 142–43, 145, 158–60, 199, 203, 213, 269, 274, 282, 285–88, 319, 324, 355, 367, 368. *See also* concubine; conquered women; "Daughter Jerusalem"; daughters of Jerusalem; daughters of Zion; foreign women; harem; queens and concubines
wordplay, 128, 212–13, 252
work, labor, toil 37, 54–55, 79–80, 83, 85–87, 92–93, 99, 106, 117, 120, 127–28, 130, 146–47, 168–69, 173, 194, 202, 209, 229
Writings, 20
Xenophon, 71
Xerxes I, 70–71, 77, 319
youth, 31–32, 107–11, 195–96, 200, 203–4, 210–12, 215, 219
Zacchaeus, 136, 138
Zenon, Zenon Papyri, 88, 90–91, 105, 118–20, 127, 130–32, 148, 172, 201
Zerubbabel, 47, 96, 200–1
Zeus, 224, 232, 263, 271, 297, 302, 311, 346, 350
Zion, 97, 144, 199

Author Index

Akin, D. L., 38, 79, 184
Alter, R., 43
Athas, G., 32, 43, 108, 122, 125, 133, 156, 239, 252, 263, 265, 285, 297, 334, 336
Austin, M. M., 120–21
Barbour, J., 59–60, 70, 73, 77, 89, 94, 98, 111, 132, 186–87, 149, 214–15
Boda, M. J., 34, 61
Brown, W. P., 61, 79, 128–29, 184, 186, 207, 211, 232–33
Caneday, A. B., 184
Carr, G. L., 254, 277, 344
Castellino, G. R., 155
Clay, A. T., 174, 186
Crenshaw, J. L., 215
Dahl, R., 192
Davidson, R. M., 265
Davis, B. C., 104
Dell, K. J., 43
Duguid, I. M., 277, 299, 300
Eaton, M. A., 37, 79–80, 103, 105, 128, 186, 204, 211
Edgar, C. C., 90, 120
Ehrensvärd, M., 26, 251
Enns, P., 156
Estes, D. J., 79, 93, 100, 102–3, 123, 128, 131, 153, 155–56, 175, 180–81, 184–85, 201, 204, 207, 211, 228
Ewald, H., 256
Exum, J. C., 254, 265, 277, 281, 299, 338, 340, 342
Fentress, J., 111
Fox, M. V., 43, 53, 58, 75, 77, 97, 104, 128, 179, 184, 207, 227–28, 249, 253, 254, 278, 279, 294, 295, 296, 299, 300, 304, 305, 318, 325, 338, 339, 342, 351
Fredericks, D. C., 26–27, 79, 93, 100, 102–3, 123, 128, 131, 153, 155–56, 175, 180–81, 184–85, 201, 204, 207, 211, 228
Frolov, S., 342
Fuks, A., 120
Gardiner, A., 215
Garrett, D. L., 277, 323, 340
George, A., 174
Gerhards, M., 253, 260, 262, 360
Gitin, S., 98
Gledhill, T., 254, 277, 279, 325, 351
Gordis, R., 107, 129, 253, 280, 300
Grainger, J. D., 110, 265
Grant, M., 43
Greidanus, S., 38, 79–80, 146, 149, 185, 211
Griffiths, P. J., 255
Haerinck, E., 70
Handis, M. W., 225–26
Hanson, K. C., 170
Hastings, J., 215
Hengel, M., 90, 120, 133, 171
Hess, R. S., 254, 273, 277
Hill, M., 363
Hölbl, G., 49
Hubbard, D. A., 37–38, 79
Jacobsen, T., 319
Jarick, J., 160
Jastrow, M., Jr., 174, 186
Kaiser, O., 260
Kaiser, W. C., 54
Keel, O., 253, 260, 263, 265, 272, 279–80, 296, 300, 305, 323, 338–39, 342
Kinlaw, D. F., 260
König, J., 225
Krüger, T., 26–27, 43, 176, 178, 184, 201, 203, 207
Kugel, J. L., 125, 128
Levine, B., 98
Lichtheim, M., 49, 198, 206
Lohfink, N., 200
Longman, T., 34, 43, 53, 61, 97, 102–3, 107, 123, 125, 129, 156, 158, 160, 178–79, 184–85, 201, 204, 214–15, 227–28, 235, 253–54, 263, 325, 338, 342, 344, 351, 355

McDonald, H., 114
Meek, R. L., 61
Mercer, S. A. B., 170
Meyer, L. de, 70
Mitchell, C. W., 280
Moore, D. G., 38, 79, 184
Moran, W. L., 170
Murphy. R. E., 100, 250–51, 265, 277, 299, 301
Ogden, G. S., 58, 159
Oikonomopoulou, K., 225
Perdue, L. G., 43
Phillips, J., 255
Pope, M. H., 253, 265, 273, 279, 298–99, 321, 323, 338, 342, 344–45, 349
Provan, I. W., 155, 252, 256, 265, 324–25, 338, 344, 357–58
Rata, C. G., 34, 61
Rezetko, R., 26, 251
Rooke, D. W., 200–1
Rudman, D., 93, 99, 115
Sasson, V., 255
Schäfer, P., 43
Schellenberg, A., 260
Schiffman, L. H., 121
Schoors, A., 95, 100, 184, 201, 203, 231
Schroer, S., 307–8
Schunck, K. D., 110
Schwienhorst-Schönberger, L., 260, 265, 275, 281
Seerveld, C., 252, 265
Segal, M. H., 254, 351
Seow, C. L., 79–80, 127–28, 148–50, 152, 183, 186, 201, 203–4, 207, 214–15, 228, 231–32
Shafer, A., 107
Shields, M. A., 43, 126, 155–56, 160, 176, 179, 187, 207
Smith, D., 265
Sneed, M. R., 43, 91, 171, 202
Sokoloff, M., 98
Staubli, T., 307, 308
Steinmann, A. E., 280
Strassler, R. B., 69
Stronach, D., 70
Tamez, E., 185
Tcherikover, A., 120
Tcherikover, V., 120, 171
VanderKam, J. C., 43, 201
Webb, B. G., 123, 265
Weeks, S., 55
West, J., 52
Whybray, R. N., 98, 184
Wickham, C., 111
Wiersbe, W. W., 91, 103
Woolf, G., 225
Young, I. M., 26, 251
Zarghamee, R., 27
Zevit, Z., 98
Zuck, R. B., 91, 100, 104, 155, 184